'Hie lert uns der meister'

Latin Commentary and
the German Fable 1350–1500

Medieval and Renaissance Texts and Studies

Volume 218

'Hie lert uns der meister'

Latin Commentary and
the German Fable 1350–1500

by

A. E. WRIGHT

Arizona Center for Medieval and Renaissance Studies
Tempe, Arizona
2001

Library of Congress Cataloging-in-Publication Data

Wright, A. E., 1963–
    "Hie lert uns der meister" : Latin commentary and the German fable, 1350–1500 / by A. E. Wright.
        p. cm. — (Medieval & Renaissance texts & studies ; v. 218)
    Includes bibliographical references and index.
    ISBN 0-86698-260-4 (alk. paper)
    1. Fables, Latin (Medieval and modern)—Germany—History and criticism. 2. Fables, Latin (Medieval and modern)—Austria—History and criticism. 3. Aesop's fables—Adaptations—History and criticsm. 4. Literature, Comparative—Latin and German. 5. Literature, Comparative—German and Latin. 6. Boner, Ulrich, 14th cent. Edelstein. 7. Avianus—Criticism and interpretation. 8. Fables, German—History and criticism. 9. Fables, Latin—History and criticism. I. Title. II. Series. III. Medieval & Renaissance Texts & Studies (Series) ; v. 218.

PA8045.G3 W75 2000
398.24'52--dc21   00-058290

This book is made to last.
It is set in Garamond,
smythe-sewn and printed on acid-free paper
to library specifications.

Printed in the United States of America

A.L.P.B.

Table of Contents

Introduction   ix

Chapter 1. *Moraliter, Allegorice, Scholastice:* Latin School
Commentary on Avian and the Anonymus Neveleti   1

Appendix. The Avian Commentary in Wolfenbüttel, Herzog
August Bibliothek, Cod. guelf. 185 Helmst.   74

Chapter 2. Corpora and Collections: The *Edelstein* and the
Magdeburg Aesop   107

Chapter 3. Aesop's Two Tongues: Secondary Bilingualism in
the *Edelstein* and the Wrocław Aesop   145

Chapter 4. Prose, Verse, and the Fable in Fifteenth-
century Vienna   169

Concluding Comment   197

Appendix. Translations of Medieval Texts Cited   199

Appendix. Latin Verse Fables Cited   255

Bibliography
    Texts   281
    Secondary Literature   283
    Manuscripts and Incunables   291

Acknowledgments

My thanks go first to the many libraries and their staffs who so kindly permitted me access to their manuscripts and printed books, first among them, the Herzog August Bibliothek, whose generous support included everything from permission to edit the fable commentaries in the Helmstedt manuscript to repeated invitations to work in residence in Wolfenbüttel. The assistance and encouragement of Wolfgang Milde, Jill Bepler, and Sabine Solf, among others, were essential to this project from the very beginning.

Financial support for work in European libraries was provided by the German Academic Exchange Service, the Fulbright Commission, and the Jagiellonian Library, Cracow; to all of them I offer sincerest thanks.

I am equally grateful for the encouragement and advice of a large number of colleagues, students, and friends, in the United States and in Germany alike. While it is impossible to name all those whose influence is reflected in this book, I am particularly indebted to Michael Curschmann, Klaus Grubmüller, Marianne Kalinke, Stephen Jaeger, Ingeborg Glier, Peter Travis, Gerd Dicke, and Ulrike Bodemann. I also owe great thanks to my research assistants, Amy Gebauer, John Martin, and Brenda Sanders, and to Jonathan Green and Alison Beringer for their many contributions to my graduate seminars.

Finally, I thank the editorial board of Medieval and Renaissance Texts and Studies for their willingness to publish my work in their series.

Introduction

On a cold dark night in the year 1360, Bono Stoppani, an Augustinian monk in the Italian monastery of Cumae, received an unexpected visitor. The traveler had come a great distance indeed: for as Bono was amazed to learn, this handsome and fashionably turned-out stranger was none other than the Roman poet Avianus, dead a thousand years. Avianus greeted his startled host in a friendly voice and comforted him, encouraging him to present his recently completed *Fabulæ mistice declaratæ* to the Pope, who would certainly see the great merit of Bono's work and perhaps even attend himself to its wider distribution:

> Cogitanti mihi sepissime, si hoc ipsum opus meum possem cum honore offerre domino pape, trepidantique, ne ut minus ydoneum sperneretur, ecce fabulator Avianus, amictu decenti et forma decorus, nocte quadam in sompniis apparuit, amicabiliter increpare et confortare me cepit, ita dicens: quid tua mens inani timore tabescit? age quod dico: sicut enim ego fabulas meas simplices et nudas optuli theodosio primo tanto imperatori, sic et tu fabulas mistice et decenter expositas offerre non metuas Urbano V, summo pastori, veluti illi qui mistici intellectus et sensus est pater et curus et auriga eius.[1]

---

[1] A. Oldrini, "L'ultimo favolista medievale: Frate Bono Stoppani da Como e le sue *Fabulæ mistice declaratæ*," *Studi medievali* 2 (1906/1907): 155–218, here 214. Note the intentional verbal echo of Avian's own dedication to Macrobius, which begins "Dubitanti mihi ..." (on this preface, see Alan Cameron, "Macrobius, Avienus, and Avianus," *Classical Quarterly* 17 [1967]: 385–399). Bono's vision predates by a century Robert Henryson's more famous posthumous interview with "Maister Esope, Poet Lawriate"; compare H. Harvey Wood, ed., *The Poems and Fables of Robert Henryson* (Edinburgh: Thin, 1978), 48–51. It

The possibility must be admitted, remote as it may seem, that Bono's report of this nocturnal visitation is disingenuous, that it was not really the shade of Avianus that appeared to him but perhaps another dead poetaster, one perhaps even more embarrassingly minor than the fourth-century imitator of Aesop; or Bono might even be lying outright, his ghostly visitor no more than a literary topos invoked in support of the petition—ultimately, to all appearances, the unsuccessful petition—for a papal publication subvention.[2] While it is plain that for Bono, the fabulist's seal of approval was intended both to flatter and to persuade the "summo pastori ... qui mistici intellectus et sensus est pater," there speaks here, too, a less banal insecurity on Bono's part as to the propriety of his method in the *Fabulæ mistice declaratæ*, a work that accommodates two hundred prose exempla, gathered from a variety of classical and contemporary sources, to a rigorous and consistent program of Christian moralization. To assuage the uncertainties of his much younger colleague, Avian's modest shade contrasts explicitly his original "fabulas ... simplices et nudas" dedicated to the Emperor Theodosius—a plain echo of the prologue to the *Apologi*[3]—with the "fabulas mistice et decenter expositas" now to be laid at the feet of Urban V, thus placing Bono satisfyingly within a tradition that encompasses *translationes* both political and literary.

However one ultimately understands the Roman fabulist's apparition—whether as figment, phantom, or fiction—Bono's account of it provides rich traces of the productive and thoroughly typical tension between the canonical texts of the classical (and *soi-disant* classical) past and their medieval readers, revivers, and redactors. In the century and a half that followed Bono's visit from Avian, that tension is increasingly discernible both within the Latin academic tradition and between the

---

seems most unlikely, however, that the Scots fabulist would have known Bono's work.

[2] Bono's *Fabulæ* are known only from the single, autograph manuscript, and do not seem to have enjoyed any wider reception; the only modern editions available remain those few excerpts transcribed by Oldrini.

[3] "Quas [fabulas] rudi latinitate compositas elegis sum explicare conatus": Antonius Guaglianone, ed., *Aviani Fabulae* (Turin: Paravia, 1958), 4. In contrast to the view held nearly universally in the Middle Ages, modern scholarship tends to identify in the patron of the *Apologi* not an Emperor Theodosius but the academic writer Macrobius. See Alan Cameron, "The Date and Identity of Macrobius," *Journal of Roman Studies* 56 (1966): 25–38, and "Macrobius, Avienus, and Avianus"; W. Robert Jones, "Avianus, Flavianus, Theodosius, and Macrobius," in *Classical Studies Presented to Ben Edwin Perry* (Urbana, Ill.: University of Illinois Press, 1969), 203–209; and, especially, Niklas Holzberg, *Die antike Fabel: Eine Einführung* (Darmstadt: Wissenschaftliche Buchgesellschaft, 1993), 76–77.

representatives of classical erudition and a new, newly assertive vernacular learning.

These conflicts and their consequences are the theme of the present investigation. To describe the unresolvable tensions between classical and modern, learned and literary, Latin and vernacular, and to demonstrate how the discomfort they caused ultimately contributed to the founding and development of an authoritative vernacular tradition of learned literature, this study relies on the evidence provided in the transmission and translation of two of the most widely read and most abundantly preserved Latin school texts of the later Middle Ages: the late-antique *Apologi Aviani* and the upstart *Aesop* of a medieval English schoolmaster known today only as the Anonymus Neveleti.[4]

At first regard, it may seem odd to accord these two works, now so little known and virtually never read, a place among the "canonical texts of the classical past." Only in the broadest possible terms can the modern literary canon be said to include the fable at all; serious adult readers at the end of the twentieth century do not take Aesop to bed or to beach, and even only moderately clever children quickly outgrow the pious morals and pastel illustrations of the fable books compiled for them.[5] Even when viewed from a more narrowly scholarly and historical perspective, neither Avianus nor the English Anonymus plays any role in the modern Aesopic tradition, which can be said properly to have begun only with the rediscovery and publication in 1594 of the first-century Latin fabulist Phaedrus, who had been for fifteen hundred years no more than a name to medieval scholarship; as has often been

---

[4] The standard editions of these texts are, for Avianus, Guaglianone, *Fabulæ*, and *Avianus: Fables*, ed. and trans. Françoise Gaide (Paris: Les Belles Lettres, 1980); and, for the Anonymus, Wendelin Foerster, ed., *Lyoner Yzopet: Altfranzösische Übersetzung des XIII. Jahrhunderts in der Mundart der Franche-Comté mit dem kritischen Text des lateinischen Originals (sog. Anonymus Neveleti)*, Altfranzösische Textbibliothek 5 (Heilbronn: Henninger, 1882), 96–137, and A. E. Wright, ed., *The Fables of 'Walter of England'*, Toronto Medieval Latin Texts 25 (Toronto: Pontifical Institute of Mediaeval Studies, 1997). Holzberg, *Die antike Fabel*, provides the most useful introductory treatment of Avianus, while by far the most informative discussion of both poets and their medieval reception is that given in Klaus Grubmüller, *Meister Esopus: Untersuchungen zu Geschichte und Funktion der Fabel im Mittelalter*, MTU 56 (Munich: Artemis, 1977), esp. 58–61 and 77–84. See also Fritz Peter Knapp, "Von der antiken Fabel zum lateinischen Tierepos des Mittelalters," in *La fable*, Entretiens sur l'antiquité classique 30 (Geneva: Fondation Hardt, 1984), 253–306, esp. 255–256.

[5] There is considerable anecdotal evidence suggesting that for nearly a generation, most American children have never had any kind of "Aesop" placed in their hands, either at home or in school; this is in plain contrast to the practice only twenty years ago, when fables were told and read in most elementary school classrooms.

correctly observed before, the Renaissance "Aesop," proud in its reliance on older, presumably more authoritative sources, swept its medieval predecessors quite happily into an almost total oblivion.[6]

In the late Middle Ages, in contrast, the Aesopic fable was not only conspicuously represented among the Latin works every *litteratus* could be expected to know, but was assigned priority of place in that canon, adduced chronologically (if not aesthetically) well before Virgil, Horace, and Ovid; indeed, it was precisely in the marginal notes to the fable books that the medieval schoolboy first encountered those august names.[7] And it must always be recalled that to the late-medieval West, still unacquainted with Phaedrus and entirely unaware of his Greek contemporary Babrius, the collections of Avianus and the Anonymus were not thought, as they are today, the curious side branches of a philological tree badly in need of pruning; they quite simply *were* the Aesopic fable.[8]

It is above all to their use in the elementary Latin curriculum of the schools that these two fable collections owed their medieval prominence.[9] The pedagogic use of the fable is attested from late antiquity on, both in theoretical texts and in some of the earliest known fable manuscripts. It is well known that both Quintilian and Priscian recommended that the young pupil's first assignments include fables for parsing and

---

[6] See, for example, the convincing exposition by Paul Thoen, "Les grands recueils ésopiques latins des XVe et XVIe siècles et leur importance pour les littératures des temps modernes," *Acta Conventus Neo-Latini Lovaniensis: Proceedings of the First International Congress of Neo-Latin Studies, Louvain, 23–28 August 1971*, ed. J. IJsewijn and E. Keßler, Humanistische Bibliothek I.20 (Munich: Fink, 1973), 659–679.

[7] Compare, as a typical example, the first preserved leaf of the Anonymus Neveleti in London, British Library, Ms. Add. 11897, fol. 2r, where the annotations on the verse prologue and the first fable already cite by name Horace, Boethius, and Ovid; considerable material is quoted as well from Isidore, although in this manuscript without specific attribution.

[8] The possibility of a source relationship between the Anonymus Neveleti and Phaedrus's books of fables has been most recently raised by Sandro Boldrini, "Una testimonianza delle 'favole nuove' di Fedro prima di Perotti: Gualterio Anglico XLVIII," *Res publica litterarum* 13 (1990): 19–26; I do not, however, find the "echoes" Boldrini identifies in the Anonymus's version of the "Widow of Ephesus" sufficiently strong or sufficiently clear to establish direct Phaedrean influence on the younger collection.

[9] The classroom use of the fable is discussed in Grubmüller, *Meister Esopus*, 87–97; to the bibliographical references given there should be added especially Eugene F. Provenzo, "Education and the Aesopic Tradition" (Ph.D. diss., Harvard University, 1976); and Edward Wheatley, "The 'Fabulae' of Walter of England, the Medieval Scholastic Tradition, and the British Vernacular Fable" (Ph.D. diss., University of Virginia, 1991).

paraphrase; that their prescriptive advice was actually followed in medieval classroom practice is early and eloquently demonstrated by the two manuscripts of the *Interpretamenta* of Pseudo-Dositheus, which preserve bilingual versions of a number of fables apparently produced by Roman pupils newly embarked on their study of Greek.[10]

Similar practices are documented in some of the earliest records of medieval pedagogy—with the important difference, of course, that the more prestigious "target language" was now no longer Greek, but Latin. In the eighth and ninth centuries, such renowned educators and scholars as Alcuin and Remigius of Auxerre are thought to have prepared fable books for the use of their Carolingian pupils.[11] By the twelfth century, Avianus—occasionally alongside an otherwise unidentifiable "Aesop"—appears regularly on the lists of official school *auctores*, a position these texts would retain well into the early modern period.[12]

In the earlier Middle Ages, the most frequently cited and most widely used fable collection was that of Avianus, whose forty-two *apologi*, as we have seen, had been translated at the end of the fourth century from the Greek of Babrius into Latin elegiac distichs.[13] Thanks to their varied vocabulary, sophisticated metric form, and syntactic complexity, Avianus's poems found favor among the schoolmasters, who found them especially suitable for the teaching of Latin; and for centuries the *apologi* seem to have gone largely unchallenged as *the* collection of Aesopic fables for pedagogic use. Beginning in the high Middle Ages, however, critics and pedagogues alike expressed increasing dissatisfaction with Avianus as *auctor*. Both the Roman poet's religious views and his literary attainments were the subject of occasionally vitriolic attack,[14]

---

[10] G. Goetz, ed., *Hermeneumata Pseudodositheana*, Corpus Glossariorum Latinorum 3 (Leipzig: Teubner, 1892); see Holzberg, *Die antike Fabel*, 34–35.

[11] See William A. Oldfather, "New Manuscript Material for the Study of Avianus," *TAPhA* 42 (1911): 105–129, here 115–117; and Edith Carrington Jones, "Avianus in the Middle Ages: Manuscripts and Other Evidence of Nachleben" (Ph.D. diss., University of Illinois, 1944), 23–29, 49–52.

[12] Carrington Jones, "Avianus in the Middle Ages," provides in her table of contents a convenient list of allusions and references to Avianus in the high and later Middle Ages.

[13] Whether the Latin poet worked directly from the *Mythiamboi* or from an intermediate redaction of Babrius's text remains a matter of dispute; see, for example, Jochen Küppers, *Die Fabeln Avians* (Bonn: Habelt, 1977), 166ff.; H. Hunger, *Die hochsprachliche profane Literatur der Byzantiner*, 2 vols. (Munich: Beck, 1978), 1: 94–96; and Holzberg, *Die antike Fabel*, 72ff. On Titianus's Latin prose fables as possibly intermediary between Babrius and Avianus, see Cameron, "Macrobius, Avienus, and Avianus," 398–399.

[14] See Aaron Wright, "*Iste auctor ab aliis differt*: Avianus and His Medieval Readers," in W. Harms and C. S. Jaeger, eds., *Fremdes wahrnehmen—fremdes Wahrnehmen* (Stuttgart: Hir-

and in the twelfth and thirteenth centuries, dissatisfied amateurs produced numerous reworkings of Avianus intended, apparently, to redeem the older collection for classroom use.[15] None of these "Novi Aviani"—the best-known among them the fragmentary recasting by Alexander Neckam[16]—enjoyed more than modest success. It was instead another collection, perhaps written in England, perhaps at the end of the twelfth century, that would come in the late Middle Ages to compete with, and eventually nearly to replace, Avianus in the pedagogic canon: the sixty fables of the Anonymus Neveleti.

It is ultimately of only little importance to the present study precisely where, precisely when, and by precisely whom this self-consciously modern "Aesop" was composed. In the following, I adhere to the practice current in German scholarship on the fable in speaking of the "Anonymus Neveleti"; in Britain, Canada, and the United States, however, the collection is occasionally referred to as the work of a certain "Walter of England." This attribution, first accepted as definitive by Hervieux,[17] has the advantage of being widely supported in the *accessus* that frequently introduce the collection in the later manuscripts.[18] The name alone, however, no matter how often it may be encountered in

---

zel, 1997), 9–19. On early clerical objections to the schoolroom use of the fable in general, see Erich Seemann, *Hugo von Trimberg und die Fabeln seines Renners* (Munich: Kastner and Callwey, 1921), 1–7.

[15] A number of these collections, most of them, significantly enough, preserved anonymously in unique manuscripts, are edited in Léopold Hervieux, *Les fabulistes latins depuis le siècle d'Auguste jusqu'à la fin du moyen âge*, 5 vols., 2d ed. (Paris: Firmin-Didot, 1893 ff.), vol. 3 ("Avianus et ses anciens imitateurs"); several additional examples are briefly described in Gerd Dicke and Klaus Grubmüller, *Die Fabeln des Mittelalters und der frühen Neuzeit: Ein Katalog der deutschen Versionen und ihrer lateinischen Entsprechungen*, Münstersche Mittelalter-Schriften 60 (Munich: Fink, 1987), xxxii. Peter Binkley's attribution of Hervieux's "Antavianus" to Henry of Avranches is most likely correct: "Thirteenth-Century Latin Poetry Contests Associated with Henry of Avranches: With an Appendix of Newly Edited Texts" (Ph.D. diss., University of Toronto, 1990 [1991]), 91 and 187. The most recent treatment of two further such collections is provided in Loriano Zurli, "L' 'Avianus Astensis' e l' 'Avianus Vindobonensis': Considerazioni sulla nazionalità dell' 'Astensis' e sulla cronologia relativa," in *La favolistica latina in distici elegiaci: Atti de Convegno Internazionale Assisi, 26–28 ottobre 1990*, eds. Giuseppe Catanzaro and Francesco Santucci (Assisi: Accademia Properziana, 1991), 63–78. See also Carrington Jones, "Avianus in the Middle Ages," and, especially, Theodore Bedrick, "The Prose Adaptations of Avianus" (Ph.D. diss., University of Illinois, 1944).

[16] Edited in Hervieux, *Les fabulistes latins*, 3: 462–467.

[17] *Les fabulistes latins*, 1: 494–495.

[18] Grubmüller's admirably cautious comment, in *Meister Esopus*, 78, n.176, appears nevertheless to underestimate both the frequency of the attribution to Gualterus in the medieval *accessus* and those texts' potential for communicating accurate historical information.

the annotations of late-medieval schoolmasters, is in fact no more informative than the more neutral designation "Anonymus." The only biographical information thus far found attached to the name "Walter" in
any medieval source is the curious suggestion, reported independently in
two apparently unrelated fifteenth-century *accessus*, that this Walter at
some point contracted leprosy, and that he was subsequently moved to
assume the name "Aesop" out of fear that as a result of his shameful
condition his book might go unread;[19] unfortunately, the search for
poetic lepers named Walter has so far gone unrewarded.

Even given the relative frequency of the name in the manuscripts,
there is absolutely no evidence for Hervieux's rather enthusiastic identification of that Walter as the chaplain of Henry II of England. It is
on that identification, though, that Hervieux bases his precise dating of
the composition of the text: apparently assuming that only unmarried
princes require Aesopic solace and advice, Hervieux concludes that
his Walter wrote these fables for the future son-in-law of Henry II
shortly before the royal wedding of 1177.[20] The manuscripts themselves offer no clues; the oldest, datable to the early thirteenth century,
merely confirm the certain *terminus ante quem non* provided already by
the earliest known citation of the Anonymus's verse prologue, in Eberhard's *Laborintus*.[21]

I am furthermore aware of no convincing evidence that might establish the nationality of the Anonymus. Curiously, even those scholars
who, in the German tradition, carefully avoid naming the work's author
have seemed largely content to accept the "Aesop" as the product of an

---

[19] Cracow, Bibliotheca Jagiellonica, cod. 2195, fol. 76v: "Secundum autem aliquos expo-
sitores causa efficiens huius libri fuit Gwaltherus qui librum istum compilauit, sed incidens
in lepram [non] audebat se suo nomine intitulari"; Donaueschingen, Fürstlich Fürstenbergische Hofbibliothek, cod. 27, fol. 1v: "Et nota quod esopus non est nomen auctoris, sed quidam asserunt magistrum Galtherum eum composuisse, sed quia lepram inciderat noluit eum
intitulare nomine suo ne liber suus ab auditoribus despiceratur." Both commentators are
unmistakably reluctant to assume responsibility for the validity of this account, referring it
rather to unspecified sources: "secundum aliquos," "quidam asserunt." See Aaron E.
Wright, "Aesop, Hyssop, and Brass: Two Late-Medieval Latin *Merkverse*," *Fifteenth Century
Studies* 31 (2000): forthcoming.

[20] *Les fabulistes latins*, 1: 494: "De la solution de ce point [namely, the question of the
identity of the fables' author] découle tout naturellement celle de la date à laquelle elles ont
été écrites. Cette date est d'un an ou deux antérieure au mariage de la fille de Henri II avec
Guillaume le Jeune. . . ."

[21] See Foerster, *Lyoner Yzopet*, xxii–xxiii.

English or perhaps Anglo-Norman poet;[22] yet that tradition rests ultimately on the same late and doubtful authority as Hervieux's incautious
identification of the author as "Gualterus." Here, too, the manuscript
tradition is less eloquent than hoped: the earliest preserved specimens, as
Foerster was already aware, are in fact of continental provenance, and
the late medieval transmission of the text suggests clearly an especially
strong reception—though, not, of course, necessarily an origin—in German-speaking central Europe. It is remotely possible that a thorough linguistic study of the fables' vocabulary and the Anonymus's distinctively
flowery style might uncover regional characteristics that have hitherto
gone unnoticed; given the collection's wide geographic distribution over
three centuries, however, and the highly artificial rigor imposed by its
verse form, neither the orthography of the manuscripts nor the syntax
of the poems themselves is likely to provide any useful clues.[23]

These uncertainties aside, what does seem plain is that the appearance of the Anonymus Neveleti's "Aesop" and its rapid integration into
an elementary Latin curriculum that already included one fable collection would necessarily have an effect on the further reception of Avianus. Where the hopeful writers of the "Novi Aviani" had largely failed
in the attempt to rehabilitate their ancient *auctor*, the Anonymus Neveleti, relying on sources other than Avianus, succeeded dangerously in
producing a fable book whose superiority was such that it threatened to
supplant the older collection in authority and pedagogical utility. Given
the traditional constraints of the genre, the two collections necessarily
overlap substantially in both their narrative content and their moral intention; their confrontation in the pedagogic enterprise finds material
expression in the many medieval manuscripts that transmit both texts in
succession, often within a single quire.

In the practice of the late medieval grammar schools, the simultaneous availability of two fable collections in the curriculum—both in
Latin, both in elegiac distichs, both with claims to a classical heritage—

---

[22] Compare, for example, Foerster, *Lyoner Yzopet*, xxii, and Grubmüller, *Meister Esopus*,
78.

[23] My thanks to Ms. Celena Peet, Carleton College, for her kindness in allowing me to
read her unpublished essay on the Latin style of the Anonymus and its possible value in lo-
calizing the text's origins ("De leone et mure: Rhetorical Devices in Aesop's 'The Lion and
the Mouse' "). A thorough description of the rhetorical devices in the Anonymus's prologue, without, however, any indication that the results might be useful in identifying the
author or place of origin of his collection, is to be had in Armando Bisanti, "L'*ornatus* in
funzione didascalica nel prologo di Gualterio Anglico," *Sandalion* 12/13 (1989/90): 139–163.

led necessarily to a radical reconstruction of the way the two texts were read. It must be recalled that the *Apologi* of Avianus had been composed in an environment where literary composition in Greek was still the standard of erudition; the fables of the Anonymus Neveleti, on the other hand, appear to have been written with the peculiar needs of the high-medieval Latinist in mind, and the competition from this new "Aesop" drew forth a predictable reaction on the part of schoolmasters anxious to defend the venerable *Apologi* against the implicit charge that that collection was not only antique but antiquated, morally and academically. For many, it was clearly difficult to stand up for a text whose disadvantages were so obvious; as, for example, the well-known comments of Hugo von Trimberg in the thirteenth century make clear,[24] the late medieval advocates of Avianus were for the most part moved not by any special fondness for the Latin poet but rather by an understandable and familiar mixture of parsimony and inertia.

Happily for those unwilling to relinquish Avianus entirely, late medieval pedagogic practice made available a hermeneutic device that allowed for the adjustment and accommodation of a troublesome text to new conditions. While interlinear glosses, *accessus*, and marginal annotation had always been integral to the graphic preparation of texts for classroom use, the enforced cohabitation of Avianus and the Anonymus at the end of the high Middle Ages seems to have coincided with the development of a new form of academic commentary, innovative in both its thoroughness and its flexibility. It has been credibly suggested,[25] though not yet convincingly demonstrated, that the "Aesop" of the Anonymus was written expressly to provide an occasion for such commentary, that in the verse fables of that collection the poet intentionally enacted a *tmesis* whose gaps virtually demanded schoolmasterly intervention to "complete" the text. It is by no means fortuitous that the commentaries on Avianus—which until the thirteenth century had largely retained the older, even more primitive *ad hoc* forms of annotation familiar from the earlier medieval tradition[26]—changed markedly

---

[24] Quoted in Grubmüller, *Meister Esopus*, 58 and n.63.

[25] Wheatley, "The 'Fabulæ' of Walter of England," *passim*.

[26] In addition to the Wolfenbüttel manuscript of Avian discussed in Chapter 1 below, see, for example, Vatican Library ms. Reg. 1424, whose Carolingian text of Avian is accompanied by interlinear glosses and marginal grammatical comments, with no apparent effort to create a coherent set of annotations. Compare the description of twelfth-century annotations on Virgil in Christopher Baswell, *Virgil in Medieval England: Figuring the* Aeneid *from the Twelfth Century to Chaucer* (Cambridge: Cambridge University Press, 1995), 53–63.

with the insertion into the Latin curriculum of the new "Aesop," and
that in the new-style commentaries given Avianus's older text in the late
thirteenth, fourteenth, and especially fifteenth centuries, there are clear
attempts to assimilate the *Apologi* to the new, higher poetological and
ethical standards created by the arrival of the Anonymus.[27] Thanks to
the appearance of the Anonymus Neveleti, the reception of Avianus in
the later Middle Ages became one of reaction and defense, motivated by
the schoolmasters' need to "save" the older text from the pretensions of
the younger.

The sites of this textual strife were the academic prose commentaries
of the later Middle Ages, and the effects of the intense commentary activity within the Latin fable tradition are described in greater detail in
Chapter 1. Up until now little regarded by historians of the fable,[28] the
commentaries—abundantly transmitted in the margins of the late medieval school manuscripts—preserve material of crucial relevance to both
the literary and the pedagogic history of the period. First and most obviously, these commentaries, based as they are in a tradition whose first
intention was to ease the reader's access to difficult verse texts in a
foreign language and then to guide his understanding of pagan poetry[29]
along a narrow, dogmatically legitimate path, provide precious insights
into current hermeneutic practice and the strategies of reading and re-
writing applied to sometimes uncomfortable texts. Second, as these fable
collections were among the first texts given the schoolboy struggling to
learn the rudiments of his Latin, many of the commentaries preserve, if
only partially, an account of late medieval pedagogic practice difficult or
impossible to find even in contemporary theoretical works. Finally, as
described in Chapter 1 below, the practice of commentary provided the
more officious readers of the fables an opportunity to vary, correct, and

---

[27] A first introduction to this phenomenon is offered by Wright, "*Iste auctor.*"

[28] The most important treatments to date of the late-medieval commentaries on Avianus
and the Anonymus are provided by Seemann, *Hugo von Trimberg*; Wheatley, "The 'Fabulæ'
of Walter of England"; and Aaron E. Wright, "The 'Nuremberg' Aesop and Its Sources"
(Ph.D. diss., Princeton University, 1991). None of these studies, however, in spite of the
large amounts of otherwise inaccessible manuscript material they present, fully satisfies the
desiderata set forth in Dicke and Grubmüller, *Katalog*, xxiii–xxiv.

[29] Avianus, of course, was almost certainly a pagan, the Anonymus Neveleti doubtless
a Christian; medieval scholars, however, often considered Avianus an early and heroic ad-
herent to the one true faith (compare, for example, Hugo von Trimberg in his *Registrum*:
"Verbis acrioribus iam dictus Avianus / Carperetur, idem si non foret Christianus," cited
in Grubmüller, *Meister Esopus*, 93), while Aesop, even in the person of the Anonymus, had
by definition and tradition to be stipulated a pagan.

elaborate texts that in the verse originals of Avianus or the Anonymus were for whatever reason found lacking. While the strictness of their prosodic form served well to insulate the verse fables from substantive interference, the stories they told were haplessly exposed to improvement (or, as frequently, mutilation) at the hands of commentators whose prose "reductions" tended, unsurprisingly, to diverge ever more from the texts they commented and ultimately to become the productive locus of narrative innovation and expansion.

The significance of this richly complex phenomenon is not exhausted, though, within the Latin school tradition. If it is to serve the elucidation of its primary text, commentary must, virtually by definition, differ substantially from the annotated work. In the case of verse texts used, as were Avianus and the Anonymus, for elementary language instruction, the schoolmasters' preparation of the texts, beginning with construe marks and interlinear vocabulary glosses and extending to the full prose commentaries themselves, necessarily involves the dismantling—even the destruction—of those distinctive linguistic and stylistic features that characterize the authentic and authoritative verse originals. Thus even within the Latin tradition, this shift proves ultimately to be more fundamental than the merely formal and easily observable one from verse into prose; the commentaries on the fables of Avianus and the Anonymus Neveleti are, as we shall see, finally tantamount to an act of intralingual translation, effecting the transfer of literary material from one highly stylized, prosodically sophisticated Latin into another whose goals are, by definition, more hermeneutic than aesthetic. In this context, expressly and pointedly presented as an alternative to more demanding poetic forms, Latin prose itself represents a first stage in a process of "de-Latinization,"[30] a process that in the fifteenth century led, repeatedly and as if on its own momentum, to the translation of fables from both Avianus and the Anonymus Neveleti into German.[31]

---

[30] "Entlatinisierung" as the first step in the process of translation and vernacularization is most impressively described by Michael Curschmann, "Marcolfus deutsch," in *Kleinere Erzählformen des 15. und 16. Jahrhunderts*, eds. Walter Haug and Burghart Wachinger, Fortuna vitrea 8 (Tübingen: Niemeyer, 1993), 151–256.

[31] For a brief introduction to the German-language Aesopica of the fifteenth century, see especially Grubmüller, *Meister Esopus*, 411–433, and Nikolaus Henkel, *Deutsche Übersetzungen lateinischer Schultexte*, MTU 90 (Munich: Artemis, 1988), 225–227, 288–290. Somewhat less accurate is the overview of the late medieval tradition given in the preliminary chapters of Adalbert Elschenbroich, *Die deutsche und lateinische Fabel in der Frühen Neuzeit: Grundzüge einer Geschichte der Fabel in der Frühen Neuzeit*, 2 vols. (Tübingen: Niemeyer, 1990).

In the lapidary "Ausblick" that concludes his ground-breaking study of the medieval Aesop, Klaus Grubmüller suggests that the principal characteristic of the vernacular German fable in the fifteenth century is its increasing reliance on traditional, that is to say Latin, models.[32] In this assertion, Grubmüller confirms for the minor genre of the fable a famous axiom set forth by Hugo Kuhn: the fifteenth century

> wird mehr und mehr das Zeitalter der Übersetzungen, Bearbeitungen, Adaptionen—so sehr, daß alle Text-Konstituentien geradezu in diesem Verbrauch unterzugehen scheinen, daß auch die Neu-Produktionen nur vom Durchscheinen rezipierter Muster her sich verstehen lassen.[33]

The present study, as much of the literary historiography produced in the last generation, finds its motto in Kuhn's proclamation, and takes as its starting point a more precise identification of the relationship between the German fable collections of the fifteenth century and the traditional Latin models they translate, rework, and adapt.

Posed in this way, the question can be seen to bring with it its own methodology. Obviously, careful source studies remain a necessary first step; absent a reasonably sure identification of the exemplar translated or imitated in a given German work, it is impossible to identify with any certainty which of the features of the translated text are genuine innovations and which are after all present already in an imperfectly known Latin tradition.[34] The more productive, and the more difficult, second

---

[32] Grubmüller, *Meister Esopus*, 411.

[33] "Versuch über das 15. Jahrhundert," in *Entwürfe zu einer Literatursystematik des Spätmittelalters* (Tübingen: Niemeyer, 1980), 79; it is of interest that one of the examples here adduced for the aggressive omnivory of the late medieval literary enterprise is the "Panchatantra," an Indian fable collection translated into Latin and various vernacular languages alike in the fifteenth century, and into Greek in what became known as the "Barlaam and Joasaph" attributed to John of Damascus. See G. U. Thite, "Indian Fable," in *La fable*, 33–60.

[34] An instructive, indeed cautionary example of the importance of a thorough understanding of the variation within a Latin tradition is provided by the German versions of the *Visiones Georgii*; while the four known vernacular translations were long thought to indulge in great freedom in respect to their putatively quite stable Latin source, recent discoveries have shown that one at least is in fact "a faithful rendering of its source text," and that "it is not unlikely that all the German translations will prove to be similarly dependent on their source texts. This ought to be considered in further research, instead of ascribing the act of adapting *a priori* to the translators." Bernd Weitemeier, "Latin Adaptation and German Translation: The Late Medieval German D-Translation of the *Visiones Georgii* and Its Source Text," in *The Medieval Translator. Traduire au Moyen Age. Proceedings of the International Conference of Conques (26–29 July 1993). Actes du Colloque international de Conques (26–29 juillet 1993)*, eds. Roger Ellis and René Tixier, vol. 5 (Turnhout: Brepols, 1996), 99–119 (here 102 and 110).

step in the enterprise is an investigation of the ways in which certain of the elements—formal and material—characteristic of the Latin texts are imported into their German-language reflexes and are there assigned new functions. It is this process of "vernacularization," of the establishment and exploitation of textual authority in a new environment for a new audience, that must form the basis for any "Literaturgeschichte des 'Machens' und des 'Lesens' " in late medieval Germany.[35]

In the case of the fifteenth-century fable, scholarly investigation of the relation between the vernacular collections—not only in German, but in English, French, and Italian[36]—and their Latin forebears has been hampered by the early identification of their putative sources exclusively among the verse texts of Avianus and the Anonymus Neveleti; the commentaries, on the other hand, that accompany those collections in so many late medieval manuscripts have long been deemed the merely derivative contributions of men of limited intellect, negligible literary skill, and enormous vanity. The founder of modern fable scholarship, writing in the first third of the eighteenth century, characterizes the work of his late medieval predecessors as a uniquely threatening mixture of intellectual presumption and moral danger:

> Illi dubiis interpretationem adjiciebant, obscuris lucem affundebant, glossas ubique interponebant, atque ut suam artem ingeniumque cirratae turbae testatum facerent, in eodem argumenti, quod pueris enarrabant, quasi certaturi cum antiquis Poëtis, vires suas experiebantur, monstrososque fœtus suos aut apponere horum operibus, aut genuinis versibus extinctis, subjicere non dubitabant. Pueri autem quibus notis atque interpretationibus veris, falsis, ineptis per lasciviem atque errorem libros suos commaculare soleant, nemo ignorat.[37]

As serious as Cannegieter's fear of corruption seems to be, more significant a factor still in the scholarly neglect of medieval fable commentary

---

[35] Kuhn, "Versuch über das 15. Jahrhundert," 81.

[36] On the significance of school commentary to Chaucer, Langland, and Henryson, see Wheatley, "The 'Fabulæ' of Walter of England." Similarly, the *Yzopet III de Paris*, a mid-fifteenth-century exemplum collection in Middle French prose, seems to rely on the conventions of Latin prose fable commentaries to establish a formal consistency among its forty-three fables; I express here my thanks to Ms. Alison Beringer, Princeton University, for her help in concluding a survey of the Old and Middle French Aesopic tradition.

[37] *Flavii Aviani Fabulae: cum commentariis selectis Albini scholiastae veteris, notisque integris Isaaci Nicolai Neveleti et Casparis Barthii: quibus animadversiones suas adjecit Henricus Cannegieter: accedit ejusdem dissertatio de aetate et stilo Flavii Aviani* (Amsterdam: Martin Schagen, 1731), 287.

has been the ways in which these texts are transmitted. While even in the later Middle Ages the original verse fables of Avianus and those of the Anonymus Neveleti are occasionally encountered in manuscripts that can only be described as luxurious,[38] those manuscripts that preserve prose commentaries on the fables tend to be decidedly unremarkable, usually small-format paper *Gebrauchshandschriften* of the sort endemic to the late medieval schools. The graphic presentation even of the verse texts in these manuscripts can charitably be described as unattractive; the marginal commentaries, however, with which those verse texts are furnished can call forth stronger language.[39] Hervieux complains repeatedly and at length that the commentaries are preserved in handwriting that is at its best "microscopic," at its more typical worst "nearly indecipherable"; he concludes, however, echoing Cannegieter, that

> tous les préambules des glossateurs se ressemblent et que dans tous on retrouve les mêmes idées ineptes exprimées en termes presque identiques,

which to Hervieux's view renders a more thorough investigation of the phenomenon useless except as a measure of the deplorably primitive literary tastes of the late medieval reader.[40] For the past hundred years, then, further inquiry has been largely put off by the not inconsiderable paleographic challenge posed by the commentaries, on the one hand, and their failure, on the other, to promise any kind of aesthetic reward. Predictably and lamentably, these considerations—again, along with the traditional assumption that the late medieval vernacular Aesops depend directly and without intermediary on the verse texts of the Latin fabulists—have likewise prevented the application of any substantial editorial effort to these merely "secondary" texts; while both Avianus and the

---

[38] Among the codices preserving the fables of Avianus, compare, for example, Vatican Library, ms. Reg. 1424, and Dijon, Bibliothèque communale, Ms. 497; both manuscripts, copied on parchment and ornamented with painted figure initials, are briefly discussed in A. E. Wright, "A Cistercian Figure Initial in Vienna," *Wolfenbütteler Beiträge* 11 (1997): 1–7, here 5–6. Even more striking are two fifteenth-century copies of the Anonymus (Berlin, Staatsbibliothek Preußischer Kulturbesitz, Ms. Diez B Sant 4 and Ms. Hamilton 6) prepared for wealthy Italian bibliophiles; both are richly painted and illuminated, and neither, tellingly, mars its vellum leaves with commentary.

[39] A conveniently accessible facsimile of a not unrepresentative manuscript accompanies A. Wright, "*Fabule vtilitatem in se continentes:* Der kommentierte Äsop der Handschrift St. God. 27," in *Bücherschicksale*, eds. Jochen Bepler et al. (Hildesheim: Dombibliothek, 1997), 255–270, here 258.

[40] Similar comments are scattered through volumes 1, 3, and 4 of the *Fabulistes latins*; see, for example, 1: 506–508, 562; 3: 97; 4: 52, 94.

Anonymus have seen their verse collections edited more than half a dozen times in the last one hundred fifty years, no prose commentary on either collection had been reprinted before 1964, when Robert G. Risse made available in his dissertation a partial transcription of a fifteenth-century Avianus commentary.[41] Apart from that single, not invariably accurate source, scholars of the fable have for nearly five centuries had recourse only to the commentaries in several of the earliest printed Aesops, in which the verse fables are accompanied by commentaries that are—most likely as a result of the not inconsiderable technological challenges to be overcome in the reproduction of complex manuscript layouts on the printed page—for the most part atypically brief, simple, and predictable.[42]

As the present study argues, the inaccessibility of these late medieval commentaries on Avianus and the Anonymus has led to serious misapprehensions about the relation between those standard Latin school texts and their vernacular translations in the late fourteenth and fifteenth centuries. Apparent differences in the structural, narrative, and hermeneutic characteristics of the Latin and German fables have too often been described as innovations of the German-language fabulists, when the process of "de-Latinization" in fact commences, as asserted above and as argued below, already within the Latin commentary tradition. Conversely, and yet more significantly, because these prose commentaries have been up until now so little known and so little studied, scholars and literary historians have not yet recognized the Aesopic fable and its transformation in the medieval commentary tradition as among the best and most representative sources of material for investigations of the process of vernacularization.

As a genre, the fable has always been constituted, from Antiquity

---

[41] Robert Gregory Risse, Jr., "An Edition of the Commentary on the Fables of Avianus in Erfurt Ms. Amplon. Q.21.: The Text and Its Place in Medieval Literary Culture" (Ph.D. diss., Washington University, 1964). See also the sources listed in note 26 above.

[42] An instructive example of the dangers encountered in relying on the commentaries printed in the fifteenth and early sixteenth centuries, most often under the title *Aesopus moralizatus*, is provided in Thomas Cramer, "Æsopi wolff," in *Festschrift Walter Haug und Burghart Wachinger*, eds. Johannes Janota et al. (Tübingen: Niemeyer, 1995), 955–966; citing in support of his judgment only the *Esopus moralizatus*, Cramer claims (p. 956) "Die lateinische Kommentartradition beschränkt sich auf eine Auslegung des Fabeltextes unter dem Gesichtspunkt des Leib-Seele-Verhältnisses, der äußeren und inneren Schönheit." The actual wide variety of explications given this fable in the commentaries as preserved *in the manuscripts* is the subject of A. E. Wright, "Readers and Wolves: Late-Medieval Commentaries on 'De lupo et capite'," *Journal of Medieval Latin* 8 (1998): 72–79.

through the Middle Ages and up to the present day, by its peculiar and distinctive combination of *prodesse* and *delectare*; the late medieval locus classicus for this principle of duality is the prologue to the fables of the Anonymus Neveleti:

> Vt iuuet et prosit, conatur pagina presens:
> Dulcius arrident seria picta iocis.
> Ortulus iste parit fructum cum flore, fauorem
> Flos et fructus emunt: hic sapit, ille nitet.
> Si fructus plus flore placet, fructum lege. si flos
> Plus fructu, florem. si duo, carpe duo.
> Ne mihi torpentem sopiret inhercia sensum,
> In quo peruigilet, mens mea mouit opus.
> Vt messis precium de uili surgat agello,
> Verbula sicca, deus, implue rore tuo.
> Verborum leuitas morum fert pondus honestum,
> Et nucleum celat arida testa bonum.

The interlinear glosses accompanying these difficult verses in many of the manuscripts decode the Latin poet's organic metaphors,[43] identifying the book's "flowers" as the *delectatio* proffered by the fables' superficial verbal beauty; the "fruits" borne by the garden are the moral *utilitates* contained in the fables' sentential epimyths. Among the most explicit statements is that preserved in a late-fifteenth-century prose commentary on the Anonymus from a manuscript now in Hildesheim:

> Nota per ortulum debemus intelligere istum librum. Et per fructum et fauorem debemus intelligere documentum fabule, et per florem debemus intelligere fabulam.[44]

In the high and later Middle Ages, this neat twist on the Horatian maxim

> aut prodesse volunt aut delectare poetae[45]

---

[43] On the use of glosses to resolve metaphorical language, compare Gernot Rudolf Wieland, *The Latin Glosses on Arator and Prudentius in Cambridge University Library, Ms. GG 5.35*, Studies and Texts 61 (Toronto: Pontifical Institute of Medieval Studies, 1983).

[44] Hildesheim, Dombibliothek, Hs. St. God. 27, fol. 25r; on the prose commentary of this manuscript, which is in some respects anomalous, see Wright, "*Fabule vtilitatem.*"

[45] *Ars poetica* 333.

becomes a commonplace in literature both Latin and vernacular.[46] In the medieval tradition of the Aesopic fable, these dualities of story and sense, of language and learning were rendered even more complex by their explicit connection with the pedagogic enterprise. Thanks to the privileged position of the fable collections of Avianus and the Anonymus Neveleti within the elementary grammar curriculum, the medieval schoolmasters, commentators, and the pupils themselves construed the linguistic "flowers" springing from the text not simply as words but— and no doubt less pleasurably—as specifically Latin words, intended in classroom practice less for delight than for recitation. The *utilitas*, too, born of those blossoms was likewise understood as necessarily bound to the young scholar's acquisition of the exclusive language of instruction. This understanding of the Aesopic fable as the first vital step in gaining access to the universally Latinate culture of the *litteratus* finds eloquent expression on the title page introducing the earliest separately published edition of Avianus:[47]

Apologus Aviani ciuis Romani adolescentulis ad mores et latinum sermonem capescendos vtilissimus. Cologne: Heinrich Quentell, 1494 (GKW 3110; University of Illinois Library x871.A8.1494).

The fable, thus, is institutionally "utilissimus" for the teaching not just of good manners, *mores*, but of good speech—that is to say, presumptively, Latin speech. For the German-language fabulists of the late Middle Ages, the challenge of translation—or, better, of vernaculariza-

---

[46] Modern critics have nevertheless not always recognized in the miraculous fruit-tree an allusion to the dual signification of figurative language; Anton Schönbach, for example, discussing the use of the image in Hartmann von Aue's *Erec*, remarks charmingly "Aus diesem schmuck, mit dem Hartmann den zaubergarten des Mabonagrin ausstattete, wird man nicht schließen dürfen, daß er damals schon in Italien gewesen sei, denn in besonders guten jahren konnte derartiges"—namely, the simultaneous presence of flowers and fruit—"auch in Deutschland gesehen werden . . ."! *Über Hartmann von Aue: Drei Bücher Untersuchungen* (Graz: 1894), 465.

[47] The *editio princeps* was that published in 1476 as part of Heinrich Steinhöwel's bilingual *Aesop*. The curious woodcut, with its haloed image of the "doctoris tanti sancti," is obviously re-used from an earlier publication; its appropriateness to the Avianus edition was suggested perhaps not just by its depiction of a scene of teaching but by the presence of the *avis* perched on the saintly schoolmaster's shoulder—originally almost certainly the inspiration of the Holy Spirit, here, however, taken wittily as eponymous for the Roman fabulist. (On the use of this cut in other incunables, see Robert G. C. Proctor, "The Accipies Woodcut," in *Bibliographical Essays*, ed. A. W. Pollard [London: Chiswick Press, 1905], 1–12.)

tion—consisted most urgently in disentangling the fable's ethically useful content from its peculiarly academic values, importing into the vernacular the more generally applicable *morum pondus* while abandoning, replacing, or re-functioning the *levitas* of the fable's *verborum latinorum*.

The strategies, gestures, and techniques employed to this end in five German Aesops of the late fourteenth and fifteenth centuries are the subject of the remainder of the present study. Following on Chapter 1's discussion of fable commentary as a Latin, academic phenomenon, Chapter 2, "Corpora and Collections," treats the significant role played by this learned commentary tradition in the conception and birth of the first vernacular German Aesop, the mid-fourteenth-century *Edelstein* of the Zurich monk Ulrich Boner. Where the transmission of the German-language fable before this time is characterized either by a nearly random *Streuüberlieferung* or, alternatively, by assimilation and association to other rhymed short forms,[48] the *Edelstein* is the first corpus of German fables conceived and transmitted as a collection. The innovative coherence of the work as a whole is the result, I argue, of the Swiss Dominican's canny recognition and skillful exploitation of potentials made available in the Latin prose commentary tradition—a source that has gone utterly unrecognized in two centuries of intensive scholarship on the *Edelstein*.[49] As the closer examination in Chapter 2 reveals, the influence of the prose commentaries extends not only to the gross structure of Boner's German-language collection, but also to the style and formal presentation of the individual fables themselves, which invoke, imitate, and successfully adapt to new, vernacular contexts and purposes a number of the distinctive features of the Latin pedagogic tradition.

The effectiveness of Boner's vernacularization—perhaps most easily measured by the collection's impressively dense and durable manuscript history[50]—stands in marked contrast to the apparently only very slen-

---

[48] See Grubmüller, *Meister Esopus*, 124–228, on the codicological distribution of the fables produced in the mid-thirteenth century by Der Stricker; only in the modern editions are the Stricker's animal texts assembled as a coherent corpus, while the manuscripts of the late Middle Ages organize the pieces on different principles, practical and poetological. See also Sarah Westphal, *Textual Poetics of German Manuscripts, 1300–1500*, Studies in German Literature, Linguistics, and Culture (Columbia, S.C.: Camden House, 1993).

[49] A first indication of the significance of the prose commentaries to the larger structure of the *Edelstein* can be had in A. Wright, "Kommentar und Übersetzung: Zur Entlatinisierung der Fabel im ausgehenden Mittelalter," *Wolfenbütteler Beiträge* 11 (1998): 53–72.

[50] See Ulrike Bodemann and Gerd Dicke, "Grundzüge einer Überlieferungs- und Textgeschichte von Boners 'Edelstein'," in *Deutsche Handschriften 1100–1400: Oxforder Kolloquium 1985*, eds. Volker Honemann and Nigel F. Palmer (Tübingen: Niemeyer, 1988), 424–468.

der success of the other principal collection discussed in Chapter 2, namely the Low German "Magdeburg" Aesop from the first decade of the fifteenth century. The reliance of the Low German fabulist on sources closely allied to the Latin commentaries is far more evident here than in the case of Boner's *Edelstein*; as shown below, nearly every fable is given an allegorical explication drawn directly from the learned tradition. Where such elements are used in the *Edelstein* to create coherence and continuity among the fables, however, the poet of the "Magdeburg" Aesop reveals a remarkable clumsiness in his efforts to integrate material from two disparate sources; the "Latinate" elements taken over from the commentary tradition are simply appended to the fables, with no effort—or at least with no obviously successful effort—to accommodate the needs of the German text's vernacular audience. The dissonances thus created quite understandably stood in the way of the "Magdeburg" collection's wider distribution; in fact, this Aesop is known from but a single manuscript, now lost.

Chapter 3, "Aesop's Two Tongues," treats the phenomenon of secondary bilingualism in fifteenth-century manuscripts of German fable collections. Scattered vernacular glosses are not infrequent in late medieval school manuscripts of Avian and the Anonymus Neveleti, and there is even a tradition in the fifteenth century of German-language epimyths within otherwise exclusively Latin commentaries on the Anonymus.[51] More striking still, however, are two Munich manuscripts discovered in the 1970s by Klaus Grubmüller in which the text of Ulrich Boner's German collection shares the leaf with excerpts from Latin school commentaries on the Anonymus Neveleti;[52] a yet more extreme manifestation of the same phenomenon is had in the fifteenth-century Latin epitome of the *Edelstein* first described by Bodemann and Dicke.[53] These manuscripts not only preserve suggestive traces of the actual use of the German-language fable at the end of the Middle Ages, but are eloquent witnesses to a contemporary awareness of the close connection between the Latin commentary tradition and the vernacular Aesop.

---

[51] See Nikolaus Henkel, *Deutsche Übersetzungen lateinischer Schultexte* (Munich: Artemis, 1988), 288–290.

[52] See Klaus Grubmüller, "Elemente einer literarischen Gebrauchssituation: Zur Rezeption der aesopischen Fabel im 15. Jahrhundert," in *Würzburger Prosastudien II: Untersuchungen zur Literatur und Sprache des Mittelalters*, Medium Aevum 31 (Munich: Beck, 1975), 139–159.

[53] "Grundzüge," 439.

The precise nature of that relationship is made clearer by the discussion in Chapter 3 of one of the most singular of late medieval fable collections, the "Wrocław" Aesop; still unedited,[54] this unique late-fifteenth-century manuscript combines the Latin verse fables of the Anonymus Neveleti, two different Latin prose commentaries, and a complete Aesop in rather undistinguished Middle German verse. Previous evaluations to the contrary, the vernacular fables are not immediately dependent on either of the manuscript's two Latin commentaries, but rather serve to provide a third distinct set of annotations. The German text thus claims an equivalence not only to the verses of the Anonymus but to the scholarly apparatus surrounding them; the simultaneous presence of all these elements on a single manuscript leaf gives graphic expression to the assimilation of the German Aesop to its Latin forebears—and the ultimate displacement of the learned tradition by its vernacular heirs.

Chapter 4, "Verse, Prose, and the Fable in Fifteenth-Century Vienna," considers that displacement under the specific aspect of poetic form. The Latin fable tradition of antiquity and the Middle Ages is characterized by the nearly regular alternation of collections in verse and collections in prose. The vernacular Aesop, on the other hand, was nearly obligatorily a rhymed genre; of the German-language collections discussed in Chapters 2 and 3—the Alemannic *Edelstein*, the Eastphalian "Magdeburg" Aesop, and the Silesian "Wrocław" Aesop—all are composed in four-beat couplets, the conventional prosodic form of short narrative in the German Middle Ages. The first attempt to render a fable collection in German prose was made in the first or second decade of the fifteenth century, in Vienna; named for a later stage in the provenance of the only known manuscript, this so-called "Nuremberg" Aesop combines word-for-word translations of two Latin prose commentaries, one on the Anonymus Neveleti and one, by a different author, on Avian. The Viennese fabulist's decision to render these sources in German prose must be considered in the light of theories then current among Austrian scholars and translators, whose works and ideas in important ways anticipate the practices of better-known prose writers half a century later. Preparing for the most part theological and devo-

---

[54] The best introduction to the text is found in Henkel, *Deutsche Übersetzungen*, 225–227; transcriptions of a small number of the German fables, nearly illegible as most of them are in the manuscript, are provided in Chapter 3 below.

tional tracts for use at the young University and the ducal court, the Viennese translators in their prologues and prefaces explicitly link prose form with edifying intention, and are at pains to reproduce in the vernacular as many of the learned gestures of their sources as possible. The translator of the Austrian Aesop found in his Latin commentary sources the ideal combination of formal rigor and moralizing content. In spite of the care and considerable skill evident in the work's attempt to replicate both for a vernacular audience, this German Aesop does not appear ever to have found the wider reception its translator had hoped; the text is preserved in but a single, apparently early manuscript, and in no later fable collection, whether in verse or in prose, can its influence can be discerned. Aesthetically, the "Nuremberg" Aesop is a remarkably attractive specimen of early New High German prose; its failure, however, must be explained as the result of a process of vernacularization that proved, ultimately, to be incomplete.

Some decades after the completion of the Austro-Bavarian prose Aesop, another poet, writing in part for the same Viennese lay circles at court and university as the earlier translator, took advantage of closely similar Latin sources. Michael Beheim, active in the middle of the fifteenth century at a number of courts in the German-speaking southeast, included among the works he composed for the Austrian Albrecht VI some three dozen fables; even a cursory examination of these texts demonstrates that Beheim's chief sources were not, as usually assumed, the verses of Avian and the Anonymus Neveleti, but rather, just as in the case of the author of the "Nuremberg" Aesop, the academic prose commentaries. Unlike his Viennese predecessor, however, Beheim—who, though demonstrably familiar with much Vienna School prose, does not seem to have known the earlier fable collection[55]—intentionally departed from the formal precedent set in his Latin sources to compose fables in singable strophes. In stark contrast to the author of the "Nuremberg" Aesop, for Beheim, verse alone was appropriate to the imparting of learned moral material in the vernacular.[56] Chapter 4 concludes with a summary discussion, based in a comparison of the treatment of com-

---

[55] Preliminary evidence supporting this conclusion is presented in Wright, " 'Nuremberg' Aesop," 311–312.

[56] This problematic is addressed under the aspect of vernacular literacy and orality by Ingeborg Spriewald, *Literatur zwischen Hören und Lesen: Fallstudien zu Beheim, Folz und Sachs* (Berlin: Aufbau, 1990). Spriewald deals (40–48), to my view unsatisfactorily, with Beheim's attitudes towards prose and verse; compare the brief review by A. E. Wright, *Journal of English and Germanic Philology* 92 (1993): 391–392.

mentary sources in the "Nuremberg" Aesop and in the fables of Michael Beheim, of the complex relationship between verse and prose, Latin and vernacular, lay and learned in the fifteenth century—a discussion whose relevance extends beyond the history of a single, minor genre.

'Hie lert uns der meister'

Latin Commentary and
the German Fable 1350–1500

CHAPTER 1

Moraliter, Allegorice, Scholastice:
Latin School Commentary on Avian and the Anonymus Neveleti

To the extent that the Latin fable collections of Avian and the Anonymus Neveleti can be said to have found modern readers at all, those brave souls have confronted the Latin texts in the profoundly anachronistic—and profoundly misleading—form of critical editions. For some two centuries, the scholarly attention paid these two collections has been almost exclusively philological, concerned in the first (and, as a rule, in the final) instance not to recover the historically attested circumstances of reading, but rather to "establish" a critically authentic text; the beginning of such efforts can be discerned as early as Isaac Nevelet's carefully compiled *Mythologica* in the seventeenth century, or even, with greater caution, in Steinhöwel's *Aesop* one hundred fifty years before.[1] In this century and the last, such scholarly reconstructions of Avian and the Anonymus have had as their principal goal the clearer understanding of the place of those texts in a diachronic tradition of the Aesopic fable; both Latin texts have accordingly been subordinated in the editorial tradition to their older, more authentic, or more interesting kindred. Thus, Avian's forty-two *apologi* have been made

---

[1] On Heinrich Steinhöwel's activities as "editor" of the Latin fables he collected, see especially Gerd Dicke, *Heinrich Steinhöwels 'Esopus' und seine Fortsetzer: Untersuchungen zu einem Bucherfolg der Frühdruckzeit*, Münchener Texte und Untersuchungen 103 (Tübingen: Niemeyer, 1994), 40–76.

available largely as an aid to the study of his principal source, Babrius, while up until now the most important editions of the Anonymus Neveleti have been those prepared as comparative appendices to editions of later vernacular collections;[2] the better to serve such purposes, both are presented in the standard editions in a form as "pure" and as nearly "original" as possible, studiously purged of the accretions of mere reception.

It is painfully obvious, however, that such critical editions, for all their considerable value otherwise, can provide at best only a partial impression of the ways the fable collections of Avian and the Anonymus Neveleti were actually used—the ways, that is to say, they were read—in the late Middle Ages and the early modern period. Antonio Guaglianone, for example, supplements his carefully prepared and clearly legible texts of the forty-two *apologi* of Avianus with an extensive and extensively learned apparatus enumerating the poet's sources and identifying apparent citations in the works of an impressive range of later classical and medieval authors. These notes are obviously intended above all to help fix Avian's place in the reception and transmission of classical knowledge in the Rome of late antiquity; such erudite annotations—Guaglianone's as well as those supplied by the other editors of the collections here under discussion—describe a process of transmission that is implicitly seen as both abstract and purely textual, a narrow line traced from author to eponymous author over the centuries. Reception, thus, is imagined in the modern editions as a network of discrete but interdependent instances of monumental writing, the origins and relationships of which are to be recovered and reconstructed by historiographic investigation.[3]

Measured against this philological standard, the late medieval manuscripts of Avian and the Anonymus Neveleti are decidedly ineloquent; when the marginal notes of the fourteenth and fifteenth centuries do cite from the texts of other authors, later and earlier, it is never obviously

---

[2] For a list of modern editions of the Anonymus, see Wright, *The Fables of 'Walter of England'*, 14.

[3] To be fair, Guaglianone's proposed investigation of Avianus in the Middle Ages would likely have gone beyond the traditional, almost positivistic approach taken in the edition as described here; I am grateful to the staff of the Herzog August Bibliothek, Wolfenbüttel, for their kind efforts in confirming that the promised study was not, in fact, ever published or even, it seems, completed. For late Antiquity, see Robert A. Kaster, *Guardians of Language: The Grammarian and Society in Late Antiquity* (Berkeley: University of California Press, 1988), esp. 170–196 on the combination in late antique commentary of exegesis and linguistic instruction.

the commentator's goal to establish a source relationship among works, but rather, in a familiarly medieval process more of association than of affiliation, to adduce additional authoritative examples of a word, a phrase, or a thought encountered in the text of the fabulist. The marginalia of the British Library's Anonymus Neveleti manuscript described in the Introduction, for instance, are not intended to assert the genetic descent of any given passage from the classical authors they cite; the annotations represent instead the first building blocks of a simple *dilatatio*, the introduction and elaboration of certain of the additional material the schoolboy can look forward to reading in the further course of his Latin studies.

As it is to be understood in the present investigation, "reception" consists in precisely these artifacts of everyday reading, teaching, and learning in the late Middle Ages. While the ultimate advantages of such an approach are easily appreciated, its results, if they are to be meaningful, cannot derive solely from the study of anything so abstract and so ideal as a "text," but must rather be based in a close understanding of the historical, material realities of reader and book.[4] In their abundance and their variety, the manuscripts of Avian and the Anonymus Neveleti produced in the fourteenth and fifteenth centuries seem to provide a picture of remarkable clarity and completeness of the ways readers were meant to use these books. While from the point of view of the traditional philologist, the texts these late medieval codices preserve may well be inauthentic, corrupt, bad, it is precisely those same additions, revisions, and officious improvements so conscientiously deleted by the modern editors that permit us to some extent to retrace the steps of the contemporary readers and translators of the Aesopic fable, and ultimately to assign the manuscript collections to, so to speak, their late medieval *Sitz im Lesen*.

With that as its goal, the remainder of this chapter will serve as an introduction to the richness of the fourteenth- and fifteenth-century commentators and their treatments of Avian and the Anonymus Neveleti. The first section offers an extensive study of the medieval commen-

---

[4] A useful introduction in English to one aspect of this "material philology," namely the study of text associations in manuscript miscellanies, is provided by the introduction to Stephen G. Nichols and Siegfried Wenzel, eds., *The Whole Book: Cultural Perspectives on the Medieval Miscellany* (Ann Arbor: University of Michigan Press, 1996). See also Baswell, *Virgil in Medieval England*, 5–9.

tary tradition, broadly tracing the reception of a single, still well-known fable of Avian's in a variety of learned contexts from antiquity through the late Middle Ages; the second section then concentrates intensively on the salient features of a number of individual commentary manuscripts from the fourteenth and fifteenth centuries, ranging for its material across a number of fables drawn from both Latin collections.

I

Seeing a pitcher, a thirsty crow swooped down, but the water level was too low to quench his thirst. Undaunted, he gathered pebbles, which he dropped one by one into the pitcher. The water level rose and at last he drank.[5]

Nearly two thousand years after its first preserved attestation, the fable of the crow and the pitcher remains among the best-known representatives of the genre. No modern child's "Aesop," of course, is without its brightly illustrated retelling; this fable, moreover, is at the same time one of the very few from the classic corpus that still occur with some regularity in contexts outside of traditional children's literature. The precise circumstances of this modern *Streuüberlieferung* can at times be startling, as, for example, in a series of newspaper advertisements from the early 1990s, where the fable, as cited above, is retold in illustration of the advantages of a particular financial strategy:

For mutual fund investors, the moral is: A consistent approach may raise the level of your reward. ... It's called dollar cost averaging. ...[6]

This "moral" may seem at first regard incongruous, even laughable. In fact, though, the lesson derived here, for all its mercenary singlemindedness, is thoroughly consistent with the epimyth deduced in more traditional versions of the fable: in the words of the first and perhaps most influential of modern "Aesops,"

Interdum id quod non potes efficere ui, efficies prudentia et consilio.[7]

---

[5] "The Crow and the Pitcher," advertisement in *The Wall Street Journal*, February 22, 1992, p. C-11.

[6] *The Wall Street Journal*, February 22, 1992, p. C-11.

[7] *Aesopi Phrygis et vita ex Maximo Planude desumpta, et fabellae iucundissimae* ... , ed. Martin Dorp (Strasbourg: Schurer, 1518), 45. On this important collection and its considerable influence on the development of the modern "Aesop," see particularly Paul Thoen,

It is plain on reflection that in no way does the advertisement's explication of the fable contradict this broad principle; what startles is not the perfectly acceptable moral tendency of the lesson, but rather the extreme particularity with which it is applied there to a very specific, very modern realm of human conduct.

The remarkably narrow focus of this moral specifically "for mutual fund investors" is far from typical of the Aesopic fable as it is understood today. Instead, the exegetic impulses of the genre are now thought characteristically to proceed in precisely the opposite direction, moving from the particular—the events recounted in the fictional narrative—to the universal—the principle asserted in the explication. The typical hermeneutic structure of the fable in its modern textual form is thus entirely inductive; the final, deductive step, in which the epimyth's general lesson is applied, is left to the reader, whose identification of a relevant situation or circumstance for application takes place outside the text, immediately subsequent to the act of reading.

In the form offered in the advertisement, the fable relies for its effectiveness on the conspicuous violation of just these generic expectations. Rather than the unidirectional exegesis described above as typical of the Aesopic fable in the modern period, the explication imposed by the newspaper ad reveals two distinct and opposed rhetorical tendencies. The interpretation given here moves first, in the familiar and traditional way, from the particulars of the crow's behavior to a general assertion about the advantages of persistence; then, however, it proceeds, by deduction from that general principle, to prescribe in detail the precise circumstances in which that virtue is to be exercised, thus pre-empting the role customarily played by the fable's reader. Indeed, if a fable is a "fictitious story picturing a truth" that "must always be a general one,"[8] then this version of the crow and the pitcher is no fable at all, but rather a sort of extended metaphor. While the narrative in its entirety is capable of supporting a broad and abstract truth—namely, that persistence can be profitable—the explication's true focus is on the particular elements of that narrative, each of which the reader is invited—or rather, is obliged—to identify, on the basis of an analogous function or position, with the equally particular elements of the real-life situation to

---

"*Aesopus Dorpii*: Essai sur l'Esope latin des temps modernes," *Humanistica Lovaniensia* 19 (1970): 241–316.

[8] B. E. Perry, "Fable," *Studium generale* 12 (1959): 17–37, here 22.

which it corresponds: the crow, accordingly, must represent the canny investor, and its thirst the profit motive; the pitcher is the economy, the water the investment return; and the pebbles, "dropped one by one into the pitcher," parallel precisely small investments regularly made until "at last" the investor's thirst is assuaged. Thus constructed on principles of correspondence and analogy, the fable becomes an allegory, and its moral a moralization.

The modern reader is as much struck by the technical novelty of such an interpretation as titillated by the unexpected confrontation of the fable and high finance; and yet this interpretive strategy is not without precedent in the history of the genre. For in the later Middle Ages, epimyths of this sort, highly specific and specifically applied, not only were frequent, but indeed came in the fourteenth and fifteenth centuries to be the dominant mode of explication in the most important Aesopic collections of the time, both Latin and vernacular. Such epimyths, many of them no less surprising in their applications than the modern example discussed above, are an especially distinctive feature of the prose fable commentaries prepared in the later Middle Ages for classroom use.

As mentioned above in the Introduction, these manuscript commentaries remain quite inaccessible to the modern reader,[9] and the rare printed texts from the late fifteenth and sixteenth centuries are for the most part considerably abridged or otherwise less useful than those in the manuscripts.[10] Before turning to an overview of the commentaries on the fable of the crow and the pitcher, it will be well to review the

---

[9] For a late fifteenth-century Anonymus Neveleti commentary, see Wright, *The Fables of 'Walter of England'*. For a fifteenth-century commentary on Avian, see Risse, "An Edition of the Commentary on the Fables of Avianus," 97–242; unfortunately, Risse's transcription is neither complete nor unfailingly accurate, as was apparent from a collation of his text with the manuscript.

[10] Two different Anonymus Neveleti commentaries (of the type commonly known as the *Aesopus moralizatus*) from prints of the early sixteenth century are now available in photographic reproduction and are more or less accurately transcribed in the appendix to Wheatley, "The 'Fabulae' of Walter of England"; both, however, are quite brief in comparison to the commentaries preserved in many manuscripts. For a cautionary illustration of the dangers in relying on such printed texts to the exclusion of the manuscript tradition, see Cramer, "AEsopi Wolf"; compare Wright, "Readers and Wolves." In contrast, the exceedingly rare *Apologus Aviani* (Cologne: Quentell, 1494), GW 3110, is exceptional in offering a prose commentary quite as thorough as any in the manuscript tradition; the prose annotations supplementing the fables there are particularly close to those of the Avian commentary in Augsburg, Universitätsbibliothek, cod. II.1.4o.27 (see Bedrick, "The Prose Adaptations of Avianus").

textual basis of this story as it was transmitted from antiquity into the Middle Ages.

Of all the most familiar examples of the genre, this fable of the crow and the pitcher is among the last to be attested. In its earliest preserved version, in fact, the story is not presented as a fable at all, but rather as a scientific curiosity: Pliny, writing in the middle of the first century, reluctantly memorializes in the tenth book of the *Naturalis historia* a raven

> visum per sitim lapides congerentem in situlam monimenti, in qua pluvia aqua durabat, sed quae attingi non posset; ita descendere paventem expressisse tali congerie quantum poturo sufficeret.[11]

It is not inconceivable that this episode, which the natural historian in his account rather archly attributes to an otherwise unidentified "quidam," was already in Pliny's day known as a fable, whether in written or oral form.[12] The earliest clearly Aesopic version that can plausibly be reconstructed, however, dates to no earlier than the second century, when it is likely that the Hellenizing Roman poet Babrius included the fable in his *Mythiamboi*. While none of the extant fragments of this oldest known collection in Greek verse includes the fable of the crow and the pitcher, two slightly later compilations, both of which are known to have borrowed other fables directly from Babrius's collection, do retell the fable in Greek prose;[13] it is, therefore, reasonable to assume that in

---

[11] *Nat. Hist.* X.43.125. On the broader medieval reception of Pliny's book, see Arno Borst, *Das Buch der Naturgeschichte* (Heidelberg: Carl Winter, 1994).

[12] "Tradendum," he says, "putauere memoriae quidam ...," plainly unwilling to take full responsibility himself for the episode's historicity (*Nat. Hist.* X.43.125). The fable is not known from either of the only two extant fable collections older than the *Naturalis Historia*, namely the Greek *Collectio Augustana* and the Latin "Aesop" of Phaedrus.

[13] These are the third-century bilingual *Hermeneumata Pseudodositheana*, number 8, edited in G. Goetze, ed., 3: 43, 98, and in Georg Thiele, *Der lateinische Äsop des Romulus* (Heidelberg, 1910), 285 (Latin text only); and the "Byzantine paraphrase" of Babrius number 200, doubtfully reconstructed by Léon Herrmann, *Babrius et ses poèmes*, Collection Latomus 135 (Brussels: 1973), 182. The *Hermeneumata*, dating from the first quarter of the third century, preserve the oldest extant Latin text in which the material is clearly cast as a fable: "cornix sitiens accessit ad hydriam et eam conabatur convertere. sed quia fortiter stabat, non poterat eam deicere. sed remedio obtinuit, quod voluit. misit enim calculos in hydriam, et eorum multitudo de imo aquam sursum effudit, et sic cornix sitim suam reparavit. sic ergo sapientia virtutem fallit." (Thiele, *Der lateinische Äsop*, 285, the readings given here those of the tenth-century Leiden manuscript; the somewhat younger Paris copy already shows the influence of subsequent versions of the fable in its substitution of "urnam" for the first "hydriam.")

this case as well the later fabulists relied on the *Mythiamboi*, and that there was indeed a version of the story among the approximately eighty Babrian fables that have not yet been recovered.[14] This assumption is strengthened by the occurrence of the fable in a third late-antique collection likewise known to have relied heavily on Babrius for its material, namely, the forty-two fables in elegiac distichs attributed to the Roman poetaster Avianus.[15]

It was as the twenty-seventh poem in this collection that the fable of the crow and the pitcher assumed what would be throughout the Middle Ages its authoritative form:

De cornice et urna
Ingentem sitiens cornix aspexerat urnam,
  Quae minimam fundo continuisset aquam.
Hanc enisa diu planis effundere campis,
  Scilicet ut nimiam pelleret inde sitim,
Postquam nulla viam virtus dedit, admovet omnes
  Indignata nova calliditate dolos.
Nam brevis immersis accrescens sponte lapillis
  Potandi facilem praebuit unda viam.
Viribus haec docuit quam sit prudentia maior,
  Qua coeptum volucris explicuisset opus.[16]

---

[14] The estimate is drawn from Holzberg, *Die antike Fabel*, 58. The early tradition of this fable is likely to remain a matter of debate so long as no more direct evidence for its inclusion in the *Mythiamboi* is available. M. J. Luzzato and A. LaPenna, *Babrius: Mythiamboi Aesopei* (Leipzig: Teubner, 1986) do not mention this fable in their discussion of the use of Babrius by Pseudo-Dositheus (xii, xxxii–xxxiii); Holzberg, *Die antike Fabel*, similarly omits this fable from his list of those whose Babrian heritage he considers unproven but "sehr wahrscheinlich" (34). Thiele, *Der lateinische Äsop* (LXVII, 284), Crusius (*Reallexikon* Sp. 2376), and Herrmann (182), on the other hand, assume a model similar to that sketched here, according to which the three earliest preserved versions of this story—in Pseudo-Dositheus, the Byzantine paraphrase, and Avian—all represent reflexes of an otherwise lost poem of Babrius. See John Vaio, "Babrius and the Byzantine Fable," in *La fable*, 197–224.

[15] In his introductory epistle, Avian explicitly identifies among his sources the older poet's "duo volumina" (Guaglianone, 4); Grubmüller, *Meister Esopus*, 59, identifies a certain Babrian source for at least 36 of Avian's 42 fables. The notion that Avian consulted Babrius through the intermediary of an otherwise unknown Latin prose translation by Titianus (see, for example, Grubmüller, *Meister Esopus*, 59) cannot be confirmed by the ambiguous passage usually cited in its support; compare Wright, "The 'Nuremberg' Aesop," 99, n.5; Luzzato, *Babrius*, introduction; and, especially, Holzberg, *Die antike Fabel*, 70–72.

[16] Guaglianone, 48–49. Two manuscripts, in which Avian's fables are presented first in the Latin original and then in French verse, go on to provide a concluding distich (labeled "Addicio"): "Omne genus uirtutum nam prudencia uincit/Virtutum mores regulat arte sua" (Paris, Bibliothèque nationale, ms. Fr. 1594, fol. 106r; London, British Musuem, ms. Add. 33781, fol. 130r); see Kenneth McKenzie and William A. Oldfather, *Ysopet-Avionnet: The Latin and French Texts* (Urbana: University of Illinois Press, 1919), 245.

For all its unlikely prosody and recherché diction,[17] Avian's was the version in which the fable would be read, memorized, and commented for over a millennium.

As has already been observed, Avian's fables owed their wide and enduring reception to their early adoption as a school text. By the eighth century at the latest, when Alcuin is said to have prepared a commentary on the fables for the use of his pupils,[18] Avian had gained a firm place in the elementary Latin curriculum alongside such well-established primers as the Distichs of Cato, the Eclogues of Theodulus, the Physiologus of Theobald, and one or another of the medieval "Aesops." As a standard component of the anthologies known as "Libri catoniani," Avian's forty-two poems were among the very first Latin works to be confronted and, ideally at least, mastered by the neophyte pupil in the cloister schools.[19]

The early and almost universal classroom use of Avian's fables in the medieval West seems in retrospect strangely at odds with the widely expressed scorn to which the high and later Middle Ages would subject their author.[20] The injunction often encountered in the manuscript *accessus*,

Fabule sunt attendende et non ymitande,[21]

may well be a gentle warning against Avian's barbarous style in the fables. For all their sometimes earthy vigor, however, the schoolmasters' objections applied in the first instance only to the Roman poet's inflated literary aspirations and his rather unsatisfactory attainments; as a practical matter, these same teachers appear to have been entirely able to overcome their aesthetic reservations in order to exploit the collection's purely pedagogic advantages. Whatever their stylistic shortcomings, the

---

[17] On Avian's use of the elegiac distich, see Holzberg, *Die antike Fabel*, 73–76, and especially Küppers, *Die Fabeln Avians*. Guaglianone, 48, discovers in just these five distichs echoes of Vergil, Claudian (but cf. Küppers), Vegetius, and Cicero, as well as a parallel to the epimyth of an otherwise lost fable of Phaedrus.

[18] See Max Manitius, *Geschichte der mittellateinischen Literatur*, 3 vols. (Munich: Beck, 1911, repr. 1974), 1: 512, and Oldfather, "New Manuscript Material for the Study of Avianus," 115–116. According to Guaglianone, ix, the last scholar to have actually seen Alcuin's manuscript commentary was K. Barth.

[19] On the use of the Aesopic fable in medieval education, see the bibliographic notes in Wright, *The Fables of 'Walter of England'*, 2–3.

[20] See the disparaging pun on the fabulist's name in Hugo von Trimberg's *Registrum*, quoted in Grubmüller, *Meister Esopus*, 58: "... Avianus / Inque suo carmine blaterans ut anus / ... / Scribens enim ut ipsius avi tonat anus."

[21] Quoted here from the fifteenth-century preface to Avian in Wolfenbüttel, Herzog August Bibliothek, cod. guelf. 185 Helmst., fol. 95r.

fables of Avian were obviously well suited to the moral education of young children, teaching as they do a variety of useful and salutary ethical lessons in an entertaining and memorable way; as has been aptly remarked in a different context, "[g]ute Lehre im Munde von Unwürdigen war dem späteren Mittelalter kein Problem."[22] Accordingly, the *accessus*, in the course of their schematic discussions of the poet's intention and his work's utility, explicitly emphasize the fables' moral content:

> Intentio huius actoris est ... instruere auditores in bonorum moralitate,

notes one such introduction, while another identifies the "utilitas" of the text

> ut perlecto libro presenti sciamus ... bonis operibus inherere.[23]

Avian's putative intention "de moribus sew virtutibus pertractare"[24] is taken in many *accessus* as a clear sign that the poet considered his work a specimen of "moral philosophy"; for example, the Avian paraphrase found in Würzburg, Bibliothek der Franziskaner-Minoriten, cod. I.42, claims that the work that follows "supponitur ethice et moralistice, quia tractat de moribus" (fol. 146v).[25] This, of course, is a commonplace in medieval *accessus* literature, which identifies in all poetic texts—not just the Aesopic fable—a bulwark against failings of an ethical nature:

> contra vicium inuenta est philosophia moralis, que sibi subalternat poetriam.[26]

While the fable's moral aspect is plainly of tremendous importance to the late medieval schoolmaster, the annotations present in many of the manuscripts point at the same time to an additional, quite different emphasis in the classroom use of Avian. While the fables' moral utilities

---

[22] Kurt Ruh, "Heinrich Wittenwilers 'Ring'," in *Festschrift Herbert Siebenhüner* ed. Erich Hubala (Würzburg: Schöningh, 1978), 59–70, here 64.

[23] Wolfenbüttel, Herzog August Bibliothek, cod. 13.10.Aug.4o, fol. 157v; cod. guelf. 185 Helmst., fol. 95r.

[24] Munich, Bayerische Staatsbibliothek, clm 22404, fol. 61r.

[25] On the prose Avian transmitted in this manuscript, see Dicke and Grubmüller, *Katalog*, lxxii.

[26] Wolfenbüttel, Herzog August Bibliothek, cod. guelf. 185 Helmst., fol. 95r. On the essentially moral nature of the poetic text in medieval literary theory, see J. B. Allen, *The Ethical Poetic of the Later Middle Ages: A Decorum of Convenient Distinctions* (Toronto: University of Toronto Press, 1982).

are never completely neglected, the clear preoccupation of most of the text's commentators is with another, more immediately practical matter: the teaching and learning of Latin. The same stylistic features that so compromised their literary worth made Avian's fables ideal for assignment to the beginning Latinist. The syntactic obscurity of the distichs provided abundant material for exercises in parsing and construction, while their sometimes outlandish diction could be exploited to enrich the young pupil's vocabulary. The interlinear glosses and marginal notes present in so many of the manuscripts let no opportunity pass to draw the reader's attention to these purely linguistic aspects of the fables; they define and distinguish new or unfamiliar words, and point out clearly the poet's observance—and his occasional violation—of grammatical rules and literary conventions. Avian writes, for example, in his very first fable

> Rustica deflentem parvum iuraverat olim,
>   Ni taceat, rabido quod foret esca lupo,

to which the commentators of three manuscripts, plainly disapproving the barbarous lapse in the poet's usage of the subjunctive in indirect discourse, rather archly respond

> Est ibi tempus pro tempore: *taceat*, id est *taceret*.[27]

The fifteenth-century author of the *Liber Esopus et Avianus* provides in his epilogue a rare explicit justification for the commentary enterprise; his book—a collection of prose fables with clear commentary antecedents—was written, he says,

> pro informacione scolarium et puerorum et pro leuitate doctorum, ut eo facilius haberent lecturam, et versos pro latino dare illos et istum librum legere breuem, quem pueri faciliter acquirere possunt, qui longos libros, scilicet Esopum et Auianum, propter prolixitatem fugiebant.[28]

Where the involved prosody of the verse originals serves only delight,

---

[27] Wolfenbüttel, Herzog August Bibiliothek, 13.10.Aug.4o, fol. 54v; Copenhagen, Kongelige Bibliotek, cod. 2136 4o; Urbana, University of Illinois Library, x871A8.1400.

[28] Budapest, National Széchényi Library, Cod. Nem. Muz. 123, fol. 46r ("for the learning of pupils and children and for the convenience of teachers, so that they might learn their text that much more easily, both to give [et . . . et] those verse texts for Latin and to read this short book, which children can learn easily who once despised the long books, namely Aesop and Avian, on account of their long-windedness").

blocking the ready understanding of the texts, prose—says the Budapest commentator—has the advantage of modernity and brevity.[29]

The fable of the crow and the pitcher is among the briefer and more straightforward of Avian's poems, and thus its annotation tends at this purely grammatical level to be less intensive than that furnished certain more challenging texts; indeed, a few otherwise heavily commented manuscripts leave this fable completely unmarked. In most of the manuscripts, however, even these relatively simple verses are accompanied at least by a set of interlinear glosses, generally lexical and syntactic in their focus.[30]

There is a plain chronological progression in both the abundance and the graphic presentation of these elements in the manuscripts. Generally speaking, the glosses and marginal notes in copies of Avian prepared in the thirteenth and early fourteenth centuries have not yet been organized along the clearly structured, "through-composed" commentary schemes typically encountered in manuscripts written in the last two centuries of the Middle Ages; instead, each explanatory element tends rather to be introduced *ad hoc*, its relationship to the verse fable text made clear both by the use of lemmata and by the placement of the note as close as possible to the passage to be commented on the manuscript page. For example, the Avian in Wolfenbüttel, Herzog August Bibliothek, 13.10 Aug. fol., written in eastern France in the last quarter of the thirteenth century, adds in the margins surrounding the verse fable of the crow and the pitcher a series of brief notes intended, at least in part, to ease the pupil's access to Avian's distichs. The first annotation, introduced by an underscored reference to the last word of Avian's fable, consists in a rhetorically pointed restatement of the moral provided in the penultimate verse:

> *Opus.* quasi dicit: melior est prudentia animi quam robur corporis (fol. 2r).

The margin next to line 6 of the verse text is occupied by a gloss on "indignata," which supplies the reader with both a definition of the word

---

[29] Fol. 46r; compare also the remarks of the second commentator in clm 16213, reproduced below.

[30] The following discussion relies for much of its terminology on the useful taxonomy of the various sorts of glosses common in medieval school manuscripts provided in Wieland, *The Latin Glosses on Arator and Prudentius*. See also Baswell, *Virgil in Medieval England*, 54–55.

and an explanation of the source of the bird's frustration: "Indignata, id est indignationem habens de hoc quod non poterat contingere fundum aque." Considered as lexical and narrative in intention, this gloss seems both incompetent and unnecessary: it is singularly unhelpful to define "frustrated" as "bearing frustration," and the source of the thirsty bird's annoyance must anyway be already apparent to all but the most desperately unskilled pupil. It seems likely instead that this gloss serves in the first instance as a grammar aid, indicating the recommended construction of the prosodically ambiguous participle with the unstated nominative subject "cornix," thus anticipating and preventing its undesirable parsing as an ablative modifying "calliditate."

Immediately following this note, but without any attempt to provide a prose context that might integrate the two annotations narratively, the glossator remarks that

bene dicit quod cornix admouit dolos;

it is unclear for the moment whether his approval is directed at the poet's apt choice of words or at the crow's clever application of stratagem. The gloss on verse 7,

lapillis. id est super lapillos,

is more plainly grammatical in intention, suggesting that "lapillis" is to be taken as a locative in the dative case; this annotation, however, confirms the suspicion raised above about the glossator's relative inexpertise as a reader of Latin verse, for—as his contemporaries well knew[31] —the noun belongs to an absolute construction with the passive participle "immersis," and must therefore properly be understood as in the ablative, "pebbles having been dropped in."

The marginal commentaries on this fable conclude in the Wolfenbüttel manuscript with a pun, an obscure schoolboy's joke copied here not, it seems, for its slender relevance to the story of the thirsty crow, but rather out of sheer delight at its cleverness:

cornix est alba si cor tollatur ab illa.[32]

---

[31] Compare, for example, the interlinear glosses given in the Darmstadt manuscript to be discussed immediately below, where "lapillis" is explicitly and correctly construed with "immersis" earlier in the same line.

[32] Leaving, in other words, only the syllable "nix": "Take away the part/ That was her heart/ And the blackest crow/ Is white as snow."

As this brief description has intended to make clear, the annotations in the Wolfenbüttel Avian are strongly paratactic, offering information and explication with no obvious effort to present in the commentary a complete and consistent retelling of the fable; instead, only a selection of elements—those, naturally, deemed most likely to confuse or mislead—are glossed, and the reader is forced to rely on the verse text itself for any fuller understanding of the fable. The marginal notes themselves make no sense alone, read singly or seriatim, but rather remain entirely subordinated to the original distichs of Avian, to which they refer explicitly with underscored lemmata and verbs of speaking—"bene dicit ..."—and without which they communicate nothing.

What appears to be an intermediate stage on the way to the more prolix commentaries of the last two centuries of the Middle Ages is preserved in two German school manuscripts, both dating from the early fourteenth century, now held in the Hessische Landesbibliothek, Darmstadt. The first, cod. 2640, has suffered considerable loss under the binder's knife, and many of the interlinear glosses originally present have, for whatever reason, been subsequently rubbed out; nevertheless, despite their fragmentary state of preservation, this manuscript's marginal glosses on the story of the crow and the pitcher attest clearly to the process of accretion that would lead, not much later, to the composition of full-blown prose commentaries on Avian's fables. Throughout his copy, the scribe of the Darmstadt codex fills the paper margins of the manuscript with odd sentences associatively adduced, revealing a clear predilection for rhymed Latin proverbs. The three separate notes copied next to the verses of Avian 27 are typical:

> – cornix alba si cor -atur ab illa.
> – lbe cornices nec meretrices – .
> – meretrix munda nec cornix alba fecunda.[33]

A later hand adds beneath these annotations the vocabulary note, likewise mechanically mutilated by trimming:

---

[33] Here and throughout, single n-dashes in my transcriptions represent material illegible or missing in the manuscripts, while the omission of material irrelevant to my discussion is indicated by points of ellipsis (...). The final sentence here is plainly garbled from that printed in Hans Walther, *Proverbia sententiaeque Latinitatis medii aevi: Lateinische Sprichwörter und Sentenzen des Mittelalters in alphabetischer Ordnung*, 6 vols. (Göttingen: Vandenhoeck, 1963), no. 16212: "Nec meretrix munda nec cornix alba fit unda."

– dolus equivocum dolus est – prudencia seu fraus – dolus
a doleo fit – vnde: sine dolo.[34]

While graphically and intellectually no more a coherent whole than
their counterparts in the slightly older Wolfenbüttel manuscript discussed above, the first set of comments in the hand of the text scribe is
of note for its casual introduction of the "meretrix," a figure, of course,
not so much as alluded to in Avian's fable. The commentator's inspiration is supplied ultimately by the pun, present also in the Wolfenbüttel
codex, which depends for its wit on the image of the heartless black bird
made white as snow; and it is this antithesis, it seems, that in turn elici-
ted the proverbial *impossibilia* that culminate in the paradoxical notion
of the "meretrix munda," the chaste courtesan.[35] As we shall see, this
connection, here made in all apparent innocence, is further developed in
surprising ways in the fuller commentaries of the fifteenth century.

The slightly younger note on "dolus" is drawn from the *Grecismus*
of Eberhard of Bethune, an important and popular thirteenth-century
textbook treating, among other grammatical topics, the proper distinction of Latin homonyms and homographs. This annotation too, like
those dealing with the "meretrix," anticipates—indeed, prepares—certain
tendencies in the later, fuller prose commentaries given this fable; for
where in Avian's verse text the crow's behavior is, in the most positive
sense of the word, exemplary, a thoroughly laudable demonstration of
the power of wit over weight, the comment drawn from Eberhard
points to the potential for a semantic and, more importantly, a moral
ambiguity in the bird's successful application of "dolos," an ambiguity
given full elaboration in those fourteenth- and fifteenth-century moralizations to be discussed below that explicate the crow, black and crafty,
in malam partem.

Some of the same elements present in this and the Wolfenbüttel
codex are included as well among the annotations on the fable of the
crow and the pitcher in a second Darmstadt manuscript. Although it is

---

[34] Eberhard of Bethune, *Graecismus*, ed. Johann Wrobel, Corpus grammaticorum medii
aevi 1 (Wrocław: Koebner, 1887; repr. Hildesheim: Olms, 1987), IX: 30.

[35] Compare also Walther, *Proverbia*, no. 1648: "Ater olor, nivea cornix, nigra nix, aqua
sicca / Inveniuntur ea citius quam pulchra pudica"; no. 1910: "Balnea cornici quid prosunt
vel meretrici?"; no. 12539k: "Instar enim corvi prius exoculant mulieres / Nos, post excere-
brant, prout ostendunt liquide res." As will be discussed below, this last proverb is likely
more closely allied to the encyclopedic natural history than to the Aesopic tradition.

most likely no younger than that just described, Hessische Landesbibliothek cod. 23b preserves marginalia and interlinearia that are denser,
more abundant, and even more revealing than those in the first Darmstadt codex.[36] This copy of Avian preserves copious interlinear glosses
for nearly all the fables, along with a large number of marginally in-
scribed vocabulary notes. Remarkably, this manuscript also includes frequent annotations treating the rhetorical aspects of Avian's fables; in
this, codex 23b is exceptional, as in only a vanishingly small number of
others is there any evidence that the late-medieval school enterprise ever
subjected these elementary texts to any investigation beyond the grammatical. Even here, however, the "rhetorical" commentators are satisfied with the simple one-word identification of the figure at hand; their
analysis is exhausted in the label identifying the figure.[37] Avian 27 in
this Darmstadt manuscript is left without any such rhetorical analysis,
but the fable is furnished with a complete set of interlinear glosses and
two marginal vocabulary notes, which, of interest in themselves, at the
same time provide important impulses that will be fully elaborated in
the allegorizations given the fable in some of the later commentaries.

Because the language of Avian's verse fable 27 is relatively easy, the
interlinear glosses accompanying it in this manuscript are accordingly
simple.

Darmstadt, Hessische Landesbibliothek, cod. 23b, fol. 157v and
173r, interlinear glosses on Avian 27, "De cornice et urna":

	Lemma	*Gloss*
v. 1	Ingentem	id est magnam
	sitiens	id est totum desiderans[38]

---

[36] Cod. 23b, too, suffered harm in the binding process, with the result that a number of
the Avian fables in this manuscript are out of place or otherwise disrupted. The current
state of Avian 27, the fable of the crow and the pitcher, is particularly unfortunate. The
copying of this text was begun on the last folio of one quire and completed on the first leaf
of the next; in binding, another gathering was erroneously placed between those two, leaving the fable to begin on fol. 157v and to end on 173r. The text is, however, complete.

[37] This is the case as well in manuscripts of the Anonymus Neveleti: compare Wright,
The Fables of 'Walter of England', 8. Even the most outrageously rhetorical of the Anonymus's fables elicit at most the identification of one or the other of the *colores* invoked; of
the almost painful *tour de force*, for example, beginning Anonymus Neveleti 1, the occasional commentator remarks only: "In isto textu committitur color decimus nonus qui dicitur
gradatio" (Prague, National Library, ms. XI.C.4, fol. 1r).

[38] "Totum" is here almost certainly a scribal error for "potum," thus "desiring a
drink"; note, however, that the gloss as executed here already casts the crow's thirst, "desiring *everything*," in a bad moral light.

	cornix	sic dicta
	vndam	urnam
v. 2	minimam	id est modicam
	fundo	supple in
v. 3	hanc	supple urnam
	enisa	supple cornix
		id est connata
	effundere	id est extra uel ex toto fundere
v. 4	nimiam	id est plus iusto
	inde	aduerbum ordinis
	sitim	id est desiderium bibendi
v. 5	viam	supple bibendi
	virtus	id est vis
	dedit	id est prebuit
	admovet	id est ad iungit
v. 6	Indignata	supple cornix
		id est irrata
	calliditate	astucia
	dolos	id est calliditates, fraudes uel prudencias
v. 7	brevis	supple vnda
	immersis	id est missis
	sponte	id est ultro, voluntarie
v. 8	potandi	id est bibendi
	unda	id est aqua
v. 9	Viribus	supple corporis
	haec	supple cornix
	quam	id est quantum, aduerbum quantitatis
v. 10	Qua	supple prudencia
	coeptum	id est inceptum
	volucris	id est cornix
	explicuisset	id est soluisset

These glosses are for the most part unexceptional, characteristic representatives of the interlinearia found in the Avian manuscripts of the late Middle Ages. Typically, glosses of two broad types predominate. Grammatical glosses communicate information about the morphology and syntax of the lemma they explicate. Clearly belonging to this category here are the explicit identifications of "inde" (verse 4) and "quam" (verse 9) as adverbs of time and quantity, respectively, as well as the parsing help provided by the interlinear preposition "in," which resolves the unmodified "fundo" of verse 2 as an ablative.[39]

Somewhat more unusual, on the other hand, is the gloss given "cornix." Most manuscripts gloss the name of the bird in this fable simply and unhelpfully "talis avis," just as they most frequently gloss the names of mammals "tale animal" and of insects, amphibians, and reptiles "talis vermis."[40] The present gloss contains no more semantic information than those decidedly reticent annotations; "sic dicta," however, makes perfect sense if it is understood as in fact a grammatical gloss, communicating to the schoolboy reader information—most notably gender—about the lemma not immediately transparent from the noun's form.

A mixed form, combining the functions of both grammatical and lexical glossing, is had in "connata," the gloss offered for "enisa" in verse 3; while the glossator's attempt to provide a synonym for Avian's participle is plain, the substitution of one deponent verb for another is likely to have been intentional, with the goal of assuring the schoolboy reader's attention to a specifically grammatical peculiarity of the lemma.

As one might expect given the use of Avian's fables in the elementary Latin curriculum, pure lexical glosses—synonyms and brief definitions of potentially unfamiliar vocabulary items—are far the most frequent type in the manuscripts. For the most part, these glosses define their lemmata in a way consonant with their use in the verse text; occasionally, however, a definition or synonym will be given that does not accord with the meaning of the lemma as it might be deduced from the context. In this Darmstadt manuscript, for example, the gloss on "nimiam" (verse 4) appears to insist on the primary classical meaning of the word, "excessive," while it is clear from the fable that Avian here in fact uses it already in its usual medieval sense of "exceeding." And the explication given "dolos" two lines later,

id est calliditates, fraudes, uel prudencias,

rather than easing the young reader's comprehension of the verse, needlessly complicates his understanding with the indication that the word can be taken neutrally, negatively, *or* positively, where both the context of Avian's fable and his conspicuous use of the noun "prudentia" in the epimyth (verse 9) in fact require a specifically positive construction. In

---

[39] On the frequent use of interlinear prepositions to mark the case of noun lemmata, see Wieland, *The Latin Glosses on Arator and Prudentius*, 54–56.

[40] For example, Munich, Bayerische Staatsbibliothek, clm 22404.

instances such as this, the gloss does not serve solely the explication of the verse fable's sense, but rather leads the reader away from the lemma's meaning as suggested by its original context.

Such apparent contradictions between the lexical explanation given in the gloss and the narrative function played by the lemma are by no means infrequent in the fable manuscripts of the later Middle Ages. These disparities are an easily understood artifact of the pedagogic use of the fable texts; while one purpose of classroom explication was, obviously, to render comprehensible Avian's difficult verses, there is an additional, more general utility discernible in the glosses: the fable texts were not only read for their narrative and moral content, but also provided the raw materials for vocabulary-building exercises. As such, the glossators' comments on individual vocables at times necessarily encapsulate a broad discussion of alternative meanings that, as here, leads the schoolboy reader away from the particular sense given the word in the fable. The centrifugal impulse provided in such glosses had ultimately a not insignificant influence on certain of the prose commentaries on this fable, as we shall see.

A somewhat different phenomenon is observed in the gloss "urnam," which annotates "vndam" in verse 1. While the words are nearly synonymous—both, after all can be taken metonymically to mean "water"—this is most likely an instance of editorial glossing, its intention to suggest the replacement of the lemma by an alternative *lectio*. In this case, the emendation is entirely appropriate, resulting as it does in the restoration of a reading superior to that here erroneously copied into the verse fable; the lemma "vndam" of this manuscript likely began as a gloss in its exemplar, whence it migrated to a position of authority within the text itself through a process not without precedent in the schoolbooks of the late Middle Ages. Indeed, it seems likely that the presence of certain, less clearly implausible variant readings in fourteenth- and fifteenth-century manuscripts of Avian's fables may have arisen from precisely such erroneous substitution of a metrically unobjectionable gloss into the original verse texts.

Most of the remaining glosses on the verse fable in the Darmstadt manuscript are narrative in nature, suppletive glosses providing elements omitted, suppressed, or postponed in the verses but nevertheless useful or necessary to the reader's understanding of the fable. Adjectives, for example, are construed by glossing them with their often remote head nouns; thus, Avian's long-winded fourth distich (verses 7–8) is rendered slightly more comprehensible by the gloss "supple vnda" given "brevis," and the nominalized participles "enisa" (line 3) and "indignata" (line 6) are both identified as modifying the unstated subject "cornix."[41] Similarly, certain metaphorical or otherwise periphrastic expressions are decoded for the reader by glossing them with a genitive noun: lest the "viam" of verse 5 be taken as somehow a literal "way," it is glossed with a genitive of definition, "supple bibendi," while the "viribus" unfavorably compared in the epimyth are specified as merely physical by the subjective genitive "supple corporis."[42]

Where pronouns might seem potentially unclear in their reference, noun antecedents are often supplied, as in verse 3 where the demonstrative "hanc" is glossed as "urnam," or in the final verse, where the relative "qua" is explicitly linked to its antecedent "prudentia." When the correct construction of a pronoun is genuinely ambiguous in Avian's verses, the interlinear gloss necessarily reflects the glossator's own judgment, and often preserves richly suggestive clues to the ways the fable texts were read in the late Middle Ages. Most manuscripts of this fable of the crow and the pitcher, for example, gloss the demonstrative "haec" that introduces the epimyth (line 9) "supple fabula," thus grounding the moral authority of the concluding sentence in the literary narrative that precedes it; in this Darmstadt Avian, however, the glossator resolves the pronoun "supple cornix," making it the crow itself whose actions, without the need for any narratorial intermediary, establish the truth of the lesson set forth. A similar variation is encountered again in the fuller prose commentaries of later decades, where the fabulist is said in some to have proved his ethical point "per fabulam," in others "per cornicem."

In this Darmstadt manuscript, certain vocabulary notes too extensive for interlinear insertion have been placed instead in the margins. Avian's use in verse 2 of the word *fundum*, "bottom," elicits a comment about the variable gender of the noun:

> Notandum quod multi dicunt quod pro "fundo aque" dicitur *hoc*
> *fundum*, sed pro "agro" dicitur *hic fundus* (fol. 157v).

---

[41] Compare the discussion, above, p. 13, of the marginal annotation on this word in Wolfenbüttel, Herzog August Bibliothek, cod. 31.10 Aug. fol.

[42] Such combinations call to mind one of the most salient features of the florid style developed by vernacular German poets in the thirteenth and fourteenth centuries; it seems reasonable to suppose that the genitive periphrastics so typical of this "geblümter Stil" had their inspiration at least in part in this specifically Latin and characteristically academic practice.

In this note, both the ending of the noun and the demonstrative adjective make plain its gender in each of its different significations; once again, however, we find the glossator offering information unnecessary to a fuller understanding of the fable, where the word itself is used as a locative, "fundo," thus making it impossible to determine whether the poet's usage is "correct" or not. A second marginal gloss is preserved at verse 9 of the fable:

Grecismus. Est dolus equivocum, dolus est prudencia siue fraus (fol. 173r).

Here the annotator of the Darmstadt manuscript provides the authority for the interlinear gloss on "dolos," citing to the ninth book of Eberhard's vocabulary text.

In spite of the best efforts of the medieval glossators, some especially complex distichs remained likely to mystify the beginning Latinist. For prosodic and stylistic reasons, many of the verses of Avian and the Anonymus Neveleti alike separate spatially words whose logical association would suggest that they belong together. A good example, and hardly unique, of the lengths to which this practice could be taken is provided by the penultimate distich of Avian's fable of the crow (verses 7–8), in which the principle of the separation of semantically related words finds nearly obsessive application: every adjective in these verses is distant at least two words from the noun it modifies, and the subject of the sentence consists of a phrase whose individual components ("brevis ... unda") are symmetrically placed as far apart as possible, as the second and the second-to-last words of the distich, framed by the subtle near-rhyme "Nam ... viam."

In many late-medieval fable manuscripts, such complex verses, whether glossed or not, are furnished with a full set of construe marks,[43] indicating especially which adjectives pertain to which substantives.[44] The simplest such systems use underscoring and overscoring to distinguish the components of each noun phrase in a given verse; such marks are occasionally encountered even in manuscripts where the task of con-

---

[43] On various graphic systems for construction, see Wieland, *The Latin Glosses on Arator and Prudentius,* and Tony Hunt, *Teaching and Learning Latin in Thirteenth-Century England,* 3 vols. (Cambridge: Brewer, 1991).

[44] It is rarer to encounter graphic systems linking verbs with their subjects, a function already performed adequately by grammatical glosses marking a noun as in the nominative case.

struction is carried out largely within the verbal glosses.[45] In manuscripts whose apparatus makes more consistent use of construe marks,
however, they are most often provided in the form of Arabic numerals
that re-order the words in such a way as to make syntactic alliances
clearer.

Often, as is the case in this Darmstadt manuscript, numerical construe marks go further to re-arrange the entire sentence, effecting a new
word order for the verses that more closely follows the "normal" sequence typically displayed by prose. The interlinear numerals in the
present manuscript suggest the following construction for verses 7 and
8 of Avian's fable:

Nam brevis vnda accrescens immersis lapillis sponte prebuit facilem viam potandi (fol. 173r).

Thus re-ordered, and further explicated by the grammatical and lexical
glosses already described above, this distich can be approached by even
the most inexperienced reader along a "facilem viam." The sentence
generated with the help of the pedagogic apparatus represents already in
its simplicity a sort of intralingual "translation," a rendering of narrative
content from a highly rhetorical, self-consciously poetic language into a
Latin that is, syntactically at least, far less stylized and far more readily
comprehensible. Moreover, the standard of syntactic straightforwardness
imposed by the construe marks of the Darmstadt manuscript is not,
ultimately, Latin at all; the new word order strives not for the periodic
syntax characteristic of Latin prose, but rather is satisfied to adhere to
patterns that are unmistakably vernacular. In this sense, the incon-
spicuous Arabic numerals ornamenting Avian's verse can even be considered, without exaggeration, to present an incipient de-Latinization, to
anticipate and to prepare the translation of the fable into German.

In the later fourteenth and fifteenth centuries, the tendencies already
observed in the interlinear and marginal annotations of these and other
earlier manuscripts of Avian and the Anonymus Neveleti gave rise to a
new and fuller commentary type. As we have seen, the glosses in the
manuscripts of the thirteenth and early fourteenth centuries tended to
be paratactic and accumulative, characterized by the accretion by association of gnomic material, grammatical comment, and editorial delibera-

---

[45] As in, for example, both the Avian and the Anonymus Neveleti found in Wolfenbüttel, Herzog August Bibliothek, cod. guelf. 185 Helmst., where occasional construe marks
of this sort are scattered through the texts, drawn in an ink identical to that used for the extensive interlinear glosses given in both collections.

tion in the margins, but not yet integrated into a well-defined "commentary" text of recognizable structural uniformity and moral or pedagogic directedness. In the last two centuries of the Middle Ages, however, these elements came to be expanded and then subordinated to stereotyped textual structures, giving the prose commentaries a certain formal and narrative autonomy. By elaborating the centrifugal impulses of many of the glosses described above, the later commentaries would eventually attain an independent authority that would allow them to compete with the verse fable collections themselves: a fact taken full advantage of by the vernacular fabulists of the fourteenth and fifteenth centuries.

A typical example of these fuller Latin commentaries of the late Middle Ages is that preserved in the Copenhagen manuscript, Gl. Kgl. Saml., 1905 4o:

> *Ingentem.* Hic docet quod ingenium preualet uiribus, et hoc per coturnicem que dum sitiret in quodam campo urnam semiplenam aqua inuenit, quam uiribus inclinare non potuit. Sed eam ingenio lapillis inpleuit et istam aquam extraxit. Fructus talis est: Melior est sapiens forti uiro (fol. 139r).

Brief as it is, this segment from a fourteenth-century commentary, copied and transmitted separately from Avian's original verses, already exhibits the formal conventions and stereotyped formulas that give the commentaries a describable textual tradition quite independent of that of the verse fables.

In typical fashion, this commentary begins with a lemma. These introductory words or phrases correspond to the incipit of the verse fable under discussion, and have as their primary goal to help the reader match commentary to commented text; they are usually somehow graphically distinct from the commentary proper, written in an exaggerated display script, rubricated, or, as here and most commonly, underscored by the scribe. The purely practical value of such cross-references in their original Latin academic setting is plain from the graphic preparation of such commentaries as that on the Anonymus Neveleti in Wolfenbüttel, Herzog August Bibliothek, cod. guelf. 185 Helmst., where lemmata are used only when the excessive length of the commentary segments requires their physical separation on the manuscript leaf from the shorter verse fables; otherwise, mere physical proximity is apparently sufficient to assure the correct association of fable and commentary.[46] In manu-

---

[46] See Wright, *The Fables of 'Walter of England',* 6 and note 25.

scripts such as the Copenhagen codex, of course, which transmits only
the commentaries without the accompanying verse *apologi*, the lemma
is absolutely indispensable, not only serving the proper alignment of primary text and annotation, but also providing the internal articulation of
the commentary accomplished in other manuscripts by the regular alternation of prose with verse fables. As we shall see below, such academic
functions are subject to radical displacement when they are taken over
into the vernacular Aesops of the fifteenth century; no longer serving
any practical purpose as cross references, the Latin lemmata present in
some German collections come instead to be markers of authenticity
and authority, vouching definitively for the "learnedness" of the material they introduce.

The lemma in the Copenhagen commentary is followed immediately
by a promyth, here introduced "hic docet"; this formula varies slightly
among commentaries, both in the particular verb and in the agency of
instruction. While the verb of instruction is most frequently "docere,"
as here, a brief review of the manuscript annotations of Avian 27 reveals
a number of different options. While "docere" is in the majority, "ostendere," "hortari," "intendere," "dicere," and "monere" all occur
more than once. This range is representative of not only the commentaries on Avian and the Anonymus Neveleti, but of the medieval tradition of academic exegesis as a whole; Geoffrey of Vinsauf, describing
the schoolmaster's task in his *Documentum*, notes that if the explicatory
text begins with a proverb or "generalis sententia," one should continue
with an expression such as "fatetur," "docet," "probat," or "attesta-
tur."[47] The subject of these verbs—the source of all this teaching,
urging, and showing—is the fabulist himself, usually called "autor" (or
"actor" or "auctor"), but occasionally referred to by name, as in this
fifteenth-century German commentary on the fable of the crow and the
pitcher:

> In hoc appollogo Auianus docet quod melior est prudencia quam
> fortitudo uel vires. . . .[48]

By thus grounding the moral validity of the fable in the verbal authority
of the fabulist, such introductory formulas effect a reduction in the

---

[47] *Documentum de arte versificandi*, ed. Edmond Faral, *Les arts poétiques du xiie et xiiie
siècle*, Bibliothèque de l'école des Hautes études 238 (Paris: Champion, 1924; repr. Geneva:
Slatkine, 1982), 269.

[48] Munich, Bayerische Staatsbibliothek, cgm 3974.

probative status of the narrative, a shift made even plainer by the commentaries' widespread introduction of promyths, concise statements of the story's lesson preceding the actual retelling of each fable. These anticipatory sentences are not originally a feature of the Latin verse fable; none of the sixty fables of the Anonymus Neveleti is furnished with a promyth, while only once does Avian anticipate his moral with a didactic summary at the beginning of one of his poems.[49] Absent or exceptional in the verse tradition, promyths are, however, a conspicuous element in many of the prose commentaries. The Munich commentary just cited is typical in offering as its promyth an obvious prose paraphrase of Avian's epimyth

Viribus haec docuit quam sit prudentia maior,

while the Copenhagen promyth just as plainly reflects the influence of interlinear glossing in its composition: "ingenium" is a ready synonym for the verse fable's "prudentia," while the verb "preualet," governing as it does the ablative, is a natural choice to gloss Avian's "sit ... maior," a construction itself requiring an ablative of comparison. Both strategies—the straightforward prosing of the original verse epimyth and its variation through the use of synonyms—are widespread in the commentaries,[50] although more liberal reformulations are by no means rare. The author of a commentary preserved in a fifteenth-century manuscript now in Wrocław finds that

in hoc appologo docemur quod multa sunt que citius fiunt per artem quam per vires,[51]

---

[49] Guaglianone, no. 34: "Quisquis torpentem passus transisse iuventam/ Nec timuit vitae providus ante mala,/ Confectus senio, postquam gravis affuit aetas,/ Heu frustra alterius saepe rogabit opem." The sentential distichs introducing three further fables (numbers 5, 7, and 8) in many younger manuscripts of Avian are certainly the additions of one or the other medieval redactor of the fables.

[50] Promyths similar to that in cgm 3974 are found in Lincoln, Cathedral Library, C.5.8.; London, British Museum, ms. add. 10090 and Harley 4967; Munich, Bayerische Staatsbibliothek, clm 609; Peterhouse, cod. 2.1.0; Vat. reg. 2080; St. Petersburg, QvCl.Lat.N.6; Stuttgart, Landesbibliothek, ms. 34; Urbana, University of Illinois Library, x872.c686.1400; Prague, Universcitní Knihovna, ms. 546. The Copenhagen promyth occurs, with minor variations, in the commentaries on this fable in, for example, Copenhagen, S.2136; Munich, Bayerische Staatsbibliothek, clm 237, clm 631, and clm 14703; Vat. pal. 1573; Vat. Regina 1556; Vienna, Österreichische Nationalbibliothek, cpv 303; Winchester, Cathedral Library, ms. III,A; and Wolfenbüttel, Herzog August Bibliothek, ms. 288 Gud.

[51] Wrocław, Bibl. univ., ms. cod. Q.126, fol. 130r.

while others expand or continue the thought to include a direct admonition to the reader:

> Hic monet nos ut studiosius acquiramus scientiam quam vires, quia magis proficit.[52]

Or:

> Hic docet auctor quod prudencia preferenda est viribus et monet nos ut studeamus omnem scienciam vel prudenciam.[53]

And:

> Hortatur nos quod plus debemus appetere prudenciam quam fortitudinem, quia cum prudencia possumus aliquando perficere quod non cum fortitudine [et] quod non perducere per vires ad effectum possumus per prudenciam ad effectum perducere.[54]

The expansion is often accomplished by the addition of gnomic material, as in the Munich manuscript cgm 3974, already cited above, where the promyth continues with what appears to be a proverb:

> Vnde: Homo sepe vincit illa per sapientiam que per vires non faceret. Eciam monet nos ut studiosius sapientia et ingenio insistamus magis quam viribus (fol. 228v).

In the extreme case, such promyths are so expansive as to assume a virtually homiletic function, as in a fifteenth-century manuscript now in Budapest:

> In hoc appollogo auctor docet nos quod queramus prudenciam, dicens "Tu debes scire quod prudencia est maior viribus et prevalet eam, quia per sapienciam vincet homo qui viribus vincere non posset." Ideo subiungit dicens quod sapiencia complet opus cuiuslibet hominis inceptum. Vnde Salomon Prouerbiorum: "Potencior est sapiencia."[55]

---

[52] Berlin, Staatsbibliothek Preußischer Kulturbesitz, cod. Q 536, fol. 9r.

[53] Munich, Bayerische Staatsbibliothek, clm 391, fol. 29v.

[54] Vienna, Österreichische Nationalbibliothek, cpv 15071, fol. 68v.

[55] Budapest, Magyar nemzeti múzeum, ms. lat. med. aev. 123, fol. 15r (citing Prov. 24:5: "vir sapiens et fortis est et vir doctus robustus et validus"). While the fables in this manuscript were most likely intended to form an independent collection, their debt to the prose commentary tradition, in both form and content, is unmistakable. See Dicke and Grubmüller, *Katalog*, xxxvii.

Even where the introductory matter of the commentaries is less prolix, in their highly stylized consistency these formal elements—mechanical, even trivial, as they may seem to modern eyes—effect a decided shift
in the status and focus of the text they introduce. In the two-parted
structure of their verse fables, both Avian and the Anonymus are strict
traditionalists, attracting the audience's attention with a narrative before
imposing a moral; thus, the reader's experience of the fables in their
original verse form is in the first instance one of literary *delectatio*, the
enjoyment of a story. The late-medieval authors of the prose commentaries, in contrast, must hardly have needed to concern themselves with
the benevolence of their already captive audience, and instead took the
liberty of directing their pupils' attention immediately to the pedagogical utility of the texts at hand. Accordingly, the repeated *inquit*-formulas
described above focus the reader's concentration not on the story, but
rather on the didactic intentions of the story-teller; the schoolboy is explicitly reminded from the start that his entertainment has, in fact, a
very serious purpose. The point is made even sharper by the commentaries' formulation of promyths anticipating the moral sense of the story
to be told. In the verses of Avian and the Anonymus, the "moral" sense
of the fable is derived; it not only follows, but follows from, the narrative that precedes it. Even this basic narrative tension is absent in the
commentaries, where a promyth gives away the "meaning" of the story
from the very beginning; suspense, it seems, was not among the pedagogic techniques preferred in the Latin schools of the later Middle Ages.
Thus in the prose commentaries, the moral lesson of each fable is presented from the beginning as a specimen of original and self-existent
truth, and this truth is no longer predicated on the result of the events
of the narration; rather, that narration is to be read as an example—an
exemplum—of that truth.[56] As presented in the commentaries, the fable
proper no longer *requires* a certain moral conclusion, but needs only to
be consistent with the general rule posited in the commentator's promyth.
The fable no longer generates moral truth, but simply illustrates it.

Consider again the Copenhagen commentary reproduced above; as
in many such texts, the transition between the commentator's promyth
and the retelling of the fable is effected by the stereotyped phrase "et
hoc per coturnicem qui. ..."[57] Thus the principal actor in the fable is

---

[56] The "Liber Avianus et Esopus" (see note 55; fol. 15r) follows its homiletic promyth
with "Exemplum Auiani de cornice: Cornix siciens ualde. ..."

[57] Similar rhetorical transitions to bring the reader back to the matter at hand are

introduced in an oblique case, the object of *per*, literally as the instrument and not the object of communication; the clever crow's exploits are retold in the commentary in a series of dependent clauses. Even grammatically, the fable narrative is rendered clearly secondary to its message.

In these ways, the prose commentaries on the verses of Avian and the Anonymus Neveleti intentionally and systematically assert, even more than generic convention would require, the special status of the fables' moral content, reducing the significance of the narrative to that of mere illustration. This inversion of the original relation between story and truth has as its ultimate effect a new fictionalization of the fable narrative; by loosening the logical connection between the fable and its lesson, the commentaries free the stories for variation, adaptation, and revision.

This tendency to narrative innovation in the prose commentaries can be seen clearly in their retellings of Avian's fable of the crow and the pitcher. As we have seen, the Copenhagen commentary, quoted above page 23, offers a very short and straightforward paraphrase of the events narrated in Avian's fable. An even simpler method for creating such "reductions" was, of course, simply to render the fabulist's verse into prose, a procedure conveniently prepared, as we have seen, by the glossator's work in many manuscripts. The prose retelling of a fifteenth-century commentary now in the University Library, Prague, for example, provides in several places little more than a slightly clumsy prose construction of Avian's verses:

> Ingentem sitiens. Hic actor ostendit quod *prudencia est* melior et *maior viribus*. Ergo studiosius admonet ut sciamus et prudenciam acquiramus, quod probat dicens: Quedam sitiens cornix volans per campum venit ad vnum fontem, quem circa vidit pendere vnam vrnam in qua modicum aque fuit, quam haurire non valebat. Post hec cupiens *effundere vrnam planis campis*, quia cornix nusquam potuit inclinare, tandem invenit sua arte calliditatem, et congregans lapillos in vrnam misit. Quibus immissis aqua sursum ascendit et sic habuit *facilem viam potandi*. . . .[58]

---

described approvingly by Geoffrey of Vinsauf in the *Documentum* II, 1, 2: "Si principium artificiale sumptum fuerit a medio vel a fine et ita recessum fuerit a naturali principio, continuandum est per nomina relativa . . ." (ed. Faral, *Les arts poétiques*, 268).

[58] Prague, Universitní Knihovna, ms. 546, fol. 22r (emphasis added).

The italicized phrases echo Avian's verses directly, while several others of the words in this prose reduction seem likely to have their origins in interlinear glosses.[59] The doublet "melior et maior" in the commentary's epimyth, for example, suggests an editorial gloss on Avian's "maior," as does the commentator's "immissis" corresponding to the poet's "immersis"; the prose text's "cupiens" may well have begun life as a lexical gloss on "enisa" in the verse fable.

Note, however, that even this commentary's brief prose retelling, for all its verbal fidelity to certain of the more difficult passages in the original verses, introduces elements of plot neither present there nor likely derived from any tradition of glossing. The conciseness of the verse fables of Avian and the Anonymus Neveleti, in each case the product of both generic convention and stylistic preference, can verge on narrative reticence, and it can in fact come as no surprise that the late medieval annotators should have taken advantage of the freedom afforded them by the conventions of their own genre to introduce into the commentaries new motivations, causalities, or simple embellishments lacking in the verse fables. Such an effort to produce a more coherent, more readable text is evident in the additions made by the author of the Prague commentary. The crow's thirst, which in Avian's poem is merely asserted in the participle "sitiens," is here explained as the result of the bird's exertion in flying "per campum." The giant "urna," likely still understood by Avian as a funerary ornament, must have seemed mysterious in the extreme to the late medieval schoolboys of central Europe, and its rather sudden presence is justified in the commentary by having the crow arrive at a well, above which there hangs what can only be a bucket. It is best, perhaps, to refrain from thinking too deeply about the role of physics in the fable as recast by the commentary, but it is worthy of note that this is precisely the image one encounters in the woodcut illustrating the fable in Steinhöwel's "Aesop," whence it has passed firmly into the modern iconographic tradition of this fable.

Some others of the innovative elements observable in the prose commentaries are the result of apparent scribal errors. The attentive reader will by now have noticed that the Copenhagen commentary cited above identifies the protagonist of Avian's fable 27 not as a crow but as a quail, *coturnix*. This is easily understood as an example of scribal care-

---

[59] Not, however, in the interlinear glosses of this manuscript.

lessness, made possible by the fact that the commentary was after all copied without the accompanying verse fable for comparison and control. It is possible, though, that even this is not the gratuitous substitution it seems: quails, on biblical authority, are desert birds, and as such are perhaps more likely to suffer extreme thirst than the average dooryard jackdaw. Whether intentional or not, the change from crow to quail is not significant in the setting of the prose commentary; either bird is as well suited as the other to demonstrate "quod ingenium preualet uiribus."

Another manuscript transmitting virtually the same commentary as the Copenhagen codex preserves a less felicitous error. The fifteenth-century scribe of the Munich manuscript clm 631, while correctly identifying the avian actor, went on to misread an extremely significant verb in his exemplar; where in the Copenhagen manuscript the bird is thirsty, *sitiret*, the copyist of clm 631 gave to the ages the unfortunate *lectio facilior*

> cum staret in quodam campo.[60]

Another Munich commentary on the same fable preserves a text that is marred by an equally improbable—but ultimately productive—error. Cgm 50 is a poorly copied Avian from the fourteenth century; the scribe, his skills best described as slight, appears to have worked from an exemplar written in a Gothic hand whose *r* and *e* resembled each other so closely as to have been at times indistinguishable. Thus, three times in the course of the commentary segment treating the fable of the crow and the pitcher, the copyist substitutes for the expected word "vrnam" what seems to be in fact "venam," "a ditch." This odd variant could be dismissed as merely a nonce reading generated by an inexperienced scribe if not for the existence of two French manuscript illustrations[61] depicting the crow standing in a field (reminiscent of clm 631's "cum staret in campo") and rather stupidly dropping stones into a shallow ditch, just as described in the commentary of cgm 50:

> Tandem collegit paruos lapides et misit in venam. ...

The bilingual manuscripts containing these illustrations do provide the

---

[60] Munich, Bayerische Staatsbibliothek, clm 631, fol. 161r.
[61] London, British Museum, ms. add. 33781, fol. 129v; Paris, Bibliothèque nationale, ms. Fr. 1594, fol. 106r.

correct reading "urnam" in Avian's Latin verses, but the French translations that follow accord with their illustrations, and so with the commentary of cgm 50, in identifying the crow's antagonist as a "rucel" or
"ourcelle." The obvious explanation is that the translator of the French
"Avionnet" had before him a Latin manuscript commentary whose
readings for "urnam," like those in cgm 50 and its (unidentified) exemplar, were uncertain, illegible, or incorrect; the miniaturist in turn,
relying on the vernacular text before him in illustrating the fable, faithfully reproduced the crow standing not before a vessel, but a ditch.[62]

No doubt partly to avoid such errors, many of the commentators of
the fourteenth and fifteenth centuries had recourse in composing their
reductions to parallel versions of the fables in prose. In the case of commentaries on the Anonymus Neveleti, such material was widely available in the various "Romulus" fable collections of late antiquity and the
Middle Ages. Where it was available, the late classical Romulus *recensio
vetus* was particularly favored, in large part because of its greater attention to the completeness and logical coherence of the events narrated in
the fables; commentaries based on the thirteenth-century Romulus LBG
were ultimately more successful, however, as it was such a text that
would in the fifteenth and sixteenth centuries be printed along with the
verses of the Anonymus Neveleti as the "Aesopus moralizatus."[63]

There is considerable variation among such commentaries in the extent to which elements taken over from the Romulus tradition have
been adapted to accord with the version of a given fable found in the
Anonymus.[64] Although there are manuscripts whose commentaries
consist almost solely of prose fables lifted from one or another Romulus
and copied *in extenso* next to the Anonymus's verse fables,[65] it is most
usual to find the commentators selecting brief passages from a secondary
Latin prose source and then paraphrasing, simplifying, and adapting that

---

[62] Compare Bruno Herlet, *Studien über die sog. Yzopets (Lyoner Yzopet, Yzopet I und
Yzopet II)* (Leipzig: Fock, 1889), 69; according to Herlet, the French translator was merely
an incompetent Latinist, who translated "urna" as "rucel" and placed the bird "en un
champ," so that "die ganze Fabel völlig sinnlos wird."

[63] On the relative frequency in the commentaries of material from the various Romulus
recensions, see Wright, "The 'Nuremberg' Aesop," 281–290.

[64] The best discussion of this phenomenon, with illustrations taken from the fable
manuscripts of the Bayerische Staatsbibliothek, remains Erich Seemann, *Hugo von Trimberg
und die Fabeln seines Renners* (Munich: 1921), 27–36. Additional analysis of the use of Romulus material in the commentaries on the Anonymus Neveleti is had in Wright, "The 'Nuremberg' Aesop," 280–289.

[65] For example, Vienna, Österreichische Nationalbibliothek, cpv 303.

material to supplement their own prose retellings. In the version of the Anonymus Neveleti, for example, the well-known fable of the dog and his reflection is terse to the point of unintelligibility:

> Nat canis ore gerens carnem. Caro porrigit vmbram.
> Vmbra coheret aquis. Has canis vrget aquas.
> Spem carnis plus carne cupit, plus fenore signum
> Fenoris. Os aperit, sic caro spesque perit.
> Non ergo debent pro vanis certa relinqui.
> Non sua si quis amat, mox caret ipse suis.[66]

While the rhetorical skill evident in these verses is considerable, the Anonymus makes no attempt to describe the motivation for the dog's wasteful behavior, leaving the reader little more than an image of the dog pawing anxiously at the waves.

Unsatisfied by such reticence, many commentators[67] availed themselves of the somewhat fuller recounting given in the prose Romulus *recensio vetus*, which records that the dog, a piece of meat in his mouth,

> cuius [that is to say, of the meat] umbram cum vidisset in aqua, maiorem suspicatus est.[68]

The prose of Romulus thus grounds the dog's foolish action more clearly in the greedy desire for an even larger pork chop. This detail serves well the more pointed moral given the fable in many commentaries on the Anonymus Neveleti: where in the verse fable the dog is deceived in believing the reflection real, in the prose fable he thinks it better, too, than what he has, just as greedy humans find greater delight in the "transitoriis huius mundi" than in the promise of salvation.[69]

A typical example of how such material is integrated into the prose commentaries is provided by the Anonymus commentary in the Wolfenbüttel manuscript 185 Helmst., where the explicit description from Romulus of the dog's avarice is quite skillfully fused with words and

---

[66] Wright, *The Fables of 'Walter of England'*, 34 (verses 2 and 4 are here emended). The edition includes the interlinear glosses on the verse fable as well.

[67] A thorough sampling of the manuscript commentaries on this fable is provided by Wright, "The 'Nuremberg' Aesop", 207–217; on an unexpected vernacular reflex of the story, see Wright, "'Le voir ne l'en osa dire': An Aesopic Reminiscence in Chrétien de Troyes," *Romance Notes* 36 (1996): 125–131.

[68] Thiele, *Der lateinische Äsop*, 23.

[69] Wolfenbüttel, Herzog August Bibliothek, cod. guelf. 185 Helmst., fol. 112v (Wright, *The Fables of 'Walter of England'*, 34–35).

phrases taken from the verse fable and its interlinear glosses, to create a prose retelling of great clarity.

> Quadam die canis quidam carnem portans in ore natauit per quendam fluuium. Qui videns vmbram et speciem carnis suspicatus est vmbram vere carnis esse maioris quantitatis meliorisque saporis quam ipsas carnes. Ideo desiderans vmbram carnis, carnem in ore habitam perdidit et vmbram non accepit.[70]

While the commentator's retelling is obviously dependent for its general plot and much of its vocabulary on the verses of the Anonymus, a comparison with the interlinear glosses present in the Wolfenbüttel manuscript reveals the considerable contribution made by those annotations to the relative coherency of the prose fable. That the dog should be not just swimming, but swimming across a certain river, is an elaboration already added by the glossator above the first word of the verse text; likewise, that the dropped "caro" of verse 4 is that which the dog actually holds in his mouth, and that the missed "spes" in the same verse refers to the meat's reflection, is already made clear by the interlinear glosses "scilicet habita" and "id est vmbra," respectively, both of which reappear in the commentator's prose. The additional Romulus material, then, is paraphrased and expanded, so that the "maiorem" of that source is explained as referring to both the imagined meat's size and taste; the result is a prose fable that is as easily understood as it is thoroughly logical.

Only exceptionally were the commentators of Avian's verses able to engage in the same procedure; where the fables of the Anonymus Neveleti were part of a broad tradition of surviving parallel collections in verse and prose, Avian had drawn principally on sources no longer accessible to his readers a thousand years later: his commentators in the fourteenth and fifteenth centuries could appeal to neither Babrius nor Phaedrus for help in composing their prose retellings. Only for those few Avian fables with parallels in the medieval Romulus tradition was such assistance available, among them the fable of the dog and the lion (Avian 37)[71] and that of the crow and the pitcher.[72]

---

[70] Wright, *The Fables of 'Walter of England'*, 34.

[71] On the commentators' use of additional sources in commenting this fable, see Seemann, *Hugo von Trimberg*, 56–57, and Wright, "The 'Nuremberg' Aesop," 262–265.

[72] Thiele, *Der lateinische Äsop*, lxvii, suggests that these fables entered the original Romulus corpus as early as the third century, their ultimate sources Babrian fables now lost.

A comparison of the Copenhagen commentary on that latter fable to the version in Avian's verses reveals a suggestive difference in the description of the thirsty bird's adversary. Avian, as we have seen, describes the uncooperative *urna* as containing just a little water in the very bottom, but the commentator here has it *semiplenam aqua*. Precisely because this deviation is so trivial and so obviously unmotivated in the narrative—it makes no difference in the fable how much water is in the pitcher, so long as it is unreachable by the crow—this minor detail assumes significance in the search for secondary sources that may have contributed to the commentary's prose retelling. In fact, the version of this fable offered in the late antique Romulus recensions describes the vessel as half-full, "dimidiam aquae,"[73] and the medieval collection known as the Romulus LBG couches that description in the same language used by the commentator:

> Cornix sitibunda venit ad urnam semiplenam. Quam evertere temptavit, ut effusam aquam sibi hauriret. Quod cum fieri non posset, quia firmiter stabat, ad alias ivit artes, calculisque viribus suis aptis studiose invectis urna prope plena, superavit aqua lapillos, et sic Cornix sitim suam revelavit [ms.: relevavit]. Moralitas. Hinc est quod dicitur: Fortior est ars viribus.[74]

It seems likely that the commentary's embellishment is owed to its author's remembering of this or another, similar prose version of the fable, just as another group of commentaries appears to reveal the influence of the Romulus *recensio vetus* in their description of the bird's efforts; the Romulus prose reads

> cornix sitiens accessit ad urnam dimidiam aquae et eam conabatur evertere ...,[75]

the same verbs used in at least three fifteenth-century prose reductions.[76] The fact that none of those manuscripts, however, makes ex-

---

[73] Thiele, *Der lateinische Äsop*, no. 87.

[74] Hervieux, *Les fabulistes latins*, no. 107.

[75] Thiele, *Der lateinische Äsop*, no. 87.

[76] London, British Museum, ms. add. 10090, fol. 6r ("... conabatur ergo cornix urnam illam effundere et euertere ..."); Munich, Bayerische Staatsbibliothek, clm 609, fol. 92r ("... conebatur eam vrnam euertere ..."); Stuttgart, Landesbibliothek, ms. 34, fol. 83r (the prose reductions of this manuscript are generally identical to those in the London manuscript just cited).

tensive verbatim use of Romulus passages leaves open the possibility that the apparent borrowings have their immediate source in interlinear glosses on Avian's "enisa" and "effundere."

Some commentators, faced with the task of composing a prose reduction for this fable, turned to a surprising secondary source: namely, encyclopedic natural history. As seen in the brief discussion at the beginning of this chapter of the story's origins and transmission, the oldest preserved Latin account of such behavior is Pliny's, who presents the episode as a natural curiosity of slightly dubious credibility. Yet whatever the natural historian's own doubts, the story captured the scientific imagination for a millennium and a half; from Pliny's younger contemporary Plutarch to the seventeenth-century editors of Vincent of Beauvais, scientists, scholars, and compilers of exotica repeated, embellished, and accepted the tale of the thirsty raven as authoritative proof "de sagacitate corui."[77] Very early in its written transmission,[78] this narrative appears to have been reanalyzed as a description of behavior characteristic of the entire species. By the time of the medieval encyclopedists, the story was related most often without any sense of its temporal particularity; and even when, as in the *Liber de natura rerum* of Thomas Cantimpratensis, it is told with explicit reference to Pliny as its source, it is reported generally "de corvis,"

> ut si aquam in aliquo profundo loco repperissent, ... ilico aggregare lapillos in aqua, quoadusque ... ascendat aqua.[79]

This enduring natural historical tradition is not, as we shall see, irrelevant to the late medieval reception of the story as a fable. In late antiquity, however, the scientific and the fictional versions of this material seem to have developed independently—coming together only in the prose commentaries on Avian, a small number of which preserve

---

[77] This is the rubric given by its early modern editors to Chapter LXIII of the *Speculum naturale: Vincentius Bellovacensis. Speculum Naturale* (Douay: Beller, 1624; repr. Graz: Akademische Druck- und Verlagsanstalt, 1964), col. 1193.

[78] Aelian, for example, writing scarcely a hundred years after the first publication of the *Naturalis Historia*, considers such behavior typical of ravens in general; they can, he notes, be observed in times of drought dropping stones into water vessels throughout the Libyan countryside. Aelian, *De Natura Animalium* 2.48, ed./trans. A. F. Scholfield, 3 vols. (Cambridge, Mass.: Heinemann, 1958), 1: 146–149.

[79] Thomas Cantimpratensis, *Liber de natura rerum*, ed. Helmut Boese, 1 vol. (all published) (Berlin: de Gruyter, 1973), 190–191.

prose reductions of the fable reminiscent of versions found in the scientific tradition.[80]

The clearest difference between the Aesopic and the natural-historical traditions of this story, of course, is the identity of the avian protagonist. In the fable, the bird is almost always a crow, *cornix*,[81] while the scientific reports, following Pliny, invariably identify it as a raven. One Latin prose commentary on Avian's fables, preserved in Wolfenbüttel, Herzog August Bibliothek, ms. 288 Gud., appears to fuse the two traditions, informing the reader in its promyth that

> In hoc apologo ostendit actor quod plus prodest ingenium quam vis et prudencia quam labor, et intendit probare per coruum ... (fol. 98v).

The prose reduction of the same commentary, however, identifies the thirsty bird correctly as a "cornix," and for most of its length recalls rather a combination of Avian's verses and a thorough set of lexical glosses:

> ... intendit probare per coruum qui sitiens reperit vrnam in cuius fundo erat parua aqua quam non posset attangere. Cornix enixa est eam effundere in campo ut ex ea bibens sitim suam minueret. Quia urna gravis et bene intacta fuit, cum non posset effundere, lapillos in fundo iniecat et immittit vt crescens vnda super lapillos potum bibendi cornici preberet (fol. 98v).

More convincingly the result of a commentator's use of natural-historical sources is the prose reduction of the fable in the Vatican manuscript Ottob. 1297. In addition to the obvious distinction in the identity of the bird, the natural-historical and the Aesopic traditions of this matter differ in their presentation of the challenge facing the crow. In Pliny and his medieval reflexes, the crow's (or rather the raven's) diffi-

---

[80] A similar development seems to have characterized the medieval tradition of the tale of the mother ape and her twin offspring, a story that likewise occurs in both numerous natural historical works and in various fable collections derived ultimately from Avian. See A. Wright, *"Fabule vtilitatem in se continentes,"* 266–267; and H. W. Janson, *Apes and Ape Lore in the Middle Ages and the Renaissance*, Studies of the Warburg Institute 20 (London: Warburg Institute, 1952), 32–37.

[81] The "Nuremberg" Aesop departs from this tradition to identify the bird as a "nachtrab," while in the sixteenth-century version of Jakob Koppelmann the story is told of an unspecified bird; the medieval Hebrew fable of Berechiah has as its principal actor an osprey. See Dicke and Grubmüller, *Katalog,* 410–411.

culty when confronted with a deep container lies in its short-necked build:[82]

> De corvis quoque compertum est, ut si aquam in aliquo profundo loco repperissent, ubi colli brevitate obstante pertingere minime potuissent, ilico aggregare lapillos in aqua. ...[83]

Elsewhere, Pliny himself serves as the authority for the bird's reluctance to go into the dark urn; the raven is said

> ita descendere pauentem expressisse tali congerie quo poturo sufficeret.[84]

Avian's and the other fables, in contrast, make no mention of the bird's dread; but they do describe an additional obstacle provided by the great weight of the *urna*. It is no accident that the Roman poet writes "Ingentem" as the first word of his fable, and the various Romulus versions, too, insist on the immovable mass of the vessel: the bird is forced to use its wits because the vase "firmiter" (Romulus LBG) or "fortiter stabat" (Romulus *recensio vetus*). This shift in emphasis is obviously motivated by the fabulists' need for a clear juxtaposition of physical weakness and mental strength, or, in Avian's words, of "vires" and "prudentia."[85]

The Avian commentary of the Vatican manuscript, while including among its epimyths the traditional assurance that

> ingenium superat vires (fol. 17r),

draws its prose retelling of the episode from the scientific tradition, and from a source very close—if not identical—to Pliny's own work. There is no mention that the "urna" is heavy, only that it is deep; the crow's inability to reach the water is explained as the result of its fear to enter into the vessel:

> Ingentem cornix. Quedam cornix habebat magnam sitim et disserendo inuenit uas in quo erat modicum aque in fundo ita quod non poterat bibere de ipsa, nec intrare uolebat timens ne cape-

---

[82] The primary taxonomic character in the medieval ornithological tradition is, in fact, length of neck.

[83] *Liber de natura rerum*, 190–191.

[84] Vincent of Beauvais, *Speculum naturale*, 1193 (citing Pliny's Book 8).

[85] The clearest statement of this dichotomy is that of the glossator of Munich, Bayerische Staatsbibliothek, clm 391, who writes in the margin next to the prose commentary "Animi vires sunt nobiliores robore corporis."

retur. Interea statim ipsa cogitauit cautelam et accepit lapides cum ore et proiciebat in uas ita quod aqua semper axcendit, emmauit, et uenit usque ad partem superiorem, et ipsa postea bibit ad suam uoluntatem sine aliquo periculo et timore (Vatican, Ottob. 1297, fol. 17r).

The commentary must rely on the scientific account of the crow at the mausoleum, taken either directly from Pliny or from an intermediate encyclopedic source such as the *Speculum naturale* of Vincent of Beauvais; as a guide to Avian's verse fable, it is not among the most successful such texts produced in the late Middle Ages.

For the majority of Avian's fables, of course, no parallel texts were conveniently available from any source, Aesopic or scientific, and most of his late medieval commentators had to construct prose reductions of their own using the verses and the interlinear glosses. An extensive commentary found in two fifteenth-century manuscripts from the southeast of the German-speaking area seems simply to expand the slight details given by the poet into a coherent prose narrative:

Quondam fuit cornix que paciebatur magnam sitim et cum libenter bibisset volauit ad fontem et invenit ibi quendam vrnam in aqua que modicum de aqua continuit ita quod ipsa ex ea bibere non poterat. Et sedens super illam ipsa multum laborauit ad hoc vt aquam biberet, et cupiebat hanc aquam fundere ad terram vt illam bibisset et magnam sitim remouisset. Quia post quam illa nulla fortitudine effundere poterat hanc aquam vt ex illa bibisset, quia debilis nimis fuerat, illa indignata admouet omnes dolos et fraudes sua sapientia et calliditate. Illa astuta multos lapides congregauit et in vrnam posuit et illa aqua in vrna crescebat et sic cornix bibit facilior (Munich, Bayerische Staatsbibliothek, clm 22404, fol. 87r).[86]

The same prose reduction, with but slight variations, is found in the former Maihingen manuscript 635 (fol. 194r), and, significantly, in the commentary accompanying Avian's verse fables in the edition printed in

---

[86] On the Avian commentary in this manuscript, see Klaus Grubmüller, ed., *Nürnberger Prosa-Äsop*, Altdeutsche Textbibliothek 105 (Tübingen: Niemeyer, 1996), xi–xii. The same prose reduction is found in Augsburg, Universitätsbibliothek, Cod. II.1.4o.27, fol. 194r, and in the *Apologus Aviani* (Cologne: Quentell, 1494).

Cologne in the 1490s. In each of these textual witnesses, the retelling is followed by a series of epimyths, drawn from disparate sources and each offering a slightly different interpretation of the fable just read:

> Vtilitas: Sapientia plus valet quam fortitudo, quia multa fiunt per artem que viribus fiere non possunt. Vnde Katho: "Consilio pollet."[87] Vnde: Melius est uirum esse sapientem quam fortem. Et ergo interdum magis vtendum est arte quam viribus (clm 22404, fol. 87r; compare Augsburg, Universitätsbibliothek, cod. II.1.4o.27 [formerly Maihingen ms. 635], fol. 194r, and *Apologus Aviani*, GKW 3110).

This gesture is typical of the prose commentaries on Avian and the Anonymus Neveleti alike, which only exceptionally offer a single, definitive moral; instead, the commentators offer their readers a selection of alternative, usually complementary, epimyths, drawing, as here, on proverbial lore, the Bible, and, especially, other texts of the elementary Latin curriculum. Some thirty different epimyths occur in various recombinations in the manuscript commentaries to this fable of crow and pitcher alone. A closely similar practice in the German *Edelstein* of Ulrich Boner—aptly styled by Grubmüller "das Epimythion als Variantenangebot"[88] —is, as we shall see, understandable only as the almost certain reflex of this feature of the Latin prose commentaries.

Many fable commentaries include an additional element following the moral epimyths, namely, an "allegorical" or "spiritual" explication of the events narrated in the prose reduction. Here, the fable actors are identified as specific types, human, divine, or demonic, whose attitudes and activities are described or denounced. In the tradition of the Latin fable, this is a phenomenon strictly limited to the commentaries and allied texts,[89] although similar tendencies can be observed in many of the independent vernacular collections of the later Middle Ages. These allegorical epimyths are of tremendous interest, reflecting as they do one of the most striking exegetic habits of the late medieval literary enter-

---

[87] *Disticha Catonis* II.9. It is worthy of note that this distich is quoted in the school poem known as the *Iocalis*, where the next verse following reads: "Sic cornix undam lapides iaciendo levavit" (Paul Lehmann, ed., "Der *Liber Iocalis*," *Sitzungsberichte der Philosophisch-historischen Abteilung der Bayerischen Akademie der Wissenschaften zu München* [1938], 55–93, lines 143–144).

[88] *Meister Esopus*, 320.

[89] Grubmüller, *Meister Esopus*, 427.

prise, seen in everything from commentary on the *Aeneid* to the *Gesta romanorum*.[90]

In the fable tradition, these explications probably have their ultimate origins in straightforward applications such as that established in an English commentary of the fourteenth century:

> Per cornicem sibi prospicientem ergo ad haustum intelligimus illos qui immensitatis articulo sibi prospiciunt hoc modo.[91]

Here, the rather unimaginative identification of the crow with those who keep their wits about them and persist in their efforts, whatever the circumstances, serves only to reiterate and apply the general sense offered in the commentary's twin promyths

> In hoc appollogo ostendit auctor quod melior aliquando prudencia quam corporis fortitudo, et quod plus agendum cum calliditate quam uiribus. Et hoc ostendit per cornicem ... (fol. 98r).

The qualities so highly praised here at the beginning of the commentary, *prudencia* and *calliditas*, are shown, as it were, in action in the epimyth. The same analogical impulse is somewhat more fully elaborated in an epimyth from a manuscript now in Wrocław, which likewise urges the use of *ars* rather than *vires*, and presents as a worthy example wise men's emulation of the clever crow:

> In hoc appologo docemur quod multa sunt que citius fiunt per artem quam per vires, et hoc probatur per fabulam de cornice, de qua in hac allegoria: Per cornicem intelligimus sapientes. Namque sicut cornix sapienter agit quia aquam quando attingere in fundo urne non poterat, tunc repleta vrna lapillis aquam ascendere sapienter fecit: sic homines sapientes angustiam et turbationem suam, ut cornix sitim, per sapientiam, discretionem, et patientiam superarent et vincerent.

These general urgings are applied less vaguely in the Erfurt Avian edited thirty-five years ago by Risse. As befits its schoolboy audience, the final epimyth in this commentary gives corvine cleverness a pecu-

---

[90] Further discussion with additional examples of the various types of allegorical epimyth appended to the fables of Avian and the Anonymus is had in Wright, "The 'Nuremberg' Aesop," 73–85.

[91] London, British Museum, Harley ms. 4967, fol. 98r.

liarly academic construction; the commentator, forefinger awag, would have the fable read "scholastice" thus:

> Licet sicud cornix non potuit effundere vrnam, sic nullus scholaris studens potest quamlibet scientiam acquirere; sed potest acquirere aliquam partem scientie si proiciat lapidem, id est si adhibet laborem et dilegenciam.[92]

The desired goal in this epimyth is no longer "sapientia" but "scientia," and it can be reached only with diligent effort in the classroom. That the Erfurt commentator was not the only medieval reader to apply Avian's lesson in this way is suggested by the unexpected epimyth in the "Novus Avianus" found in two fifteenth-century manuscripts:[93] after retelling the fable in leonine rhymes, the fable's "renovator" (verse 1) concludes, somewhat surprisingly,

> Versus cev scribit, taliter arte bibit (line 10).

Here the act of writing itself is described as a process of patient accretion similar to the crow's gathering of pebbles; it is this fable, and this interpretation of the fable, that was responsible, as well, for an otherwise incomprehensible dictum in Geoffrey of Vinsauf's *Documentum*. Discussing the proper methods for the rhetorical *amplificatio* of a text or an idea, Geoffrey urges his reader to concentrate on the steady accumulation of one element at a time, until at last

---

[92] Erfurt, Stadtbücherei, Amplon.Q.21, fol. 35r. The prose reduction and morals read:

Hic ponit talem apologum: Cornix valde quondam citiens vidit in campo vrnam iacentem, in qua aqua — . Quam multociens temptauit effundere propter citim extingwendam, sed non poterat per vim aquam adhipisci ex vrna. Ex quo cogitavit istum modum quod accepit lapides paruos proiacere in vrnam, et sic aqua existens in fundo vrne ascendit ad orificium eius. Quo facto cornix citim extinguit per aquam. Ex isto apologo probat quod subtilitas et astutia seu sapiencia prevalet fortitudine. Sepe enim prudencia acquiramus quod fortitudine non possumus acquirere.

The second epimyth here is found also in the commentaries on this fable in Wolfenbüttel, Herzog August Bibliothek cod. guelf. 185 Helmst. (see appendix below for a full transcription of the Avian commentary in this codex); and Kampen, Archief der Gemeente, no sign., fol. 36v. The prose reduction in the Erfurt commentary, while identical over its length to no other, most closely recalls the paraphrases in the Wolfenbüttel manuscript 185 Helmst. and Budapest, Magyar nemzeti múzeum, ms. Lat.med.aev. 123.

[93] "Novus Avianus," Munich, Bayerische Staatsbibliothek, clm 14703; and Vienna, Österreichische Nationalbibliothek, cpv 303; edited in Hervieux, *Les fabulistes latins*, 3: 443.

sic ex modica maxima crescit aqua,[94]

a clear but hitherto unrecognized allusion to the fable of the crow and
the pitcher and its academic explication.

Success of a different sort is the goal of another set of allegorical epimyths, more widespread in the prose commentaries. Here the crow is
identified not as the struggling scholar but as the penitent sinner, and
the water in the pitcher is not worldly knowledge but the font of redemption. In the words of the second allegorical epimyth in a manuscript described earlier in this chapter,

> Allegorice per cornicem intelligimus peccatorem, qui niger est ut
> corvus de peccatis; per aquam uero Christum uel baptismum; sed
> per lapidem confessionem et bona opera. Quia cum peccator wlt
> desistere a peccatis, non potest accedere ad Christum nisi per con-
> fessionem et elemosinam et alia bona opera.[95]

The explication of the Budapest "Liber Avianus et Esopus" provides a
figural identification for nearly every element in the fable, insisting,
however, on contemplation rather than on works, mental rather than
physical exertion, as the source of salvation:

> Allegorice per coruum intelligitur peccator denigratus in peccatis.
> Sitiens primam [?] venit ad fontem fidei et habet modicum de hu-
> more in vrna cordis sui, scilicet sapientiam; id est, filio Dei debet
> uti et recipiere lapillos, id est wlnera Christi, et pendere in cor
> suum ut aqua accrescat, id est vna lacrima contriciones eueneret
> sursum, id est ad Christum; et cum bibit illum potum angelorum,
> videlicet lacrimam de corde emissam, non sitiet in eternum.[96]

Precisely this allegory is found at the end of the fifteenth century in the
vernacular in the so-called Magdeburg Prose Aesop, a Low German
translation of Steinhöwel's compilation with additional epimyths drawn
from the Latin commentary tradition:

---

[94] *Documentum de modo et arte dictandi et versificandi*, ed. Faral, 265–320, 283: "Si
autem velimus hanc seriem extendere, sumamus clausulam narrationis, . . . et eam confir-
memus rationibus et rationis confirmationibus" (II,2,63).

[95] Darmstadt, Hessische Landesbibliothek, ms. 2780, fol. 37r. Compare also the Avian
commentary in clm 14703, fol. 10v: "Allegoria. Per cornicem sicientem intelligimus peccatorem, qui Deo cupit satisfacere suo ingenio, per confessionem, fidelem contricionem, et
satisfactionem."

[96] Budapest, Magyar nemzeti múzeum, ms. Lat.med.aev. 123, fol. 15r.

De ghestlike syn: De dar begheret to drinkende den borne der innicheit, de dar nicht en vind wen me wil, men me mot ene vakene vletende maken mit starker betrachtinghe vnde vele; vnde vakene to lesten kumpt he aueurlodigen, dar me mede loschet den dorst der sele vnde werd ghereyneghet van den sunden.[97]

The identification of the crow as the sinner, of course, finds wide support in patristic exegesis as passed to the Middle Ages in the encyclopedias, where it most often finds its impulse in the bird's color; Gregory the Great, on the other hand, in a passage of relevance to the fable explications just quoted, identifies the crow's "nigredo" as at once both a reminder of human sinfulness and a sign of repentant conversion.[98]

Where the foregoing explications take the crow of the fable *in bonam partem*, interpreting its desire for the water as true contrition, another, found as the first spiritual epimyth in the Erfurt manuscript excerpted above and in the heavily commented Avian of the Wolfenbüttel cod. 185 Helmst., identifies the bird's actions as a vicious, indeed demonic, attempt to turn men from God:

Allegorice per istam aquam in vrna existentem intelligitur cor hominis, quod stat in corpore tanquam in vrna.[99] Per cornicem intelligitur dyabolus, qui immittit lapidos, id est prauas cogitationes in cor hominis sua astucia et fraude, ut ipse bibat aquam, id est ut removet cor hominis a bonis operibus (Erfurt, Stadtbücherei, cod. Amplon. Q.21, fol. 35r).

Suddenly the crow of Avian's fable, once the exemplar of virtue and the love of wisdom, is the enemy of every good Christian. The multiplicity of interpretations is anticipated in the exegetic tradition,[100] but the contrast is particularly jarring where, as in this Erfurt manuscript, a

---

[97] Wolfenbüttel, Herzog August Bibliothek, Alleg. 17524, fol. O.viii, "De xx fabule van der dorstighen kreyn."

[98] *Moralia in Job* 10, 30. The rich tradition of patristic and medieval interpretations of crows, ravens, and magpies, fascinating though it be, must await separate treatment. A convenient introduction to the topic is provided by Dietrich Schmidtke, *Geistliche Tierdeutung*; see also Giovanna Maria Pintus, "Il Bestiario del diavolo: l'Esegesi biblica nelle 'Formulae spiritalis intelligentiae' di Eucherio de Lione," *Sandalion* 12–13 (1989–90): 99–114, here 106–107.

[99] Compare Prov. 20:5: "Sicut aqua profunda sic consilium in corde viri, sed homo sapiens exhauriet illud."

[100] Compare, for example, the aviary of Hugh of Folieto, in which the raven is identified as "doctor predicans," "peccator," *and* "diabolus." *PL* 177: 13–155; I,35.

single commentator invokes them both, smoothing their startling juxta-position only by assigning each to a different type of explication, here the "allegorical" and the "scholastic" (as throughout this commentary). The author of the annotations in another, contemporary manuscript makes only a weak effort to reconcile the two:

> Vtilitas quod quondam sapientia multis viribus prevalet. Alle-gorice per cornicem duo intelligimus: per colorem magis dyabo-lum, quem debemus fugere; per opus cornicis sapientiam et illam appetamus.[101]

The commentator's unease at the contradiction is apparent, but was not sufficient to discourage a nearly contemporary reader from adding in the margin of the same leaf yet another epimyth on this fable:

> Allegoria: per cornicem meretrix intelligitur, que licet paruas ha-beat vires, tamen multas habet astucias, quibus suos amatores semper vallere [for Classical Latin *fallere*] conatur.

This epimyth, very widespread in the prose commentaries on Avi-an,[102] is of complex origin. It identifies the crow as a woman of ill re-pute, the bird's cleverness as the wicked wiles with which she deceives men foolish enough to take up with her. Similarly incongruous epi-myths can be encountered in the commentaries on other fables where women play, as here, no role whatsoever; thus, a common explication of Avian's fable of the boy and the thief[103] identifies in the child's wicked cleverness feminine duplicity,[104] where Avian in his own verses makes no mention of a woman at all.

The misogynous epimyths supplementing the fable of the crow and

---

[101] Munich, Bayerische Staatsbibliothek, clm 609, fol. 92r.

[102] Misogynous explications are appended to the commentary on this fable in Prague, Universitní Knihovna, ms. 546; Augsburg, Universitätsbibliothek, cold. II.1.4o.27; Munich, Bayerische Staatsbibliothek, clm 22404; Munich, cgm 3974; Darmstadt, Hessische Landes-bibliothek, ms. 2780; Vatican, Ottob. 1297. On its use in the vernacular, see Wright, "The 'Nuremberg' Aesop," 270–275; and, if somewhat obliquely, Mireille Schnyder, " 'sunder ich pin ein armer rab': Zu einer autobiographischen Anekdote in Konrads von Megenberg 'Buch der Natur'," *Wirkendes Wort* 1/94 (1994): 1–6, here 2–3.

[103] Guaglianone, no. 25. A thief approaches a boy weeping at a well, who tells him that he has lost a golden cup in the water. Hoping to recover and steal the precious vessel, the thief undresses and enters the well, whereupon the child—his story a lie—takes the thief's clothes and runs away.

[104] See the prose commentary of Wolfenbüttel, Herzog August Bibliothek, cod. guelf. 185 Helmst., reproduced below in the appendix to Chapter 1.

the pitcher in so many commentaries seem to be made possible in the first instance by the peripeteia of the feeble crow's victory in the fable. That the eventually triumphant *cornix* is both weak and (grammatically!) feminine may well have recalled a dictum present in several commentaries, where it is given various attributions; the Vatican manuscript Ottob. 1297 ascribes it to Pamphilus:

> Heu michi, quam paucas habet omnis femina uires, et licet fragilis sit, tamen astuta fallet.[105]

The appropriateness of such allegories is further confirmed by the moral ambivalence, already discovered by the interlinear glossators, of the qualities so highly praised by Avian: the bird of the verse fable avails herself not only of *prudentia*, but also of *calliditas* and *dolos*, which—as the manuscript annotations discussed above demonstrate—can be understood with but little effort as deceitful slyness and fraud. Given the lexical ambiguity of these terms, the mental capacities they describe, given so unequivocally positive a reading in the verse fable, can come to seem suspect themselves, vicious trickery better suited to the devil or to women than to dutiful scholars and penitents. The epimyths *in malam partem*, treating the devil or the wicked woman, are ultimately a writing out of the ambiguities discovered by the glossators in Avian's use of the equivocal noun *dolus*, "prudencia siue fraus."

There is furthermore the possibility that the misogynous explications of the crow's behavior are yet another result of contact between the Aesopic and the scientific traditions. While in its encyclopedic transmission this story is not, to my knowledge, furnished allegorical interpretation, others of the anecdotes told there about crows and ravens are. Thomas Cantimpratensis, for example, immediately following on the account of crows and their thirst in his *De natura rerum*, tells of an exotic race of Oriental ravens, which peck out the eyes of cattle and horses and then feed from the slaughtered carcasses of the livestock they have thus rendered useless,

> sicque improba avis fortia animalia vincit; et improba mulier fortes viros deicit.[106]

---

[105] The Prague ms. 546 cites somewhat differently, and attributes the quotation to Paul: "licet habeat paucas vires, ut testitur Paulus, dicens Heu mihi quam plorant fidem habeat omnis mulier hec enim quamvis sit fragilis tamen habet multas astucias fallendi."

[106] Boese, 190–191.

By the late Middle Ages, the comparison has become proverbial:

> Instar enim corvi prius exoculant mulieres
> Nos, post excerebrant, prout ostendunt liquide res.[107]

In the course of transmission, this misogynist reading was freed from its original context and reassociated with the story of the crow and the pitcher, a transfer responsible for the epimyths in the Latin commentary tradition and, as we shall see below in Chapter 4, in a vernacular German collection of the early fifteenth century, the so-called "Nuremberg" Aesop.

II

Startling as their conceits can be, in none of the Latin commentaries on Avian and the Anonymus Neveleti do the allegorical epimyths mark an effort to make of the fable collections a systematic exposition of dogma. The animal actors are identified for the most part *ad hoc* according to their role in the fable narrative or, as we have seen above, the better to suit the demands of the explication; the Aesopic fox, to take a random example from an Anonymus Neveleti commentary, can be equated in a single commentary—indeed on a single manuscript page—first with every "bonus homo" who

> ieiunando, vigilando, et orando incendit facem, id est invenit gratiam Spiritus Sancti, et liberat pueros suos, id est bona opera, a potestate diaboli;

and then, not a folio later, with the devil himself, who

> semper laudat hominem et incendit ipsum per superbiam.[108]

Nor is there any effort discernible in the epimyths to generate a thematic continuity in the fables, to create, as it were, a catechetic Aesop.[109] This is most easily apparent on an examination of two types of allegorical epimyths whose ideological content would seem, from the late medieval perspective, to be particularly apt to programmatic use, name-

---

[107] Walther, *Proverbia*, 12539k.

[108] Wolfenbüttel, Herzog August Bibliothek, cod. guelf. 185 Helmst., fol. 115r–v.

[109] Where there is such an exceptional attempt to do just this in the Anonymus Neveleti commentary in clm 16213, it is fiercely resisted by a later reader; see the discussion of clm 16213 below.

ly, the misogynous and the anti-Semitic. Both groups, women and Jews, are frequently and bitterly criticized in the fable commentaries. Misogynous explications are particularly frequent, as mentioned above, in the Avian tradition in the commentaries on his fables 1, 25, and 27, while such explications are broadly scattered through the commentaries on the Anonymus. Anti-Semitic material is even more widespread, and can be found in the allegories on sometimes astonishing texts.

The fable commentaries in the Wolfenbüttel manuscript 185 Helmst. —the one available in edition, the other supplied below as an appendix to this chapter—are by no means atypical in interpreting the figures of five fables (out of the total of one hundred two texts in both verse collections) as the "Iudeorum congregacio." The commentators describe the Jews as vicious slanderers, who, when God sent them the longed-for messiah (*ad* Anonymus Neveleti 22), refused to recognize him, and instead denounced him and had him killed (Anonymus Neveleti 2, 22); they derided Christ in his passion (Avian 10,[110] with the odd detail of the Jews' plucking hairs from his beard), not knowing that it was they who were in fact damned for persisting in their pernicious beliefs (Avian 14, Anonymus Neveleti 37).

Ludicrous, even offensive as these images are, they are nevertheless not sufficient to brand this commentary, or fable commentary in general, as an anti-Semitic tract. In the commentaries on the fables listed above, the merest narrative parallel, the slightest verbal suggestion are enough to call forth a diatribe *contra Iudeos*; surely, had it been the commentators' principal intention to inculcate such ideas into their schoolboy readers, they would have had no difficulty in finding similar parallels and suggestions in other fables as well, making of *every* treacherous wolf, every silly toad, every boastful mosquito a Jew. No such effort can be observed in any of the fable commentaries preserved from the late Middle Ages; the anti-Semitism of the commentaries is, as so much medieval anti-Semitism, breathtakingly matter-of-fact, a convenient material for exposition and not its purpose.[111]

This circumstance (which, of course, does not make the anti-Jewish

---

[110] On Latin and vernacular explications of this fable ("bald knight"), see K. Grubmüller, "Fabel — Exempel — Allegorese," in *Exempel und Exempelsammlungen*, ed. Walter Haug and Burghart Wachinger, Fortuna vitrea 2 (Tübingen: Niemeyer, 1991), 58–76; and the discussion below (120ff., 140–141) of the fable in Boner and the Magdeburg Aesop.

[111] I am grateful to John D. Martin for sharing with me the fruits of an unpublished study on Jews in the vernacular fable of the fifteenth and sixteenth centuries in Germany.

epimyths any easier for the modern reader) is made especially plain in
the commentary tradition on one of the fables of the Anonymus Neveleti, in whose verses one of the principal figures is identified expressly as
a Jew.[112] Fearing robbers along the road, he requests the company of
a royal cupbearer, who, however, on discovering that the Jew is carrying a great treasure, kills him. The cupbearer is eventually found out
and punished, leading the Anonymus to warn

> Vt perimeas quenquam, nullum tibi swadeat aurum.
> Nam decus et vitam mesta ruina rapit.

Thus the fable, in the Anonymus's version, is about the cupbearer's
treachery, not about the purely incidental and neutrally described religious identity of his victim; the prose reductions of the commentaries,
too, without a single exception, simply identify the Jew without negative remark. Most importantly, however, in all of the preserved allegorical epimyths on this fable, the murdered Jew is given a positive signification. For example, the Wolfenbüttel commentary reads

> Moraliter per Iudeum intellige fidelem animam, que timens accu-
> sationem huius seculi vadit ad regem, id est Deum, petens ab eo
> conductorem. Deus autem dat ei pincernam, id est corpus incli-
> natum ad delectaciones, quod corpus interfecit animam auferendo
> sibi diuicias magnas. Tandem autem in cena, id est in die iudicii,
> perdices, id est peccata, accusabunt corpus, et tunc rex dampnat
> corpus cruci, id est eterno supplicio.[113]

It is easy to imagine the vileness with which a commentator bent on
promulgating stereotypes could have seized on the Jew's cowardice,
wealth, and weakness; yet even the commentator of this Wolfenbüttel
manuscript, who hardly shies otherwise, passes up the opportunity in
favor of a quite predictable discussion of the problematic relationship of
body and soul, a matter he has addressed in the commentaries on three
other fables as well.[114]

The same observation can be made about the misogynist material in
the fable commentaries. Not only do the commentators present no con-

---

[112] Anonymus Neveleti 59, "De Iudeo et pincerna," Wright, *Fables of 'Walter of Eng-land'*, 151–153.
[113] Wright, *Fables of 'Walter of England'*, 154–155.
[114] Numbers 3, 48, and 57.

sistent program of misogyny, but they often fail to take advantage of what seem obvious opportunities for the expression of such sentiment. The verse collection of the Anonymus Neveleti includes two fables whose express theme is the unreliability of women. Thus, the Anonymus concludes his version of the "Widow of Ephesus"[115] with the cynical observation that

> ... Nil fidei mens mulieris habet.
> Sola premit viuosque metu penaque sepultos;

in the fable immediately following, "Thais," he warns of the true source of a woman's affection:

> Fallere vult hodie si qua fefellit heri.
> Thayda si quis amat, sua non se credat amari.
> Thays amore caret, munus amantis amat.[116]

The commentators dutifully take these sententiae into their promyths, but most take a different direction in their spiritual explications; again, typical and eloquent examples can be found in the Wolfenbüttel commentary of 185 Helmst. In the allegory of this commentary, the figure of Thais is in fact given a negative role; the commentator does not, however, advance the surely most obvious figural identification with the gold-digging temptress, but instead interprets the woman of the verse fable abstractly, as the seductive allurements of youth:

> Moraliter per iuuenem intellige quemlibet hominem iuuentuti deditum. Per meretricem intellige ipsam iuuentutem, que uaga et inconstans est et homini sic adulatur: 'Iuuenis es, vtere iuuentute tua in delectacione et voluptate. Multi tibi adhuc supersunt anni quibus viuere possis. Nam cum senueris tunc primum ad vitam religiosam magis aptus eris. ...'[117]

With this explication, the commentator, like all others, leaves unrealized the potential for calumny created in both his promyth and his ultimate summary of the fable's "doctrina":

---

[115] On the treatments of this matter in the Middle Ages, see Gerlinde Huber, *Das Motiv der 'Witwe von Ephesus' in lateinischen Texten der Antike und des Mittelalters* (Tübingen: 1990); Huber does not discuss the career of this "motif" in the fable commentaries.

[116] Wright, *Fables of 'Walter of England'*, 127, 130.

[117] Wright, *Fables of 'Walter of England'*, 131.

Presens appollogus docet nos ne mulieribus instabilibus et mere-
tricibus fidem adhibeamus neque ipsis amorem inpendamus. ...
Quilibet homo ab amore mulieris se retrahat, quia non ipsum sed
bona sua meretrix amat (131).

Other mentions of women in the fables of the Anonymus likewise go
unexploited in the commentaries. The verse from the fable of the
mountain and the molehill,

   ... Pene perit sexus vterque metu,

could conceivably have provided an impulse for misogynist tirades; instead, the commentator of the Wolfenbüttel Anonymus takes the phrase
rather unconvincingly in his allegory to mean "alios homines," a decidedly bland reading and one that reveals no interest in seeking opportunities to denounce the wiles of women.[118]

The commentaries on the Anonymus's fable "De muliere qui suspendit virum suum" pass by an even easier opportunity for misogynist expression. Again, they recapitulate the verse fable's warning against the
treacherous words and deceitful weeping of women in their promyths:

Hic docet nos actor ne uerbis et lacrimis mulierum credimus,[119]

a logical lesson to be drawn from the story of a woman who exhumes
and mutilates the corpse of her recently deceased husband in order to
save the life of the man she has seduced beside his grave. In the most
frequent allegorical epimyth appended to the fable, however, the woman
is taken as a figure of pious correction:

Moraliter per mulierem intellige animam bonam, per virum bona
opera et castum corpus quod mors, id est dilectacio mundi, ducit
ad peccatum mortale tanquam ad tumulum. Et quando in vanitatibus huius mundi sepiliuit ipsum, anima residens circa tumulum
flet deuote, et tandem custos furis, id est angelus cuiuslibet
hominis, intelligens fletum adiungit se ei perswadendo per diuinum instinctum ut dimittat corpus mortuum vanitatibus mundi
deditum. Et si tunc ipsa mulier corpus mortuum per peccatum

---

[118] Wright, *Fables of 'Walter of England'*, 76–77; on the medieval trasmission of this fable
in the French and German traditions, see A. E. Wright, "Hartmann and the Fable: On *Erec*
9049 ff.," *Beiträge zur Geschichte der deutschen Sprache und Literatur* 116 (1994): 27–36.

[119] Berlin, Staatsbibliothek Preußischer Kulturbesitz, ms. Diez B. Sant. 4, fol. 36r.

suspendit in patibulo, euellens dentes eius per remorsum con-
sciencie, tunc angelus sumit eam ad celestem patriam.[120]

Once again the commentators refrain from misogynist outbursts when
in the context of the fable narrative they would be most expected.

In the commentaries on Avian, a further striking example is to be
had in the annotations on the first fable of that collection, "De rustica
et lupo."[121] Avian himself deduces a misogynous lesson from the
wolf's disappointment similar to that just described for the story of the
widow of Ephesus:

> Haec sibi dicta putet seque hac sciat arte notari,
> Femineam quisquis credidit esse fidem.[122]

Later medieval readers and redactors of the text greatly relished the expansion of the epimyth into a universal truth:

> Adam Samsonem, regem David et Solomonem
> Femina decepit, cepit et arte sua.
> Ingemiscit egens ubi non est femina, saltem
> Femineus dulcis omnia vincit amor.

While the commentators, too, give vent to their fears in their promyths,
they are of one accord in the allegorical moralization they give it. The
standard allegorical gloss is this, reproduced in the appendix below from
the words of the fifteenth-century Wolfenbüttel manuscript 185 Helmst.:

> Per rusticam intelligitur ecclesia et per lupum diabolus. Sed per
> puerum flentem intelligitur peccator qui, si non voluerit cessare
> de peccatis suis, rustica, mater eius, id est sancta mater ecclesia uel
> confessor in persona sancte matris ecclesie, minatur ipsum pue-
> rum quod velit eum dare lupo, id est diabolo, si non voluerit de
> peccatis suis desistere.[123]

A few alert and casuistically gifted commentators attempt to reconcile

---

[120] Compare the substantially identical commentaries on this fable in Mainz, Stadtbibliothek, cod. I.540, fol. 22r; and Munich, Bayerische Staatsbibliothek, clm 7680 and clm
16213.

[121] The following discussion relies on the more thorough treatment of the commentaries
on this text and their role in rendering Avian a "safe" school author in Wright, "*Iste
auctor.*"

[122] Guaglianone, fable 1; there also the spurious epimyths cited immediately below.

[123] Wolfenbüttel, Herzog August Bibliothek, cod. guelf. 185 Helmst., fol. 95r.

this interpretation of the commentaries with Avianus's original epimyth; as disingenuous as they are subtle, these glossators simply assign each to a different class of application, calling the one "allegorical" *sensu stricto*, the other merely "ethical" or "tropological":

> Allegorice per rusticam intelligeri [debet] ecclesia, per puerum plorantem peccatorem, per lupum diabolum ... Ethice autem hortatur nos auctor iste ne nimis credamus verbis mulieris.[124]

Others, particularly brash, justify their practice on the basis of Avian's tendency to spread his epimyths over two verses,

> ex quo quelibet fabula ... habet duplicem sensum, vt pute tropologicum, id est moralem, et allegoricam, id est misticum.[125]

Most, however, seem unmoved by the utter incompatibility of this spiritual explication with the lesson originally derived by Avian—a lesson that would have provided more ideologically intent glossators the perfect opportunity for misogynist outpourings.

As these examples show, the allegorical epimyths in the prose commentaries on Avian and the Anonymus were not systematically intended to disseminate any particular ideological content. Their function in the texts is better understood instead as furthering two goals of specific relevance to their use in the late medieval classroom. First, the "spiritual" explications demonstrate, using material familiar to even the youngest grammar school pupil, the basic workings of figurative thought, a preoccupation only natural to commentators of texts belonging to an ostentatiously metaphorical genre. And second, in reaction to pressures applied by the academic reading of the "modern" Anonymus Neveleti, the commentaries seek to redeem the older author Avian for classroom use.

The commentators' interest in the modes of figurative thought—and so ultimately in the workings of the very texts they annotate—is evident already in the *accessus* introducing the commentaries. In many of these prefaces, the commentators go beyond the simple discussion of the genre of their texts[126] to address the rhetorical modes of their signification,

---

[124] For example, Copenhagen, Kongelige Bibliotek, Gl. Kg. S. cod. 1905 4o, fol. 138v.

[125] Munich, Bayerische Staatsbibliothek, clm 22404, fol. 62v.

[126] A discussion most often limited in any event to etymologies; see Ulrike Bodemann, *Die Cyrillusfabeln und ihre deutsche Übersetzung durch Ulrich von Pottenstein*, Münchener Texte und Untersuchungen 93 (Munich, Artemis, 1988), 35–37.

often adducing the very highest academic authorities for their expositions. The particularly dense *accessus* in the Wolfenbüttel Anonymus
Neveleti 185 Helmst. quotes at great length from the Aristotle commentary of Aegidius Romanus, concluding that

> ex predictis patet quod sermo appollogus quo autor vtitur per
> totum librum reducitur ad modum assimilatiuum,[127]

a metaphoric mode distinguished by its use of analogy:

> Si enim iuuentus appellatur ver et senectus yems, metaphora sit
> siue transsumptio. Si vero superaddimus quandam proporcionem
> dicendo sic: 'Sicut se habet ver ad annum, ita iuuentus ad ciui-
> tatem, assimilacio dici debet' (p. 23).

The commentator claims here to be describing the procedures followed
by his author; in fact, though, the verse fables only rarely avail themselves of such specific formulations, and it is rather in the commentaries,
particularly in the allegorical epimyths they so prominently feature, that
comparisons are regularly and consistently made in this way. The Wolfenbüttel commentator, in purporting to describe the workings of metaphor in the verse fables, in fact justifies the rhetorical strategies of his
own prose.

The Avian commentary in the same manuscript insists equally on
the need for a figural reading of the fables:

> noticia presentis materie habetur ut perlecto libro presenti scia-
> mus veritatem fabularum cognoscere et per eas bonis operibus
> inherere et viciis alienari.[128]

As many commentators note, this truth is hidden; it is their task, then,
to

> ostendere veritatem . . . sub tegmine fabularum latentem et instru-
> ere auditores in bonorum moralitate.[129]

The role of allegory in revealing that truth is described explicitly by

---

[127] Wright, *Fables of 'Walter of England'*, 23.

[128] See the complete commentary cited in the appendix below.

[129] Copenhagen, Kongelige Bibliotek, cod. 1905 4o, fol. 1. The noun "auditores" is of
special interest here, suggesting that the commentaries were presented to young scholars in
the course of their teachers' oral expositions, rather than being assigned for the pupils' independent reading.

a number of commentators. The mid-fifteenth-century manuscript clm 16213, for example, in the course of discussing the duality of the fable, reminds the reader

> Nota quod autor in isto libro presenti duo considerat, scilicet delectationem et vtilitatem. Delectatio pendet ex fabulis, in quarum recitatione omnes audientes delectantur. Vtilitas vero consistit ex fructu allegoriarum et fabularum, que mores docent et virtutes informant (fol. 292r).[130]

These apparently simple sentences in fact are richly suggestive of the ways the commentators understood and wished others to understand their activities as explicators of figural language. The verbal doublets typical of commentary style here create a scheme of overlapping oppositions between delight and utility, fable and allegory, speaking and writing, and morals and virtue. In the system propounded here, literary pleasure is exclusively narrative and oral; it is had from the stories themselves, and is in the first instance a function of their aural reception.

Utility, on the other hand, significantly considered here with the help of the organic metaphor "fructus," is more complex. The learning provided in the fables is situated in two locations, in the allegories and in the fables themselves; the clear implication is that the commentator understands his contribution to the text—a contribution made, by definition, in writing—as distinct from the author's, the supplying of an additional level of meaning beyond the ideas already present in the verse texts. The commentary asserts its own power to promulgate "mores" and "virtutes," effecting a clear shift in textual authority from the verse fable to the prose annotation, and introducing at the same time an uncertainty about the identity of both "autor" and the "liber presens." For the careful reader of this *accessus*, it is no longer entirely clear whether the "author" is an eponymous Aesop or his later interpreter, while the "book" under discussion seems to be not merely the verse fables, but the fables as revealed by the good offices of the commentator's prose. The reader's attention is drawn away from the verse stories and towards their interpretation, away from narrative and towards allegory.

---

[130] Compare also in the commentary on the Anonymus Neveleti's verse prologue: "[the fable] delectat, scilicet audientem quo ad ipsas fabulas; et prosit, scilicet audienti quo ad percepcionem vtilitatum in mistificacionem allegoriarum proveniencium" (fol. 292v).

This privileged status of the commentary is especially pronounced in clm 16213, a manuscript copied around 1450 for the library of the Augustinian canons of St. Nikola in Passau; it entered the collections of the Royal Library in Munich (now the Bayerische Staatsbibliothek) on the secularization of the monasteries in 1803.[131] In its material presentation, clm 16213 is unremarkable, a bulky, cheaply bound volume in small folio, its 336 thick paper leaves covered by a single hand writing a competent but unlovely bastarda. As a physical artifact, the book belongs to an enormously familiar fifteenth-century type, the "Gebrauchshandschrift"; with the exception of the Anonymus Neveleti at the end of the codex, the texts it transmits are just as typical of a manuscript genus particularly common in the German-speaking southeast. Following a thematic program developed at court and university in Austria in the late fourteenth century, these manuscripts bring together catechetic and devotional works, generally of nearly contemporary composition, in German or simple Latin prose, their purpose the moral and religious edification of growing numbers of devout but academically inexpert readers.

The selection of works that makes up the bulk of the St. Nikola manuscript, while not encountered in identical form in any other codex, nevertheless serves well as a representative of similar constellations in any number of contemporary mansucripts. Clm 16213 begins with a Latin explication of the mass, compiled in the 1340s by Bernard of Parentini;[132] this is followed by the manuscript's oldest work, the *Meditationes de interiore homini* of Bernard of Clairvaux. There follows a short anonymous tract *De penitentia*, whose date of completion, 1448, provides a credible *terminus ante quem non* for the entire manuscript. A brief Latin florilegium drawn from Suso's *Horologium* is followed, then, by an unattributed *Dialogus inter hominem et animam*; the dialogue leads naturally to a well-known *Ars moriendi* dating from the second or third decade of the fifteenth century. This tract, falsely attributed here to Jean Gerson and elsewhere commonly ascribed to Nikolaus von Dinkels-

---

[131] On the history of the manuscripts from St. Nikola, see Paul Ruf et al., eds., *Mittelalterliche Bibliothekskataloge Deutschlands und der Schweiz*, 4 vols. (Munich: Beck, 1918–1977), 4.1: 47–56; the present manuscript bore the shelf-mark S.Nic.213 in the cloister library.

[132] See Adolph Franz, *Die Messe im deutschen Mittelalter* (Freiburg, 1902; repr. Darmstadt: Wissenschaftliche Buchgesellschaft, 1963); Franz discusses Bernard and mentions this manuscript, 502–503.

bühl,[133] is preserved in the Munich manuscript in two versions, one in Latin prose, the other a German translation of Viennese provenance.

Familiar as such combination is in the fifteenth century, the final work of clm 16213, a thoroughly commented Anonymus Neveleti,[134] is far from an expected component of the period's mass-produced pop-theological manuscripts. The Aesop is not, however, a codicological afterthought; copied by the same hand that writes the remainder of the texts, it begins in the middle of a quire, and, in the strictness of its graphic format, carefully maintains the formal two-column layout of the manuscript's other texts. Likewise, the codex's contemporary table of contents registers the fable collection in precisely the same way as the more conventional works that precede it, leaving the reader with the un-mistakable impression that its inclusion is, in fact, programmatic, and that the fables themselves are meant to contribute to the catechetic in-tention served by the remaining texts of clm 16213.

The Anonymus Neveleti of this manuscript is accompanied by a very full commentary, availing itself of prose reductions combining material drawn from the parallel texts of both the Romulus LBG and the Romulus *recensio vetus*.[135] It is the prose commentaries accom-panying the fables of the Anonymus that permit their assimilation into this manuscript's otherwise alien textual environment of spiritual in-struction. Where the original verse fables are often suspicious, even cyni-cal in the worldly wisdom they offer, the commentaries, particularly in their allegorical epimyths, let the fables serve purposes similar to those of the other texts in the compilation, making of them no longer simply moral, but religiously moral, works for their readers' edification.

A striking example is provided by the manuscript's transmission of the Anonymus's fable of the crow and the eagle.[136] Uncertain what to

---

[133] See Rainer Rudolf, "Der Verfasser des Speculum artis bene moriendi," *Anzeiger der Österreichischen Akademie der Wissenschaften, phil.-hist. Klasse* 88 (1951): 387–398; and Her-bert Kraume, *Die Gerson-Übersetzungen Geilers von Kaysersberg*, Münchener Texte und Untersuchungen 71 (Zurich: Artemis, 1980), 41. The St. Nikola codex is not included in the manuscript lists furnished by Alois Madre, *Nikolaus von Dinkelsbühl: Leben und Schriften*, Beiträge zur Geschichte der Philosophie und Theologie des Mittelalters 40,4 (Münster: Aschendorff, 1964).

[134] This copy of the Anonymus is briefly discussed in Dietmar Peil, *Der Streit der Glie-der mit dem Magen*, Mikrokosmos 16 (Frankfurt: Peter Lang, 1985), 42, 44–45; and Seemann, *Hugo von Trimberg*, 29–30, 32–35. See also Hervieux, *Les fabulistes latins*, 1: 564, and Dicke and Grubmüller, *Katalog*, xxxviii.

[135] Compare Seemann, *Hugo von Trimberg*, 49.

[136] Foerster, *Lyoner Yzopet*, no. 14.

do with a turtle it has captured, an eagle follows the crafty crow's advice and drops it from great height onto stony ground; the shell breaks, revealing the flesh. The Anonymus offers a bitter warning against foolish credulity:

> De se stultus homo subuersus turbine lingwe
> Corruit, et fortes ista procella rapit.

In a manuscript compilation such as this, consisting of texts that purport to give only good advice, this epimyth amounts to a potentially disruptive invitation to skepticism. Accordingly, the warning against bad or self-interested counsel disappears completely in the prose commentary, where it is replaced by an allegorical reading that offers both a thoroughly moral caution about sinful pride and a not insubstantial bit of biblical history:

> *Pes aquile.* Fabula talis est, quod aquila quedam testudinem rapiens inter altas nubes petauit. Testudo autem in concha latens nullo ledi potuit periculo. Sed aquila nesciente quid preda valeat, cornix eidem obviauit et dixit: "Optimam fers predam, sed ea uti non poteris viribus sine consilio." Tunc dedit ei consilium: "Volate," inquit, "super alta aera et respice deorsum vbi fuerit saxosa loca et demitte quod fers, et sic conchis confractis vteris esca." Sic fecit aquila. Allegoria: Per testudinem Luciperum intelligimus; per aquilam superbiam, per quam multi cadunt ad interitum; per cornicem virtutem Dei. Quia Luciper per superbiam voluit aquilonem ostendere. quod erat contra naturam suam, quia creatura non valet similari suo Creatori. Quod virtus Dei videns, deiecit eum in infernum (fol. 299v).[137]

Only by utterly ignoring the sense of the verse fabulist's epimyth—a procedure that, as we have seen, is not at all rare in the commentaries—could the commentator produce such an allegory.

Thus annotated, however, the fables of the Anonymus are rendered similar to the remaining texts of clm 16213, resembling them in edifying intention and unsubtle catechetic propensity;[138] the commentaries,

---

[137] The moralization of the eagle *in malam partem* was no doubt suggested by the mock-etymological pun on "aquila" and "aquilo."

[138] My assertion above that the epimyths of the prose commentaries do not make a systematic presentation of religious dogma is not contradicted; for even in this manuscript, which comes closer than any other to subjecting the fable to a catechetic scheme, the alle-

too, unlike the verse work they annotate, share a very important formal
feature with the texts in the remainder of the codex. By generic neces-
sity, the commentary is written in a prose of very slender sophistication,
manifestly pitched to the modest skills of the neophyte Latinist; this
stylistic trait fits well with the other works of clm 16213, with their
programmatic concentration on simple prose, whether Latin or German.

At another level, the confrontation in clm 16213 of the verse fables
and their commentary is a further manifestation of a larger theme that
links several of the other works in the manuscript: namely, a typically
fifteenth-century focus on the modes of interpretation of texts and
events. Considered in this way, the fable commentary at the conclusion
of the manuscript provides a logical counterpoise to the liturgical exposition that began it: just as Bernard interprets the mass, so the commentator interprets the fables of the Anonymus. There is an additional
symmetry in the positioning of the fables directly after the manuscript's
two redactions of the *Ars moriendi*. The relationship between verse text
and prose commentary in the fable collection recalls that between Latin
and vernacular prose in the paired versions of the devotional tract, the
only difference being that the juxtaposition is in the first case one of
prosody, in the other one of language.

Thanks to its transformation through commentary, the fable collection of clm 16213 fits its manuscript context both substantively and for-
mally. In so thoroughly exploiting that transformation, the compiler of
the codex has reversed the relationship between the verse fables of the
Anonymus and their annotations: where in their original academic habitat, the commentaries were intended to help the beginning pupil in his
struggles with the difficult Latin verses, the compiler of the Munich
manuscript grants the prose commentary primacy over the verse text
from which it was originally derived, and its significance shifts from the
margins of a purely pedagogic enterprise to the very center of this
manuscript's religious program. The fables of Aesop in this manuscript
are the commentary, the Anonymus's verses serving only to anchor it in
a traditional authority.

This displacement of the commentary is not only metaphorical, but
has in clm 16213 a remarkable codicological effect as well. Where most
school manuscripts of Avian and the Anonymus give plain graphic ex-

---

gories of the commentary leap from subject to subject, without effort to present a thematically coherent summary of edifying content.

pression to the secondary, derived nature of the commentaries, the mise-
en-page of this section of the Munich manuscript is strikingly dominated
by the prose commentaries, while the verse texts give the impression of
simply tagging along. As usual, the verses do occupy the central columns
of each opening, leaving the commentaries to fill the margins and the
bottom of each leaf; the distichs of the Anonymus do not, however, give
the leaves their visual structure. They are copied continuously through
the folios, each following immediately on the one before, regardless of
its position on the page. Thus, a given verse fable may begin on a recto
leaf, continue on to fill the entire verso, and then end in the middle of
the following recto; immediately, then, set off only by a small rubricated initial, the next verse fable will begin on the same leaf. Graphically, the verse texts begin and end essentially at random; it is no more
likely that the top of a leaf will coincide with the beginning of a text
than that the text will end at the bottom of the next.

The layout of the Munich manuscript's commentaries, in contrast, is
considerably more formal, and it is around the commentary segments,
not the authoritative verses, that the leaves of this section are organized.
Each new commentary segment begins on a new folio. The longest commentaries take up an entire opening; in these cases, the scribe has carefully calculated the number of lines eventually required by each segment, and divides his prose text precisely so that the opening presents a
uniform appearance with the same number of lines symmetrically positioned on each recto and facing verso; the visual structure of the Aesop
echoes the equally carefully planned two-column layout of the remainder of the codex, further integrating the fable collection into its *Mitüber-
lieferung*. This physical integration is effected by the layout of the commentaries, not of the verses; graphically as well as substantively, the prose
annotation has replaced the fables themselves, arrogating to itself the functions of the primary verse text and making of the margin a new center.

The reason for this displacement is, in my view, clear. The original
owners of the Munich manuscript were members of a preaching order;
their interest in texts of a pastoral nature shines brightly through the
selection preserved in clm 16213, and that manuscript's Aesop is no exception: for the prose commentary that accompanies the verse fables
there prepares them for the homiletic use of the canons of St. Nikola.

This adaptation is substantively effected in the allegories. As one
would expect from the manuscript context, they are here almost all
"spiritual," treating a wide variety of religious matters both doctrinal
and personal. Most frequent are explications from biblical history, as the

example cited above from the commentary on the eagle and the tortoise; others, of a type already familiar, urge the Christian to mindfulness of what is of real importance in the world, as the allegory on the Anonymus's fable of the dog and his reflection:

> Allegoria. Per canem intelligitur homo auarus, per carnem regnum celorum, per vmbram transitoria huius mundi, per flumen istum mundum vel corpus cuiuslibet hominis. Caue ergo ne propter voluptates et transitoria huius mundi de quibus intenti sumus amittamus regnum celorum, quod certum et perpetuum est, quod paratum est nobis ab origine mundi (fol. 294r).

Most eloquent are those allegories that explicitly thematize the act of religious teaching, making of the stories they annotate "fables of the fable."[139] Thus the commentary on the Anonymus's fable of the swallow identifies the "hirundo" as the preacher and its avian fellows as sinners too foolish to heed his warnings, an explication very common in the late Middle Ages in both Latin and the vernacular.[140] Likewise, in the allegory of Anonymus Neveleti 29, the mother goat—in other commentaries typically identified as Christ[141] —is a figure for the "pater spiritualis," whose counsel to every good Christian (figured in the fable by the obedient kid) is to avoid the blandishments of the wolf, who unsurprisingly represents the devil.[142]

More striking still is the moralization given the narratively complex fable of the father and his disobedient son, Anonymus Neveleti 50. This fable is one of a small number in the Latin verse tradition featuring a narrative frame:[143] frustrated by his son's wild behavior, a man takes out his exasperation on his servants, until an acquaintance tells him a

---

[139] Compare Klaus Speckenbach, "Die Fabel von der Fabel: Zur Überlieferungsgeschichte der Fabel von Hahn und Perle," *Frühmittelalterliche Studien* 12 (1978): 178–229. See also Wright, *"Iste auctor,"* on a similar phenomenon in the tradition of commentary on the fables of Avian.

[140] The commentary of clm 16213 is here very close to that of the Wolfenbüttel manuscript 185 Helmst. (Wright, *Fables of 'Walter of England'*, 63–65). On vernacular adaptations of this allegory, see Grubmüller, ed., *Nürnberger Prosa-Äsop*, 91–93; and Edward Wheatley, "Scholastic Commentary and Robert Henryson's *Morall Fabillis*," *Studies in Philology* 91 (1994): 70–99.

[141] Representative of the tradition is the commentary reproduced in Wright, *The Fables of 'Walter of England'*, 82–84.

[142] Clm 16213, fol. 310v.

[143] See also the vernacular epimyths from the Wrocław Aesop discussed in Chapter 3 below.

fable about a young ox who, while balky at first, eventually learns to plow by observing the example of an older colleague. The Anonymus concludes (in his usual obscure Latin)

> Proficit exemplis merito cautela docentis
> Maiorique sua credat in arte minor.[144]

The verse fable's concentration on effective instructional technique is obvious, a focus repeated in general terms by most allegorical commentaries on the fable. In the allegory provided in clm 16213, however, the father is identified as canny

> patres spirituales ... scilicet predicatores, qui corrigentes peccatores remouent ipsos a via iniquitatis et erroris, docentes ipsos exemplis sanctorum, ut illa sequentes cessent a peccatis et iuste atque virtuose viuentes eternam benedictionem mereantur obtinere (fol. 324r).

While the activity of teaching was of clear interest to the compiler of this manuscript, the fact that the commentaries on the Anonymus are, by force, copied out in the original order of the verse collection prevents them from making a systematic presentation of dogma; the English Aesop's fables were written with a different purpose, and there is no orderly progression of spiritual ideas or religious concerns as one reads through it. To assist the reader in locating the edifying content scattered through the fable commentaries, each commentary segment in the manuscript is given a conspicuous caption, much more detailed than those found in most other manuscript commentaries. Where in other copies the captions are usually limited to a recitation of the fable's *dramatis personae*, those of clm 16213 recall the extensive promyths so often a feature of the commentaries; indeed, they may well have originated as just such anticipatory summaries within the body of the commentary text and been removed in this manuscript to the head of each folio for the convenience of the priestly reader. Compare, for example, the caption given in this manuscript to the Anonymus's third fable with the briefer title and promyth introducing the prose annotation on the same fable in the Wolfenbüttel codex Helmst. 185. The latter manuscript

---

[144] Wright, *Fables of 'Walter of England'*, 133 ("The lesson of a teacher is effective [when properly accompanied] by examples; and so let the young man rely on the knowledge of his elder").

heads the leaf succinctly "De mure et rana"; the body of the commentary, following the verse fable in the same column, offers as twin promyths

> ne promittamus prodesse cum volumus obesse, et generaliter docet nos diligenter providere cui credamus.[145]

The Munich manuscript, in contrast, has no promyth at all in the commentary on this fable, beginning simply and abruptly "Fabula talis est: quedam mus . . ."; but the rubricated caption at the top of the leaf reads

> De mure uolente natare per lacum et rana veniente ipsam iuuare docemur ne cogitemus aduersa de alterius salute et non promittamus nos uelle prodesse cum velimus obesse (fol. 293r).

Clearly, the scribe of clm 16213 has combined the captions and the promyths of his commentary exemplar to ease the search for exemplary material, providing for the reader's convenience not only the (relatively unhelpful) list of fable actors but a brief summary of the narrative situation and a suggestion for the fable's moral application.

There are additional changes in the texts of the fable commentary to adapt them for homiletic use. The commentary excerpts thus far reproduced in this chapter have been typical in the exclusively jussive nature of their exhortations: rather than directly command the reader, they are content to urge on him the exemplary behavior of the generalized good Christian, almost always couching their admonishments in the third or the first person plural. In the commentary of clm 16213, on the other hand, there are numerous and repeated instances of direct second-person address, anticipating rhetorically the public and oral nature of the sermon. The Anonymus's fable of the unforgiving serpent, for example, introduced by the extensive caption

> De serpente inhabitante domum rustici, quem rusticus securi wlnerauit, docemur vt non teneamus fidem cum infidelibus, et semper habeamus illos suspectos qui nos aliquando ledere sew offendere voluerunt in rebus, corpore, et honore (fol. 310r),

is accompanied by the following prose commentary:

> Rustica. Fabula talis est: Serpens vnus cuiusdam rustici domo conswetus erat habitare vt nutriretur ibi. Sed non longo tempore rusticus cepit odire serpentem. Quem et securi wlnerans, post

---

[145] Wright, *Fables of 'Walter' of England'*, 30.

modicum tempus rusticus cecidit in paupertatem. Qui credens serpentem esse causam sue paupertatis, et existimans se esse diuitem iterim si serpens parceret ei peccatum quod fecerat, supplicabat ergo ei. Cui ille ait: "Quia penitus parco tibi, sed antequam cicatrix dorsi mei clausa et sana fuerit, non swadeo fidem integram te habere mecum. Redibo enim in graciam tecum si obliuiscatur securis in perfidiam." Wersus hoc tempore scribo: "Tu prudens aspice lector, ne sis securus, suspectus sit tibi lesus." Allegoria: Quicumque offendisti Deum, et si penitenciam facis, Deus parcit tibi, sed tamen semper peccata tua sunt in conspectu Dei donec pro eisdem fiet satisfactio. Et ergo per serpentem debemus intelligere dÿabolum, per rusticum quemlibet hominem qui cum peccat nutrit dÿabolum in corde peccatis suis. Sed cum confitetur, nititur eum expellere de domo, id est de corde, sed dÿabolus aduc exire recusat, quousque homo accepta vera penitencia necat eum tanquam cum securi.

Similarly, the commentary often introduces its allegorical explications not with the familiar formulas "intelligere possumus" or "intelligi potest," but with an imperative:

Allegoria: Hic intellige quod fides est tenenda, quia promisimus Deo fideliter seruire cum omni deuocione,[146]

words that could easily be taken over directly into a sermon.

The function of the Anonymus Neveleti in clm 16213 has been completely displaced from the pedagogical to the religious; this shift is accomplished by the use of a commentary whose epimyths, while not a systematic summa of dogmatic lore, nevertheless concentrate on matters spiritual. The revaluation of caption and promyth as an indexing tool, and minor changes in the text of the commentaries, ease the preacher's access and adaptation of the edifying material "discovered" by the allegorical explications. The result is a fable manuscript completely dominated by the commentaries, reversing the original, academic hierarchy between text and annotation.

As we shall see in chapters 3 and 4 below, the codicological habitat and catechetic intention of the fables in clm 16213 are closely similar to those of two other fifteenth-century fable manuscripts, this time, however, in the vernacular. Cgm 3974, thoroughly described some twenty-five years ago by Klaus Grubmüller, is a mid-fifteenth-century copy of

---

[146] Munich, Bayerische Staatsbibliothek, clm 16213, fol. 313r.

the Anonymus Neveleti, in which the verse fable collection is accompanied for most of its length by a Latin prose commentary and the
parallel fables from Ulrich Boner's German-language *Edelstein*; the investigation above of clm 16213 provides valuable corroboration for Grubmüller's still tentative assertion that the German texts in his bilingual
Aesop constitute a "Rückpräparierung in die Volkssprache" for use in
vernacular sermons, and suggests, as discussed at greater length in Chapter 3, that the production of the vernacular fable was viewed by at least
some fifteenth-century readers as allied in important ways to the enterprise of Latin prose commentary on the Anonymus and Avian.

Although it is fifty years younger, clm 16213 also exhibits a revealing
similarity to the early fifteenth-century German collection known as the
Nuremberg Aesop. Produced for the same Viennese court circles who
formed the primary audience for many of the simple Latin and German
devotional works composed by the scholars associated with Nikolaus
von Dinkelsbühl, that text is preserved in a manuscript whose content,
like that of clm 16213, includes several catechetic works and an Aesop;
as discussed below, the German Aesop is at home in that otherwise
unusual context by virtue of its direct reliance not on the verses of
Avian or the Anonymus Neveleti, but rather—again like the fable collection of clm 16213—on a prose commentary on the fables. The greater
youth of clm 16213 notwithstanding, the contextual structure of that
manuscript and the independence it accords fable commentary can be
seen as standing for the lost Latin exemplar of the Nuremberg Aesop.

While the privileging of the commentary was ultimately productive
for vernacular fabulists, the procedure did not meet with the approval of
one of the later readers of clm 16213. A closer look reveals that the fable
collection in that codex was subjected to further annotation in a slightly
younger, but still fifteenth-century hand. Where the intention of the
manuscript's original compiler was, as we have seen, to exploit fully the
spiritually edifying potential of the fables, largely to the exclusion of
their traditional pedagogical use, the second hand is equally intent on
wresting the Aesop out of its innovative environment and reasserting its
value as a purveyor of more mundanely practical wisdom. To borrow
the formula of Avian's early editor,[147] the original compiler of clm
16213 read his fables "ad mores," while the notes left in the manuscript

---

[147] See Introduction above, p. xxv.

by its later reader reveal a single-minded insistence on the stories' utility "ad sermonem latinum."

In keeping with this program, the younger annotator—who has left traces in no other of the manuscript's texts—begins by aggressively reasserting the primacy of the Anonymus's verse texts. Essentially irrelevant to the original purposes of the codex, the verses were copied there with a mechanical neatness that demonstrates their failure to capture the interest of the original compiler, unglossed and likely unread. The younger reader, on the other hand, fills the interlinear spaces with all the apparatus of the grammar schools as already described. He adds interlinear glosses of a variety of types, lexical, grammatical, and editorial; he provides vernacular equivalents for the names of plants and animals, and frequently indulges in excursus on such matters as botany, architecture, and musical instrument construction.[148] As if to insist that they are as readable and as important as the prose commentaries, he construes the Anonymus's verses with numbers and underscoring, and corrects readings that he finds inferior.

Neither does this industrious reader leave the prose commentaries unmarked. To align them more closely with the primary verse texts, the corrector carefully restores details omitted from the commentaries' retellings; in the commentary on the fable of the eagle and the crow, for example, this second hand faithfully re-inserts a detail suppressed in the commentary, marking the point of omission in the commentary with a dark cross and adding his own blunt account of corvine gluttony:

† Cornix autem protinus affuit et istam concham in proprio stomacho sepeluit (fol. 299v).

Quite apart from its indelicacy of expression, this addition to the commentator's prose greatly problematizes the allegorical epimyth that identifies in the crow divine wisdom:[149] surely it is not God, but the Luciferian tortoise who gobbles up unrepentant sinners.

This introduction of additional dissonances between the prose re-

---

[148] Fol. 300r: "Saxifrago: Nomen herbe frangentis lapidem in vesica, wlgariter stainprech"; the nearly illegible note in the margin to fable 22 is about architectonic strain; to the fable, cited above, of eagle and turtle he adds that "testudo" can be the name of a musical instrument as well as an animal.

[149] Interestingly, this equation was attacked eight centuries earlier by Isidore as a vile superstition: "Magnum nefas haec credere ut Deus consilia sua cornicibus mandet." *Isidori Hispalensis Episcopi Etymologiarum sive Originum Libri XX*, ed. J. W. M. Lindsay, 2 vols. (Oxford: Oxford University Press, 1911), 2: XII.vii.44.

tellings and the allegorical epimyths of the commentaries is neither isolated nor unintentional. Instead, it is part of a programmatic effort to nullify the carefully effected moral assimilation that permitted the inclusion of a fable collection in this manuscript in the first place, and an effort to return the Aesop to its "proper" function as a pedagogic text teaching broadly applicable morals. This is apparently the meaning of the anti-*accessus* added by the second annotator at the top of the first folio of the Anonymus Neveleti:

> Titulus huius libri est: Incipit Apologus Esopi. Et apologus est sermo rusticalis de brutis animalibus agens ad instructionem hominum coaptatus. Et scientia presentis libri pertinet [?] ad allegorias nihil sed ad sensum moralem. Subordinatur philosophie morali (fol. 292r).

Fragmentary and in places only with difficulty legible, these sentences appear to be the second commentator's avowal of the superiority of the Anonymus Neveleti's verse epimyths ("sensum moralem") over the "allegorias" of the prose commentator. This impression is strengthened by a series of comments with which the second hand concludes the manuscript; the verse morals are to be preferred for their authenticity, their brevity, and their suitability as *Merkverse*:

> [Autor] wlt tamen quod fructus vniuscuiusque fabule comprehendatur in duobus versibus in vltimo locali eiusdem fabule positis. ...[150] Racio vero secunda, vidilicet quare magister huiusmodi doctrinas hic narratas comprehendit tantum in duobus metris, est ista: Quia cum fabule hic narrate aliquando sunt satis longe, immo si doctrina consimiliter fuisset longa, ipsa non fuisset grata neque leuiter apprehensa. Et propter breuitatem et facilitatem retinende finis comprehendit tenorem in duobus versibus (fol. 333v).

Here speak clear schoolmasterly interests: the value of the fables is in the moral content given them by Aesop, *autor* and *magister*, and not in their secondary, derived explication by a modern; and that value can be attained by the scholar only through direct confrontation with the verses. To refocus the reader's attention on the original texts, the second

---

[150] There intervenes a long discussion of the different functions of prologues and epilogues, in which the principal authority cited is Aristotle's *Rhetorica*.

commentator often provides short prose epimyths, based on the Anonymus's verse morals, as alternatives to the lengthy allegories of the commentary; these are invariably introduced with a scornful "recte." On the fable of the eagle and the tortoise, for example, he writes in the margin next to the original compiler's allegory

> Recte. Primus fructus: Propter falsa consilia pluries innocentes et pauperes et aliquotiens diuites opprimuntur. Secundus fructus: Homo ad aliqua perficienda minus expertus et insufficiens doctiorem se consulere debet (fol. 299v).

What is identified in the prose commentary as the wisdom of God is here the treacherous counsel of those desiring to take advantage of the innocent; this reading is far more closely consonant with the sense of the Anonymus's verse fable,

> De se stultus homo subuersus turbine lingue
> Corruit et fortes ista procella rapit.

Both commentators of this manuscript would be likely to grant the validity of the second alternative epimyth given above; where they would differ, one suspects, would be in just who the "doctior" is that one should consult. It is this issue, the identity of the "meister," that will recur in the German Aesops of the fifteenth century.

For the original compiler of clm 16213, prose commentary on the Anonymus Neveleti permitted the re-evaluation of pedagogic utility as religious edification. Many of Avian's late medieval commentators took advantage of the form with another purpose in mind, namely, to redeem their unfashionable author in the face of competition from the new, proudly "modern" Aesop of the Anonymus. As I have sought to demonstrate elsewhere,[151] one of the goals of the Latin commentaries on Avian in the fourteenth and fifteenth centuries was to defend the Roman poet against increasingly vociferous charges of poetological and moral inferiority. Morally, they sought to rescue their poet by making of a clear pagan a doubtful Christian, an enterprise greatly furthered, of course, by the practice of allegory described above: the commentators in their "spiritual" explications purport to reveal what Avian truly intended to say. Where, as not infrequently, the worldly cynicism of the Roman poet's verse epimyths cannot be reconciled with the religious

---

[151] See Wright, "*Iste auctor*," 9–10.

wisdom of the prose, the commentators draw explicit, if disingenuous, distinctions. The author of the Avian commentary reproduced in the appendix below, for example, concedes defeat in the face of the verse fable's decidedly un-Christian moral,

> "Nam miserum est, inquit, praesentem amittere praedam,
> Stultius et rursum vota futura sequi."[152]

The commentator admits the possibility of conflict between this practical sentiment and the Christian duty to forbearance, but explains to his reader

> Nec est contra autorem quod omnia mundana debemus delinquere pro celestibus futuris, quia dictum autoris intelligitur de inferioribus et non de superioribus (Wolfenbüttel, Herzog August Bibliothek, cod. guelf. 185 Helmst., fol. 103r).

It is striking here that the commentator defends expressly not the fable but the fabulist; it is the *autor* whose orthodoxy is to be asserted against the contrary evidence of the text.

Both moral and poetic objections are answered in many of the commentaries on Avian's first fable.[153] A mother warns her squalling child that he will be thrown to the wolves if he does not stop weeping; believing the woman's words, a wolf waits outside the door, only to be disappointed when the child finally falls asleep.

> Ista fabula potest alegorice sic exponi ita quod per rusticam intelligitur sancta mater Ecclesia. Per puerum intelliguntur peccatores, per lupum ipse dyabolus, quia sicud lupus de rapinis viuet et multum gulosus ad rapiendum, sic et dyabolus conatur capere animas peccatorum. Vnde rustica, id est sancta mater Ecclesia, minatur, id est minas imponit, peccatoribus, quod ipsa dabit peccatores lupo, id est dyabolo, nisi taceant, id est nisi peccatores dimittant

---

[152] The later spurious epimyths added to the verses in many manuscripts echo Avian's original sentiment: "Incerta pro spe non munera certa relinque,/ Ne rursus quaeras forte nec invenias./ Unum quod tendis praepono duobus habendis,/ Plus valet 'hoc tribuo' quam 'tribuenda duo'"; "Quisque tenet, teneat quod cepit dextera prompta,/ Ad praesens ova sunt meliora feris"; "Iudicio plebis non fallit 'habes,' sed 'habebis,'/ Plus 'hoc unum tribuo' quam 'tribuenda duo'."

[153] Again, this is discussed at greater length in Wright, "*Iste auctor*." A typical example is in the commentary of the appendix below; a broad sampling of prose annotations on this fable is in Wright, "The 'Nuremberg' Aesop," 122–131.

peccata. Et cum puer, id est peccator, tacet, id est non peccat, tunc rustica decepit lupum, id est dyabolum, quia non dat peccatores dyabolo.[154]

This allegory is all the more striking for the fact that in the Erfurt manuscript just cited and in innumerable others it follows immediately a long recital of misogynous *dicta*; the figure identified as holy Church is also, and on the same manuscript folio,

> insatiabilis bestia, viri confusio, dampnum amabile, amor odibilis, fetus mendacii, orrigo litium, hominum mancipium, dampnum cottidianum, sarcina in via, et ad omnem nefas causa.

Yet this potentially jarring contrast was, it seems, of no concern to the commentators. Plainly intended to bring the Roman poet into the fold of the orthodox, this explication likewise remedies a grave formal defect noted by many of Avian's commentators; in the succinct words of the author of the Budapest *Liber*,

> Avianus prohemium non habet.[155]

The precise nature of this failing is demonstrated in the contrast between the commentaries furnished Avian and the Anonymus Neveleti in the Helmsted manuscript already discussed. The verse prologue of the Anonymus is read by the commentator as a prooemium to the entire collection:

> In parte prohemiali quatuor facit. Primo intentum proponit, materiam libri, finem, et vtilitatem describens. Secundo causam compilacionis presentis libri subiungit. Tercio katholicum se ostendens diuinum inplorat auxilium. Quarto auditores attentos reddit et beniuolos (Wright, *Fables of 'Walter of England'*, 21).

Similarly, the collection itself as a whole displays an internal structure; the commentator notes at the beginning of his remarks on the fable of the frogs and Jove

> secundum quosdam, hic incipit liber secundus.

---

[154] Erfurt, cod. Amplon. Q.21, fol. 18v (see Risse, "Commentary on the Fables of Avianus," 105–107, for an approximate transcription of the manuscript's entire commentary on this fable).

[155] Fol. 46r.

The Avian commentary of the same manuscript is pointed in its contrast; absent any type of formal *propositio* in Avian's collection, the commentator is left to conclude rather helplessly that

> iste liber presens diuiditur in tot partes quot fabule seu appollogi in eo habentur (fol. 95r).

The commentator of the Erfurt Avian edited by Risse is even more forthright:

> autor iste morem aliarum poetarum non seruet, quia non proponit nec invocat, sed solummodo narrat.[156]

Plainly, Avian suffers in comparison with his younger competitor's Aesop. With the help of the spiritual allegory on his fable of the woman and the wolf, however, Avian's commentators rehabilitate him by supplying the formal elements he failed to provide himself. In its radical rereading, the ingenious and incongruous "spiritual" epimyth reproduced above makes of Avian's original verse text an explicit discussion of a specifically Christian act of teaching and learning: the first fable of the collection is reanalyzed in the commentaries as an invocation, a profession of adherence to moral dogma of strictly orthodox origin. Likewise, the fable as interpreted in the commentaries comes to take the place of Avian's missing *propositio*, providing the reader his first guidance in the application of the lessons to be learned in the verse texts that follow. Avian may fail to invoke, he may fail to propone; but his late medieval commentators do not.

An additional, and somewhat surprising, strategy for asserting the Roman poet's legitimacy can be observed in the Erfurt commentary. Throughout the classical and medieval tradition of the fable, the authority of the genre was grounded ultimately in its place in the biography of its founder, Aesop. The prose Romulus collections of late antiquity frequently place their epimyths in the Phrygian slave's own mouth; even in the verses of the Anonymus Neveleti, composed a good millennium after any knowledge of a *vita Esopi* had been lost to the west, the narrator of several of the fables is identified still as Aesop, "ille sapiens."[157] This close link between the authority of the fable and the authenticity

---

[156] Erfurt, cod. Amplon. Q.21, fols. 17v–18r.
[157] Interlinear gloss, Wolfenbüttel, Helmst. 185: Wright, *Fables of 'Walter of England'*, 69.

of the fabulist was greatly reinforced, naturally, by the rediscovery in the fourteenth and the translation in the fifteenth century of the Greek romance treating the life of Aesop.

In contrast, there was no such biographical tradition in antiquity or the medieval period identifying in any of his fables episodes from the life of Avian. Instead, as the letter of dedication accompanying the fables makes clear, Avian considered himself a purely "literary" fabulist. His goal, as he explains to his colleague Theodosius, was to make a name for himself in the world of letters; the fable seemed an amusing genre,

> huius ergo materiae ducem nobis Aesopum noveris,

and his own contribution in the *Apologi* consists in having recast forty-two of the master's texts "elegis."[158] Avian's medieval readers took him at his word, and assert his secondary status repeatedly in their commentaries, if somewhat more bluntly than their author:

> Esopum actor iste imitatur in hoc opere.[159]

The Erfurt commentator attempts to counter this dismissive view of the poet as merely the epigone of his great Greek predecessor by providing in his prose commentary a biographical frame for the fables, the rudiments of a *Vita Aviani* to rival the life of Aesop then newly sweeping across western Europe. This is effected first in the commentary's *accessus*, which combines circumstances from Avian's own dedicatory epistle with material borrowed from the biographical sketches of the life of Aesop found in the commentaries on the Anonymus Neveleti:

> Causa efficiens scientie huius libri est duplex, scilicet mouens et mota. Mouens fuit quidam imperator Romanus nomine Theodosius, qui videns Auianum esse peritum in arte poetica rogauit eum ut sibi quasdam fabulas in quibus delectaretur conscriberet. Mota fuit quidam ciuis vrbis Romane nomine Auianus, qui a predicto imperatore rogatus ut sibi librum iocosum componeret,

---

[158] Guaglianone, *Fabulae*, 4. See also Cameron, "Macrobius, Avienus, and Avianus."

[159] A marginal note in Wolfenbüttel, Herzog August Bibliothek, cod. 13.10. Aug 4o, fol. 246v; compare also, for example, the *accessus* in Würzburg, Bibliothek der Franziskaner-Minoriten, cod. I.42; Hannover, Stadtbibliothek, ms. mag. 15; Copenhagen, Kongelige Bibliotek, ms. 1905 4o, and NKS cod. 2136 4o; Munich, Bayerische Staatsbibliothek, clm 391. Conrad of Hirschau, in his *Didascalion*, likewise identifies Avian as a "follower" of Aesop (*Dialogus super Auctores*, ed. R. B. C. Huygens, Collection Latomus 17 [Brussels: Latomus, 1955], 26).

hunc librum de fabulis et apologis dicitur composuisse. ...[160]

From Avian's own statements about his work, the commentator has taken the name "Theodosius"; here, however, the addressee of the fables is identified as a Roman emperor.[161] The ruler's request, and Avian's acquiescence, are without parallel in the letter of dedication. The account of these circumstances has its most likely origin instead in contemporary commentaries on the Anonymus Neveleti, where material ultimately traceable to the prose Romulus redactions of late antiquity is integrated into a brief history of the Aesopic fable; compare, for example, the following, typical description from an Anonymus commentary now in Munich:

> Erat autem istud opus in greco sermone compositum, quod haud interpretatum latuit, donec Tiberius, imperator Romanorum, Esopum poetam petiit ut sibi aliquas iocosas fabulas ad remouendas curas exteriores compilaret (Munich, Bayerische Staatsbibliothek, clm 14703, fol. 68v).

Eager to assert Avian's equality, the Erfurt manuscript transforms Theodosius so as to give the Roman poet an emperor of his own, and attributes to his fables precisely the function assigned those of Aesop in this Munich commentary.

The construction of a life for Avian continues in a number of the individual commentary segments from this Erfurt manuscript. While in none of his verse fables does Avian present his account as from experience, his fifteenth-century commentator is at pains to ground the authority of the fables in the Roman poet's life. Just as the *Vita Aesopi* presents the fables as rhetorical reactions to specific situations in the biography of the Greek fabulist, the Erfurt commentary explains the *appollogi* as Avian's response to the moral shortcomings of those around him. The first fable, for example, is said to have been written as a topical warning against the allures of loose Roman women:

> Notandum quod cum in urbe Romana vigeret studium philosophie, multi scholares cupientes tendere ad facultatem scientiarum

---

[160] Erfurt, cod. Amplon. Q.21, fol. 17r–v.

[161] On the commentators' varying efforts to deal with this name, see Wright, "The 'Nuremberg' Aesop," 117–118. See also Baswell, *Virgil in Medieval England*, esp. 108–120.

liberalium, pro amore mulieris multipliciter decipiebantur. Quos
ipse Auianus per hunc apologum cupit castigare (fol. 18r).

In his second fable, too, Avian addresses a burning issue in late fourth-
century Rome:

> Tum vidit tempore suo quam plures scholares et alios homines in
> flatura superbie tumescere et ultra proprium statum valde ascen-
> dere, quod non est licitum, cum ipsa superbia maximum est impe-
> dimentum ipsis scholaribus et aliis, quia cum ultra modum nimis
> volunt alte tendere, contingit eos sepe grauiore lapsu inferius
> cadere; et istud autor declarat per testudinem . . . (fol. 19r).

And the third fable, that of the hypocritical crab, is directed explicitly
at those who, able to ignore their own transgressions, reproach others
for their faults:

> Ex quo autor tempore suo videt quam plures alios reprehendere
> qui ad enormia facta eorum nolebant attendere, ideo dictum po-
> suit documentum (fol. 20r).

The commentary does not consistently assert the biographical context
of each fable after these first three; neither would that be necessary,
though, as the reader is by now himself so accustomed to the procedure
that it might be expected that each of the remaining thirty-nine fables be
read with a hypothetical *vita autoris* in mind.

Prose commentary, as I hope to have shown, provided its practitioners in the fourteenth and fifteenth centuries a flexible and creative
instrument for dealing with texts that would otherwise have proved
dogmatically or aesthetically intractable. The remaining chapters of this
book will have as their theme the way that that flexibility was exploited
by the new fabulists of the late Middle Ages—writing not in Latin, but
in their own German vernacular.

Appendix:
The Avianus Commentary in
Wolfenbüttel, Herzog August Bibliothek,
Cod. guelf. 185 Helmst.

For a description of this fifteenth-century manuscript, see the introduction to my edition of the Anonymus Neveleti,[162] itself originally
intended as an appendix to the present study. The fables of Avianus immediately precede those of the "Englishman" in the codex, where the graphic presentation of glosses and commentary is identical to that of the
younger collection. The present appendix gives only the prose commentaries to the fables, following largely the editorial practices described
in my edition of the Anonymus. Thus I have retained the orthography
of the manuscript, preserving the somewhat capricious alternation of *c*
and *t* and *u* and *v*, respectively; the manuscript's frequent *ij*, however, is
rendered in the edition *ii*. All of the text's abbreviations have been
resolved without comment, and always in adopting the scribe's apparent
practice when writing the same or a similar word in full (for example,
I have resolved the very common abbreviation *m'* as *michi*, in keeping
with the scribe's invariable preference for *nichil*). Except for obvious
homeoteleuta, which are simply deleted, any words and letters whose
omission makes sense are enclosed in square brackets, while editorial
insertions and corrections are placed in angled brackets. The numbering
and the titles heading each commentary segment are those to be found

---

[162] Wright, *The Fables of 'Walter of England'*, 5–9.

in Guaglianone's edition of Avian; for easy comparison with parallel versions, each fable is also given a "D"-number, corresponding to the entry in Dicke and Grubmüller's *Katalog*, and a page citation ("R") to Risse's transcription of the Erfurt Avian.

[ACCESSUS; R97]

[*fol. 95r*] Sicut ex dicto sapientis habetur, fabule sunt attendende sed non ymitande. Sunt enim attendende quia in eis ostenditur vitacio malorum et imitacio bonorum operum seu moralium. Vnde: Quatuor sunt impedimenta que impediunt humanam naturam, scilicet ignorancia, taciturnitas, vicium, et defectus. Contra itaque ignoranciam inuentum est quadriuium siue sciencie quadruuiales, ut sunt musica, arismetica, astronomia, et geometria. Sed contra taciturnitatem inuentum est triuium siue scyencie triuiales, ut sunt gramatica, loyca, et rethorica, que tractant de sermone. Sed contra defectum invente sunt artes mechanice, vt pelliparia, sutoria, pistoria. Sed contra vicium inuenta est philosophia moralis, que sibi subalternat poetriam. Et sic patet quod noticia presentis materie habetur ut perlecto libro presenti sciamus veritatem fabularum cognoscere et per eas bonis operibus inherere et viciis alienari. Pro titulo autem presentis materie habetur: "Incipiunt fabule uel appollogi uel libri ipsius Auiani." Vnde: Auianus erat quidam Romanus prepollens scientiis, qui ob peticionem cuiusdam nobilis nomine Theodosius presentem materiam conscripsit. De aliis autem generalibus dicendum, videlicet de causis, dicetur sicut alibi.

[Avian I, DE NUTRICE ET INFANTE; D647; R105]

[*fol. 95r*] Iste liber presens diuiditur in tot partes quot fabule seu appollogi in eo habentur.[163] Vnde primus appollogus habet duas partes. In prima recitat fabulam. In secunda infert fructum fabule, et eodem modo facit in quodam appollogo. Sciendum quod in presenti appollogo docet nos autor ut non adhibeamus fidem credulam verbis mulieris.

Et hoc probat per quendam rusticam que habebat puerum flentem a fletu desistere nolentem. Cui rustica dixit: "Si non cessaueris a fletu, dabo te ad deuorandum lupo." Lupus vero stans foris ante ianuam credit verbis mulieris expectans promissum istius rustice. Puer autem fatigatus ex nimio fletu obdormiuit. Tunc lupus vidit se deceptum a muliere; va-

---

[163] On the function of such remarks in the commentators' efforts to establish the formal unity of Avianus's collection, see Wright, "*Iste auctor differt ab aliis,*" 12.

cuus recessit ad sua [*fol. 95v*] lustra siluarum. Cui lupa occurrit inter-
rogans cur ita longo tempore fuisset et nil penitus attulisset. Tunc lupus
respondit: "Non mireris, o bona lupa, nam dulcia verba mulieris dece-
perunt me."

Ex quo autor vult inferre quod verbis mulieris raro est credendum.
Nam: "Sicut non est caput super caput serpentis, ita nec fraus super
fraudem mulieris."[164] Versus: "Stultus eris si credideris verbis mulierum."

Allegorice enim per rusticam intelligitur ecclesia et per lupum diabolus, sed per puerum flentem intelligitur peccator, qui si non voluerit
cessare de peccatis suis, rustica, mater eius, id est sancta mater ecclesia
uel confessor in persona sancte matris ecclesie, minatur ipsum puerum
quod velit eum dare lupo, id est diabolo, si non voluerit de peccatis suis
desistere. Quam cito autem cessauerit ab iniquitate suo, tunc restituitur
pristine gracie et sic de laqeuo diaboli eripitur, id est liberatur. Vnde Ecclesiastes: "Fili, memorare peccata tua et peniteas et in eternum non pec-
cabis uel peribis."[165] Item quod mulieribus non est credendum patet
rursum per metristam; versus: "Adam, Sampsonem, David, Loth, et Sa-
lomonem femina decepit; quis modo tutus erit?"[166]

[Avian 2, DE TESTVDINE ET AQVILA; D7; R110]
[*fol. 95v*] Hic autor subdit alium appollogum seu fabulam que est talis
quod cum ipsa testudo vidit pecudes in terra velociter ambulare et aues
repente volare, multum contristata est, quod cum esset leuissima inter
res mobiles et quod naturaliter tamen esset tarda. Videns vero aquilam
omnibus volatilibus altius volare, promisit ei multa, scilicet conchas et
lapides preciosos, ut eam in aerem tolleret. Sed quia promissum soluere
non poterat, aquila eam deorsum cadere permisit. Et sic testudo inter
media aera gemens mortua est.

Isto quidem appollogo autor docet ne aliquis metam sue nature exce-
dat, sed quod viuat contentus propriis rebus, quia quamuis alta petit,
sepe descendit ad yma. Quanto enim gradus altior, tanto casus grauior.[167]

Allegorice autem per testudinem Luciferus primus angelus designa-

---

[164] Compare Ecclus. 25:22–23.

[165] Citation not found in Eccl.

[166] This distich, here relegated to the commentary, is frequently encountered in the late
medieval manuscripts as an additional epimyth appended to Avian's verses; compare
Guaglianone, 6.

[167] Walther, *Proverbia* 23589.

tur, qui non fuit contentus propria claritate; Deo altissimo, qui per aquilam denotatur, fieri similis concupiuit, dicens: "Ponam sedem meam ad aquilonem et ero similis altissimo."[168] Qua propter iste cum ceteris angelis secum conspirantibus cecidit in iehennam, et sic de angelo lucis factus est princeps tenebrarum.[169] Versus: "Actibus et verbis, homo, tu quicumque suberbis, [*fol. 96r*] hoc retine verbum: Deus destruit omnem superbum."[170] Eciam in presenti appollogo docemur fugere vanam gloriam huius mundi, que animam suffocare consueuit. Si enim prothoplastus, id est primus homo, fugisset vanam gloriam, vtique humanum genus stabilitum fuisset. Sed modo per superbiam cecidit, que est radix omnium viciorum.[171] Versus: "Si sapiencia, si tibi gloria formaque detur, sola superbia destruit omnia si comitetur."

[Avian III. DE CANCRO ET MATRE; D364; R114]

[*fol. 96r*] In isto appollogo autor docet nos ne quis reprehendat alium de quo ipse reprehendi possit. Vnde Bernhardus: "Cuius vita despicitur restat quod eius predicacio contempnatur." Vnde Catho: "Que culpare potes, ea tu ne feceris ipse. Turpe est doctori cum culpa redarguit ipsum."[172] Item Antigameratus: "Tunc alios culpa cum tu fueris sine culpa."[173] Item: "Dogma tuum sordet cum te tua culpa remordet."[174] Item patet eciam ex ewangelio, quo dicitur: "Cepit Ihesus facere et docere."[175]

Et hoc probat autor per quendam cancrum iuuenum et per eius genetricem. Iste iuuenis cancer redarguebatur a matre sua propterea quod semper retrorsum procederet. Respondit autem matri sue: "O bona mater, si precesseris me, irem, et iuste ego gressus tuos sequar." Que cum deberet preire retrocedebat quemadmodum iuuenis retrorsum monebatur.

---

[168] Compare Is. 14:13–14.

[169] On this widespread allegory, see Robert G. Risse, "The Augustinian Paraphrase of Isaiah 14.13–14 in *Piers Plowman* and the Commentary on the *Fables* of Avianus," *Philological Quarterly* 45.4 (1966): 712–717, here 713–714.

[170] Compare Walther, *Proverbia*, 303; compare also Prudentius, *Psychomachia*, 285.

[171] Compare, for example, Hugh of St. Victor, "De fructibus carnis et spiritus," *Patrologia latina* 176: 997–1010, here 997C.

[172] Compare *Disticha Catonis* I.30.

[173] Edwin Habel, ed., "Der Antigameratus des Frowinus von Krakau," in *Studien zur lateinischen Dichtung des Mittelalters: Ehrengabe für Karl Strecker* (Dresden: Baensch, 1931): 60–77, l. 96.

[174] Walther, *Proverbia* 6232.

[175] Acts 1:1.

Ex ista ergo fabula patet quod iste non debet redarguere uel corrigere alium pro aliquo excessu quo ipsemet corrigendus est. Nam qui hoc fecit, videlicet qui mala agit et bona docet, similis est candele ardenti qui aliis lucet et se ipsam consumit. Item Paulus: "Fratres, estote factores verbi Dei et non auditores."[176] Item de tali iudicio viciorum hominis dicitur in ewangelio: "Eice primo trabem de oculo tuo et vide vestucam de oculo fratris tui."[177] Versus: "Qui vult alterius oculo reprehendere labem, eruat a proprio cicius ipse trabem."[178]

Item allegorice per cancrem intelligitur diabolus, qui fecit filios hominum retrocedere a fide catholica. Sed cum temptatus ab ipso resistet, cum oportet ipsum diabolum retrocedere, sicut est scriptum quod ipse circueat "velut leo rugiens et famelicus, querens quem devoret,"[179] id est a fide katholica seducet. Vel alio modo per cancrum intelligimus sacerdotes et predicatores in quibus lex Dei dependet, quorum vita debet esse talis ut omnibus sit exemplum. Et per filium cancri intelligimus subditos istis prelatis qui insipienter velut superiores mala opera faciunt. Iuxta illud: "A boue maiore discat arare iunior."[180]

[Avian IV. DE VENTO ET SOLE; D532; R119]

[*fol. 96v*] Hic habetur alia fabula, cuius sentencia est quod cum ipse Boreas et Phebus fuissent inimici comparauerunt coram magno deo, videlicet Ioue. Et conuenerunt ibidem quod quilibet eorum deberet excercere secundum ultimum sui posse vim suam et quis eorum forcioris virtutis fuisset gaudere deberet de triumpho. Isto compacto sic posito erat quidam viator ambulans per iter sibi conswetum. Qui dixerunt quis eorum vestes viatori prius reciperet forcior esse deberet. Tunc Boreas excitauit maximos ventos cum maxima turbine et frigidissima tempestate, quibus mediantibus pallium viatori deponere putabat. Sed viator magis et magis palleo se circumdabat. Phebus autem postquam expulsa fuerit tempestas paulatim radios suos spersit cum calore super istum viatorem sic quod ipse viator pre nimio calore sudescere incepit. Et tandem pori eius maxime aperti fuerunt sic quod ipsum pre nimio calore et sudore palleo deposito resedere in terra oportuit. Et sic Phebus victoriam obtinuit.

---

[176] James 1:22.
[177] Matt. 7:5.
[178] Walther, *Proverbia* 24936.
[179] 1 Peter 5:8.
[180] Anonymus Neveleti 50.10.

In presenti appollogo instruimur ne de facili propter aliquas minas ab incepto bono opere resiliamus, sed pocius forti animo minas pertranseamus et licito operi assistamus. Vnde Poeta: "Non venit ad siluam qui cuncta rubeta veretur."[181] Sic eciam homo modica perficeret si omnium minarum verba multum timeret. Et sic in presenti appollogo innuitur quod per gerrulitatem[182] non sequitur sepe victoria, quia sic aliquis garrulator deberet esse maioris victorie quam discretus homo. Item in presenti fabula duplex est fructus. Primus est quod nemo debet se opponere forciori ne extingwatur ut lucerna. Vnde Katho: "Cede locum lesus fortune, cede potenti."[183] Item cedere maiori non est pudor inferiori. Secundus vero fructus est quod pocius aduersarios nostros vincere debemus paciencia et mansuetudine quam cum minacionibus et austeritatibus. Iuxta illud dictum: "Paciencia vincit maliciam."[184] Item: "Disce pati si vis vincere."[185] Versus: "Nulla virtus tanta fertur patiencia quanta." Quare dicit Iacobus in canonica: "Deus humilibus dat graciam, resistit autem superbis. Subditi ergo estote Deo et resistite diabolo ut fugiet a vobis."[186]

Allegorice seu moraliter per Boream intelligimus insipientes, per solem autem sapientes. Vel per Phebum intelligimus Deum omnipotentem, per Boream vero Luciferum, qui se Deo comparare voluit dicens: "Ponam sedem meam ad aquilonem et ero similis altissimo."[187] Vnde maxima lis erat inter Boream et Phebum in passione Christi vbi Christus vicit diabolum. Isti enim simile litigauerunt pro veste [*fol. 97r*] viatoris, id est pro anima humana. Sed Phebus mitis et mansuetus sua sapiencia Boream, id est diabolum seuerem hostem humane uite, deuicit et superavit.

[Avian V. DE ASINO PELLE LEONIS INDUTA; D117; R124]
[*fol. 97r*] In presenti fabula seu appollogo docemur quod nullus hominum debeat sibi vsurpare aliquem honorem quam habere non potest, quod declaratur de quodam azino. Vnde: Erat quidam azinus qui invenit pellem leonis inter se istos dicens sermones: "Ego volo me induere pellem leonis ut videar esse leo." Illo autem facto valde horribilis apparuit

---

[181] Walther, *Proverbia* 18688.
[182] Classical Latin *garrulitatem*.
[183] *Disticha Catonis* IV.39.
[184] Compare Walther, *Proverbia* 20833f.
[185] Compare Walther, *Proverbia* 5865.
[186] James 4:6–7.
[187] See notes 169 and 170 above.

et fuit inimicus omnibus timidis animalibus perturbando ea modis quibuscumque potuit. Tandem quidam vir cognovit ipsum per magnas et longas aures quod fuerat azinus et corripuit eum tam verberibus quam verbis, dicens: "Tu potuisses multos sic fallere per tue vocis imitacionem, sed ego in eternum te pro azino habebo." Et abstracta sibi pelle azinum esse demonstrauit.

Doctrina presentis fabule est quod nemo debet sibi asscribere virtutem seu dignitatem quam non promeruit, quod si fecerit, magnum dampnum et vicium ex inde pacietur.

Vnde allegorice per azinum intelligitur diabolus, qui mundum et homines in eo existentes ante adventum Christi voluit sibi subiugare. Quod Dominus videns nos sua morte ab eius domineo redemit. Vel aliter per azinum intelligitur quilibet diues et potens qui gloria et virtute sua tumescit et aliis hominibus terrescit. Tandem rusticus, id est dominus suus, scilicet diabolus, ipsum eternaliter puniendo induebatur pelle leonina, id est quod antichristus veniat sub pelle, id est specie diuina, fidem nostram destruendo, christianos necando et semper hoc propter nimiam eius superbiam, quare superbie multum diligenter est resistendum. Vnde dicit sapiens: "Deus humilibus dat graciam, resistit autem superbis."[188] Versus: "Est verum verbum: Deus destruit omnem superbum."[189] Item nichil est peius homini superbo qui fuit humilis. Versus: "Asperius nichil est humili cum surgit in altum."[190] Item: "Dum surgunt miseri nolunt miserum misereri."[191] Item effectus fabule presentis patet in hiis metris: "Flagra ferens azinus detracto pelle leona te monet ut laude potieris non aliena."[192]

[Avian VI. DE RANA ET VULPE; D164; R128]

[fol. 97v] In presenti fabula autor nititur nos instruere ne iactemus nos de illis que perficere non valemus. Et hoc probat per quendam ranam que ascendens super montes herbosos [et] vidit ibi gregem ferarum quibus dixit: "Ego sum bonus medicus et scio consulere grauibus morbis, et non vidi aliquem medicum cui velim cedere in arte medicinali." Et fere ibi congregate illud verum esse putabant. Sed vulpes deridens simplici-

---

[188] James 4:6; compare also Prov. 3:34.
[189] See note 171 above.
[190] Walther, *Proverbia* 1565.
[191] Walther, *Proverbia* 6740.
[192] The commentator here and in the next fable ("Vulpes qui docuit . . .") has apparently had recourse to a medieval reworking of Avian's fables in rhyme.

tatem earum dixit: "O vos stulte creditis verbis rane. Ipsa enim nititur vos decipere maligna fraude. Ymmo videtis quod ipsa pallida est ac si esset ydropica; color enim talis non conuenit aliquibus sanis. Si enim sciret morbos curare, maxime se ipsum curaret." Et sic vulpes auertit feras de tali credulitate.

Ista fabula monet nos quod nemo debet sibi assumere scienciam quam non habet et non debet promittere quod non potest per ipsum reduci ad effectum.

Allegorice per ranam intelligimus mundum presentem, qui promittit nobis longam vitam et tranquillam et spacium penitendi, in quo sepe decipimur. Tandem digne deridemur a sapientibus et religiosis qui vulpibus comparantur. Versus: "Vulpes qui docuit ranam medicamine vanam te docet ut solitum non fingas esse magistrum."

[Avian VII. DE CANE; D306; R132]

[*fol. 98r*] In presenti fabula autor presens nititur nos instruere ne superbiamus propter munera nobis collata. Nam dubitatur sepe et de facili scire non potest scilicet an dantur nobis propter nequiciam vel an dantur propter bonitatem nostram. Et hoc ostendit per quendam fabulam de quodam cane. Erat enim quidam canis solens hominibus cum caude sua applaudere ut silenter sine latratu eos dentibus suis morderet. Quod considerans dominus istius canis seu eius possessor apposuit collo istius canis quendam nolam, id est paruam campanam, que nola motu suo signum hominibus intimaret vt audientes sonum eiusdem nole morsus ipsius canis euitarent. Iste autem canis propter nolam suo collo alligatam ultra modum superbiuit, putans istud munus habere ortum ex sua virtute et esse signum honoris. Quod videns quidam senior canis ipsum superbum canem aggrediens huiusmodi verbis dixit: "Vere tu nimis fatuus es, stultissime canis, qui putas, qui enim estimas hec munera, id est nolam, propter honorem fore data. Ipsa enim nola est tibi data propter neqwiciam tuam et propter fraudulentam inuasionem quia inuadere solebas homines eos horribiliter mordendo."

Fructus enim huius fabule est ut nos discernamus quod quando nobis aliqua dona seu munera dantur, an nobis tribuantur propter maliciam uel propter virtutem, quod tamen quam plures non faciunt utique in procuracionibus et causidicis quibus propter maliciam eorum homines quandoque reddunt stipendia, que quidem stipendia ipsi putant eis dari propter honorem.

Allegoria: Vero per canem intelliguntur homines nequiciosi et superbi, per nolam vero canis collo alligatam intelligitur potestas superbis

concessa et data. Sicut enim canis non poterat discernere quare talis nola
suo collo esset alligata, sic homines nequicii et superbi non apprehen-
dunt beneficia ab eorum superioribus ipsis collata, sed quando aliqua
beneficia eis dantur, ex malicia eorum putant ex inde eos fore reperta-
turos honoris altitudinem.

[Avian VIII. DE CAMELO; D329; R137]

[*fol. 98r*] Hic autor per fabulam presentem nititur nos instruere ut petamus ea que iusta sunt et que de iure negari non possunt, quod probat
per quendam camelum qui conquestus est Iovi, videns alia animalia habere defendicula, ut leones et ursi vngues, boues vero et cerui cornua;
ipse autem omnibus istis defensionibus est destitutus, quare dilegen-
tissime rogauit ipsum Iovem ut daret ei cornua. Iupiter autem derisione
subsannauit istum camelum, dicens: "Non sufficiunt tibi dona dei, et
[nec] ergo merito aures parue pro tuis magnis sunt tibi dande." Sustulit
igitur Iupiter longitudinem eius aurum, dicens: "Vive eternaliter minor,
quia noluisti esse contentus de donis fortune."

Docet itaque autor in presenti appollogo ne aliquid iniuste [*fol. 98v*]
petamus ne refulsionem paciamur, quia qui iniuste petit non meritur
exaudiri. Vnde Katho: "Quod iustum est petito uel quod videatur ho-
nestum."[193] Item mater filiorum Zebedei de iniusta peticione non est
exaudita.[194] Vel in presenti appollogo docemur quod simus contenti istis ornatibus corporum que nobis sint tributa a natura. Vel eciam ex eodem appollogo habetur ut non simus cupidi aliarum rerum, sed contenti
simus propriis rebus, quia cum aliquis cupit aliena acquirere, sepissime
perdit propria, vt uidemus per experigenciam cottidianam de furibus et
latronibus qui cupiunt ditari et perdunt propriam vitam pro diuiciarum
acquisicione.

Allegorice vero per camelum intelligitur homo cupidus et auarus, qui
sepe petit et desiderat habere plura quam sibi expediunt. Iupiter vero, id
est Deus gloriosus, qui cuncta creauit ex nichilo, indignatur ex iniusta
peticione et aufert tali homini auar‹o› omnem fortunam, inferendo ei
disfortuniam uel mortem, per quam mundi cuncta entia reliquuntur.
Versus: "Est rota fortune rota mobilis ut rota lune. Crescit, decrescit, in
eodem cistere nescit."[195] Fortuna dicitur respondere ad ista metra tali

---

[193] *Disticha Catonis* I.31.
[194] Compare Matt. 20:20–23.
[195] Read "sistere"; Walther, *Proverbia* 7874.

modo: "En ego fortuna non sum sors omnibus vna. Si non mutarer, nunquam fortuna vocarer."

[Avian IX. DE DUOBUS SOCIIS ET URSA; R142]
[*fol. 98r*] In hoc appollogo autor docet nos quod nemo de facili debet sibi assumere socium ignotum, quod ostendit de duobus sociis qui sibi invicem promiserunt quod uellent pati mutuo singula occurrencia eis tam prospera quam aduersa et e contra. Quibus sic conuenientibus occurrit quidam ursa horribilis, quam vt vnus sociorum videret fugiens ab isto ascendit quendam arborem et suspendit se cum manibus ad ramum quendam vt vrsa eum non videret. Alter vero videns se non posse euadere cecidit ad terram, fingens se esse mortuum. Quem cum vrsa vidisset ipsum leuauit cum pedibus anterioribus, et cum se non moueret nec penitus spiraret, credidit esse fetidum cadauer, et eo dimisso reuersa est in speluncam. Tunc socius [*fol. 99r*] fugax descendens de arbore ad socium suum dixit: "Socie karissime, dic michi que secreta retulit tibi ex quo diu murmurauit tecum." Cui respondens dixit: "Multa quidem michi dixit, sed inter cetera maxime michi precepit quod nunquam assumerem societatem ignotorum, quod firmiter facere intendo."

Per istam igitur fabulam docemur quod plus debemus esse sociales notis quam ignotis, quia hominis noti amicicia est approbata sed ignoti hominis est dubia. Vnde Katho: "Ignotum tibi tu noli preponere notis. Cognita iudicio constant, incognita casu."[196] Item Alanus: "Sepe viatorem noua non vetus orbita fallit, sic socius socium non vetus ymmo novus."[197]

Allegorice vero per istum socium qui finxit se esse mortuum intelligitur saluator noster, et per socium fugientem intelliguntur discipuli eius, qui fugerunt ab ipso.[198] Et per ursam intelligitur diabolus, nam sicut iste recessit sine lesione ab ursa, sic Christus diabolum vicit tercia die a mortuis resurgens. Vel aliter per socium qui ascendit arborem intelligitur corpus, quod sepe nititur deliciose viuere tam superbiendo quam altiora acceptando. Sed per illum qui cecidit super terram, fidelis anima intelligitur, quia ista semper quantum est de se tendit ad salutem, videlicet ad humilitatem, contricionem et castitatem et continenciam. Vnde beatus Ieronimus docens contra perfidiam hominum viciosorum dicit: "Enim

---

[196] *Disticha Catonis* I.32.
[197] Alanus ab Insulis, *Liber parabolarum* I,13–14, in *Patrologia latina* 210: col. 581.
[198] Compare Matt. 26:56.

vnusquisque de proximo se custodiat et pre omni non habeat fiduciam
quia frater supplantat fratrem. Et omnis amicus fraudulenter incedit in
ore suo pacem cum amico loquitur, sed occulte ponit ei insidias. Et in
presencia ostendit se verum amicum, in absencia tamen seuissimus est
persecutor, quare societas singulorum non est acceptanda, sed solum cog-
nitorum."[199] Versus: "Calles, antiquos, veteres seruabis amicos."[200]

[Avian X. DE CALVO EQUITE; R148]

[*fol. 99r*] Hic autor per appollogum presentem docet nos quod si ab
aliquibus derideamur, non debemus cum iracundia depellere risum sed
cum risu. Quia sepius fit cum quis deridetur, quanto quis irascitur, tanto
magis risus augmentatur. Quod probat per fabulam presentem, quod fuerat quidam miles caluus qui alligauit capiti suo crines equinos. Contigit
isto facto sepius quod venit ad campum splendidis armis et cepit velo-
cem equum flectere frenis. Qui cum esset inter magna gaudia, ventus,
scilicet boreas, veniens ab aduerso suo flatu deposuit sibi comam anne-
xam. Populus autem veniens[201] hunc militem caluo capite conuersus
fuit in maximum risum. Miles vero percipiens se derisum a populo simul
cum eis ridere incepit, dicens: "Non est mirum annexos a me capillos
fugisse cum naturales me dimiserunt." Et risum hominum cum suo risu
depulit a se.

Fructus autem presentis fabule est ne faciamus istud per quod possumus derideri, et ne curamus artificialia durare cum naturalia durare
non possunt.

Allegorice per istum militem [*fol. 99v*] Christum intelligere possumus,[202] per comes vero annexos humanitatem eius, que mortua et elapsa fuit et a Iudeis derisa sic dicentibus: "Alios saluos fecit, se ipsum salu-
are non potest."[203] Et per resurrexionem eius risum Iudeorum deleuit.
Vel aliter per turbam deridencium intelliguntur Iudei qui euellendo barbam militis, id est Christi, eum deriserunt, quod gratanter accepit quia
omnes euntes per viam caput mouerunt[204] in signum derisionis, sed
ipse verbis suauibus coram eis se defendit.

---

[199] See Jerome's commentary on Jeremiah 2, *Patrologia latina* 24: cols. 741–742.

[200] Compare Walther, *Proverbia* 2242.

[201] Read "videns."

[202] On the Christological allegories of this fable, see Wright, "The 'Nuremberg' Aesop,"
142, and Grubmüller, "Fabel — Exempel — Allegorese." Ulrich Boner's mid-fourteenth-
century German version of the story is discussed below, Chapter 2.

[203] Compare Matt. 27:42.

[204] This is an allusion to Lamentations 1:12 and Psalm 22:7.

[Avian XI. DE GEMINIS OLLIS; D559; R151]

[*fol. 99v*] Hic autor ponit aliam fabulam de duabus ollis et est talis, quod aqua cuiusdam fluminis impetuose currentis duas ollas diuersas, scilicet vnam eream et aliam terream, secum eripuit. Quibus pariter natantibus in aqua ista lutea olla fugiebat eream, timens ab ea ledi et frangi. Erea vero dixit ad luteam: "Cur fugis amicam tibi indigenti paratam subuenire?" Cui ea respondit: "Scio quod fiducia debilis cum maiori pauca est, et quamuis me securam reputas verbis et iuramentis tuis, tamen timor non poterit ex animo meo excludi et euelli. Siue enim aqua ducit me ad te siue te ad me, semper ego ero subjecta periculo."

Subdit autor fructum istius fabule, dicens quod pauper et inpotens vitabit societatem potentium, quia pauper potentibus malignantibus resistere non potest. Dicitur enim prouerbialiter: "Dampna reportabit cattus, qui cum cane ludit."²⁰⁵

Allegorice enim per ollam eream, qui fortis est, intelligitur diabolus, humani generis inimicus, qui durus est et callidus. Sed per ollam terream intelligitur homo debilis et fragilis, qui cum diabolo trahitur seu temptatur ut secum ambulet et suam voluntatem faciet, debet omnino eum fugere et suis suggestionibus nunquam assentire. Et sic patet quod dispar‹ibus› in moribus non valet mutua conuersacio. Nam dicitur quarto Ethicorum quod ex viuere cum bonis fit quedam assimilacio in opere virtutis.

[Avian XII. DE RUSTICO ET THESAURO]

[*fol. 100r*] Hic autor ponit aliam fabulam que talis est quod quidam agricola volens aratro suo terram suam vertere invenit in sulco, id est eyn voer,²⁰⁶ maximum pondus auri purissimi. Statim animo indigno reliquit aratrum, adduxit suos boues ad meliora sata vel frumenta et erat multum supplex seu deuotus et cepit agro suo construere templum, quia ager seu terra sibi gazam sponte obtulisset. Fortuna vero, videns hunc rusticum ita laborare pro construxione templi, dixit: "Cur non des illa dona meis templis sed magis honoras alios deos? Nam tamen meo dono sis ditatus, sed inposceris cum faciem meam a te auertens et fueris effectus pauper, tunc me primo supplici prece solicitabis."

Fructus autem huius fabule est quod quicumque acceperit aliquod

---

²⁰⁵ Walther, *Proverbia* 4903.

²⁰⁶ This is the only instance of a vernacular phrase in the commentary; the word "sulsis" in Avian's verses is glossed only with the preposition "in," apparently as an indication of its case.

beneficium ab aliquo et regraciatur alteri et non illi, multum grauiter peccat cum vicium ingratitudinis sit valde malum et detestabile vicium. Vnde Seneca: "Ingratus est qui negligit beneficium, ingracior qui non reddit, ingratissimus enim qui obliuiscitur benefici accepti."²⁰⁷

Allegorice autem per rusticum intelligitur homo diues, qui putat de labore proprio habere diuicias et non a fortuna, id est a Deo, sine quo tamen nichil habetur in hac vita. Et si tunc graciarum actiones sibi non reddamus uel referamus, in fine aufert a nobis thezaurum regni eterni propter ingratitudinem a nobis sibi commissam.

[Avian XIII. DE TAURO ET HIRCO; D443; R157]

[*fol. 100r*] Hic autor subdit aliam fabulam per quam docet quod nemo terreat proximum suum cuius causa est,²⁰⁸ ne forte ab ipso in posteris ledatur. Hoc declarat auctor per quendam hircum et thaurum, dicens quod quondam quidam thaurus erat agitatus a quodam magno leone. Tunc iste thaurus cepit querere tuta antra in diuersis montibus. Reperit tandem vnam speluncam quam quidam oleus, id est fetens, hircus possidebat, et leuato capite trusit ipsum in talem antrum. Hircus fetens vero videns hunc terruit ipsum per suam longam barbam, quare fugam [*fol. 100v*] cepit talis thaurus. Hircus autem interim exiens speluncam alloquebatur thaurum, dicens: "Mea audacia expulit te ab antro mea, et iurgia mea faciunt te timere." Thaurus vero respondit, dicens: "O fetide et putride, tuam barbam dimissam non timerem, si iste abesset qui sequitur gressus meos. Nam si ipse decesserit a me quem timeo, tunc tu pessime notes vires thauri quantum discrepant a viribus hirci."

Fructus istius fabule est quod non noceamus illo quem vel cui nocere possumus ut non noceat nobis. Vnde Katho: "Quem superare potes, interdum vince ferendo. Ledere qui potuit aliquando prodesse valebit."²⁰⁹

Item allegorice per thaurum intelligitur homo iustus, per leonem vero diabolus, qui non cessat homini inferre continua nocumenta. Per hircum vero intelligitur peccator, qui nolebat thaurum dimittere ire in antram quando a leone fagebatur, quia mali semper inpediunt bonum et inferunt obprobria bonis hominibus.

---

²⁰⁷ Seneca, *Epistolae morales* III, 1–3.
²⁰⁸ The manuscript appears to omit an adjective here.
²⁰⁹ *Disticha Catonis* I.38.

[Avian XIV. DE SIMIA; D12; R160]

[*fol. 100v*] Hic autor ponens aliam fabulam docet nos quod nemo debet se ipsum laudare, nam laus propria iudicatur esse sordida. Quod declarat per fabulam presentem, quod quodam tempore ipse Iupiter, volens scire quis pulcriorem natum haberet in toto orbe, fecit vocare omne genus volucrum, bestiarum, pecudum et piscium, similiter et hominum. Quibus conuocatis venerunt ad Iovem et omnes vno ritu consederunt. Tandem symea venit et adduxit suum natum, petendo Iovem ut daret ei victoriam propter pulcretudinem sui nati, affirmans ipsum esse ceteris animalibus pulchriorem. Quod audiens Iupiter ductus est in risum, et motus in iram dedignatus est exaudire preces symee. Et cum diu fatigasset suis precibus, Iovem non tamen proficiens, cum magno dolore recessit.

Fructus huius fabule est quod nemo debet sibi asscribere laudem suo iudicio, quia est stultorum et non sapientum. Similiter ex presenti fabula habetur quod nemo debet corrumpi prece uel precio, nec fauore nec odio, quin iudicet veritatem et equitatem.

Item allegorice per symeam debemus intelligere synagogam et per alias feras quaslibet alias gentes. Modo synagoga dicet fidem suam esse meliorem, cum tamen ita non sit, et sicut symea clamat ad Iouem, ita Iudei et heretici nituntur destruere fidem nostram christianam, dicentes fidem ipsorum esse optimam, cum tamen sit pessima.

[Avian XV. DE GRUE ET PAVONE; D362; R164]

[*fol. 101r*] Hic autor docet quod nemo debet cum alio pugnare verbis vel factis faciliter. Similiter ostendit quod nemo debet se iactare de pulcritudine sua. Hoc enim probat per gruem et pauonem, dicens: Erat quidam pauo de pulcritudine sua nimium se extollens. Cum venerit inter alias aues, affirmat se omnes excellere in decore. Grus autem, audiens hoc, dixit qualiter hoc posset fieri. Qui respondit: "Nam meis pennis templa deorum ornantur, et eciam sum auis domini Iouis. Sed tue penne reddunt te vilem esse, quia nullum in se habent decorem. Ideo te in pulcritudine excello." Grus vero ad hoc respondit mitibus verbis: "Licet ego habeo viles et difformes pennas, tamen ego superero proxima syderibus, et quamuis tu habes pulchras pennas, tamen tu geris tua florida terga iuxta terram."

Fructus huius fabule est quod pulcher non spernat difformem. Versus: "Cum tu sis pulcher, difformem spernere noli."

Item allegorice per pauonem intelligimus diuites seculares, et per caudam eius diuicias seculares. Sed per gruem intelligimus viros religiosos ad diuina officia deputatos, spernentes bona temporalia. Isti ergo deridentur a pauonibus, id est a diuitibus secularibus, eo quod diuicias non habent. Sed possunt respondere quod liceat careant diuiciis temporalibus, tamen alte volant et semper habent cor erectum ad celum, vbi sunt diuicie celestes et perpetue. Sed diuites seculares manent in terris et habunt cor depressum per diuicias seculares, ita quod non veniunt ad alta et ad diuicias celestes desiderandum. Et hoc similatur pauoni, qui in cauda multos habet oculos sed nichil vidit mediantibus illis.

[Avian XVI. DE QUERCU ET HARUNDINE; D81; R169]
[*fol. 101v*] Hic autor docet nos ut simus humiles et modesti ad resistendum cum humilitate, quod plus valet quam cum molestia et peruersitate, quod probatur per quercum et cannam quendam. Quercus enim stabat extensis ramis in alto monte et omnes ventos supervenientes impedivit sua magnitudine. Et dum sic staret secura, boreas veniens suis magnis flatibus ipsam ab alto monte deicit. Quam aqua quedam suis fluctibus arripiens ipsam duxit per alta flumina. Que tandem venit inter cannas et suis ramis ibi adhesit. Videns cannas resistere ventis, dixit: "Qualiter potestis resistere forti boree cum sitis exigui corporis? Nam ego habeo fortes ramos et magnas vires, similiter magnas radices; ei tamen resistere non potui." Quod audiens vna canna: "Noli mirari, quia quamuis sumus parui corporis, tamen veniente aliquo vento locum ei damus. Et sic ventus nobis parcit. Tu vero cum sis magna, te opponebas vento et victa ruebas."

Moralitas huius fabule est quod quivis debeat euitare elacionem, nam secundum Senecam, per humilitatem et pacienciam melius habetur victoria quam per elacionem et molestiam. Quare dicitur: "Disce pati, si vis vincere."[210]

Allegorice per quercum intelligitur superbus, per cannam vero intelligitur humilis. Nam humiles et mediocres preceptis Dei obedientes declinant se ab inpetu superbie et humiliant se maioribus suis. Sed diuites et superbi preceptis Dei inobedientes potencioribus se resistunt. Sed in fine euelluntur et suppeditantur. Nam Dominus viam peccatoris disperdet[211] et precipue superborum. Vnde: "Deus humilibus dat graciam, resistit autem superbis."[212]

---

[210] Walther, *Proverbia* 5865.
[211] Psalm 145:96.
[212] James 4:6.

[Avian XVII. DE VENATORE ET TIGRIDE; D323; R173]

[fol. 101v] Hic autor ponens aliam fabulam reprehendit eos qui nimium confidunt de sua fortitudine quod nemo possit eis nocere. Quod declarat de quodam venatore qui sumpsit secum sua arma, videlicet sagittas, et intrauit quandam siluam multum densam *[fol. 102r]* more consueto. Et videns diuersas feras per nemora vagari, tetendit arcum suum et eas fugauit. Tigris autem videns eas fugere incepit ipsas timentes consolari, dicens: "Nolite timere, ego namque vobis conferam clippeam protectionis." Quo facto venator accepto iaculo tigridem in pedem sagittauit. Voluit enim tigris dare fugam, sed nimius dolor vires eius arripuit ita quod vis attraxit spiritum. Venit itaque vulpes quedam videns ipsam lesam et cepit eam blandis verbis circumvenire, sic dicens: "O tigris, dic michi quisnam contulit tibi tanta dampna." Cui respondit tigris: "Cum sic irem ad alias feras defendere vellem,[213] sum lesus tam magno vulnere, et a quo penitus ignoro." Cui respondit vulpes, subsanatiue dicens: "S‹c›is enim quod telum in te missum ostendit aliquem virum hic fuisse." Venator vero, stans in abschondito loco, tacito sermone dicebat: "Iste nuncius manifestabit qualis ego sum," et mox telo transfodit viscera illius animalis, scilicet tigridis.

Fructus huius fabule est quod nemo periculum sue vite propter alium intret, ne periculo suscepto aliis fiat derisio. Vnde Katho: "Sic bonis esto bonus, ne te mala dampna sequantur."[214]

Allegorice vero per venatorem intelligimus diabolum, qui nos reperit in silua, id est in voluptatibus huius seculi, et vulnerat nos suis telis, id est per malas suggestiones quando nos a voluptatibus retrahere non studeamus vel alios voluptatibus inherentes. Vnde: "Sicut silva est refugium ipsis feris, sic voluptates sunt refugium corpori."

[Avian XVIII. DE QUATTUOR IUVENCIS ET LEONE; D450; R176]

[fol. 102r] Hic ponit autor aliam fabulam, que talis est quod quondam quator boues erant vinculo amicicie adeo uniti quod inter se talem fecerunt confederacionem, quod equaliter tollerare vellent quodcumque eis per fortunam eueniret, siue bonum siue malum. Quibus ad pascua euntibus quidem leo famelicus obuiabat eis in siluis. Videns autem leo eos fore vnitos et confederatos, eos timuit inuadere ex quo solus erat. Quare

---

[213] The accusative "alias feras" is to be read as in a construction *apo koinou*.
[214] *Disticha Catonis* I.11.

nitebatur eos separare ab invicem, suis verbis fallacibus inter ipsos discordiam seminando. Boues igitur confidentes leoni sunt distincti et separati, et sic leo vnumquemque diuisim invasit et interfecit. Quartus autem bos, videns suos socios interfectos et se statim interficiendum a leone, prorupit in hec verba: "Quicumque seruare voluerit vitam quietam et pacificam, ex nostra morte potest dicere²¹⁵ ne cito credat fallacibus verbis. Et secundum Senecam, blanda verba habent venenum permixtum, eciam debet discere ex nostra morte quod non dimittat veterem fidem siue amiciciam propter nouam."

Vnde Alanus: "Sepe viatorem noua, non vetus, orbita fallit; sic socius socium non vetus, ymmo nouus."²¹⁶ Item Katho: "Ignotum tibi tu noli proponere notis. Cognita iudicio constant, incognita casu."²¹⁷

Allegorice per leonem [fol. 102v] intelligimus diabolum, et per quator boues possumus intelligere quator virtutes cardinales. Quantum diu homo coniunctus est quator virtutibus cardinalibus sic quod agat virtuose et eciam uivet secundum eas, tam diu leo, id est diabolus, non potest sibi inferre aliquod nocumentum. Sed postquam ipse dimiserat istas virtutes statim erat subiectus diabolo.

[Avian XIX. DE ABIETE ET SPINO; D550; R179]

[fol. 102v] Hic autor ponit aliam fabulam que est talis: Abies quedam radicata et stans inter dumos, videns se erectam in longitudine ultro dumos, incepit dumos deridere, dicens quod ipsa abies de iure non deberet poni inter dumos quia ipsa longa et pulchra esset et naues de ea componerentur, sed dumus difformus esset et asper et nullius vtilitatis, et propter hoc homines videntes dumos non curant eos, sed potius pretereunt ipsos tanquam despectos. Quod audiens, dumus respondit: "O abies, quamuis multum longa sis et procera, non tamen debes omnia nostra mala allegare ad tantum tuas laudes exprimendo. Sed tempus adhuc veniet quod rusticus te visitabit et cum securi te detruncabit; tunc bene volueris quod spinas nostras habuisses ut te defendisses."

Doctrina autem huius fabule est quod nemo debet nimis superbire de sua pulchritudine nec se debet exaltare de aliqua virtute eius, ne postea illo privatus honore doleat. Similiter ex fabula presenti habetur quod si tu fueris pulcher, non debes spernere difformem, quia quanto aliquis

---

²¹⁵ Read "discere."

²¹⁶ Alanus ab Insulis, *Liber parabolarum* I, 13–14.

²¹⁷ *Disticha Catonis* I.35.

fuerit pulchrior, tanto cicius cadit forma. Enim et pulchritudo est bonum valde fragile.

Sed allegorice per abietem intelliguntur elati. Solent deridere et spernere humiles et letantur in tantum de sua superbia quod in fine destruuntur totaliter vbi humiles stare videntur.

[Avian XX. DE PISCATORE ET PISCE; D143; R182]

[*fol. 103r*] Hic autor ponit alium appollogum quod talis est: Quidam piscator vadens piscari paruum piscum cum hamo suo extraxit. Cum autem extraxisset hamum ab ore pisculi, statim iste pisculus lacrimosa voce supplicat piscatori quatenus demitteret eum, dicens: "O piscator, de meo paruo corpore non habetis magnum lucrum, quia iuuenis sum et mater mea statim peperit me et iussit me ludere in aquis. Mitte me ergo crescere quousque aptus sum ad comedendum, et tunc ego sponte redibo pigwior ad hamum tuum." Piscator autem, credens esse stulticiam quod dimitteret rem certam pro incerta, eum non dimisit nec acquievit promissis pisculi.

Subdit pro documento quod nullus demittere debet rem certam pro re incerta, nec presencia debet quis dimittere pro futuris, licet res futura multo melior estimetur, quare proverbialiter "Plus valet in manibus passer quam sub dubio grus."[218] Nec est contra autorem quod omnia mundana debemus delinquere pro celestibus futuris, quia dictum autoris intelligitur de inferioribus et non de superioribus.

Allegorice per piscatorem intelligimus doctorem spiritualem alios regentem, et per pisculum peccatorem intelligimus. Peccator igitur correptus per sacerdotem, licet dicat se velle abstruere a peccato, nichilominus tamen bonus doctor non acquiescens promissis ipsius peccatoris incitabit eum quatenus dimisset erroribus siue procrastinacione, adhereat bonis moribus et quatenus inprouido[219] cum incederit in peccata emendet se sine mora quia mora est alimentum peccatoris. Quare Ovidius in De remedio amoris hortatur nos quatenus obstemus principiis dicens: "Principiis obsta, sero medicina paratur. Cum mala perlongas conualuere moras, sed prospera nec te venturas differ in horas. qui non est hodie cras minus aptus erit."[220]

---

[218] Walther, *Proverbia* 21805.

[219] This word unclear in the manuscript. The commentary edited by Risse offers a similar text for this passage, but reads "in principio."

[220] Ovid, *Remedia amoris*, ed. A. A. R. Henderson (Edinburgh: Scottish Academic Press, 1978), lines 91–94.

[Avian XXI. DE PARVULA ALITE ET SUIS NATIS;
D569; R185]

[*fol. 103r*] Hic ponitur alia fabula seu appollogus qui talis est: Erat quidem rusticus bladum habens viride in quo auis quidam parua, scilicet
alauda, nidificavit et secundum cursum nature suos pullos educavit.
Videns autem rusticus segetem suam maturam, vi [*fol. 103v*] cinos suos
rogauit ut eum adiuuarent ad metendum suas segetes. Pulli autem existentes adhuc inplumes, id est sine plumis, audientes vocem rustici quousque iuuamen vicinorum secundario imploraret. Item rusticus videns
segetes maturiores rogavit vicinos secundario et conturbauit pullos, quos
mater ut prius consolata est. Tercio igitur rusticus videns vicinos suos
multum tardare in eius iuuamine propriam manum apposuit segetibus
eas metendo. Quod videns, mater pullorum cito cucurrit ad nidum, dicens suis pullis: "Currite et relinquite nides vestras. Iam enim tempus
est. Rusticus enim propriis manibus falcem accepit."

Documentum huius fabule est quod homo non debet ab aliis auxilium petere cum ipse potest sibi sufficere. Similiter docemur quod nemo
veritatem et iusticiam occultare debeat propter amicos alterius.

Allegorice vero per auem intelligimus diabolum et per rusticum peccatorem et per blada corda hominum, quibus ipse diabolus prauas cogitaciones et peccata inmittit, licet igitur rusticus, id est peccator, hortatus
fuerit ab aliis ad deponendum peccata latentia in corde suo. Tamen hoc
minime prodest nisi homo velit se ipsum castigare.

[Avian XXII. DE CUPIDO ET INVIDO; R189]

[*fol. 103v*] Hic ponitur alius appollogus qui est talis: Jupiter quodam vice
volens cognoscere ambiguas mentes hominum misit Phebum de celo ut
exploraret animos hominum. Phebus autem obtulit se admodum duo-
rum hominum, quorum vnus erat invidus, alter avarus, dicens quod pe-
terent aliquid et quantumque vnus peteret, alter duplicatum conseque-
retur. Auarus autem distulit peticionem, cogitans: "Socius meus maxima
rogabit munera, et ego statim duplicata accipiam." Inuidus enim e contra cogitauit intente quomodo hoc quod auarus expectebat mutaret in
supplicium. Inuidus ergo accedens stetit paratus ad peticionem. Auarus
autem attentus inhiabat ut duplicatum acciperet quantumque invidus
petisset. Petit igitur inuidus ut ipsemet vno privetur oculo ut auarus
vtraque careret. Et sic factum est. Phebus autem multum mirabatur de
tanta malicia humana, videlicet quod vnus cum gaudio obtauerat supplicium proprii corporis ut alter in duplo puniretur, et ista sic facta Iovi
retulit.

Documentum huius appollogi est quod non debeamus letari de infortunio seu dampno aliorum.

Allegorice per Iovem intelligitur Deus omnipotens, qui misit Phebum, id est Christum, qui ‹est› vera lux, in hunc mundum. Sed per invidum intelligitur diabolus, qui petit priuari vno oculo, id est maiorem optat penam sustinere ut humanum genus ad penam trahat perpetuam.

[Avian XXIII. DE VENDITORE ET MERCATORE; D62; R192]

[*fol. 104r*] In appollogo hic proposito dicitur quod quidam mercator quandam pulchram ymaginem factam de marmore ad similitudinem ipsius Bachi, qui erat deus vini, in foro vendendum exposuit. Venerunt igitur duo nobiles ciues uolentes illam ymaginem emere, vnus ut poneret eam super sepulcrum patris sui mortui, alter vero vt poneret eam in templo ut ibi adoraretur ab hominibus. Hoc autem videns ymago alloquebatur venditorem, sic dicens: "Cum ita sit quod tu potes michi honorem conferre vendendo me illi qui positurus est me in templum ut adorarer ab omnibus, potes eciam michi vituperium facere vendendo me illi qui me ponet super sepulcra patris sui. Pocius debes honorare quam vituperare."

Per istum enim appollogum docemur quod in cuius potestate est prodesse et nocere, pocius debet prodesse quam nocere. Vnde Katho: "Si potes, ignotis eciam prodesse memento."[221]

Allegorice per istam ymaginem possunt intelligi diuicie temporales [quarum] que acquiruntur ut ipsarum vsus sit finaliter ad seruicium Dei ordinatus. Aliqui vero acquirunt sibi diuicias seculares propter honorem mundi seu propter cupiditatem. Cum ergo primum istorum sit laudabile, secundum vero vituperabile quare pocius laborare debemus ad acquirendum diuicias ad gloriam Dei omnipotentis et non propter honorem seculi ut sint diuicie mater superbiendi.

[Avian XXIV. DE VENATORE ET LEONE; D390; R195]

[*fol. 104r*] Hic ponitur alius appollogus qui talis est: Quidam venator et leo socii erant et amici, sed ex quo inter bonos amicos quandoque discordia oritur, ideo isti quadam vice disceptantes erant de nobilitate et audacia eorum. Quibus sic disceptantibus, id est litigantibus, venator ayt leoni: "Veni mecum et ostendam tibi quis nostrum nobilior et forcior

---

[221] *Disticha Catonis* II.1.

est." Venerunt ergo ad quendam villam in qua depictum fuit in quodam pariete circa sepulcrum cuiusdam nobilis viri qualiter homo leonem interfecit. Ostendit itaque venator leoni hanc picturam, dicens: "Ecce quantum forcior est homo leone." Cui respondit leo: "Quis hanc picturam fecit, vtrum homo vel leo?" Venator respondit quod homo. Leo autem inquit: "Vera quidem refers. Homo enim quando vult pingere potest, leo vero pingere nescit. Sed absque dubio, si leo sciret pingere sicut homo, tunc optime videres quod homo deuictus et oppressus esset a leone ex solo murmure et rugitu leonis."

Documentum huius fabule est quod nulli testimonium de se ipso dicenti uel de suis credendum est.

Allegorice autem per venatorem intelliguntur homines seculares pro rebus mundanis laborantes et solliciti. Per leonem vero intelliguntur homines simplices a curis humanis abstracti et deuoti. Sed per ymaginem intelliguntur diuicie seculares, que non sunt verum bonum, sed solum apparens. Vnde venator, id est homo qui in hoc seculo acquisiuit sibi multas diuicias, credit se esse digniorem leone, id est hominibus simplicibus et abstractis a pompis huius seculi. Et ergo propter suas diuicias uolunt ab eis honorari, quod tamen non deberet fieri quia diuicie huius mundi sunt multum caduce, ex quo fluunt et refluunt, et quare dicit Psalmista: "Diuicie si affluunt, nolite cor apponere."[222]

[Avian XXV. DE PUERO ET FURE; R198]

[*fol. 104v*] Hic ponitur alia fabula in qua dicitur quod puer quidam flens sedebat circa puteum et quidam fur accessit, querens causam fletus ipsius. Puer autem mira calliditate mendacium confinxit, affirmans funem esse preruptum cum quo aquam haurire deberet et auream vrnam in profundo putei cecidisse. Fur autem ex isto dampno lucrum suum crescere cogitauit et dampnum pueri asscripsit sue felicitati. Depositis igitur vestibus in puteum descendebat, non attendens quod dolum puer ingeniose prepauerat. Puer autem collatis vestibus furis inposuit ‹eas› humeris suis et abschondit se inter latebras spinarum. Fur autem videns quod frustra laboraret exiuit puteum, videns puerum cum vestimentis suis recessisse, quare tristis sedit. Hoc modo infortunum suum conquestus est: "Quicumque de cetero crediderit quod vrna aurea natare posset in liquidis aquis, bene custodiat vestimenta sua ne perdat, ut ego credulus ‹perdidi› ea."

---

[222] Psalm 61:11.

Moralitas huius fabule est quod cupidi et auari cum concupiscant aliena, plerumque amittunt sua propria, et sepe aliquorum simplicitas deludit vesuciam aliorum. Vnde dicit autor quod nullus debet cupide desiderare alienas res, nam si hoc fecerit, forte perdat quod habuerit.

Allegorice per puerum flentem possunt [*fol. 105r*] intelligi male mulieres et deceptorie. Et per furem intelliguntur homines eis credentes, per vrnam vero bona et clenodia intelliguntur. Interdum namque mala mulier cupiens decipere virum lugubres voces emittit, dicens: "O tenue amice, propter amorem tuum amisi cadum aureum, id est omnia bona mea, amicos meos et honestatem meam, quasi nichilipendi ut te ad amorem meum sic allicere valeret." Et sic per lacrimas nititur capere amantem. Vnde Katho: "Nam lacrimis struit insidias dum femina plorat."[223] Sed prudens et discretus vir non debet solide credere lacrimis mulierum. Nec debet intrare puteum, id est non debet manere in miseris et peccatis consensiendo mulieri ad amorem illicitum, vt sic intrando per viciose puteum amoris ne perdat vestimenta sua, id est virtutes et alia bona ex quo luxuria est multum consumptiua virtutum et bonorum operum.

[Avian XXVI. DE LEONE ET CAPELLA; D386; R201]

[*fol. 105r*] Hic ponitur alia fabula. Ista videlicet quod quidam leo esuriens vidit [vidit] capram in quodam alto monte pascua querentem et dixit ei: "Dimitte ardua montis, nec quere pascua ammodo in irsutis iugis, id est in asperis collibus montium, sed descende ad prata virida, vbi invenies salices et optimos flores et virides herbas pro tuo nutrimento tibi congruentes." Respondit capra: "O leo, precor te diligenter ut dimittas me in mea securitate, licet enim vera dicas, tamen tu celas maiora pericula. Si enim descenderem de monte, forte me deuorares."

Fructus autem huius fabule est quod nemo debet faciliter credere verbis blandis siue adulatoriis alicuius, licet enim talia verba quandoque aliquod veritatis tangant. Tamen bene debet respici in quem finem dicantur.

Allegorice autem per leonem intelligitur diabolus nocte dieque nos insequens ut ad suam miseriam seu penam nos trahat. Sed per capram intelligitur quilibet homo qui dimisset peccatis et contritum transfert se ad bonas operaciones et ad arduam penitenciam. Per montem vero intelligimus Deum omnipotentem uel vitam celestem, videlicet speculacio-

---

[223] *Disticha Catonis* III.20.

nem. Per croceum florem intelligimus delectaciones friuolas huius mundi. Leo enim, id est diabolus, consulit capre, id est homini conuertenti se ad Deum, ‹non› ut ipse ascendat montem, id est faciat penitenciam pro peccatis suis, sed quod descendat ad virides herbas, id est ad delicias friuolas huius mundi et ad ista terrena que sunt sensibus delectabilia.

[Avian XXVII. DE CORNICE ET URNA; D360; R203]
[*fol. 105v*] Hec est alia fabula in qua docetur quod quidam cornix magnam sitim abuit et vidit in campo vrnam quendam iacentem, in qua modicum aque fuerat. Quia ex ea potare non potuit, voluit ergo vrnam effundere uel ad terram inclinare propter sitim extiguendam. Sed ista debilis existens hoc facere non potuit. Parvim excogitat illa alium modum subtilem, videlicet quod accepit multos lapidos parvos quos proiecit in vrnam ut aqua existens in fundo vrne ad orificium eius se leuaret vt sic sitim suam extigueret et bibit de aquis vrne.

Ex ista autem fabula patet quod subtilitas seu astucia plus valet fortitudine. Sepe enim per prudenciam seu astuciam acquiritur quod per fortitudinem solam acquiri non potest.

Allegorice enim per cornicem intelligimus diabolum continue nos sequentem. Sed per aquam existentem in vrna intelligitur cor hominis, quod stat in corpore tanquam in vrna. Per lapidos vero intelliguntur mala opera seu prauas cogitaciones quas diabolus in corde humano per suam astuciam infigit ut bibat aquam, id est remoueat cor a bonis cogitacionibus et operibus. Debet ergo quilibet prudens homo sibi cauere ne cornix, id est diabolus, per suam astuciam et fraudem mittat lapidos, id est mala seu peruersa desideria, in vrnam, id est in cor ut ipse sic bibat aquam.

[Avian XXVIII. DE RUSTICO ET IUVENCO; D51; R205]
[*fol. 105v*] Ista fabula est de quodam rustico qui habebat iuuenem thaurum multum rebellem, dominum suum, scilicet ipsum rusticum, suis cornibus percutientem. Dominus autem, scilicet rusticus, cupiens eum castigare abscidit ei cornua sua et ligat eum ad aratrum, credens eum sic domare. Thaurus autem detraxit vincula quibus ligatus erat et videns quod non posset nocere cornibus suis, proiecit terram cum pedibus [cum pedibus] ad caput rustici et sic deturpauit crines eius et totum caput domini sui, scilicet rustici sequentis eum. Rusticus autem ita deturpatus dixit: "Non est mirum quod ipse, videlicet thaurus, sic faciat, quia naturaliter malus est et ergo a sua malicia non potest refrenari."

Documentum istius fabule est quod homines naturaliter mali seu in maliciis habituati de facili non possunt remoueri ab ista malicia.

Allegorice autem per rusticum possunt intelligi iudices seculares. Et per thaurum rebellentem intelliguntur homines mali, sicut fures, latrones, qui quanto plus castigantur, tanto plus in sua malicia indurantur ex quo sunt habituati in malicia ac si esset eis innata. Ex quo consuetudo altera natura esse dicitur.[224]

[Avian XXIX. DE VIATORE ET SATYRO; R208]

[*fol. 106r*] Ista fabula est quod tempore yemali cum asperis frigus totam terram occupauerat quidam viator ibat in medio campi et erat ventus contrarius. Laborabat ergo viator in difficultate itineris in asperitate nimium et ventoris turbine. Quem videns satirus, id est custos nemoris, fortitudinis eius miratus est et compaciebatur eum et invitauit eum in antrum suum ut se calefaceret et necessariis reficeret. Viderat autem sathirus dum esset in itinere quomodo congelatos digitos afflatu oris calefaciebat et calore intrinseco frigus extrinsecum expellebat, de quo multum mirabatur et tanta esset virtus caloris naturalis. Postquam autem cum simul intrauerunt antrum et ipse sathirus commendaret istum viatorem suo hospicio, delicias ruris et nemorum et vit‹e› egreste[m] dedit ei in cibum. Tandem obtulerat ei ciphum plenum vino calido vt calor vini infusus frigidis membris hospiti subveniret. Viator autem cum bibere deberet primo cum calidam testam ori apposuerat, horruit et celeriter ab ore remouit et flatum vento ore suo concitans vinum calidum temperauit. Quod ut vidit sathirus quasi monstrum exhorruit hominem illum qui antea frigus depulit flatu oris sui et postea eodem ore intemperatum calorem refrigerare studuit, quare ipsum depulit de antro suo dicens: "Volumus te abesse hiis silvis nec amplius in antro nostro recipieris ‹quia› duo tanta diuersa ora in vno capite geras."

Moralitas huius fabule est quod homines biligwes bona et placencia in aliorum presencia dicentes, mala autem in absencia, diligenter sunt vitandi. Nam secundum Boecium: "Nulla est pestis efficacior ad nocendum quam familiaris inimicus."[225]

Allegorice per sathirum intelligitur quilibet existens in consilio alicuius principis, qui homo dicit vnum aperte et aliud occulte. Et cum

---

[224] Compare Walther, *Proverbia* 850.
[225] Boethius, *De consolatione philosophiæ* III, pr. 4, 41–42.

vnum dicat aliud intendat. Debet ergo iste homo expelli a consilio, quia multum nocere potest ex reuelacionibus sibi in consilio factis.

[Avian XXX. DE SUE ET ILLIUS DOMINO; D281; R211]
[*fol. 106v*] Ista fabula est de quodam rustico qui custodiens quendam agrum in quo multa semina creuerunt inuenit quendam suem in illis seminibus cui abscidit vnam aurem ne amplius rediret in suum campum. Idem tamen sus secundario reprehensus est in eodem campo et ideo aliam amisit aurem. Tercio enim rediit et tunc rusticus totaliter ipsum interfecit et domino suo presentauit ad comedendum. Qui vlterius eum tradidit coco precipiens ei quod ipsum membratim diuideret et bene prepararet. Tandem dominus comedens de isto suo quesiuit cor eius et non inuenit. Cur cepit acriter inquirare cocum, dicens quod ipse comedisset cor suis uel furatus esset. Quod audiens rusticus dixit: "Vero domine, cor non habuit. Si enim cor habuisset, non tam sepe redisset ad locum ubi amisit membra sua."

Moralitas enim huius est quod similiter illi qui solent cottidie peccare difficulter possunt abstinere a peccatis. Non enim curant dampna que eis ex inde sequuntur.

Allegorice autem per rusticum intelligitur quilibet vir ecclesiasticus castigans et monens peccatorem ut a peccato desistat. Per suem vero quilibet peccator intelligitur qui primo currens ad segetem, id est ad delicias peccatorum, amittit vnam aurem, id est priuatur pro isto peccato a Deo quandoque per infirmitates uel alias tribulaciones diuersas. Et si tunc secundario peccauerit, item priuatur consimili modo. Si vero tercio, dominus noster viderit quod nulla correctio proderit, tunc tandem finaliter interfecit eum et mittit eum in iehennam ignis vbi est fletus et stridor dentium.[226] Quilibet ergo lapsus in peccatum peniteat tempestiue, emendendo peccata commissa ‹et› amplius non comittendo ea, quia pluries peccare est animam amplius aggrauare.

[Avian XXXI. DE MURE ET BOVE; D445; R213]
[*fol. 107r*] Hic docetur qualiter quidam mus paruus leditur cum exiguo dente magnum bouem in suo pede et postquam ipsum momordit statim cucurrit ad antrum suum. Bos autem lesus incepit irasci et minari; non tamen sciuit quis lesisset eum. Mus autem audiens minaciones bouis ta-

---

[226] Luke 13:28.

cuit et abschondit se in antro suo quousque iam bouis recessisset. Postquam autem ira eius mitigata mus dixit ad bouem: "Licet parentes tui
magna membra tibi dederunt, non tamen dederunt tibi magnum effectum et fortitudinem in membris tuis. Ergo debes addiscere quantum parua corpora possunt, ne amplius ea opprimas sed fideliter adimpleas
quidquid parua turba a te petit et desiderat."

Fructus autem huius fabule est quod non sit faciendum ut diuites
solent, nam cum non possunt subdire sibi debiles et pauperes irascuntur
et tument quare pauperibus et impotentibus non est resistendum cum
perteruitate. Dicit namque Catho: "Corporis exigui vires contempnere
noli. Consilio pollet cui vim natura negauit."[227]

Allegorice autem per bouem intelliguntur diuites et potentes, per
murem vero debiles et pauperes. Quando autem videtur potentibus quod
aliquo modo a pauperibus molestentur tunc incipiunt multum fremere
et minas imponere pauperibus. Sed pauperes et humiles illis temporibus
tacent quousque diuitum et potentum ira recedat et sic dissimulabunt
hoc tempore. Nam per talem dissimulacionem plus ledunt diuites et potentes quam si multa uerba loquerentur.

[Avian XXXII. DE HOMINE ET PLAUSTRO; R215]
[*fol. 107r*] Fabula ista est qualiter quidam rusticus ducens currem suum
bobus suis vexit eum in qu‹en›dam vadum luteum de quo boues currum
tradere non valebant quia currus multum fortiter adherebat luto. Et videns iste rusticus cecidit ad terram lacrimando inuocans omnes deos et
precipue ipsum Arculem ut sibi in tali necessitatis articulo subsidium
prestare vellet. Arcules vero dixit rustico: "Surge et appone proprias
manus et verbera equos tuos et boues, et si tunc non profeceris, iuuabo
te pigrum. Enim dii non succurrunt nisi proprias manus ad opus po-
nant." Rusticus vero acquiescens monitis Arculis surrexit et proprias
manus apposuit et statim currus exiuit.

Ex isto appollogo colligitur hec doctrina quod diuinum auxilium in
rebus agibilibus non est nobis solum inuocandum, sed eciam nostras
operaciones et studia debemus apponere.

Allegorice enim per rusticum intelligimus peccatorem, per vadum
luteum corpus humanum, per currum in eo stantem animam existentem
in corpore. Peccator ergo volens iuuari a Deo non solum debet inuocare
auxilium, sed debet apponere propriam voluntatem abstinendo se a pec-

---

[227] *Disticha Catonis* II.9.

catis, peccata sua confitendo et penitenciam agendo. Et sic ipse poterit
iuuari per graciam Dei.

[Avian XXXIII. DE ANSERE ET SUO DOMINO; D229; R217]

[*fol. 107v*] Hic docetur de quodam homine multum cupido qui habebat
aucam omni die producentem vnum ouum aureum, et fuit talis nature
quod non potuit simul duo oua vno vice proferre. Dominus autem istius
auce ex quo auarus erat libenter fuisset ditatus subito, et credens quod
auca haberet in se multa ova aurea, eam interfecit. Qua interfecta nulla
ova invenit, quare dominus spe sua frustratus multum doluit.

Documentum enim huius fabule est quod homo non debet esse nimis
cupidus nec nimis auarus, ne per auariciam et cupiditatem propriam
incurrat dampnum. Item aliquis volens aliquid opus complere non debet
mentem suam ad multa applicare. Iuxta illud Metriste: "Amittit totum
qui tendit ad omnia votum."[228]

Allegorice enim per istum dominum auce intelligitur domini seu prelati. Per aucam vero subditi intelliguntur a quibus prelati nutriuntur,
quos quidam subditos quandoque spoliant prelati seu domini bonis suis,
quod ammodo lucrum eis prestare non possunt.

[Avian XXXIV. DE FORMICA ET CICADA; D35; R220]

[*fol. 107v*] Hic autor per fabulam presentem incitat nos ad laborandum.
Que fabula est qualiter formica prouidens sibi tempore estiuali de necessariis sue vite que recludit in suum antrum ut tempore yemali non peri-
ret fame. Vnde cum quodam vice formica sic colligisset fructa in antrum
suum, venit cicada tempore yemali ad istam formicam et petiuit auxilium ab ea, dicens quod pateretur magnum defectum in necessariis. Cui
respondit formica: "Quid operata es in estate, quando ego et familia mea
fuimus in labore magno currentes et congregantes in horreis nostris vnde
viuamus in yeme?" Respondit cicada: "Ego tunc cantaui illis qui tunc
laborabant et nichil marcedis ab eis recepi." Tunc ayt formica: "Con-
sulcius egisses, si in estate fuisses prouida future necessitatis quam quod
yemis inclementia modo cogit te ad nostra hostia mendicare. Si [one
illegible word] ego indigerem aliquibus que michi porrigere non posses,
restaret michi mors. Et ergo restat tibi iam mors, quia prior vita tua pe-
racta est intencionibus tuis et quia nil cogitasti de futuro, nil tibi dabo."

---

[228] Walther, *Proverbia* 972.

Allegorice enim per formicam intelligitur quilibet vir prudens et sapiens, sed per estatem iuuentus et per yemem senectus. Et per cicadam homo fatuus et peruersus intelligitur. Quilibet ergo vir sapiens [*fol. 108r*] acquirit in iuuentute necessaria quibus uti poterit in senectute. Cicada vero, id est homo fatuus, non curat tempore iuuentutis sibi prouidere de illis quibus indigebit tempore senectutis. Vnde Salomon: "Vsque piger dormis, surge sompno tuo, o piger, vade ad formicam et disce ab ea sapienciam qui parat in estate escam et congregat in messe cibum quem comedat in yeme."[229]

[Avian XXXV. DE SIMIA ET NATIS; D13; R223]

[*fol. 108r*] Hic ponitur alius appollogus, et est talis, quod quedam erat symea duos habens filios, quorum vnum dilexit et alium odio habuit. Que quidem symea veniens ad nemus agitabatur a canibus, suscepit ergo ambos filios dissimili tamen amore seu modo, quia dilectum recepit in manibus et in brachiis suis, non dilectum vero in dorso, ut si canes venirent pocius non dilectum caperent quam dilectum. Cum ergo paruo tempore fugisset a facie venatorum, dilectus filius quem in manibus habuit currere non potuit. Mater timens venatores dilectum filium dimisit ut ipsa citius curreret. Quod videns filius non dilectus amplexus est matrem cum brachiis suis in tantum quod mater non potuit ipsum abicere. Cum ergo zimea non haberet nisi vnicum filium, incepit illum maxime diligere quem tamen prius non dilexit.

Moralitas enim istius fabule est quod multa sunt in presencia neglecta et spreta et refutantur tanquam vilia, postea vero efficiuntur multa dilecta.

Allegorice enim symea habens duos filios est peccator, filius enim magis dilectus est mundus et bona temporalia, qui brachys, id est affectibus astringit. Filius vero minus dilectus est spiritus suus, quem quasi in dorso proicit quia paruum de eo curat. Cum ergo venator, id est mors que homines prosequetur, venerit, tunc compellitur dilectum filium, id est mundum et terrena, dimittere, et spiritus, de quo non cucurrit, a peccatis grauatus a demonibus capitur et ad eternalem interitum ducitur.

[Avian XXXVI. DE VITULO ET BOVE DOMATO;
D328; R225]

[*fol. 108v*] Ista fabula est qualiter quidam vitulus erat pulcher et sine la-

---

[229] Compare Prov. 6:6–8.

boribus, vitam ducens delicatam. Hic vidit bouem continue arantem et dixit ei: "Non pudet te ita continuo laborare, cum ego curram ad diuersa pascua spaciatum quocumque voluero secundum libitum meum?" Bos autem illis verbis non est compulsus ad iram sed arabat ulterius more solito donec liberatus esset a iugo. Et tunc bos tacens in prato herboso vidit vitulum duci ad sacrificandum ipsis diis. Tunc dixit bos: "Illam mortem pateris propter tuas delic‹ias›. Non enim oporteret te pati hanc mortem si laborasses ut ego."

Quare ex predicta fabula pro eius doctrina infertur quod melius cuilibet homini valeat quod laboret quam quod ocietur ne postea propter ocia pereat. Eciam pro doctrina presentis fabule habetur quod mors cicius adveniat diuitibus et ociosis habentibus vitam laboriosam.

Allegorice enim per bouem in labore perseuerantem intelliguntur homines delicate uiuentes, qui post mortem puniuntur eternaliter propter istas delicias. Quantum enim homo plus deliciis intentus fuerit, tantum statur ei locus tormentorum grauior.

[Avian XXXVII. DE CANE ET LEONE; D625; R228]

[fol. 108v] Ista fabula est quadrupliciter. Quidam canis domesticus multum pigwis occurrit leoni macro, dicens ei: "Nonne vides quam pigwis ego sum? Collum meum valde spissum est et totum corpus meum pigwe. Accipio enim pascua de mensa domini mei et largo ore accipio cibum meum. Tu vero multum macer es et pererras quasi mortuus multa lustra siluarum quousque aliqua preda offerat se tibi." Canis eciam remouet instanciam quam leo posset sibi facere, sic: "O leo, posses querere quare haberem vinculum in collo, respondeo quod ideo ne domus domini mei maneat incustodita. Tu vero leo cum multum macer es et quasi mor[b]ibundus, fac concilium meum et subdas cathenas collo tuo et sic faciliter promereri poteris dapes." Leo vero multum irascebatur et dixit cani: "Vade et habeas nodum in collo tuo pro meritis tuis et dura vincula conpescant tuam famem. Quamuis enim ieiunus sim et macer, tamen curro vbicumque michi placuerit. Et ergo michi non recommenda illas epulas pro quibus libertatem meam dare deberem."

Doctrina enim huius fabule [fol. 109r] est quod nemo propter delicias debet vendere libertatem suam. Vnde Salomon in Proverbiis: "Melior est buccella panis cum gaudio quam domus plena victimis cum iurgiis."[230] Vnde: "Melius est viuere in paupertate et habere libertatem quam viuere

---

[230] Prov. 17:1.

in deliciis et carere libertate." Vnde Esopus: "Non bene pro toto libertas venditur auro. Hoc celeste bonum preterit orbis opes."[231]

Allegorice enim per leonem intelligitur homo religiosus non curans ista mundana sed cottidie diuino cultui insistens, quod est summa libertas. Vnde Crisostomus: "Non est omnino curis solitus ac liber nisi iste qui Christo uiuit et seruit. Nam Christo seruire est regnare." Sed per canem intelliguntur homines voluptuosi et delicate viuentes qui libenter ad eorum societatem allicerent homines penitenciam agentes, quibus resistere debet quilibet homo religiosus.

[Avian XXXVIII. DE PISCE ET PHOCA; D159; R231]

[*fol. 109r*] Ista fabula est de quodam pisce qui nutritus erat in dulci stagno sed coactus est propter impetuosum cursum cuiusdam torrentis interare aquas marinas ubi se extulit super alios pisces marinos, dicens se esse nobiliorem. Foca autem, id est porcus marinus, non potens sustinere superbiam istius piscis extranei reprehendit eum, dicens quod piscis ferret multa mendacia. Nam hoc probare vellet quod mendacia protulisset: "Quia si piscator ceperit nos ambos suo hamo, tunc nobiles et diuites ement me pro magna pecunia. Pauperes vero ement te pro parua pecunia. Ergo tu non es nobilior me."

Doctrina enim huius fabule est: Homo existens in terra aliena non debet iactare de nobilitate sui generis nec extraneos suppeditare debet.

Allegorice enim per piscem intelliguntur homines instabiles de vno loco ad alium vagantes. Et per focam intelliguntur homines constantes et in bonis operibus perseverantes, qui debent arguere et corrigere instabiles ne nimium exaltent per superbiam, qui est radix omnium viciorum.

[Avian XXXIX. DE MILITE ARMA CREMANTE; R233]

[*fol. 109v*] Ista fabula est de quodam milite qui timens in bello se succumbere vouit Deo et omnibus sanctis eius quod si posset a morte liberari, amplius nunquam vellet pugnare et quod omnia arma sua vellet igne comburere. Postquam autem sanus ad terram rediit propriam, memor istius voti omnia sua arma proiecit ad ignem. Volens autem iste miles lituum suum, id est tubam, ad ignem proicere, excusauit se, dicens quod nullo in bello nocumentum intulisset, sed quod solum excitasset homines ad bellum. Cui respondens miles: "Licet tu nichil potuisti attemptare nec enisus fuisti, tamen plus peccasti quam alii ex quo incitasti

---

eos ad bellum tuis cantibus et melodiis. Ergo debes merito puniri maiori pena."

Doctrina enim huius fabule est quod non solum illi puniendi sunt qui malum faciunt, sed eciam illi qui alios ad peccandum incitant. Vnde Paulus: "Facientes et consensientes pari pena puniendi sunt."[232] Versus: "Si quis delinquit, ut Paulus apostolus inquit, Qui consentit ei fit reus ipse rei."[233]

Allegorice enim per militem intelligitur Deus omnipotens. Per arma peccata hominum intelliguntur et per lituum ligwa hominum. Et sic Deus, volens vindicare peccata hominum, mittit peccatores ad ignem iehenne. Sed lituus, id est ligwa, libenter se excusaret, dicens: "O Deus, fac ut membra qui commiserunt peccata puniantur, sed ego nullum peccatum perpetraui." Deus autem respondebit: "Licet actualiter non perpetrasti aliquod peccatum, tamen consilio tuo et sermone induxisti alia membra ad peccandum, quare merito cum aliis membris debes puniri."

[Avian XLI. DE IMBRE ET FICTILIBUS VASIS; D368; R239]
[*fol. 109v*] Ista fabula est quod ymber impulsus per ventum cucurrit per campos magna velocitate et invenit quandam ollam luteam iuxta quendam fluuium ponitam ad exsiccandum per solem. Quesiuit enim ymber nomen istius olle. Olla vero cupiens videri magna dixit: "Ego vocor amphora." Sed quia ista olla iactanter ista dixit, imber assumens eam secum in aquam totaliter destruxit eam, quod fecerat propter iactantiam sui nominis.

Documentum enim huius fabule est quod nullus debet sibi assumere maius nomen uel dignius quam sibi de iure competat. Eciam pro doctrina habetur quod ‹non› reputare debet se meliorem et magis generosum quam sit.

[Avian XL. DE PARDO ET VULPE; D373; R236]
[*fol. 110r*] Iste appollogus est de quodam pardo qui propter multas maculas diuersorum colorum quas habebat in corpore leonem et cetera animalia sic distincte non colorata despexit, dicens leonem esse miserum animal et se ipsum esse nobiliorem leone. Quare vulpes astuta istum pardum reprehendens ayt: "Licet tu sis extrinsecus coloratus, tamen tu cares intrinsecus sapiencia et sciencia. Modo sapiencia mentis plus commendanda est quam corporis pulchritudo."

---

[232] Compare Romans 1:32.
[233] Walther, *Proverbia* 28993.

Moralitas enim huius fabule est: Plus debemus laudare et recommen-
dare illos qui in mente sunt ornati virtutibus et scientiis quam illos qui
habent pulchritudinem corporalem. Vnde Metrista: "Dat probitas spe-
ciem, sed species non probitatem."[234]

Allegorice enim per pardum intelligitur homo superbus in bonis ex-
terioribus habundans. Sed per vulpem potest intelligi homo abstractus a
curis mundanis, qui si spernatur a superbo potest ei respondere quod
bona exteriora non sunt curanda sed magis interiora.

[Avian XLII. DE LUPO ET HAEDO; D65; R241]

[*fol. 110r*] Iste est ultimus appollogus huius libri, de quodam hedo vadens
ad pascua. Petiuit pascua propinquiora domibus et ‹veloci› cursu sepe
lupum decipiebat. Postquam vero pascua sua quesiuit tetendit ad urbem
cum ceteris ouibus. Lupus autem sequebatur ipsum ad medium ciuitatis
et dixit hec verba ipsi edo: "Nonne vides quod socii tui et alia animalia
interficiuntur et sacrificantur ad honorem deorum, et per eorum cruorem homini saciunt terram? Si igitur mortem velis vitare et esse securus,
venias mecum ad campum." Edus autem respondit lupo, dicens: "O
inprobe lupe, precor quatenus deponas curas tuas et viles misericordias,
quia multum melius est quod ego fundam cruorem meum ad honorem
deorum quam saturem et repleam famem tuam."

Documentum enim huius fabule est quod inter duo mala minus
malum est eligendum, quod secundum Aristotelem in Topicis, minus
malum respectu maioris mali videtur habere racionem boni uel ponitur
in genere boni.

Sed allegorice per istum lupum intelligitur diabolus, sed per hedum
petentem arua intelligitur peccator. Et per cruorem intelligitur penitencia, et per urbem intelligitur ecclesia. Quando enim diabolus videt
peccatorem currere ad ecclesiam ad agendum penitenciam, tunc totis
viribus et subtilitatibus nititur peccatorem retrahere ne agat penitenciam
pro pecccatis suis, dicens ei: "Veni, vera penitencia que iniungetur tibi
erit nimis aspera et dura, quare enim non poteris perficere. Sed veni
mecum ad campum, id est vade item ad delectaciones mundanas, et frua-
ris deliciis huius mundi." Quibus suggestionibus est multum diligenter
resistendum. Resistit ergo nichil [*fol. 110v*] interim demonibus sicut
deuota memoria passionis Domini nostri, Ihesu Christi, qui cum matre
sua et omnibus sanctis in secula seculorum sit benedictus. Amen.

---

[234] Walther, *Proverbia* 5006.

CHAPTER 2

Corpora and Collections:
The *Edelstein* and the Magdeburg Aesop

In the early 1460s, not two decades after the introduction of mechanical printing to the European west, the Bamberg press of Albrecht Pfister offered for sale his first printed book in the German language. The text Pfister selected for this still parlous enterprise was one that had already proved its durability; to judge by the nearly three dozen surviving manuscript witnesses of the work, it had already been widely copied and continually read since its composition in the mid-fourteenth century. And in fact, the Bamberg printer had judged both his text and its prospective market well: for three years after its initial appearance in Pfister's bookshop, Ulrich Boner's *Edelstein* became the first book in the German language to require a second printing.[1]

The incunable editions of the Swiss poet's work are of note, too, in that they are among the first European printed books whose text is accompanied by a full set of illustrations, woodcut designs based, as one would expect, in a manuscript fable tradition, and handsomely colored in the unique copy that survives of each Pfister printing. While the illustrations to the fables themselves have long drawn the attention of art historians and historians of the book, the simple cut with which both old prints close has attracted less interest. This final illustration is of a familiar type. It presents the portrait of a bearded author, seated on a boxy

---

[1] On the printing history of the two *Edelstein* incunables, see the introduction to Doris Fouquet, *Ulrich Boner: Faksimile der ersten Druckausgabe, Bamberg 1461* (Stuttgart: Metzler, 1972).

cathedra, with a large book under one arm and the other hand raised in a gesture of speech; a blank scroll extends from this outstretched hand. This is obviously a depiction of the fabulist of antiquity, Aesop himself; his authority is grounded in the book of his authorship, while his influence is figured in the scroll, which reaches to the edge of the illustration and beyond.

From the art-historical perspective, this picture may be uninterestingly mundane; used, however, in illustration of precisely this text, the scene of transmission it depicts is of great significance. In his epilogue, Boner describes his collection expressly as a translation:

> und der, der ez ze tiutsche brâcht
> hât von latîn, des müez gedâcht
> iemer ze guote werden . . .;[2]

earlier in his collection, the German fabulist has carefully identified his Latin sources by name, attributing the first sixty-two fables of his collection to Aesop, the remaining texts to "dem Âviân."[3] Given the text's programmatic insistence on its debt to the Latin tradition, the woodcut suggests, if it does not explicitly illustrate, the transmission of traditional material to a new and newly literate audience, an issue of obvious interest to the publisher of any book printed in the German language.

Viewed not merely as a conventional graphic colophon, this concluding woodcut raises a number of questions about the work it accompanies. How precisely is one to understand the learned content represented by the uninscribed scroll in the hands of the sage? What is the mechanism by which it is communicated to the reader of the vernacular text? And, most importantly, who is the second figure in the illustration, finger raised to point to "Aesop"? These are ultimately questions about the sources Boner relied on for his translation, and their answers may provide new ways to consider the Swiss fabulist's accomplishment in creating the *Edelstein*, the first coherent fable collection in German.

Boner's source for his "Aesopic" fables—those, that is to say, with their most immediate parallels in the Romulus strand of the medieval

---

[2] Franz Pfeiffer, ed., *Ulrich Boner: Der Edelstein* (Leipzig: 1844), 185, lines 41–43.

[3] Pfeiffer, *Edelstein*, 110, fable 62, line 87; fable 63, line 2. Not all of the fables in the first section of the book have their origins in Romulus, just as Avian is not the only exemplar used for the last thirty-eight; on Boner's Latin sources, see below, and the convenient overview in Grubmüller, *Meister Esopus*, 298–302, 310–319.

Latin tradition—was long ago identified as the collection of the Anonymus Neveleti,[4] a fable book that owed its familiarity, as we have seen, to its early and lasting success in the late medieval schoolroom. In the fifty-three fables the Anonymus and the *Edelstein* have in common, Boner follows his Latin verse exemplar faithfully, agreeing with the Anonymus so closely that the Latin original of many verses could easily be reconstructed from the German. Many examples of such nearly identical passages could be added to those adduced by Reinhold Gottschick;[5] in a few cases, the German fable nearly reproduces the Latin verses for most of its length, leaving little doubt that the translator was in fact reading the poems of the Anonymus and not any other parallel version, in prose or in meter.[6]

In a few passages, however, the alterations and additions made in the *Edelstein* suggest its author's access to supplementary material. In four of the fables from the Anonymus Neveleti, Boner has made minor changes that, while seemingly arbitrary and unmotivated, in fact have parallels in the Latin academic tradition, indicating that his manuscript of the Anonymus was, like most, a school manuscript, its texts prepared for the use of the young and the inexpert. Boner himself fit into neither category, of course, but it should be no surprise to find him relying occasionally on an interlinear gloss or marginal comment.

In his fable number 25, for example, that of the frogs who pled for a king, Boner gives the sinister monarch a new identity. Where in the Anonymus, Jove, exasperated, sends a "hydrus" to teach the frogs to rue their bondage, in the *Edelstein*

> dô Jupiter den geschrei vernan,
> ein storken sante er hin dan,

---

[4] See Grubmüller, *Meister Esopus*, 298–299; there too is found a useful concordance of the fables of Boner and the Anonymus.

[5] "Ueber die Quellen zu Boners Edelstein," *Königliches Gymnasium zu Charlottenburg Jahresbericht* 6 (Berlin, 1875): 1–13, here 2–3.

[6] Compare, for the most striking examples, Boner's fables 20 and 27 with the corresponding texts of the Anonymus, numbers 17 and 23. It is perhaps worthy of note that both of these so faithfully rendered fables have as their positive protagonists well-behaved housedogs; Boner, of course, as a Dominican, might have been expected to be especially attentive to texts depicting dogs: the pun on *Domini canes* is likely behind the explication he gives his fable (number 93) of wolves, shepherds, and sheepdogs as well: "des hundes truwe, die sint grôz,/ . . . / sîn zunge wunden heilen kan;/ sîn kel die wolfe billet an./ er wachet vast und hüetet wol,/ . . . / die selben triuw der lêrer hât./ der lêre zunge diu ist guot,/ si heilet lîp, sêl unde muot./ er wachet dur den hêrren sîn" (Pfeiffer, *Edelstein*, 166).

der ir künig solte wesen.
der küng ir keinen liez genezen;
sîn munt was offen, sîn mag wan,
er verslant alz, daz im bekan.[7]

The substitution of the stork for the exotic and somewhat mysterious
"hydrus" is widely attested already in the Latin manuscript tradition of
the Anonymus Neveleti, particularly in the glosses of the school copies;
a mid-fifteenth-century manuscript in Hildesheim, in a note on its interlinear gloss "siconia," explains:

Nota auctor vocat ciconiam idrum per similitudinem,

because both prey on frogs.[8]

Another of the *Edelstein*'s additions, too, can be sensibly explained
by comparison to the Latin annotation of the corresponding fable in the
Anonymus. The Latin fabulist's story of the hares' foolish timidity depends for its moral point,

Sepe facit metui non metuenda metus,

on the actual harmlessness of the noise that sets them to flight; in the
Anonymus, it is the sound of the wind rushing through the trees:

Silua sonat.

Boner's fable, however, in common with a number of other vernacular
versions of the tale, explains the hares' fear differently:

In einen walt ein jeger kam
mit sînen hunden. daz vernam
von dem gedœn der hasen schar.[9]

Thus motivated, the hares' flight makes perfect logical sense:

si vluhen vast: daz tet in nôt;
si wânden al geligen tôt.[10]

Because his rabbits flee for good reason, Boner has accordingly to

---

[7] Pfeiffer, *Edelstein*, 39, lines 33–38.
[8] Hildesheim, Dombibliothek, ms. 27 St. God., fol. 33v. On the commented Anonymus
Neveleti in this manuscript, see Wright, "*Fabule vtilitatem in se continentes*," 255–271.
[9] Pfeiffer, *Edelstein*, 47, lines 1–3.
[10] Lines 25–26.

change the focus of his epimyth from the Anonymus's original concentration on needless fear to a meditation on hopefulness. Boner effects this necessary modification only in part, however, retaining at the conclusion of his fable the observation

> wer verzwîvelt *âne nôt*
> dem möchte wæger sîn der tôt,

an assertion that fits far better the verses of the Anonymus than his own.

The source of this alteration, if it is not to be attributed to narrative ineptitude on Boner's part, is likely to be sought in those Latin manuscripts of the Anonymus that explain the frightening noise in the forest as "sonum ventorum," the howling of the winds. As I have explained in a different context elsewhere,[11] this gloss was later misread as "sonum venatorum," the clatter of hunters; this added detail in turn inevitably gave rise to the hunting scene, complete with baying hounds, that eventually found its way into Boner's fable, with less than felicitous result.

An even greater departure from the Latin source is exhibited in Boner's fable "von einem arn und einem sneggen," corresponding to Anonymus Neveleti 14. In the Latin poem, briefly discussed in Chapter 1 above, the eagle is able to eat its prey only on following the crow's advice to break the shell:

> Quod geris in conca, cibus est. tibi surripit illum
> Conca cibum. concam frange cibusque cadet.
> Vt concam lanies, pro uiribus utere sensu.
> Hanc, si celsa cadat, saxea franget humus.[12]

The eagle does so, and the fabulist notes that just as the tortoise, so, too, are many people ruined by the malicious advice of meddlers:

> De se stultus homo subuersus turbine lingue
> Corruit et fortes ista procella rapit.

Where the Anonymus Neveleti directs the reader's attention to the fate of the tortoise, Boner's epimyth concentrates explicitly on the eagle; for in the *Edelstein*, the fable goes on to show the crow profiting from

---

[11] For a complete survey of the school commentaries on this fable, see Wright, "The 'Nuremberg' Aesop," 232–242.

[12] Foerster, *Lyoner Yzopet*, 103.

the officious advice he has offered. The eagle drops the "snegg,"

> ... diu schal zerbrach:
> zuo vuor diu krâ und was vil vrô
> der spîs: den sneggen az si dô.[13]

There is no corresponding thievery in the Anonymus Neveleti: however harmful to the tortoise, the crow's intentions toward the eagle were sincere. Boner, however, to make his fable more clearly one "von bœsem râte,"[14] needs a clear demonstration of the crow's treachery. Precisely this was available to him in a commentary, similar to the additional annotations in clm 16213, discussed above, which insist

> Cornix autem protinus affuit et istam concham in proprio stomacho sepeluit (fol. 299v).

What has until now been accepted as an innovation in the German *Edelstein* in fact has parallels in the Latin commentary tradition.[15]

Most telling are the variations Boner introduces into his version of Anonymus Neveleti 1, the fable of cock and pearl. While it is true that the fable of the *Edelstein* closely resembles its Latin source,[16] the specific reference to the hungry cock's disappointment at having found a gemstone rather than "ein gerstenkorn" or "ein haberkorn" is not prepared in the Anonymus's verses; it is, however, a frequent feature of the Latin commentaries on this fable. The "minus cara" described by the Anonymus is routinely glossed in the school manuscripts of the late Middle Ages "scilicet granum tritici";[17] many of these same manuscripts expand the idea in the prose reductions of their commentaries:

> Sed quia nec ego tibi nec michi conueniens es, qui magis rem invenissem minus cara, puta paruum granum quod stomachum meum saturasset.[18]

---

[13] Pfeiffer, *Edelstein*, 27, lines 20–22.

[14] So the caption given this text in Pfeiffer's *Leithandschrift*.

[15] It might at this point be objected that Boner's *Edelstein*, composed in the early 1350s, is a hundred years older than the Latin manuscript here adduced in comparison. It must be remembered, however, that the commentaries represent an accumulation of schoolmasterly material beginning in the late thirteenth century, making it seem likely that many of the elements not at present known to be attested in the manuscripts before the fifteenth century were in fact widely circulated already in the fourteenth.

[16] See Speckenbach, "Die Fabel von der Fabel," 197; Robert-Henri Blaser, *Ulrich Boner: Un Fabuliste suisse du xivᵉ siècle* (Mulhouse: Baly, 1949), 58.

[17] For example, Wright, *The Fables of 'Walter of England'*, 18.

[18] Munich, Bayerische Staatsbibliothek, clm 19667, fol. 37r. The prose reductions of the

The grain so eagerly desired by the bird of Boner's fable is likely to have had its origin in such a gloss.

Especially significant in the case of this fable is Boner's apparent familiarity with the standard allegorical explication given the text in the Anonymus Neveleti commentaries of the fourteenth and fifteenth centuries. While Boner maintains the thematization of wise and foolish reading common to all antique and medieval versions of this fable, making of it here too a "Fabel von der Fabel,"[19] he introduces in the middle of his epimyth a new distinction, alien to the verses of the Anonymus that were his putative source. The cock declined to profit from his discovery of the pearl;

> alsô stât ouch der tôren gir,
> ir sitte und ir begêrde
> ûf üppekeit der erde.[20]

The "minus cara," the grain of wheat preferred by the foolish cock, is thus in the German fable worldly splendor; Boner implies in these sentences that the wise man should seek rather the spiritual brightness of heaven. Precisely this contrasting pair is the subject of the allegories given this fable in the manuscript commentaries:

> Per gallum intelligitur stultus, per fimum intelligitur iste mundus, per iaspidem regnum celeste uel gratia Spiritus Sancti. Nam quemadmodum gallus non curauit iaspidem, licet valuisset mille grana tritici, ita insipiens et insensatus non curat regnum Dei.[21]

Or:

> Per gallum isti designantur qui per vitam activam, in sterquilinio et in fine lucri temporalis siliquis et fauillis temporalium rerum inhyantes, negligunt ymmo spernunt contemplacionem, preciosam margaritam, et futuram vitam, que recte per iaspidem intelligitur.[22]

Anonymus Neveleti in this manuscript belong to a widespread group including those in clm 7680; Wolfenbüttel, Herzog August Bibliothek, cod. guelf. 185 Helmst.; Wrocław, Biblioteka Uniwersytecka, ms. IV.Q.81.

[19] See Speckenbach, "Die Fabel von der Fabel," on the history of this fable and its interpretation.

[20] Pfeiffer, *Edelstein*, 4, lines 32–34.

[21] Wrocław, Biblioteka Uniwersytecka, ms. IV.Q.81, fol. 497r.

[22] Prague, Statní knihovna, ms. XI.C.4, fol. 141r.

Where the Anonymus identifies in the

    gallo stolidum, ... iaspide pulcra sophie/ Dona ...,

Boner agrees with the school commentators in the specific and
specifically spiritual construction he gives the "gifts of wisdom." In the
words of his prologue, that wisdom consists in the pious certainty

    daz man dich, hêrre, minnen sol.[23]

The *Edelstein*'s displacement of Aesopic utility from the moral-peda-
gogical to the spiritual is, in this fable at least, effected in ways that
recall closely the similar shifts described in Chapter 1 for the academic
commentaries.

In the case of the fables from the Anonymus Neveleti, Boner's reliance on the learned apparatus of his school manuscript sources seems, all
the same, to have been limited. By far the majority of the "Aesopic"
fables in the first part of his collection follow the Anonymus's verses
closely, almost slavishly, and with the exception of the last example discussed above, the contribution to the vernacular text made by commentaries and interlinear glosses seems relatively slight. An investigation
of Boner's treatment of the fables he borrows from Avian, on the other
hand, yields a quite different picture. Here, it is quite certain that the
Swiss fabulist's exemplar was a manuscript containing a full commentary
on the verse *Apologi*; and it was from his work with that Latin commentary that Boner drew the ultimate inspiration for the formal unity of his
own vernacular collection.

Of the one hundred German verse fables that make up the *Edelstein*,
fourteen owe their inspiration to Avian. For the last century and a
quarter, it has been generally accepted—some earlier speculations to the
contrary—that Boner relied directly on the original Latin verses without
recourse to any Latin prose reworking of the Roman fables; where
Schönbach had written

    ich halte es auch für ... sicher, daß nicht der reine text Avian's
    die quelle der bezüglichen fabeln des Edelsteins war,[24]

Gottschick a year later found in none of the deviations of the *Edelstein*

---

[23] Pfeiffer, *Edelstein*, 1, line 29.
[24] A. E. Schönbach, "Zur Kritik Boners," *Zeitschrift für deutsche Philologie* 6 (1875): 251–
290, here 276–277.

from Avian's verses compelling evidence for the vernacular poet's use of any intermediate or additional source.[25] The most recent opinion is noncommittal: the divergences between Avian and Boner are attributed either to Boner's use of an intermediate prose redaction or to innovations on the German fabulist's part. As the following discussion hopes to show, Grubmüller's cautious speculation that Boner may have had before him a prose collection, "die dem alten Text näher steht als den überlieferten Auflösungen,"[26] is quite literally true; Boner's prose intermediary was most likely a commentary, standing immediately next to the "old text" in the margins of a school manuscript.

Several hitherto unexplained features revealed by Boner's versions of the fables from Avian are also typical of the Latin commentary tradition. Narrative deviations in a number of the German fables, at first regard unmotivated, are no longer so mysterious when considered with their parallels in the commentaries. In the second of the fables Boner translates from Avian, for example, the tortoise makes quite a different proposition to the eagle from that in the Latin verse fable; where in Avian the earthbound animal promises

> Si quis eam volucrum constituisset humi,
> Protinus e rubris conchas proferret arenis,[27]

Boner in the *Edelstein* changes both the reward and the request; says the tortoise,

> wölt ir mich lêren vliegen,
> ich wölt iu âne liegen
> golt und edel gesteine geben.[28]

The wish for flying lessons—ultimately suggested, perhaps, by Avian's distich

> Indignum sibimet, tardo quod sedula gressu
> Nil ageret toto perficeretque die —

is not infrequent in the prose reductions of the school commentaries, where it often occurs with the identification of Avian's unspecified

---

[25] R. Gottschick, "Über die Benutzung Avians durch Boner," *Zeitschrift für deutsche Philologie* 7 (1876): 237–243.

[26] Grubmüller, *Meister Esopus*, 300.

[27] Guaglianone, *Aviani Fabulæ*, no. 2.

[28] Pfeiffer, *Edelstein*, 112, lines 11–13.

"conchas" as gold or precious stones.[29] While these changes make admittedly little difference in the structure of Boner's fable or its interpretation, they do suggest that the question of his sources is more complex than generally believed.

A further example of commentary influence is found in Boner's fable 91, the translation of Avian's tale "de viatore et satyro." Although the vernacular text follows its Latin source quite closely, it does differ in identifying the satyr of the original as a "waltman," an apparent *lectio facilior* resulting from the Swiss fabulist's failure to understand his source. In fact, however, this reading reflects the gloss given "satirus" in at least one fifteenth-century manuscript, where the supernatural creature is rather prosaically identified as "custos nemoris."[30]

A number of the moral sentences in Boner's epimyths with parallels in neither Avian nor the spurious morals appended to the Latin verses in the high Middle Ages can likewise be traced to the late medieval commentary tradition. Avian's fable of wind and sun[31] serves in its Latin original to warn against boastful language; Boner, in his epimyth, reanalyzes the fable as an example of the inappropriateness of violence, "unvuoge" and "vrevel."[32] The same focus is apparent in a number of commentaries, including the Helmst. text reproduced in the Appendix above; in addition to the warning against verbal "gerrulitatem," that commentary offers the observation

> quod pocius aduersarios nostros vincere debemus paciencia et mansuetudine quam cum minacionibus et austeritatibus.

Similarly, the *sententia* in the epimyth to Boner's fable 68,

> lop, daz von eigem munde gât,
> daz ist nicht lop . . . ,

---

[29] See, for example, the Avian commentaries in Berlin, Staatsbibliothek Preußischer Kulturbesitz, cod. 177; Copenhagen, Konglige Bibliotek, ms. 1905 4o; Munich, Bayerische Staatsbibliothek, clm 14703; Stuttgart, Württembergische Landesbibliothek, cod. vi.128 and xii.40; and Wolfenbüttel, Herzog August Bibliothek, cod. guelf. Aug. 4o 34. A fuller survey of the Latin commentaries on this fable is found in Wright, "The 'Nuremberg' Aesop," 133–139.

[30] Erfurt, cod. Amplon Q.21, ed. Risse, "Commentary on the Fables of Avianus," 208; see also p. 97 above.

[31] Guaglianone, *Aviani Fabulæ*, no. 4

[32] Pfeiffer, *Edelstein*, 115–117, lines 50–64.

is the translation of a Latin sentiment that occurs frequently in the school commentaries on Avian's fable 14:

nemo debet se ipsum laudare, nam laus propria iudicatur esse sordida.[33]

The admonishment in Boner's fable "von einem löwen und von einer geize,"

> du solt des râtes end an sehen,
> waz von dem râte müg beschehen,[34]

likewise corresponds to none of Avian's verses; it does, however, occur in the Latin prose commentary on Avian 26 preserved in the Helmstedt manuscript:

Tamen bene debet respici in quem finem [verba] dicantur.

Much of the narrative expansiveness of certain of Boner's fables from Avian points as well to a reliance on the Latin prose commentaries. In the second section of the *Edelstein*, the vernacular poet reveals a tendency to create relatively detailed backgrounds, prehistories against which he then recounts the events of the fable proper. For example, Avian himself provides no introduction to his fable of the oak and the reed, relating simply

> Montibus e sumis radicitus eruta quercus
> Decidit, insani turbine victa noti (Guaglianone, no. 16).

In Boner's version of the same fable, in contrast, more than one-fourth of the narrative is devoted to a description of the fable's principal characters *before* the fatal storm's arrival:

> Ûf einem berge stuont ein eich,
> diu keinem winde nie entweich,
> wan si was stark, lang unde grôz.
> under dem berge was ein môz,
> dur daz vlôz ein küeler bach,
> da man mang rôr wachsen sach;
> dâ stuonden bluomen unde gras.
> diu eich vil wol gewurzet was:

---

[33] Wolfenbüttel, Herzog August Bibliothek, cod. guelf. 185 Helmst.
[34] Pfeiffer, *Edelstein*, 160, lines 39–40 (rendering Avian 26).

si stuont vast âne wenken.
wer möchte daz gedenken,
daz si sölti vallen nider?
dâ waz ir kraft vil vaste wider.[35]

Similar elaborations, setting the epic scene before the actual narrative commences, are discernible in fully half of the *Edelstein*'s fables from Avian;[36] strikingly, there are no examples of such epic expansion in the German fables with sources in the Anonymus Neveleti. This consistent difference is better explained as a relic of the *Edelstein*'s Latin sources than as an innovation on Boner's part; whatever other liberties he may have taken with the texts before him, the Swiss fabulist would have had no reason to introduce a discrepancy of this sort or to maintain it so rigorously. It is likely instead that the divergence visible in the two groups of fables reflects a difference in Boner's principal sources, the distichs of the Anonymus on the one hand, and a relatively expansive commentary on Avian on the other.[37]

Departures from Avian within the fable narrative proper are less frequent in the *Edelstein*; where such differences can be observed, however, they too suggest the translator's use of a commented manuscript. The German fable "von einem esel und eins löwen hût" translates Avian 5, still today one of the best-known texts in the Aesopic canon. Boner's vernacular fable begins with a genre scene, not present in Avian's verses, depicting the harsh life and hard labors of the jackass:

Ein esel der hât erbeit grôz,
der sînen meister nicht verdrôz.
er leit im ûf vil mangen sak,
dâ von sîn rugge dik erschrak.
ouch hôrt ich von dem esel sagen,
er muoste ziehen unde tragen:
erbeit muost er grôze hân.[38]

The donning of the lion's skin, the jackass's presumptuous behavior, and the fear of the other animals are then narrated largely as in Avian's

---

[35] Pfeiffer, *Edelstein*, 146, lines 1–12.

[36] In addition to the example just cited, see Pfeiffer, *Edelstein*, nos. 67, 78, 81, 83, 84, and 88.

[37] On a startlingly similar phenomenon in the two parts of the Nuremberg Aesop, see Wright, "The 'Nuremberg' Aesop," 68–71.

[38] Pfeiffer, *Edelstein*, 117, lines 1–8.

verses; the German fable departs again, though, from its Latin parallel in its account of the donkey's exposure. In Avian, the jackass is accidentally discovered by a certain unnamed "rusticus," who on encountering the disguised beast recognizes him by his long ears and mocks him:

> At mihi, qui quondam, semper asellus eris.[39]

Avian's terseness is replaced in the German fable by a lengthy description of the peasant's search for his missing animal:

> sîn meister der hât grôzen pîn;
> er wand den esel hân verlorn:
> daz was im nicht ein kleiner zorn.
> sîn esel er suochen began;
> er vant sîn nicht da er sölte gân,
> und suochen sîne weide.
> er gieng ûz ûf die heide,
> er suocht in verre unde nach. . . .[40]

While some Latin commentaries echo Avian's reticence,[41] others provide a vignette similar to that in the *Edelstein*:

> Rusticus autem facta undique inquisicione cum suum eveniret asellum casu. . . .[42]

This commentary agrees further with the *Edelstein* in the peasant's insistence that the donkey is specifically *his* donkey:

> du muost mîn esel sîn (*Edelstein*);
> mea estimacione semper eris asellus meus sicut ante fuisti
> (fol. 21v).

In Boner's vernacular text, such changes give the fable a narrative roundness lacking in the excessively elliptical verses of Avian; the donkey ends where he began, carrying heavy "sek" for his master. The inspiration for these changes was an Avian commentary similar to that preserved in the Erfurt manuscript, which shares with the *Edelstein* a concern for both clarity and narrative breadth.

---

[39] Guaglianone, *Aviani Fabulæ*, no. 7.

[40] Pfeiffer, *Edelstein*, 118, lines 28–35.

[41] For example, the Helmstedt commentary reproduced in the Appendix above identifies the jackass's nemesis as simply "quidam vir."

[42] Erfurt Q.21, fol. 21v.

Boner's familiarity with school commentary on the fables also makes
more comprehensible the *Edelstein*'s otherwise mystifying retelling of
Avian 10, "de calvo equite."[43] The narrative portion of the German fable
resembles closely that in Avian's verses, with the exception that in the vernacular, it is not the wind but the blow of another knight's lance that
deprives the vain rider of his toupée.[44] At its conclusion, however, the
knight's witty retort to those laughing at his suddenly revealed baldness,

> "Quid mirum, referens, positos fugisse capillos,
>   Quem prius aequaevae deseruere comae?"

serves in Boner's fable as the introduction to an unexpected series of
disapproving comments on

> batstubenvarwe diu zergât,
> sô diu natiurlîche gestât.[45]

This theme is utterly unanticipated in Avian's verses, which focus entirely on the wisdom of the bald knight's response to the ridicule of
others:

> Ille sagax, tantis quod risus milibus esset,
>   Distulit admota calliditate iocum.[46]

The *Edelstein*'s epimyth begins with a similar thought:

> Er dunket mich ein wîser man,
> der alsô spot zerstœren kan
> mit schalle. daz ist bezzer vil,
> denn er mit worten drôwen wil.[47]

Boner continues, however, with a theme alien to Avian's verse fable,

---

[43] The allegorical commentaries on this fable are discussed in Grubmüller, "Fabel —
Exempel — Allegorese." See also Wright, "The 'Nuremberg' Aesop," 140–142.

[44] Avian: "Huius ab adverso Boreae spiramina praeflant/ Ridiculum populo conspiciente
caput"; Boner: "nu vuogt sich von geschichte daz/ daz im ab gestôzen wart/ der helm; und
ûf der selben vart/ verlor er ouch die hûben sîn."

[45] Pfeiffer, *Edelstein*, 134, lines 33–34.

[46] The high-medieval epimyths appended to this fable (reproduced from Guaglianone's
edition in the last appendix below, pp. 258–259) likewise address only the need to repel
scorn with laughter.

[47] Pfeiffer, *Edelstein*, 134, lines 41–44. Boner's immediate source for these lines may have
been the spurious epimyth present in some manuscripts of Avian: "Se risu quicumque novo
sciat esse retentum, Arte magis studeat quam prohibere minis" (Guaglianone, *Aviani Fabulæ*,
21).

namely the erratic and unpredictable course of life and luck; the Swiss fabulist avails himself of the familiar metaphor of the wheel of fortune:[48]

> hiut ist er arm, der ê was rîch:
> daz glücke rât louft ungelîch.
> wer stât, mag er, der valle nicht nider;
> velt er, vil kûme kunt er wider.
> an dirr welt ist kein stætekeit.[49]

No such thought is present in Avian's fable, where the loss of the wig serves only as an opportunity for the knight's quick-witted rejoinder; a similar confrontation of themes does occur, however, in the school commentaries on this text:

> Docet nos quod si ab aliquibus derideamur, non debemus cum iracundia depellere risum sed cum risu. ... et ne curamus artificialia durare cum naturalia durare non possunt.[50]

Even more closely reminiscent of Boner's epimyth, the Erfurt commentary excerpted above thematizes the transitoriness of earthly goods in both its allegories:

> Notandum quod alegorice per istum militem possumus intelligere quemlibet sapientem virum qui est stabilis etiam aduersitatibus rerum temporalium. Et per capillos capiti aligatos intelligimus bona temporalia qui cito veniunt et etiam cito recedunt. ... Notandum quod scholastice per militem intelligimus virum ecclesiasticum doctrina et virtutibus armatum, sed per capillos intelligimus dignitatem. Dum ergo talis vir propter iusticiam obseruandam pugnat, si tunc priuetur honore et dignitate, ipse non dolebit de tale perdicione.[51]

This fable in the *Edelstein* is further remarkable for apparently preserving traces of the influence of another Latin allegorical epimyth. Boner concludes his explication with the couplet

---

[48] Note that this motif occurs in the Latin commentaries on Avian's fable of Jove and the camel, a text that typically occupies the folio immediately before Avian 10; compare the commentary edited in the Appendix to Chapter 1, pp. 82–83.

[49] Pfeiffer, *Edelstein*, 134, lines 45–49.

[50] Wolfenbüttel, Herzog August Bibliothek, cod. guelf. 185 Helmst., fol. 98v.

[51] Erfurt, cod. Amplon. Q.21, fol. 25v.

der hêrre verlor der hûben kleit,
daz ist der welte unstætekeit.[52]

The fabulist's sudden use of the title "hêrre" is a first indication of a
disruption of the unity of the epimyth;[53] in the rest of his fable, Boner
follows Avian's usage exclusively in labeling his protagonist a "ritter."
A closer reading reveals that the Swiss poet's allegorical identification of
the wig with the world's inconstancy cannot ultimately be derived from
the fable narrative or the other explications given it in his epimyth.
Taken to its logical conclusion, the equation asserted in these final lines
suggests that in losing his hairpiece the gallant rider has overcome the fic-
kleness of the world; in the fable narrative, however, that loss itself illustrates "der welte unstætekeit," and not its successful transcendence, which
is more properly figured by his retort to the laughter of the spectators.

This puzzling couplet, if it is not to be considered simply a *lapsus*, is
better regarded as an element taken over from a Latin fable commentary, in the context of which it made better sense than in Boner's fable.
In fact, the most widespread allegorization of this text in the commentary tradition is precisely one in which a *dominus* sheds his disguise to
leave earthly bonds behind:

Allegorice per istum militem Christum intelligere possumus, per
comes vero annexos humanitatem eius, que mortua et elapsa fuit
et a Iudeis derisa.[54]

Boner's couplet is best viewed as the fossilized reflex of a similar allegorical explication in his Latin source, taken over into the vernacular fable
by virtue of its emphasis on secular inconstancy, but ultimately not
easily reconcilable with the remainder of the Swiss fabulist's epimyth.

As I have sought to show in these examples, it seems certain that
Ulrich Boner's source for his Avian fables was a school manuscript with
a full prose commentary, its prose reductions generally close to the
verses of the Roman poet, but with occasional additions and deviations
that have in turn left discernible traces in the vernacular texts of the

---

[52] Pfeiffer, *Edelstein*, 134, lines 55-56.

[53] In both of the other fables of the *Edelstein* (numbers 62 and 85) involving a knight,
Boner consistently uses the word "ritter." "Hêrre" is very frequent in the epimyths to
other fables, where it means exclusively "lord," "master," in contradistinction to "man,"
meaning "subject" or "vassal."

[54] Wolfenbüttel, Herzog August Bibliothek, cod. guelf. 185 Helmst., fol. 99r-v; the entire commentary is reproduced in the Appendix above.

Edelstein. This observation casts new light on several hitherto unexplained features of the vernacular collection, and suggests new ways to understand others.

Boner's was the first German Aesop to proclaim itself a coherent fable collection; where the fables of the *Spruchdichter* were scattered among their larger œuvre, the Swiss poet assures the reader of his prologue that

> Diz büechlîn mag der edelstein
> wol heizen . . . ,[55]

and concludes with a similar assertion:

> . . . Ein ende hât
> daz buoch, daz hie geschriben stêt.[56]

It was the tradition of Latin fable commentary—on Avian, if not on the Anonymus as well—that suggested to Boner a number of the techniques that helped the vernacular poet establish the "bookishness" of his collection. Forms and gestures adopted from the Latin commentary tradition give the German fables a certain uniformity of presentation, whatever their ultimate sources.[57] This is plain, for example, in the transitional formulas Boner employs for the passage between promyth and fable narrative; using patterns we have already seen in the Latin prose commentaries, the vernacular fabulist begins with a general, proverb-like statement of wisdom:

> Waz von natûr ist angeborn
> der krêatûr, wirt daz verlorn,
> daz muoz tuon gewonheit grôz.[58]

This is followed by an introduction to the illustrative story that follows:

> als hie an dirr bîschaft beschach.[59]

---

[55] Pfeiffer, *Edelstein*, 2, lines 64–65.

[56] Pfeiffer, *Edelstein*, 184, lines 31–32.

[57] Contrast Grubmüller, *Meister Esopus*, 302: "Die Integration dieser Quellen zu einer neuen einheitlichen Sammlung bleibt Boners Werk."

[58] Pfeiffer, *Edelstein*, 113, lines 1–3.

[59] Pfeiffer, *Edelstein*, 114, line 11. Compare also the introductory material to fables 3, 17, 19, 42, 95, and 96; fables 14, 22, and 43, in contrast, provide no transition between their promyths and the fable proper.

Boner here follows the prescriptions of the medieval schoolmasters, precisely as they are carried out in the Latin commentaries.[60]

The captions that accompany the fables in most manuscripts of the *Edelstein* serve too to generate a coherence in the presentation of the individual texts. They identify first the principal characters of each fable,

von einem jeger und einem tigertier,

and then suggest a realm of moral application for the story:

von hinderrede.[61]

As described in Chapter 1 above, similar head matter is encountered in many of the commentaries on Avian and the Anonymus Neveleti, where it serves the systematic functions of index and cross-reference. Here, in the vernacular *Edelstein*, these captions point out Boner's organizational principle of grouping fables with similar characters and similar moral lessons, and thus help establish the links between individual texts necessary to make of the whole an integral collection.

The consistent form of Boner's epimyths, too, contributes to the formal unity of his collection. The vernacular fabulist's transformation of the epimyth has been identified as one of the most striking characteristics of the *Edelstein*; where in the Latin verse collections, the moral typically takes the form of a terse description or confirmation of the pattern of behavior illustrated in the fable, the epimyths of the German collection exhibit "die kumulative Reihung von Erfahrungssätzen und daraus abgeleiteten Ratschlägen oder Handlungsanweisungen," what Klaus Grubmüller has so aptly called "das Epimythion als Variantenangebot."[62] This feature as well, however, is likely to have been inspired by practices the Swiss poet first encountered in the Latin fable commentaries. As we have seen, the commentators of Avian and the Anonymus Neveleti alike heap their moral lessons into long series of equivalent, proverb-like statements, at the beginning as promyths or at the conclusion of their texts as epimyths, with great tolerance for apparent inconsistency, irrelevance, and even contradiction. Boner's use of a similar technique is unique in the German fable tradition, but it is not the independent innovation Grubmüller suggests. The epimyths of the

---

[60] See Chapter 1, p. 24, above.
[61] Pfeiffer, *Edelstein*, 5.
[62] *Meister Esopus*, 332, 326–328.

Edelstein—just as the explications given the animal exempla of the Stricker a hundred years earlier[63]—are instead better considered instances of the vernacular appropriation of a phenomenon already established and widespread in the learned Latin tradition.

The tendency of Boner's epimyths to proceed from the general to the specific in some of the fables of the *Edelstein* likewise recalls the progression of the morals in those Latin commentaries that end with allegorical explications. Although the Swiss fabulist never offers the same full allegorical equations as those found in the commentaries, he does frequently round off his epimyths with an explicit assertion of the analogy between the animal actors of the fable and the human groups whose behavior is criticized in the moral:

> waz diu natûr hât gegeben,
> dem mag der mensch kûm wider streben.
> dem hündlîn stât sîn klugheit wol,
> der esel secke tragen sol;[64]

writes Boner at the conclusion of his fable of the donkey and the lapdog; and the presumptuous are warned at the end of his fable of the swallow:

> die gar ze sicher wellent wesen,
> die mügent etswenn kûm genesen,
> als ist den vögellîn beschehen,
> daz si wol möchtin hân versehen.[65]

These carefully constructed parallels between fable narration and explication recall in their specificity the allegorical epimyths of many Latin commentaries; in Boner's collection, they serve to emphasize the unity of fictional story and moral sense.

The most important contribution of the Latin academic tradition to the formal integrity of the *Edelstein* is apparent in the programmatic frame Boner gave his collection, beginning it with a series of four fables of reading, and concluding it with a punning epilogue "von dem ende diss buoches."[66] Three of the four introductory fables are presented in the *Edelstein* in ways that recall their treatment in the commentary tra-

---

[63] Compare Henkel, *Deutsche Übersetzungen lateinischer Schultexte*, 55–56.
[64] Pfeiffer, *Edelstein*, 32, lines 55–58.
[65] Pfeiffer, *Edelstein*, 36, lines 43–46.
[66] See Grubmüller, *Meister Esopus*, 304.

dition;[67] the epilogue, whose sources have to my knowledge never been the subject of scholarly investigation, is based on a theoretical discussion of the fable transmitted with several commentaries in the fifteenth century.

The apparent commentary influence on Boner's fable of the eponymous gemstone has been discussed above; while its customary interpretation as "die Fabel von der Fabel" was developed independent of the fable's reading in the pedagogic tradition, it is in the commentaries that the fable received the allegorical explication reflected in Boner's distinction between secular and worldly ambition, a distinction that makes the fable particularly well suited to the vernacular fabulist's spiritual program.

While the fable of cock and pearl is the first text in many Aesops, Latin and vernacular,[68] Boner's displacement of Avian's fable of the tiger and the hunter to the beginning of the *Edelstein* is without parallel in any other medieval collection. The vernacular fabulist varies his text slightly from that given by Avian; the hunter, for example, armed in the Latin verses with a javelin, here carries a bow, and the dogs that apparently accompany him in the German fable[69] have no counterpart in Avian's text. Both of these innovations, as expected, are widely attested in the prose commentaries as well,[70] suggesting once again the translator's use of a manuscript that contained such a text. More remarkable, however, is Boner's adaptation of the fable as a programmatic introduction to his entire collection.[71] In both his promyth and epimyth, Boner pleads for the reader's sympathetic accommodation of his work's faults, suggesting that those who are unsatisfied after the first three fables lay the book aside:

> wem mîn geticht nicht wol gevalt,
> ez sî wîp, man, jung oder alt,
> der lâz mit züchten ab sîn lesen;

---

[67] The fourth, "von einem boume ûf einem berge," is rather a sort of nature analogy than a narrative fable; Gottschick's suggestion ("Quellen," 12) that it constitutes a further explication of Boner's second fable is plausible.

[68] See Speckenbach, "Die Fabel von der Fabel."

[69] Their existence must be inferred from the tiger's foolhardy assertion "ich sihe weder man noch hunt" (Pfeiffer, *Edelstein*, 6, line 29); as he learns immediately thereafter, the hunter is present, and so, most likely, are the unseen hounds.

[70] See the numerous examples adduced in Wright, "The 'Nuremberg' Aesop," 144–149.

[71] This matter is briefly discussed in A. E. Wright, "Kommentar und Übersetzung: Zur Entlatinisierung der Fabel im ausgehenden Mittelalter," *Wolfenbütteler Beiträge* 7 (1998): 53–72.

wil er, sô lâz ouch mich genesen,
und wâ diz buoch gebresten habe
ûf keinen sin, den nem er abe.[72]

In contrast, Avian gives his Latin poem neither promyth nor epimyth; the medieval commentators make of it variously a caution against pride:

autor reprehendit illos qui adeo confidunt in rebus suis in palibus et in viribus suis quod putant in ira nichil esse quod eos nocere possit;[73]

or a warning against human treachery:

quamuis quedam animalia bruta sint metuenda, tamen homo plus cunctis animalibus est metuendus, quia cum homo fuit factus et creatus, tunc mediante sua astucia super omnia animalia exultatus erat;[74]

or a reminder of the foolishness of self-sacrifice:

nemo periculum sue vite propter alium intret, ne periculo suscepto alijs fiat derisio.[75]

Among all this variety,[76] one fourteenth-century commentary from Austria preserves a suggestive set of epimyths. After a complicated spiritual explication that identifies the hunter as the Antichrist, the tiger as various Old Testament prophets, and the fox as Jews and heretics, the commentator offers the "fructus" that man is the beast most to be feared, as he unlike other animals can work harm even when physcially absent, "detrahendo et diffamando."

Item docet etiam autor quod verba [illegible] multa sunt timenda, quia latenter trahunt in permane. Et plus ledunt quam si palam fierent eo quod homo sic nullum habet locum defendendi. ...

---

[72] Pfeiffer, *Edelstein*, 7, lines 65–70.
[73] Stuttgart, Württembergische Landesbibliothek, cod. HB xii 4o, fol. 116r.
[74] Ottobeuren, Stiftsbibliothek, Ms. 0.82, fol. 212r.
[75] Wolfenbüttel, Herzog August Bibliothek, cod. guelf. 185 Helmst., fol. 102r.
[76] The interpretive diversity extends to the allegories given the fable as well, in which the tiger is identified variously as the vainglorious, as the apostle Peter, as the sinner, as the prophet Enoch, and as the greedy man; the hunter who wounds him is given significations ranging from Christ to the devil. See Wright, "The 'Nuremberg' Aesop," 144–149.

Etiam loquitur propheta ubi dicit in Psalmo qui exacuerunt ut gladium ligwas suas et cetera qui secuntur.[77]

This commentator, a contemporary of the Swiss fabulist, reads Avian's fable as a fable about words and their power, and so in the academic tradition prepares Boner's use of the same text in the vernacular as a proleptic response to the "hinderslân" and "hinderred" of those who read and criticize his book.[78]

Boner's second frame fable, "von einem affen und von einer nuz," does not occur in either Avian or the Anonymus Neveleti; although similar tales can be located in other late medieval promptuaria,[79] no immediate source has been identified for the fable in the *Edelstein*. In fact, the story does occur within the Latin commentary tradition on the Anonymus Neveleti, and in a function and position reminiscent of those it enjoys in Boner's German collection. The *Liber Esopus et Avianus*, a fifteenth-century Latin collection based closely on commentary sources, ends with a series of remarks on the proper reading of the texts it includes; in illustration of the admonition to attend closely to the fables' lessons, the commentator tells the story in reproach of the careless reader,

statim vnum folium peruertens ... ut symea facit que cum ascendit in arborem et in ea nuces gustat et senciens testam amarem, proicit eam cum nucleo dulci et suaui, quam si degustaret non proiceret a se sed comederet. Sic aliqui faciunt qui visa superficie verborum simplicium et invtilium bona et utilia spernunt et paruipendunt.[80]

Just as in the *Edelstein*, the rudimentary fable presented here in its Latin version provides a programmatic standard for the proper application of all the other texts in the collection; to emphasize the universal applicability of the guidelines it promulgates, it is moved to a conspicuous position outside the collection proper. Obviously, Boner could not have known the mid-fifteenth-century *Liber Esopus et Avianus*, but it seems

---

[77] Salzburg, St. Peter, ms. b.ix.l, fol. 208v (compare Psalm 63:4–6: "Qui exacuerunt quasi gladium linguam suam tetenderunt sagittam suam verbum amarissimum ut sagittarent in absconditis simplicem; subito sagittabunt eum et non timebunt").

[78] Pfeiffer, *Edelstein*, 5, lines 5–6.

[79] For a tabular list of parallels, see Grubmüller, *Meister Esopus*, 312.

[80] Budapest, National Széchényi Lib., Cod. Nem. Muz. 123, fol. 46r–v.

probable that the treatment of this fable in both depends on practices long current in the medieval Latin academic tradition.

The same Budapest manuscript preserves in its afterword a clue about the source of Boner's epilogue. Anxious lest his readers lose themselves in "diu getât"—the mere narrative plot—of his stories, the vernacular fabulist reminds them

> Wer die bîschaft merken wil,
> der setz sich ûf des endes zil.
> der nutz lît an dem ende gar
> der bîschaft, wer sîn nimet war. . . .
> . . . Ein ende hât
> daz buoch, daz hie geschriben stât.[81]

What seems a rather limping pun on "ende," meaning both "conclusion" and "purpose," "finis" and "intencio," has in fact learned antecedents in the commentary tradition. Both the Budapest *Liber* and the Munich manuscript clm 16213 conclude their expositions of the Latin verse fables with a discussion of the need to concentrate on the texts' moral content; and both provide a thorough theoretical justification of the site of that content "in fine fabule." Rather than behaving as the foolish ape, the wise reader

> finem debet considerare. Quia dicitur in Ethicorum: "Bona principia non sunt laudanda, nisi sunt ydoneo fine terminata." Ideo ad finem prospiciens cognosces rerum quarumlibet qualitates. Nunc autem de fine est dicendum. Finis est gracia cuius aliquid sit. Et est duplex, intra et extra. Intra est ut cognoscamus ea que docentur in hoc libro et exempla mente ascribamus. Extra est ut cognoscentes ea que hic dicuntur, mala fugiamus et bona cupiamus.[82]

The second St. Nikola commentator reminds us (and none too legibly) that Aesop

> concludendo librum suum ponit modum inquirendi fructus vniuiusque fabule, hoc est quomodo ipsa debet referri ad moralitatem, id est applicare ad vitam nostram. Et wlt tamen quod fructus vniuscuiusque fabule comprehendatur in duobus versibus in

---

[81] Pfeiffer, *Edelstein*, 184, lines 1–4, 31–32.
[82] Budapest, National Széchényi Lib., Cod. Nem. Muz. 123, fol. 46v.

vltimo locali eiusdem fabule positis. Racio prima quare magister
fructum cuiuslibet fabule ponit in finem est ista: ... in proposito
autor noster volens nos hortari ad bonos mores primo enim pre-
mittit preludia et deinde subiungit doctrinas ... Etiam quia omnia
a fine denominanda sunt, vt inquit Aristoteles in libro De anima.[83] Sed finis et intencio autoris est vicia corrigere et bonos
mores introducere. ... Et propter breuitatem et facilitatem reti-
nende fine comprehendit tenorem in duobus versibus. ...[84]

Here again, in his programmatic epilogue Ulrich Boner appears to
rely on material whose original context is Latin and learned, and which
is imported into the *Edelstein* to serve the coherence of a new vernacular
fable collection. Bringing the book full circle, Boner's epilogue combines
a simplified theoretical discussion taken from his presumed Latin source
with brief recapitulations of each of the programmatic fables with which
he opens the *Edelstein*; their functions thus transformed, it is elements
from the Latin commentary tradition that give the new vernacular text
its formal integrity.

In the woodcut that concludes Albrecht Pfister's *editio princeps* of the
Edelstein, the figure of the author passes learning on to an unseen audience in the form of a blank scroll. The passage of wisdom from an
established tradition to one as yet unformed appears in this depiction to
be seamless, a frictionless *translatio* from the fabulists of antiquity to the
reader. In fact, however, as the discussion above has attempted to demonstrate, the chain of transmission with the *Edelstein* at its end was more
complex than that image suggests. Boner relied for his access to the authoritative sources of his fables in part on texts prepared by the medieval commentators, whose explications and emendations of the authentic
texts of Avian and the Anonymus Neveleti have left traces not only in
the individual fables of the Swiss poet, but in their formal integrity as a
collection.

Given the commentator's vital function in the process of translation
and transmission, it would seem only fair that he, too, be given a portrait in the Bamberg *Edelstein*. And so he is, repeatedly, in the illustration to each of the individual fable texts. The hooded figure who stands

---

[83] Compare W. D. Ross, ed., *Aristotle's* De anima (Oxford: Oxford University Press,
1963), 407a, ll. 26–27; the imprecision of the reference in clm 16213 may suggest the use of
a Latin commentary on the *De anima*.

[84] Munich, Bayerische Staatsbibliothek, clm 16213, fol. 330v.

to the left of each Aesopic scene, and who points to the classical authority embodied in the seated figure of the fabulist, can be read as not Aesop, not Boner, but the medieval explicator of the Latin fables, pointing to the texts he interprets with the gesture of the commentator: hic docet autor, et hoc probat per fabulam sequentem. . . . The *meister* of the *Edelstein* is ultimately a schoolmaster, his text a commentary.

II

Where the influence of the commentary tradition on Boner's *Edelstein* must be deduced from scattered words, phrases, and attitudes in the vernacular text, the reliance of the Low German Magdeburg Aesop[85] on similar learned sources is evident on even the most superficial comparison. Of the thirty-four fables in that collection with parallels in the Anonymus Neveleti, not one is obviously translated directly from the Latin verses; the eight fables from Avian are even more liberally rendered, some of them sharing little more than their narrative conceit with the older text of the Roman poet. Both groups, however, do reveal their author's[86] familiarity with the academic practice of fable commentary: as the German Aesop's editor correctly noted a century ago, the narratives of the collection's Romulus fables rely frequently on an Anonymus Neveleti commentary whose prose paraphrases borrow extensively from the thirteenth-century Romulus LBG, while certain details in the texts from Avian bear comparison with elements introduced in the schoolmasters' annotations. Where in Boner, however, material and structural principles borrowed from the commentaries ultimately give the vernacular text its form, they are included in the Magdeburg

---

[85] On this early fifteenth-century collection—not to be confused with the vernacular prose Aesop printed in Magdeburg in the 1490s—see especially Grubmüller, *Meister Esopus*, 420–422; Adalbert Elschenbroich, *Die deutsche und lateinische Fabel in der frühen Neuzeit: Grundzüge einer Geschichte der Fabel in der Frühen Neuzeit*, 2 vols. (Tübingen: Niemeyer, 1990), 1: 10; Adalbert Elschenbroich, " *'von unrechtem gewalte'*. Weltlicher und geistlicher Sinn der Fabel vom 'Wolf und Lamm' von der Spätantike bis zum Beginn der Neuzeit," in *Sub tuo platano: Festgabe für Alexander Beinlich* (Emsdetten: Lechte, 1981), 432–433; Klaus Speckenbach, "Magdeburger Äsop," in *Die deutsche Literatur des Mittelalters: Verfasserlexikon*, 2d ed., ed. Kurt Ruh et al. (Berlin: de Gruyter, 1977ff.), 5: 1125–1127; and W. Seelmann, ed., *Gerhard von Minden*, Niederdeutsche Denkmäler 2 (Bremen: Kühtmann, 1878).

[86] The occasionally somewhat awkward periphrases with which I identify the poet of the Magdeburg Aesop arise from my unwillingness to use the name "Gerhard von Minden" in any context whatsoever; given the frequent use of the name in the secondary literature to identify the author of the Wolfenbüttel Aesop, and the considerable bibliographic confusion generated by Seelmann's not entirely convincing refutation of the title of his own edition, I prefer to avoid the name altogether in favor of the lengthier formulations I use here.

Aesop for a different reason: seven decades before the publication of the Ulm philologist's Aesop, the Low German fabulist set about compiling a *Gesamtausgabe* of the Aesopic fable, apparently drawing on every collection, Latin and vernacular, available to him. In the density and complexity of its source relationships,[87] the Magdeburg Aesop is unparalleled in the German tradition before Steinhöwel.

The identity of those sources, as already mentioned, is clear. The narrative portions of the German fables are so similar to those of the Latin Romulus LBG as to make the identification of that collection among the sources certain. Compare, for example, the vernacular fable of the dog and his reflection with the versions given in two Latin collections:

> Bi enem dorpe gink ein vlêt,
> dat was dêp unde mate brêt,
> ein bretstech ôk darover lach,
> dar men over to gânde plach.
> Mit enem kese gink ein hunt
> darover ôk to ener stunt,
> den helt he vaste an sînem munde.[88]

This scene has little in common with the description given by the Anonymus Neveleti:

> Nat canis ore gerens carnem,[89]

but accords precisely with the Latin prose of the Romulus LBG:

> Canis per pontem transivit perspicui et puri fluminis et caseum in ore tulit.[90]

---

[87] Compare Seelmann, xxviii: "Gerhard hat nun bei der bearbeitung dieser fabeln sich nicht auf die benutzung einer einzigen quelle und die getreue wiedergabe der überlieferten erzählung beschränkt, sondern hat in freister weise aus jeder vorlage ausgewählt, in contaminirendem verfahren teile und züge der verschiedenen ihm vorliegenden fassungen mit einander verbunden und nicht selten nach eigener erfindung geändert und zugetan." Seelmann's description is accurate as far as it goes; the question to be posed here, however, is one about the anonymous fabulist's motivations in combining and contaminating his sources.

[88] Seelmann, 9, lines 1–7.

[89] Wright, *The Fables of 'Walter of England'*, 34.

[90] Hervieux, "Romuli anglici cunctis exortae fabulæ," in *Les fabulistes latins* 2: 564–649, here 567. On the role played by this fable collection—itself largely a back-translation of the *Ésope* of Marie de France—in the generation of Latin prose commentaries on the Anonymus, see Wright, "The 'Nuremberg' Aesop," 247–248.

Indeed, this German fable agrees for its entire length with the version given in the prose collection:

> Des kese schemen he sein begunde
> unde hopede, dat he an dem grunde
> ôk enen anderen kese vunde,
> gelîk ome edele und gût.
> Up den wân sprank he in de vlût,
> he dede girlîk up den munt,
> de kese entfêl ome uppe de grunt,
> unde verlôr dorch giricheit beide
> kese unde scheme. . . .[91]

These events are narrated similarly by the author of the LBG:

> Cuius dum umbram in aqua perspexit, alium esse caseum existimavit. Saltu igitur rapido se in flumen precipitans, dum illum apprehendere voluit, ipsum quem tenebat amisit.

There can be no doubt that these Low German verses depend on the Latin prose retelling; nevertheless, certain small divergences in the narrative and the epimyths given the fable suggest that that principal source was modified—in the language of textual criticism, "contaminated"—by the introduction of material from the Anonymus Neveleti. In the LBG, it is the dog's ill-considered leap into the water that costs him his prize; in the Magdeburg Aesop, the loss of the cheese is redundantly motivated: not only does the dog jump from the narrow "stech," but once in the water he opens his mouth as well, a circumstance that recalls the foolish behavior of the Anonymus's swimming dog. Likewise, the self-evident fact that he loses both the cheese and its reflection, a point conspicuously made in the German text by the use of the word "beide" in end-rhyme, is unmentioned in the LBG; the Anonymus, on the other hand, devotes an entire distich of his brief fable to the dog's loss of both his booty and his hope:

> Spem carnis plus carne cupit, plus fenore signum
> Fenoris. Os aperit, sic caro spesque perit.[92]

Unlike either of the Latin fabulists, the German text puts a first epimyth in the now-empty mouth of the dog:

---

[91] Seelmann, 9, lines 8–16.
[92] Wright, *The Fables of 'Walter of England'*, 34. Compare Seelmann, 172.

> ... Do wart ome leide,
> unde sprak: 'Hedde ik nu minen weder,
> nicht mêr ik hir sprunge neder;
> to sokende is he mi unwis,
> wente hir dat water vletende is' (lines 16–20).

This brief physics lesson is followed by the author's own moral explication:

> Aldus de girige vorleset
> dat sîn, als he dat vromede irkeset
> unde des mit unwîsheit begeret;
> sîn egen gût van om veret
> mit schanden unde mit schaden darmede,
> also de kese dem hunde dede (lines 21–26).

The vital opposition here between one's own and the property of others is given only weak expression in the prose Romulus,

> Sic homines avidi sua sepius amittunt et aliena optinere nequeunt,[93]

whereas the pointedness of the vernacular text is readily recognizable as the reflex of the pithy moral of the Anonymus Neveleti:

> Non sua si quis amat, mox caret ipse suis.[94]

There are numerous other examples in the German text of an apparent contamination of Latin sources; such mixing proceeds along no apparent principle, sometimes combining a narrative from the LBG with an epimyth more closely allied to the Anonymus,[95] at other times appending a moral taken from the prose collection to a retelling with affinities to the Latin verse fable.[96] Particularly in the longer fables, elements from the two sources come nearly to alternate within the vernacular collection's retellings;[97] a clear example is had in the German

---

[93] Hervieux, *Les fabulistes latins*, 2: 568.

[94] Wright, *The Fables of 'Walter of England'*, 34.

[95] Compare, for example, fable 22, "van dem lamme unde wulve," with Anonymus Neveleti 21 and Romulus LBG 23.

[96] Compare, for example, fable 24, "van dem perde unde van dem lowen," with Anonymus Neveleti 42 and Romulus LBG 26.

[97] Particularly striking examples are provided as well by Magdeburg Aesop 10, corresponding to Anonymus Neveleti 12 and Romulus LBG 11, and Magdeburg Aesop 15, corres-

fable "van twên musen." The beginning of the vernacular text is taken directly from the Romulus LBG:

> Ût enem dorpe gink ein mûs,
> gevôt an enem riken hûs,
> unde wolde ein ander dorp besein.[98]

Compare:

> Mus quidam de villa sua, in qua natus et educatus fuit, ad aliam villam transire voluit.[99]

The town mouse's praise of her rural host's generosity, however, is rendered from the verses of the Anonymus, and has no counterpart in the prose LBG:

> De andere de sprak: "Vil sere ik prise
> spise unde hûs, mer juwe môt
> unde juwe gunste is so gût,
> dat mi is alles hungers bôt,
> went werdes gunste unde willich lât
> vor allerhande werschup gât" (verses 38–43).

In the words of the Anonymus Neveleti:

> In mensa tenui satis est inmensa voluntas.
> Nobilitat viles mens generosa dapes.[100]

The source of danger in the city mouse's own rich larder is described as well in the terms of the Anonymus Neveleti. According to the Romulus LBG, it is the voice of the master of the house that sets the two mice to flight; in both the German fable and its counterpart in the Anonymus, on the other hand, a servant enters the cellar and rattles his keys:[101]

> Ecce sere clauis inmurmurat: hostia laxat.[102]

---

ponding to Anonymus Neveleti 17 and Romulus LBG 18. Compare also Seelmann's commentary (171–172) to Magdeburg Aesop 3.

[98] Seelmann, 15.

[99] Hervieux, *Les fabulistes latins*, 2: 571.

[100] Wright, *The Fables of 'Walter of England'*, 45.

[101] This detail was much beloved of the medieval commentators on the Anonymus, whatever their ancillary sources; see Wright, "The 'Nuremberg' Aesop," 169.

[102] Wright, *The Fables of 'Walter of England'*, 45.

> Ein knape, do se dit gesprak,
> in dat slot den slotel stak.[103]

The parting words of the frightened country mouse, however, are borrowed from the Romulus LBG. Where in the Anonymus Neveleti she leaves her host with general reminders of the value of freedom from fear, the LBG paints the dangers of city life in especially vivid detail:

> Sed modo video pericula vestra et multiplices malorum causas; homines enim et laqueos timere debetis, et mustelam hostem habetis; catti quoque precipue cavend[e] sunt insidie, quia ve vobis, si in manus catti incideritis.[104]

Its German reflex reads

> De gast sprak: "Mi môt irbarmen
> dîn wolp, dat du vor den harmen,
> vor hunt, vor katten unde vor vallen
> unde jo vor den luden allen
> dîn lîf most hoden to allen stunden."[105]

Plainly, the source of the Magdeburg Aesop was not the Romulus LBG alone. Instead, the LBG is here combined with material from the Anonymus Neveleti in ways that are frequent in the Latin fable commentaries of the fourteenth and fifteenth centuries; on geographic grounds, too, it would be expected that an Anonymus Neveleti commentary available to a translator in the Low German area[106] would base its prose reductions in the Romulus LBG, as that text appears to have been more widely known to the north and west than either of the older prose Romulus recensions.[107]

Certain as it is that such a commentary was among the sources of the Magdeburg Aesop's Romulus fables, it is equally plain that the principal Latin collection used by the Low German translator was the LBG itself, which he thus had before him twice, as it were: once in the slightly modified form of a commentary on the Anonymus Neveleti, and again in its "pure" form as an independent collection. There is no other way

---

[103] Seelmann, 15, lines 68–69.
[104] Hervieux, *Les fabulistes latins*, 2: 573 (reading "cavendi").
[105] Seelmann, 16, lines 106–110.
[106] Seelmann ("Einleitung," xxx) suggests plausibly that the German text was written in western Westphalia not far from the border with the Netherlands.
[107] See Grubmüller, *Meister Esopus*, 74–75.

to explain the fact that in spite of the clear and unmistakable traces of the commentaries in the German text, the unique manuscript of the Magdeburg Aesop follows—or rather followed[108]—in its presentation of the first forty-five fables not the order of the Anonymus Neveleti, but rather the sequence of fables as preserved in independent manuscripts of the Romulus LBG.

Magdeburg Aesop	Romulus LBG
1–5	1–5
6–20	7–21
21–22	22–23
23–27	25–29
28–29	73–74
30	30
31	56
32–33	31–32
34–36	34–36
37–44	38–45
45	48
46–48	50–52
49	55
50	92
51–52	90–91

Thus, for nearly the entire first half of his collection, the Low German translator seems to have worked from a manuscript of the LBG, adducing his other sources only as supplements to that text. The first twenty German fables correspond precisely to twenty of the first twenty-one in the Latin prose collection; the Latin collection includes two variants (numbers 6 and 7) of the fable of the lion's share, while the German text makes do with only one, more closely modeled on the second than the first version present in the Latin source. The next eight fables are likewise identical in the two collections, with one displacement in the vernacular: Romulus LBG 24, an alternative version of the fable of the frightened hares,[109] is moved in the German text to a position (as number 83) immediately preceding another fable "van dem

---

[108] The manuscript was not returned to the Magdeburger Stadtbibliothek after 1945, and must be considered lost.

[109] Boner's version of this text is discussed above.

hasen" (Seelmann, no. 84). Fables number 28 and 29 in the German Aesop correspond to numbers 73 and 74 in the Latin; their shift of position in the vernacular collection is easily explained as the result of the compiler's desire to group thematically related texts, as these fables and the two surrounding them in the Magdeburg Aesop all treat marriage.[110] The thirty-first fable in the German collection is anomalous in several respects; it leaps ahead some two dozen texts in the presumed Latin source (Romulus LBG number 56), which it then renders in a version unlike that in either the verses of the Anonymus or the prose Romulus. The German fable—"van der nachtegalen unde havike"—is assimilated somewhat to those around it in its new position: the epimyth of the fable immediately preceding begins with a bird proverb

> Ût enem stricke ein vogel entvlogen,
> nicht lichter wert de echt bedrogen;[111]

the one immediately following, "van dem weder unde wulve," shares with number 31 the narrative motif of parental protection against a deceitful predator. These similarities may have suggested the displacement of the fable, whether to the author of the Magdeburg Aesop or already to his source.

After fable 45, and particularly beginning with fable 50, the order observed by the German fabulist becomes increasingly erratic. Twice, in his fables 54 to 58 and 67 to 69, the translator appears to rely on the sequence of fables in the Wolfenbüttel Aesop,[112] a late fourteenth-century vernacular collection the Magdeburg Aesop quotes liberally throughout;[113] even so, these texts do not reveal any particularly striking textual assimilation to the corresponding fables in the older German collection, borrowing no more liberally than others in the Magdeburg Aesop.

The question of the translator's motivation remains. Why, if the principal source before him was from the beginning of the entire enterprise the Romulus LBG, should he have gathered his other sources, a

---

[110] Number 27, "van enem ridder und einer vrouwe"; 28, "van dem manne unde sinem wive"; 29, "van enem manne unde sinem wive"; 30, "van enem wive unde manne."

[111] Seelmann, 46, lines 47–48.

[112] These clusters in the Magdeburg Aesop correspond to fables 120–124 and 71–73, respectively, in the older German work.

[113] See Grubmüller, *Meister Esopus*, 420–421, and the notes to the individual fables in Seelmann's edition.

commented Anonymus Neveleti and the vernacular Wolfenbüttel Aesop? While for Ulrich Boner commented manuscripts of the Anonymus and Avian provided more readily comprehensible, narratively more coherent versions of the fables to be translated, the Low German fabulist had in the LBG before him a Latin prose text that already met every criterion of intelligibility and integrity;[114] he could easily have been content with rendering that single, already quite extensive source into German, as had been the author of the Wolfenbüttel Aesop some thirty years earlier.

That course is rejected, however, in the prologue of the Magdeburg Aesop, where the poet subtly chides his vernacular predecessor:

> Sint heft an dudesch ôk ein here
> *ein dêl* bracht dusser besten mere. . . .[115]

The clear implication is that this older German author had left some of these exemplary tales untold, an omission now to be remedied in the Magdeburg Aesop. This claim to exhaustiveness is responsible for the younger poet's reaching to sources beyond the Romulus LBG, even where—as most clearly in the case of the LBG-based Anonymus Neveleti commentary he used—the overlap among them was great. Recognizing the additional material provided in the Latin commentary's retellings, and no doubt grateful for the assistance of the older German Aesop at hand, the compiler of the Magdeburg Aesop set about to create a collection of Aesopica up until then without parallel, in Latin or the vernacular.

This same impulse is responsible for the inclusion of eight fables from the Avian tradition, none of them with parallels in the Romulus LBG or the older Wolfenbüttel Aesop. These eight—only a small fraction of the forty-two transmitted in most manuscripts of Avian—are scattered among the last fifteen texts of the Magdeburg Aesop, and in an order that only once and briefly reproduces that of the Latin verse originals;[116] furthermore, most of them are present here in versions that suggest only the most distant familiarity with Avian's own fables.[117]

---

[114] On the greatly underestimated literary quality of the Romulus LBG, see briefly Grubmüller, *Meister Esopus*, 72.

[115] Seelmann, 1, lines 33–34, emphasis added.

[116] Magdeburg Aesop 8–88, 93–94, 98, and 100 (Seelmann's numbering) correspond to Avian 14, 29, 10, 16, 5, 6, 3, and 22 (Guaglianone's numbering).

[117] Only the very brief story of the crab and her son (Magdeburg Aesop 98, cor-

It seems probable that the author of the Magdeburg Aesop had his Avian fables not directly from a manuscript of the school poet, but rather from an exemplum collection for the use of preachers, in which a narrow selection of material drawn from the standard Latin fabulists was integrated into a generally "spiritual" context. The German fabulist claims expressly, here as elsewhere, to be relying on a written source; of the wolves who await the treacherous traveler in his fable 86 (loosely based on Avian 29), he says

> Wo de er dink mit ome ankleven,
> daraf ne vinde ek nicht gescreven.[118]

In others, however, the gestures of oral presentation shine clearly through the written text, a feature to be expected in a promptuarium for homiletic use. Here much more frequently than in his other fables, the German fabulist, in the first person, assures his readers that the moral lessons of his texts match his own experience. The mother ape of fable 85 is rivaled in foolishness by many human parents,

> des môt ik wârliken gein (Seelmann, 124);

in fable 93,

> ik hân gevreschet ichteswanne

that the presumptuousness of some "ammechtmanne" has been the ruin of their masters (Seelmann, 141). This grounding of textual authority in personal experience takes an extreme form in the Magdeburg Aesop's aberrant retelling of the fable of the bald knight:[119]

> Dusse mere is wâr unde it geschach,
> des is bi wane mannic dach.

The musings of the text's editor to the contrary,[120] it is exceedingly unlikely that the German fabulist believed this story—familiar to every literate European from the classroom use of Avian—to be true. Instead,

---

responding to Avian 3) is here told in a version close to that of Avian. This fable, however, as its fundamental theme of teaching by example is of such obvious and lasting interest to readers and redactors, is subjected anyway to only relatively slight variation throughout its medieval tradition, learned and vernacular.

[118] Seelmann, 126, lines 85–86.

[119] Seelmann, no. 87, 129, lines 95–96. Compare Boner's version, discussed above.

[120] Seelmann, 185: "liegt, wie der dichter glauben macht, . . . noch ein von ihm erlebtes oder ihm berichtetes ergebniss vor?"

this is an assurance of the sort frequently encountered in the sermon, where the "truth" of the exemplum is established on criteria peculiar to the homiletic situation.

The Magdeburg Aesop's version of Avian 5, the well-known fable of the donkey in the lion's skin (Boner's version of which has already been briefly discussed) treats the story in a way that recalls the allegorical fable reworkings of Michael Beheim half a century later.[121] The Low German fable is exceedingly free in its narrative, beginning with an account alien to the broader tradition of the fable:

> Et wônde ein man to Judea,
> de hadde enen lowen da,
> grôt unde ungevôch,
> darbi tam genôch.
> He was nutter dan de hunde,
> want he bewaren kunde
> an velde unde an wolde
> sîn quek, wanne he scholde.[122]

When the lion dies, his bereaved master outfits his donkey in the skin and sets him to guard his herds (lines 13–26). A fox, however, betrays his disguise:

> de wart snelle des geware,
> dat it ein esel was,
> wente he at de stengel unde gras,
> ôk sach he dat bi den oren (lines 34–37).

Once denounced, the donkey is at the mercy of the wild beasts who had feared him as a lion;

> de wulf den esel bêt,
> unde al an stucke splêt (lines 57–58),

a fate far more grisly than that reserved to him in any parallel version. The differences to Avian's original are striking, but their motivation

---

[121] See chapter 4, below.

[122] Seelmann, 139, lines 1–8. The comparison with the house dog may be a reminiscence of the Anonymus Neveleti's fable "de cane et asino": "'Me catulo prefert vite nitor, vtile tergum'" (Wright, *The Fables of 'Walter of England'*, 56); the Magdeburg Aesop here reads "'Sint ik to allen werken/ bin minem heren nutter vele,/ den de hunt is ...'" (Seelmann, 22, lines 8–10).

comes clear in the epimyth, which begins yet again with a distinctively oral, even homiletic formula:

> Nu provet leven lude,
> wat dut mere bedude (lines 59–60).

This introduces an epimyth, at forty verses long even by the standards of the Magdeburg Aesop, in which the narrative portion of the text is subjected to a complex and detailed allegorical explication:

> De rike man bedudet de heren
> unde de vorsten, dede mit eren
> alle ore herschop vorstât,
> darto des ammechtmannes rât
> môt helpen unde sîn dât,
> icht he sîn dink wol anevât.
> Oft he van dode ofte van live
> sîn man nicht lenk en blive
> unde mit eren tredet ût
> unde sîn here des lowen hût
> tut enem esele an
> unde maket enen ammechtman
> enen bûr van older art,
> dede gût, wîs, truwe nu ne wart,
> de mit des esels rochte
> wolde gerne, icht he mochte,
> dat volk vorjagen unde vorveren
> unde engestliken geberen.
> Wen ein man wart vrom unde wîs,
> des mach he hebben ere unde prîs;
> wen he aver ene hût up sek drôch,
> dor sine dôrheit ungevôch
> wert he bekant vor enen doren,
> also de esel bi den oren;
> so wert om afgebroken
> name unde gût; sus wert he gewroken.
> Sîn dorperlige dât
> dem bosen, untruwen sus irgât.
> Ik hân gevreschet ichteswanne,
> dat van enem bosen ammechtmanne
> neman vullen loven kan,

> bi deme bestât des heren hof
> an ganzen eren unde sîn lof,
> de sin gût bewaret, sin lant behût
> unde aldus to den eren is gût (lines 61–98).

The fable narrative, with the additions and variations described above, is constructed to accord as closely as possible with this allegory; the epimyth determines the structure of the fable, rather than being derived from it. This shift in the function and relative significance of the fable's traditional components was originally prepared, as we have seen, in the allegorical explications of the school commentaries, the form of which remains recognizable even in the highly deviant substance of this fable.

That the source of the Magdeburg Aesop's Avian fables was indebted to the tradition of school commentary is even plainer in the version it provides of Avian 16, the fable of the oak and the reed. Just as Boner in his *Edelstein* had relied on a prose commentary to supply a pre-history to his fable,[123] so too the poet of the Low German Aesop provides considerably more preliminary detail than is present in Avian's verses:

> Up enem berge stunt ein êk,
> de nu vor dem winde en wêk,
> wente se was stark unde grôt.
> Der breden wortelen se genôt,
> dat se vorstunt vil mannigen stôt,
> de or de wint vil dicke bôt.[124]

The subsequent conversation between the felled tree and the cattails is similarly expanded, nearly thirty lines in the German fable corresponding to eleven in Avian's poem. The epimyth, then, represents an elaboration of the Roman fabulist's moral,

> Haec nos dicta monent magnis obsistere frustra,
> Paulatimque truces exsuperare minas,

on the allegorical principle common in the school manuscripts. Just as the commentaries in the Wolfenbüttel manuscript edited in the Appendix above and in the printed *Apologi*,[125] the fabulist of the Magdeburg Aesop informs his reader that

---

123 See above, p. 117.
124 Seelmann, 129, lines 1–6.
125 Seelmann, 185–186, reprints the commentary on this fable from the incunable.

De êk bedudet den stolten man. ...
Dat rôr bedudet de ôtmoden,[126]

and reinforces his explication with a quotation from "Salmon":

... de wisheit hevet,
mit duldicheit he an gude levet (lines 73–74).

This invocation of biblical authority is, as we have seen, common to both the sermon exemplum and the academically prepared fable of the commentaries.

Concealed behind the simple lines of descent asserted in its prologue, the Magdeburg Aesop is the record of an act not of composition but of compilation, the translator working first from one source, then from another, selecting among his manuscripts on the principle of universal inclusion. Seldom so clearly traceable in their particularity, the complex source relationships of the Low German fable collection thus provide a stunningly concrete example of those processes of contamination and cross-fertilization that seem in so many other cases barely graspable by the literary historian.

---

[126] Seelmann, 131, lines 51 and 67.

CHAPTER 3

Aesop's Two Tongues:

Secondary Bilingualism in the *Edelstein* and the Wrocław Aesop

B oth the *Edelstein* and the Magdeburg Aesop had as their goal the assertion of the vernacular text. In the middle of the fourteenth century, Ulrich Boner proudly pronounced his German-language collection a "buoch," thus claiming simultaneously his work's independence from its sources and its essential equivalence to the established Latin tradition; fifty years later, the anonymous Low German compiler gathered all the fables available to him to create the first exhaustive edition of medieval Aesopica—and this in his own language. As the preceding chapter has sought to show, the efforts of both poets were furthered by their use of materials and techniques from the Latin academic tradition; by adopting the gestures of their learned sources, the German fabulists lent to their vernacular collections some of the integrity and prestige enjoyed by their classical and would-be classical predecessors.

Considered from our vantage point six centuries later, both Boner and the Westphalian anonymous succeeded admirably in composing independent and self-sufficient German-language Aesops; the modern student and the modern scholar can read and enjoy both collections without recourse to their antecedents in the medieval school tradition. In the late Middle Ages, however, readers still largely considered the fable an obligatorily Latin and learned literary type,[1] and in the fifteenth century,

---

[1] See Grubmüller, *Meister Esopus*, 415.

scribes and compilers repeatedly attempted to resubordinate the vernacular Aesop to its Latin sources. One of the tools available to re-establish the dominance of the older tradition was the Latin prose commentary; the very force that had enabled the composition of coherent German-language collections in the first place became in the fifteenth century a method for the re-assertion of a textual hierarchy in which the vernacular was deemed clearly inferior to the formal Latin of teaching and learning.

I

The medieval manuscript transmission of Ulrich Boner's *Edelstein* is rich and varied; in their prolegomena to a new edition of the text,[2] Ulrike Bodemann and Gerd Dicke describe no fewer than thirty-eight fourteenth- and fifteenth-century witnesses to the collection's widespread popularity. A number of these manuscripts preserve traces of contemporary efforts to re-assimilate the Swiss fabulist's work to the Latin tradition out of which it sprang, ranging from occasional and casual interpolations to full-scale and invasive reorganizations of the text to fit it to new contexts and new functions,[3] a phenomenon similar to that described above as taking place already within the Latin tradition in the mid-fifteenth century.[4]

The late-fourteenth-century *Edelstein* manuscript "C"[5] preserves in its vernacular miscellany only Boner's version of the fable of the cock and the pearl; the scribe seems to have been aware, however, that he was in fact copying only an extract from a larger collection, as he adds to the Swiss fabulist's epimyth the couplet

[2] "Grundzüge einer Überlieferungs- und Textgeschichte von Boners 'Edelstein'," in *Deutsche Handschriften 1100–1400: Oxforder Kolloquium 1985*, ed. Volker Honemann and Nigel F. Palmer (Tübingen: Niemeyer, 1988), 424–468. My thanks to the authors for their kindness in permitting me access to their collection of *Edelstein* manuscripts in facsimile.
[3] For a thorough discussion of one particularly striking example (cgm 3974), see the ground-breaking study by Klaus Grubmüller, "Elemente einer literarischen Gebrauchssituation: Zur Rezeption der aesopischen Fabel im 15. Jahrhundert," in *Würzbürger Prosastudien* II, ed. Peter Kestig, Medium Aevum 31 (Munich: Fink, 1975), 139–159. The most recent discussion of the manuscript is found in Curschmann, "Marcolfus deutsch," in *Kleinere Erzählformen des 15. und 16. Jahrhunderts*, ed. Walter Haug and Burghart Wachinger, Fortuna vitrea 8 (Tübingen: Niemeyer, 1993), 180–183.
[4] Compare the discussion in Chapter 1 of the two commentators of clm 16213.
[5] Colmar, Bibliothèque de la Ville, ms. 78; see Bodemann and Dicke, "Boner's 'Edelstein'," 430. The text occupying the remainder of the manuscript is a vernacular exemplum collection.

Jm mag der frucht werden nicht
Alss man von einem affen gicht (fol. 122v),

a clear reference to the fable of the ape and the nuts that in most manuscripts of the *Edelstein* follows this first programmatic text. What is of greatest interest, though, is the fact that the scribe does not end the fable here, but appends to the German poem a Latin distich, immediately identifiable as the epimyth of the parallel text in the Anonymus Neveleti:

In gallo stolidum tu jaspide dona sophÿe
pulchra notes stolido nil valet illa seges (fol. 122v).

The bilingual presentation of this fable in manuscript "C", in which the Latin moral of the Anonymus functions as the final and definitive epimyth of Boner's German fable, recalls a circumstance not infrequent in the Latin school manuscripts. In a number of fifteenth-century commentaries on the Anonymus Neveleti, German vernacular couplets—introduced by a formula such as "unde vulgariter"—are inserted into the "doctrina" section of the prose annotations.[6] Here the pattern undergoes an inversion: the fable narrative and its first epimyths are German, the concluding moral in Latin. Where the German epimyths within the Latin commentaries functioned as *Merkverse* for schoolboys—and indeed, were eventually published separately for that very purpose[7]—the effect of the Latin interpolation in "C" is more far-reaching. The Latin distich serves to situate the origins of Aesopic wisdom outside the text of the vernacular fable, making its moral content depend for its authority and credibility on the *Edelstein*'s explicit connection to the Latin source from which it descends. The Latin verse, by its very Latinity, lays claim to a greater participation in the traditions of learning, and at the same time makes pointedly plain the merely derived status of the vernacular reflex.

The subordination of vernacular reflex to its Latin source is even more drastic in two Alemannic manuscripts that—unlike the single fable transmitted in manuscript "C"—preserve the *Edelstein* as a more or less complete corpus.[8] As Grubmüller notes, both the Basel codex and the

---

[6] See the examples given in Wright, "The 'Nuremberg' Aesop," 204, and Henkel, *Deutsche Übersetzungen lateinischer Schultexte*, 288–290. Similar vernacular couplets would eventually be extracted from the commentaries and printed separately in the fifteenth century as the *Moralitatum carmina*; see Henkel, *Deutsche Übersetzungen lateinischer Schultexte*, 288, and Grubmüller, "Elemente," 153–154.

[7] See Henkel, *Deutsche Übersetzungen lateinischer Schultexte*, 288.

[8] See Grubmüller, "Elemente," 153.

now-lost Zürich manuscript used in the first scholarly *Edelstein* edition

> fügt[en] jeder Boner-Fabel das interpretierende lateinische Schluß-
> distichon des Anonymus Neveleti, also der Vorlage Boners, in
> einer sehr aufwendigen Auszeichnungsschrift an.

Thus what is an isolated phenomenon in "C" becomes in these manuscripts a codicological principle. Repeated after each of the German
fables, the Latin epimyths in these manuscripts inevitably take on the
appearance of a key to an older and presumable more authentic inter-
text, namely, the verse fables of the Anonymus; they function, in other
words, as a peculiar sort of lemma, directing the vernacular reader's
attention back to the fact that the German poems are not original, but
translations. In their consistency, they come to present the vernacular
fables of the *Edelstein* as secondary and dependent, inviting or even requiring reference to works from the Latin tradition to establish their
credibility.

Structurally, the graphic presentation given Boner's fables in these
three manuscripts assigns to the vernacular text the same place, and the
same status, as that enjoyed by the prose retellings in the Latin commentaries. Just as in the Latin school texts, the German fables of the *Edelstein* in these manuscripts are literally surrounded by an interpretative
frame, opened by the titles and captions given the German texts and
then closed by the Latin epimyths taken from the verses of the Anonymus Neveleti. Its reading governed by its position between these elements, the German fable is reduced—just like the prose "reductions" of
the commentaries[9]—to the status of an accessible illustration, one exemplum among many potential others, for the authoritative rule promulgated in the Latin distichs of the Anonymus.[10] While Ulrich Boner had
sought to provide an independent German *Edelstein*, the texts of his
vernacular collection are presented in these fourteenth- and fifteenth-

---

[9] See the discussion in Chapter 1 above of the reduction in status of the fable narrative.

[10] Compare also the treatment of the *Edelstein* in Munich, Bayerische Staatsbibliothek,
clm 19826, where the German texts are reduced to Latin digests and assigned specific
situations for application. The homiletic intentions of the compiler are plain not only from
the content of the remainder of this fifteenth-century manuscript (for a description, see
Bodemann and Dicke, "Boners 'Edelstein'," 439), but also from the frequent use of direct
second-person address. Remarkably for the late-medieval tradition of the Latin fable, several
of the digests appear to assume a female audience; consider, for example, the manuscript's
treatment of Anonymus Neveleti 26 (Foerster's numbering), interpreted "de falsa promis-
sione" (fol. 109v): "Despicit lupum agnus sed pocius sequitur capram; Sic virgo despiciat
juuenem multa vouentem."

century manuscripts as retellings of "real" texts, that is to say, the Latin poems of the Anonymus. Paradoxically, both Boner's attempt at literary integrity and its frustration at the hands of later compilers and scribes owe much to a familiarity with the forms and gestures of Latin fable commentary.

Such attempts to re-assert the traditional relationship between Latin and the vernacular did not always succeed. In the Munich manuscript clm 4409, written in the mid-fifteenth century, the German texts of the *Edelstein* are at first not only graphically but hermeneutically subordinated to their counterparts from the Latin pedagogic tradition.[11] As the manuscript proceeds, however, the fables of the Anonymus Neveleti and their Latin prose commentary, originally conceived as the central texts in the bilingual assemblage the manuscript presents, cede their place of textual priority to the other elements of the compilation, namely Boner's vernacular fables and their illustrations. In the progression from subordination to equality to primacy, the shifting status of the vernacular texts in this manuscript's Aesopic complex recapitulates the late medieval development of the genre as a whole; the scribe of clm 4409—if unwittingly, still impressively—has left a richly suggestive record of the emergence of vernacular authority from a Latin learned tradition.

The manuscript begins its Aesop[12] at folio 87r with the verse prologue of the Anonymus Neveleti; the Latin distichs are unaccompanied by any interlinear glossing, but they are followed by a brief, badly copied excerpt from a commentary *accessus* of a familiar type, based closely on the prose of the Romulus collections and clearly revealing its pedagogic origins:

> Rumula filius Tibernio de ciuitate autentica salutem. Esopus quidam homo grecus ingeniosus natus fuit in Frigia et claruit ibi honeste viuens per [illegible]. Ego vero Romulus transtuli hunc librum de greco in latinum. Titulus huius: Incipit Esopus, liber fabulorum ab Esopo compositus atheniosi magistro. Nota: Causa finalis enim poetarum consistit in utilitate vocabularum vel in

---

[11] See Bodemann and Dicke, "Boners 'Edelstein'," 432, for a brief manuscript description. The first description of the *Edelstein* as preserved in clm 4409 is to be had in Grubmüller, "Elemente," 153.

[12] As is usual in manuscripts of the Anonymus, clm 4409 identifies the text simply "incipit esopus" (fol. 87r).

delectatione materie, quia poete deversa narrant. Vnde Oracius:
Aut prodesse volunt aut delectare poete (fol. 87r).

After a space left for an unexecuted illustration, there follows the first
fable of the Anonymus Neveleti, accompanied by a Latin prose commentary "in einer feinen und zierlichen Schrift";[13] exceptionally, the
manuscript provides only the fable of the Anonymus and does not
append Boner's version to this fable of cock and pearl. Beginning with
the second text, however, the fable of wolf and lamb (Anonymus Neveleti 2), a pattern of graphic presentation begins that continues through
Anonymus Neveleti 19 (fol. 115r). For these first eighteen folios, each
fable is introduced by an illustration, which is followed immediately by
the verse fable of the Anonymus; the epimyth of each Latin fable is
given the marginal identification "Utilitas" in the hand of the commentator. The Latin prose commentary and the corresponding German fable
from the *Edelstein* follow, this last set off by a rubricated initial two
lines high.[14]

The Latin commentary and the vernacular fables are both written by
the identical delicate hand,[15] and both in a brown ink paler than the
relatively powerful black used for the Latin verse fables. Given their
graphic assimilation one to the other, it can be assumed that the German
texts and the Latin commentaries in this manuscript stand each in a
similar relation to the "primary" Latin verse fables they accompany.
Both the Latin prose of the commentaries and the German verse of
Boner's *Edelstein* must make a distinct contribution to the manuscript;
the vernacular texts must bring something to the understanding of the
fables that neither the Latin verses nor the Latin prose versions they accompany can provide.

Some idea of what that peculiar contribution might have been can be
deduced from a note at the end of the manuscript's Latin prose commentary on Anonymus Neveleti 8, "De lupo et grue" (fol. 95v). This
commentary ends, as do all others, with a statement of the fable's moral
lesson:

---

[13] Grubmüller, "Elemente," 153.
[14] Although space is consistently left for the initials of the German fables, they are
actually executed in only half the texts.
[15] Compare Grubmüller, "Elemente," 153, styling the script a "typisch[e] Kommen-
tarschrift."

Vtilitas: Non prodest seruire aut bene facere hominibus malis,
quia totum ab eo res commodum sit [crossed out] proditur cum
sint immemores beneficij accepti et grates non retentes (fol. 95v;
transcription unemended).

The conspicuous label "Utilitas" within the commentary text serves to
remind the reader of the link between the commentaries and the verse
texts, whose own epimyths, it will be recalled, have been furnished the
same designation. Normally, the fable from the *Edelstein* should immediately follow this commentary segment; instead, though, the fable is
given a second illustration, and as a result the beginning of the German
fable is delayed to the top of the following folio, 96r. The commentator,
or the scribe, anxious lest the vernacular text be overlooked, reminds
the reader at the conclusion of his Latin prose explication

   Sequitur rithmus (fol. 96r),

by which is obviously meant the rhymed text from the *Edelstein*.

   This identification of the German fables as "rithmi" focuses the
reader's attention on their purely formal distinctness from the other
texts in the fable assemblage of clm 4409, and suggests a desire on the
manuscript compiler's part to gather as many prosodically distinct reali-
zations of the same material as possible. The Latin verses of the Anonymus are proudly and self-consciously metric, alternating pentameters and
hexameters constructed with the greatest care; the commentaries insist
equally on the programmatic nature of their prose form. It seems likely
that it was in the original intention of the compiler of clm 4409 to
supplement this modest variety of Latin expression with a text in the
vernacular, one whose prosody overlapped with neither the metric
verses of the English schoolmaster nor the prose of his late medieval
commentator.

   Clm 4409 benefited further from the inclusion of the Swiss Aesop in
its physical ornamentation: for it was in the manuscript exemplar of this
codex's *Edelstein* that the exemplars for its illustrations were encountered. The Munich manuscript has been described by art historians and
others as an illustrated Anonymus Neveleti;[16] in fact, however, the

---

[16] See Bodemann and Dicke, "Boners 'Edelstein'," 442–443; Grubmüller, "Elemente,"
153 and note 46; Adolph Goldschmidt, *An Early Manuscript of Avianus and Related Manuscripts*, Studies in Manuscript Illumination 1 (Princeton: Princeton University Press, 1947),
54; and Thiele, *Der lateinische Äsop*, cxxxiv.

watercolor miniatures of clm 4409, though they are physically closest to the fables of the Anonymus they introduce, more accurately illustrate the German texts from Boner's *Edelstein* than either the manuscript's Latin verse fables or their prose commentary, as is obvious on any closer investigation.

The fable of the wolf and the crane, to take a particularly clear example, has, as mentioned above, two illustrations, both of which reveal definitively their origins in the manuscript tradition not of the Anonymus but of the German *Edelstein*. The first miniature, placed on folio 95v in the expected position immediately before the Latin verse fable, shows the wolf, open-mouthed, as he is about to partake of the severed head of a goat; the prey animal's legs lie scattered on the ground below.[17] The identity of the wolf's unfortunate victim is not to be had from the Latin verses; the Anonymus, whose distichs are given to terseness in any event, apparently recognizes the irrelevance of such a detail and dispatches both the wolf's prey and the entire matter in an ablative absolute, "osse retento." The Latin glosses and commentaries, including that of clm 4409, tend simply to expand that compact construction into a straightforward prose clause, likewise leaving the origin of the offending bone unstated:

> Ossa dum lupus deuoraret, vnum ex eis gutturi eius adhesit. . . .[18]

Unlike the Latin parallel texts, Ulrich Boner's *Edelstein*—in one of the pre-histories owed, as I have argued above, to the Swiss fabulist's reliance on the traditional patterns of prose commentary—identifies the wolf's prey:

> Ein wolf kam nâch sîner art
> hungrig ûf des roubes vart.
> schiere wart er dâ gewert
> des roubes, des sîn herze gert.

---

[17] Such scenes of violent dismemberment are common in this manuscript; for example, the illustration to the next fable, Anonymus Neveleti 6, likewise shows a butchered stag strewn across the landscape. Compare the illustration to the same text from cgm 3974 in Grubmüller, "Elemente," facing page 148.

[18] Clm 4409, fol. 95v. Compare also the interlinear gloss on "osse retento" in Wolfenbüttel, Herzog August Bibliothek, cod. guelf. 185 Helmst., fol. 113r: "id est quando retentum os fuit in collo."

In der geschicht kam im ein geiz:
vil vrâzlich er dô in si beiz. ...[19]

The illustrator plainly follows the German text here in preference to
either of the Latin alternatives.

The second miniature, occupying the position usually taken by the
vernacular fable, follows the commentary on fol. 96r; it shows the stork
(or crane) with its head and long neck plunged deep into the wolf's
mouth. This double illustration, exceptional in clm 4409, appears to be
part of an attempt to give graphic expression to two distinct morals.
This second picture is a warning against too eagerly helping the ungrate-
ful, a traditional interpretation of this fable included in the epimyths of
all three of the fable texts given in the manuscript. The earlier illustration, however, if it does not simply arise from the painter's evident
delight in the grisly, suggests a different way to read the fable, as an admonition against gluttony, the sin, after all, that led to the wolf's distress in the first place. Dietary continence, of course, is not a theme in
the verses of the Anonymus, and neither does it appear to be elaborated
in any of the Latin prose commentaries on this fable.[20] Boner, however, on recounting the wolf's excessive appetite for goat, indulges in an
excursus on precisely this matter:

> hæt er so vrâzlich nicht genomen
> die spîs, ez wær im nicht beschehen.
> ich muoz es bî der wârheit jehen,
> ich wölt, daz vrouwen unde man,
> die sich vrâzheit nement an,
> beschæch, als ouch dem wolf beschach.[21]

The first miniature in clm 4409 illustrates this disapproving outburst in
Boner's fable, relying on the vernacular text both for its general moral
import and the identity of the wolf's dinner.

The recognition that the miniatures in clm 4409 illustrate the
German texts more faithfully than any of their Latin counterparts suggests that the vernacular fables, in spite of their graphic affinity to the

---

[19] Pfeiffer, *Edelstein*, 17, lines 1–6.

[20] Suggestive, though, are such remarks as this, from the Helmst. manuscript (Wright,
The Fables of 'Walter of England', 39; emphasis added): "Quadam vice lupus deuorauit carnes
nimis auide ..." Even so, the commentary promyths and epimyths maintain an exclusive
concentration on the wolf's ingratitude rather than his greediness.

[21] Pfeiffer, *Edelstein*, 17, lines 12–18.

manuscript's Latin commentaries, are in fact not subordinated to the
verses of the Anonymus in the same way as the prose annotations,[22]
but instead enjoy some more central position in the compiler's original
program. This suspicion is confirmed by the changes in the manuscript's
layout and content beginning with the manuscript's eighteenth fable
(fol. 113r). While every text up to and including this tale of the mouse
and the lion (Anonymus Neveleti 18) has been accompanied by a marginal version in Latin prose, from fable 19—the sick kite and his
mother—the commentator falls abruptly and completely silent, leaving
the metric fables of the Anonymus and the rhythmic poems of the *Edelstein* to fill the manuscript page. More remarkably still, ten folios later,
the Latin verse fables, too, disappear, and the remainder of the manuscript—through the fable of the sheep and the hart (*Edelstein* 35)—becomes *de facto* a vernacular fable book, including only Boner's German
fables and their (increasingly sketchy) illustrations.[23] It is evident that
this was not the scribe's ultimate intention: the fables from the *Edelstein*,
even where they are unaccompanied on the manuscript leaf, are still
relegated to the tops and margins of their pages; on several leaves, the
central space left blank is pricked and ruled as if in preparation for the
copying of the Latin verse fables. Nonetheless, that the scribe of clm
4409 finished the copying of the German fables rather than concentrate
on the completion of the Latin texts of the Anonymus suggests strongly
that his own interest or the interests of the manuscript's early owners[24]
lay more firmly with the vernacular fable than with its learned antecedents, and makes of this manuscript an emblem of the complex relationship between the Latin tradition and its German reflexes in the fifteenth
century.

II

Some one hundred years after the composition of the *Edelstein*, a
scribe in a Silesian monastery was set the task of copying one of the
most complex fable books ever assembled. The Wrocław Aesop fills its
no fewer than seventy-one paper folios[25] with a tangle of diverse and

---

[22] Compare Bodemann and Dicke, "Boners 'Edelstein'," 439: "in der Schulhandschrift
M1 [fungieren] die Boner-Fabeln als Kommentare zum lateinischen 'Anonymus Neveleti'."
[23] The German fables present in clm 4409 are listed in the table in Bodemann and
Dicke, "Boners 'Edelstein'," 446–447.
[24] The codex is from the famous monastery of Ulrich and Afra, Augsburg.
[25] The earliest reference to this collection is the brief description in Alfons Hilka, "Bei-

at times barely legible textual elements: it is in the main

> eine schulmäßig mit Interlinear-Glossen und Kommentar ausge-
> stattete Abschrift des Anonymus-Neveleti-Textes aus dem Jahr
> 1461, die neben den lateinischen Distichen eingetragen (oder
> diesen abschnittsweise folgend) eine ostmitteldeutsche Reimpaar-
> Übertragung enthält. Der (lateinische) Kommentar enthält auß-
> erdem eine von der Gesamtübersetzung verschiedene deutsche
> Reimpaar-Fassung der Epimythien (... «Proverbia Esopi»).[26]

For all its comprehensive density, Henkel's description barely hints at
the multidimensional complexity of the Aesop in this manuscript; compare the manuscript's presentation of Anonymus Neveleti 1, the fable of
cock and pearl, beginning with a commentary:

> Cum rigido fodit. Ista est secunda pars prohemialis istius libelli in
> quo magister exsequitur intentum suum, scilicet detractandum de
> hys que dicit continere in presenti opusculo; scilicet de flore de-
> lectabili, puta de fabulis, et de fructu multum vtile, scilicet de alle-
> gorys in ipsis fabulis designatis. Et diuiditur in tot partes quot
> magister ponit fabulas et apologus. Et primo adducit fabulam
> vnam de gallo in qua reprehendit illum qui sapienciam, philoso-
> phiam paruipendat. Et ita per opusculum instruit nos ut non si-
> mus debetas[27] sed intelligentes, non fatue sed sapientes. Dicens
> in simili quadam vice cum quidam gallus querens escam in fimo
> vidit iacere quendam lapidem preciosum quo vti non valens sic
> locutus est ad eum: "O tu preciosa res et mire pulcritudinis, quo-
> modo tu iaces hic in isto loco vetedo?[28] Qui michi nullius est
> vtilitatis, sed si quis te invenisset qui te vti posset, tunc nitor sive
> splendor tuus augmentaretur. Sed quia nec ego ‹tibi› nec tu michi

---

träge zur mittelalterlichen Fabelliteratur," *Jahresberichte der Schlesischen Gesellschaft für vaterländische Cultur* 91, Abt. IV, Sect. C (1913), 1–21. See also Speckenbach, "Die Fabel von der
Fabel," 199; Grubmüller, *Meister Esopus,* 415–416; Elschenbroich, "'von unrechtem gewalte'," 435; and, especially, Henkel, *Deutsche Übersetzungen lateinischer Schultexte,* 225–227.

[26] Henkel, *Deutsche Übersetzungen lateinischer Schultexte,* 226. Speckenbach's early description ("Die Fabel von der Fabel," 199) of the German translations as "eine Interlinearglossierung des Anonymus Neveleti" applies with qualification only to the presentation of
the Latin poet's prologue, and badly oversimplifies the status and function of the vernacular
fables in this manuscript.

[27] Read "ebetes." The apparent feminine ending on the nonce form "debetas" accords
with the feminine plurals "fatue" and "ipse" that follow.

[28] For classical Latin "fetido."

convenis, et ergo ego pocius vellem invenisse pro te rem minus caram, puta paruum granum tritici, quod saturaret sthomachum." Et tunc subdit sic: Eciam multi homines stulti inducti[29] cum audiunt dicere de ipsa philosophia et artibus moralibus et virtuosis actibus, in quibus tamen nichil proficiunt, nec ipse curant eos sed magis minus bona, scilicet delectacionem corporis. Et hoc eciam est quod wolgariter dicitur: "Eyn thor eynem han gleiche ist, der eyne perlen vindit in deme mist. Also her das achtit nicht, also worsmeet der thor was meyn[30] ÿm list."[31] Et hoc alligorice: Et ergo per gallum intelligitur stultus, per fimum intelligitur mundus iste, per iaspidem regnum celeste per[32] gracia spiritus sancti. Quia qu‹e›madmodum gallus non curauit iaspidem, licet valuisset mila grana tritice, ita insipiens et insensatus non curat regnum dei. Juxta illud: Ad regnum celi non tendit mente videns insipiens, et cetera; sed homo sapiens ille vendit omnia que habet et emit eum et postponit omnes delectaciones humanas et intendit soli deo cum virtute seruiens. Et taliter regnum celorum et graciam dei percipit.[33]

Immediately following this commentary, the manuscript presents the first distichs of the Anonymus, heavily glossed and construed with fine Arabic numbers:

.i. quando scz gallus .i. - uel   rustro   3   .i. quando   .i. cibum

1   .i. duro vel aspero 4   2 uertit   5 .i. stercus terre   6   7 .i. diligenter querit   8

Dvm rigido fodit ore fimum dum queritat escam

---

[29] Read "indocti."

[30] "Man."

[31] Compare the verses of the "Proverbia Esopi," quoted in Henkel, *Deutsche Übersetzungen lateinischer Schultexte*, 290. It is quite in keeping with the intensive textuality of the Wrocław Aesop that the original reading *der weisen list* "the cleverness of the wise" is transformed in the Silesian manuscript to *was meyn ÿm list* "whatever one reads to him."

[32] Read "vel."

[33] Fol. 256r–v. Because the text is unedited (and, in light of the difficulty of reading many of the passages in this manuscript, likely to remain so), my discussion quotes the German and Latin fables of the Wrocław Aesop more extensively than in the case of the other collections I treat.

- .i. quando 3   4   5   2   6

1   .i. ameratur .i. reperta   tale gemma   s. ipse   s. tunc .i. dixit

vm³⁴ stupet inuenta iaspide gallus ayt

.i. nobilis 6   5   .i. splendidi   .i. ornatus

1 gemma s. o   .i. abiecto spacio 3 2 .i. et   4

Res vili preciosa loco nitidi que decoris

.i. eciam .i. in loco luteso .i. prostraueris scz gallo .i. vtilitatis   s. non .i. ferens uel portans

      8   7   10 .i. nullum 12   11   9

Hac in sorde iaces nil michi messis habens

scz ille loquitur [?]   scz homo .i. foret uel - -   .i. inventor

    3 .i. pro te 2   2   4   5   6   7

Si tibi nunc esset qui debuit esse repertor

scz -   .i. lotum   .i. in se r-et .i. decoraretur .i. per   s. tunc .i. splendor tuus

4   5   6   1   3 artificium 1

Quem limus sepelit viueret arte nitor

.i. non s. ego gallus .i .congruus sum   s. congruus scz ego gallus .i. proficio

1   2 scz iaspidi   4 scz tu iaspis   5 scz gallo 6   8 scz iaspidi 7

Nec tibi convenio nec tamen michi nec tibi prosum

scz gallo   scz iaspis .i. vales   .i. magis s. ego gallus .i. minus preciosa sicut pisum uel

     3   1   2   5   .i. diligo 4 7   6   granum etc.

Nec michi tu prodes plus amo cara minus.

Below these verses—which make up only the narrative portion of the Latin fable of the Anonymus Neveleti—and bounded by a dark line on their left, are the rhymed couplets of the anonymous Middle German translator:

> Eyn han lebitte in deme fawlen miste
> vnd zuchte speyse noch seyner list.
> Eyn ediln iaspis her do want,
> des wunders her derschrag.

---

³⁴ The initial "D" or "C" is not executed in the manuscript.

"O edil war," her vorbas sprach,
"Im köthe leystu, alz ich eyn sach.
Keynen fromen brengistu mir.
Ach, were dyn zucher komen dir,
dem du soldist werdin von rechte,
hoch wirdig hilde her dich al slechte.
Her cleyte dich mit goldis gesmeyde.
Nicht magistu an frewden bleiben.
Noch ich dir, der notcz ist cleyn
Vnsir beyder wir nicht obir eyn."[35]
Kleine wormme, ap dy hy wern,
an dy welde ich mich liber keren.

These verses are followed immediately by the Anonymus's Latin epi-myth; these distichs too are heavily annotated:

s. lector .i. per gallum .i. fatuum inadvertentem .i. per gemmam .i. documenta
1   3   2   4 scz notas 8 nobilem   6 7 .i. philosophie uel sapiencie

Tu gallo stolidum tu iaspide scripta zophie

.i. -   scz .i. intelligas .i. fatuo uel .i. proficit uel non .i. doctrina philosophie et sapiencie
5   1   4 ignaro   2 vtilis est 3   1   1

Pulcra notes/ stolido nil valet ista seges,

and are followed by a second set of vernacular verses, this time labeled "degressio" in the hand of the scribe:

Den fremden schymp durch ersten sen
Saltu, lesir, alzo versten:
Iaspis dyse weise lere bedewte,
Der han dy unuorstendige lewte.
Zottene thoren tyser weisheit rot
vnechtig halden durch ein spoth.
Des gleichen her Salomon spricht:
Hostu gute czu horcher nicht,
vil liber sweigen dir dirkews,
vnd cluge worth nicht von dir gews (fol. 257r).

---

[35] The German text, though legible, seems here to be corrupt.

Further complicating the reader's task in deciphering the manuscript page, the scribe has copied the Latin prose commentary to the next fable, Anonymus Neveleti 2, parallel to these German verses, only the slightly nonsensical lemma "Est lupus est" forestalling hopeless confusion on the part of the schoolboy reader.

Recent scholarship on the medieval fable has reached no agreement about the sources of the German verse Aesop in the Wrocław manuscript. Speckenbach,[36] apparently familiar with only the manuscript's presentation of the Anonymus's verse prologue,[37] describes the German text as an "Interlinearglossierung" of the Latin verses, thus implying that the vernacular fables' not infrequent prosodic clumsiness is

---

[36] "Die Fabel von der Fabel," 199; at the time of the publication of Speckenbach's groundbreaking essay, the Wrocław manuscript was not easily accessible to western scholars.

[37] Like a large number of other fifteenth-century commentary manuscripts, the Wrocław Aesop breaks the Latin prologue into sections of one or two distichs, which are then explicated by the commentator and, in this manuscript, translated into German; the vernacular verses are, thus, in a way "interlinear." The prologue is rendered thus:

Den lesirn czu lost vnde fromen
Ist das buch czur gemeyne kome
Ernste wort werden susze czu letczte
Wenne ich sy mit schympe dir setcze

yn dem buchelen alz yn eynem garthen
Bluthe vnd fruchte saltu sarthen
dy blute schon ist rothis vol
dy frucht speyst deyne zele wol

Libstu dy blute obir dy frucht
lys aws dy blewte mit zocht
hostu lost czu den fruchten bas
Erzewch sy heyn dach nym an has
Frucht vnd blute czu eyner gabe
Nymstu sy beyde ich das lobe.

das icht meyn hercze sey vordroszin
vnd dorch trocheit gantcz czu sloszin
Zo sal ys czu czeiten wachen
vnd dys buch den schulern machen

das aws meynem ackir gerynge
fruchtig getreyde stark offdrynge
dirfewchte o got dy worthe meyn
durch dy gnade des gyests deyn

an den worten ist das buch gar leichte
ydach loscht vndir dem selbigen getichte
erzuchtig zere brichstu off den kern
zusz is smackis wil he dich gewern.

owed to their having begun life as a primitive word-for-word translation of each vocable in the Anonymus Neveleti. Grubmüller,[38] half a decade later, describes the German text with greater caution, though perhaps equal imprecision, as a close "translation" of the Anonymus, a view repeated shortly thereafter by Elschenbroich in his investigation of the manuscript's treatment of the fable of wolf and lamb.[39] Henkel alone protests: although he appears content to identify their source as the distichs of the Anonymus, he finds the German fables

> gegenüber der lateinischen Vorlage weitschweifig und ungelenk. Die Epimythien werden—nahezu predigthaft—zerdehnt und stehen in auffälligem Gegensatz zur Prägnanz der lateinischen Verse. ...[40]

Henkel's description is both accurate and richly suggestive: for precisely the same terms can be applied to the treatment of the fables the Anonymus in the late medieval prose commentaries. On closer inspection, the German fables of the Wrocław Aesop are revealed to be the verse contrafact of just such a Latin commentary, the typical form and characteristic content of which are largely preserved in the manuscript's vernacular rendering.

Consider, for example, the Wrocław Aesop's versions of the fifth fable of the Anonymus, the story of the dog and the bone:[41]

.i. transnatat 1   .i. in ore .i. portans .i. frustum scz ipsa .i. dat uel facit .i. vmbrositatem uel

aquam 2 tale animal 5 scz suo 3   4   carnis   6   7   8 apparenciam

Nat canis ore gerens carnem caro porrigit umbram

s. .i. vmbrositas .i. adheret   .i. in aquis   scz ipse .i. mordens   .i. has vndas

scz carnis 1   2 uel apparet   3   6   4   apprehendit 5 vmbrosas 7

Vmbra coheret aquis / has canis vrget aquas

---

[38] *Meister Esopus*, 415.

[39] Elschenbroich, " 'von unrechtem gewalte'," 435: the German fables constitute "sich an den Originalwortlaut eng anlehnende Versübersetzungen." Elschenbroich's knowledge of the manuscript seems to rely entirely on the brief account of it in Grubmüller, *Meister Esopus*, 415ff.

[40] Henkel, *Deutsche Übersetzungen lateinischer Schultexte*, 226–227.

[41] Fols. 261r–262r. Compare also the versions of the *Edelstein* and the Magdeburg Aesop, briefly discussed in Chapter 2 above.

.i. vmbram scz ipsius .i. magis .i. quam 5 .s. canis 1 .s. canis scz .i. dulci .i. similitudinem carnis

2 uel similitudinem 3 4 ipsam carnem .i. optat uel esuriet cupit 6 8 vtilitate 7 uel figuram

Spem carnis plus carne cupit plus fenore signum

261v

.i. talis lucri scz suum s. ipse canis .i . sicut scz ipsa .i. umbra ipsius carnis .i. anichilatur

3   3   2   .i. reserat 1   4   5   6   7 .i. et 8   uel evanescit

Fenoris / os aperit / sic caro spes que perit

.i. propter tale factum   .i. pro transitorijs .i. propria et .i. obmitti

3   per se 1   4   5   et invtilibus 6   vtilia 2 7

Non igitur debent pro vanis certa relinqui

.i. aliena   .i. aliquis .i. gliscit .i. subdite .i. priuatur scz homo .i. hominis proprijs

3   4   1 1   2   7   6   5   8

Non sua si quis amat mox caret ipse suis

The annotated verses stretch across the leaf, fol. 261v–r, and are followed, in two parallel columns, by the vernacular fable and the Latin prose commentary. The commentary is one widespread in fifteenth-century manuscripts, with evident affinities to the prose of the Romulus *recensio vetus*[42]:

> Nat canis. In hoc apologo, autor arguit omnes cupidos et avaros qui aliquando ob spem modici boni consequendi non ponderant magna dampna que eis eueniri possit. Et docet nos ut in acquirendis necessarijs non dimittamus rem certam pro incerta consequenda, ne cariamus proprijs dum ea que aliena sunt petimus aut petere volumus. Et pro isto introducit talem fabulam, dicens quod quadam vice quidam canis portans carnem in ore suo natabat per qu‹e›ndam fluuium, et videns vmbram carneam in aquis, suspicatus est vmbram carnis esse melioris quantitatis et saporis quam ipsas carnes. Qua re patefaciens os suum et desiderans vmbram carnis accipere, carnem in ore habitam perdidit et vmbram non accepit. Sic etiam sepe contingit quod isti qui non volunt contentari, sed die noctuque pro acquirendis instant et laborant diuicijs, gracia quorum se et sua diuersis exponunt periculis. Tan-

---

[42] Compare the survey of commentaries on this fable in Wright, "The 'Nuremberg' Aesop," 207–217.

dem non acquisitis alienis etiam perdunt illud quod habent de
proprijs. Quare magister hoc redarguens dicit: Non igitur debent
etc., volens quod bona certa non debent reliqui sive dimitti pro
hijs que sunt dubia, racione quia quicumque nimium amat aliena,
huic sepe euenit quod perdit sua propria. Wersus: Perdere quisque suam sortem [?] de iure meretur, quia si placeant plus aliena
sive non sua qui cupiunt, que sua sunt cito perdunt. Et in volgare
dicitur: Vor eyttil ding sal nicht off erden gewest ding gelossen
werden, wenne welch man fremde gut begert der wirt offte an
dem seinen geserth. Allegorice per canem intellige auarum hominem, per carnem regnum celorum, per vmbram transitoria huius
mundi.[43]

The vernacular fable, in a somewhat finer, lighter script, occupies the
half leaf immediately to the left of the commentary's beginning:

> Eyn rode obir eyn geflute swam,
> Eyn bretig fleisch he mit ym nam.
> Das fleysch ym wassir den schynen gab,
> Do noch der hunt that manchin swamp.
> Me luste en des broten scheyn
> Wenn das fleysch das yo was seyn;
> He lobete eyn czeichin obir das phant.
> Der slung gante off czu hant,
> Seyn broete wart balde vorlorn,
> Dor czu das hoffin falsch derkorn (fol. 261va).

The next two couplets of the German text are given the marginal label
in the hand of the text scribe "hic applicat apologum":

> Nicht zolde wir lozen gewisse ding
> durch vnsicher gutter entspring.
> Des seyne gelost mit rechte der man,
> der yo noch fremden gutten wil stan;

the same marginal comment occurs in other texts of the Wrocław Aesop next to the morals of the Anonymus as well (compare, for example,
the promyth of the next fable, fol. 262r, next to which the scribe has

---

[43] Fols. 261vb–262rb.

noted "Hic applicat apologum ad moralem sentenciam"). The final five lines of the German fable are given the marginal caption "degressio":

> Das dy redde war sy alzo
> Bekenne by recht, o meyster Katho!
> Du sprichst: Der vil vorleysen
> vor geweis, das ist allezeit
> weis [?], stet dy ebin tewir gar breit.[44]

The rather startling apostrophe to "meister Katho" is paralleled in the other German fables of this collection, in the morals of which a number of canonical school authors—"der werde tichter Gamfredus," for example, or "Aristoteles, du meyster yn kunsten weyt gesprochen"[45]—are directly, and familiarly, addressed.

In considering the German verse fable, one is struck first by the extremely intimate reliance of the vernacular poem's narrative on the verses of the Anonymus. While Speckenbach's suggestion about their originally interlinear habitat plainly goes too far, it is equally clear that the narrative plots of the German fables depend very closely on the "original" Latin verses. Particularly the description of the dog's fatal error in judgment,

> Me luste en des broten scheyn
> Wenn das fleysch das yo was seyn;
> He lobete eyn czeichin obir das phant,

can only be the immediate reflex of the Anonymus's decidedly recherche lines

> Spem carnis plus carne cupit, plus fenore signum
> Fenoris. . . .[46]

Likewise, the vernacular epimyth is closely related to its Latin counterpart in the verses; throughout his German Aesop, the translator consistently adheres to the practice of rendering each single Latin verse by a rhymed German couplet.

---

[44] The "degressio" of this fable is among the less legible passages in the manuscript.

[45] Geoffrey of Vinsauf is the school author most often cited in the vernacular *degressiones*; Aristotle is here (fol. 307v) most likely translated from a commentary, as is the usual case in the Latin fable commentaries as well.

[46] The scribe of the Wrocław Aesop marks the Latin poet's sophisticated enjambement with a virgule.

Far greater independence, however, is apparent in the *degressiones* with which the vernacular fabulist concludes his poems. Where both narrative and epimyth of the relatively brief fable of the mountain and the mouse[47] accord closely with the version of the Anonymus, for example:

> Ein erde an eyme hobit czu swoll
> vnd clagte durch wemmerytczin [?] schal,
> Sy sulde eyn jvngis han.
> O wy derschrocken des frawen vnd man,
> dy erde wolde merwunder gebern,
> do von das volk nicht mochte entpern.
> Grawsam forchten das völk czu bereyn
> Begunde, wy wol ys gerne wer blos eyn.
> Uorne dor bey ydoch dy forchte
> flucht das pofils [?] slechlich worchten.
> Dy forchte czu honys weyse quam,
> dy erde swanger noch weybis scham
> Gebar eyne maws. Do wart eyn schymp
> der grosen forchte vnd ungelimpe.
> Dy lewte offte gar cleyns enden,
> dy mit worthen mich vollen blenden.
> Ser offte von geryngem sachen
> wil man grose forchte machen;

the conspicuously labeled "degressio," on the other hand, departs from the fable to introduce new material from external sources:

> Meister Gamfred, gib vns den zehen.
> Du sprichst: los gache, wor czu gehn.
> Deyn wort volge noch der töt.
> Wer vil ramys yn ym hot,

---

[47] Fols. 281r–v; the German is particularly difficult to decipher, but can be seen nonetheless to match well the fable as told by the Anonymus Neveleti:

> "Terra tumet, tumor ille gemit gemituque fatetur
>   Partum. Pene perit sexus vterque metu.
> Cum tumeat tellus, monstrat se monstra daturam.
>   Sic homines trepidant et prope stare cauent.
> In risum timor ille redit, nam turgida murem
>   Terra parit. Iocus est quod timor ante fuit.
> Sepe minus faciunt homines qui multa loquuntur.
>   Sepe gerit nimios causa pusilla metus."

Seyn gut lop swecht he methe.
Des andern gleich spricht Gots prophete
Her Dauid: Sy derbebitten do vor vorchte,
Do en nymand leidis worchte.[48]

The additional material here is present in neither the verses of the Anonymus nor the Latin prose commentary transmitted in this manuscript; it is instead adduced from other texts of the elementary Latin curriculum, and appended to the fable narrative on the model of the Latin fable commentary. The German text's narrative corresponds structurally and, as we shall see, functionally to the prose reductions of the academic commentaries; the verses identified as the poet's "application" of his story are the counterparts to the Latin *Doctrina* sections. The final verses of each vernacular fable expand on and vary the Latin poet's epimyths—often revealing a specifically spiritual bent in their amplified explications[49]—in a way familiar, too, in the commentaries that were, if not the German fabulist's source, then at least his inspiration.

The identification of the exemplars of the German fables of the Wrocław Aesop in the Latin commentary tradition suggests an obvious answer to questions about the functions of the vernacular texts in the fable assemblage as a whole. To the collection's first modern discoverer, Alfons Hilka, the vernacular verses were simply a "deutsch[er] Kommentar,"[50] whose straightforward goal—along with that of the manuscript's interlinear glosses, construe marks, and Latin prose annotation—was to ease the young reader's access to the canonical verse fables of the Anonymus; this view is repeated by both Grubmüller and Elschenbroich, who see in the German fables "ein Arbeitsmittel zum schulischen Gebrauch."[51] Again, it is Henkel who objects:

> Daß der deutsche Text ... 'als Verständnis- und Auswertungshilfe für die lateinischen Distichen dienen' sollte ..., halte ich für unwahrscheinlich. Wer Kommentar und Glossen benutzen konnte, brauchte keine—zumal so ungenaue—Verständnishilfe durch die deutschen Reimpaare.[52]

---

[48] Fol. 282r.

[49] Compare Elschenbroich, " 'von unrechtem gewalte'," 435.

[50] Hilka, "Fabelliteratur," 13.

[51] Elschenbroich, " 'von unrechtem gewalte'," 435; see Grubmüller, *Meister Esopus*, 415–416.

[52] Henkel, *Deutsche Übersetzungen lateinische Schultexte*, 227 (quoting critically Grubmüller, *Meister Esopus*, 415).

The suggestion that the German verses of the Wrocław Aesop are somehow inaccurate, "ungenau," in their rendering of the Latin fables of the Anonymus is a mistaken one; as the examples already adduced demonstrate, the East Middle German fables, for all their occasional awkwardness, are far more faithful a translation of the Latin texts than any other verse Aesop of the Middle Ages, going far beyond the preservation of the mere outlines of the fable plots, and they must have served (and could still serve) the German-speaking reader admirably as a parallel text on her or his first encounter with the challenging distichs of the Anonymus.

Neither should the idea be immediately accepted that the German fables represent somehow a redundant element in the compilation as a whole. It is true that the Latin prose commentaries and, especially, the interlinear glosses and aids to construction provide a ready and reliable access to the primary texts; but as Henkel himself notes, that is true only for those already in possession of sufficient Latin to use them. It is not difficult, though, to imagine the youngest pupils' being introduced to the fables of the Anonymus gradually, first—before they had any Latin at all—with the assistance of the close, nearly "literal" renderings in the German text, and then—as their skills improved—in the relatively simple form of the prose commentaries; only after some time might they be set the task of parsing and construing the verse fables with the help of the manuscript's interlinear apparatus. By including all of these diverse elements, in verse and prose, Latin and the vernacular, the compiler of the Wrocław Aesop assured the utility of his collection to wider audience possessed of varying proficiency in the language of instruction.

The vernacular fables of the Wrocław Aesop make a further contribution to the manuscript's bilingual compilation. In the strictness of their articulation, with a distinct and distinctly labeled plot, moral application, and scholastic or spiritual elaboration, the German texts replicate the form of the Latin commentaries they share the leaf with, increasing the reader's awareness of the need for explication, and providing him with a clear pattern for the generation of new interpretations. In their very redundancy, these second "commentaries," as the vernacular fables must be considered, thematize the act of reading and interpetration, inviting the reader to emulation.

Such an imitation of worthy models is the theme of the Anonymus Neveleti's short fable 50, the ox and the calf. The Wrocław Aesop (fol. 307r) furnishes the text with all the elements described for the other fables above; the distichs of the Anonymus are glossed and commented,

and a lengthy (and only partially legible) German verse retelling follows
the narrative portion of the Latin verse fable. The Anonymus's epimyth,

> Proficit exemplis merito cautela docendi
> Maiorque sua credit in arte minor,

is equally faithfully translated:

> Snelle bessert sich des menschen mut
> wo man gut beyspel thut.
> Ouch sal der iungen gehorick seyn
> yn der kunst dez meyster seyn,

and is followed by the usual "Degressio," addressed this time to an
unusually high authority:

> Aristoteles, du meyster yn kunsten weyt,
> gesprochen hostu wor langer czeit:
> So wir gute exempel geben,
> So merkin vm dy iunger ebin.
> Wil der selbir recht seyn gelert,
> So mus her dor czu seyn gekert
> Gancz czu glewben des meysters ler,
> do won wachs kunst, dy lengir [illegible] mer.

Exactly this is the intention of the compiler of the Wrocław Aesop: to
provide an example, in the vernacular as well as in the received language
of scholarship, of the careful reading and the thorough explication of the
Aesopic fable.

CHAPTER 4

Prose, Verse, and the Fable in Fifteenth-century Vienna[1]

The diversity of prosodic form tolerated in the Latin Aesops of the Middle Ages had no parallel in the early development of the vernacular fable. Particularly in the "Romulus" strand of the Latin tradition—culminating but not ending with the Anonymus Neveleti in the twelfth century—there was an almost regular alternation of prose collections and verse retellings; in the European vernaculars, however, the fable continued to resist the advance of prose until nearly the end of the Middle Ages, well after many other genres had capitulated. In France, a true prose tradition for the fable begins only after the middle of the fifteenth century;[2] Italy was not far ahead with two prose translations of the Anonymus Neveleti dating from the late fourteenth century, while in England the first unrhymed vernacular collections were written for the printing press.[3]

The persistence of verse in the German translations of other Latin schooltexts has been described as the result of literary inertia:

---

[1] Portions of the first section of this chapter are drawn from a revision of chapters 2 and 5 of my 1991 Princeton dissertation, "The 'Nuremberg' Aesop and Its Sources."

[2] The author is at present engaged in a study of the "Yzopet III de Paris" in an attempt to determine the role played by Latin commentary traditions in the composition of that vernacular prose text.

[3] See Barbara Tiemann, *Fabel und Emblem: Gilles Corrozet und die französische Renaissance-Fabel*, Humanistische Bibliothek 18 (Munich: Fink, 1974), 25; Kenneth McKenzie, "Note sulle antiche favole italiane," in *Miscellanea di studi critici in onore di V. Crescini* (Rome: Stagni, 1910), 59–72, esp. 60; Grubmüller, *Meister Esopus*, 83–84.

> Erstens ist die literarische Form, in der lehrhafte Aussagen in deutscher Sprache formuliert werden, bis ins 16. Jahrhundert fast ausschließlich der paarig gereimte vierhebige Vers gewesen. ... Zweitens sind für das Spätmittelalter ... Texte in Reimpaaren von offenbar kanonische Bedeutung für die didaktische Dichtung gewesen.[4]

The long resistance of the German fable to prose can be convincingly explained in the same terms. The "canonical" Aesop of the fourteenth and most of the fifteenth centuries was, as we have seen, Boner's *Edelstein*, a text in rhymed couplets. More generally, the fable's traditional association with other literary types similar in theme and didactic intent led to the maintenance of the received prosodic form; indeed, the fable first appeared in the German vernacular as a set piece within a longer rhymed work, and even as they attained greater independence, texts in the new genre were classified, logically enough, with several miscellaneous short forms themselves composed in rhymed couplets. Grouped and transmitted among these didactic works, the fable, too, came to seem an obligately rhymed genre.

In German, the relaxation of this generic norm did not take place until the first decade of the fifteenth century, with the composition of the first Aesop in prose. Klaus Grubmüller has identified the forces responsible as originating for the most part from outside the Aesopic tradition:[5] thus, verse precedent was first broken by the Viennese translator Ulrich von Pottenstein, who in 1408 translated the Latin allegorical exempla attributed to Cyrillus, a collection of texts resembling the Aesopic fable in their didactic intent and inanimate characters, but, in their novelty, not bound by the generic expectations burdening more familiar fable texts. Pottenstein, in Grubmüller's view, created new possibilities for translators, who were now free to subject the Aesopic fable as well to prose.

Other scholars have turned their attention rather to late medieval developments within the vernacular fable tradition itself, concentrating on an apparent new awareness in the fourteenth and early fifteenth centuries of the generic distinctness of the Aesopic fable. Rüdiger Schnell, treating German fable collections, and Barbara Tiemann, considering in the first instance the French prose Aesops of the fifteenth and sixteenth

---

[4] Henkel, *Deutsche Übersetzungen lateinischer Schultexte*, 123.
[5] See *Meister Esopus*, 436.

centuries, both identify the likely impulse for prosodic change in the use of the fable as illustrative material in vernacular sermons; as a result, the Aesopic texts were reanalyzed as more closely allied to the homiletic *exemplum* (typically in prose) than to the *mære* and *bîspel* (exclusively in verse) with which they had conventionally been associated.[6]

Appealing and plausible as both explanations may be, each can do nothing more than account for the weakening of the exclusive hold of verse form on the fable; neither, however, provides any positive reasons for the adoption of prose form in any given vernacular fable collection. The late medieval recognition of the fable's generic integrity made possible, but could not itself cause, a shift from verse to prose; neither did the realignment of the fable with new literary genres lead necessarily to such a change. The choice of unrhymed form for the Nuremberg Aesop was eased in part by the forces described above, but its inevitability was due to the composition of the work in a literary environment where German prose alone was deemed adequate to the translation of Latin works themselves in prose: here, of course, commentaries on the Aesopic fables of Avian and the Anonymus Neveleti.

I

Although no single known manuscript of Avian or the Anonymus preserves the immediate Latin sources of the Viennese collection now known as the Nuremberg Aesop, the translator's two exemplars can be reconstructed with some considerable confidence.[7] For the first thirty-nine of his fables, those with antecedents in Avian's collection, the Austrian translator had recourse to a Latin commentary on the *Apologi* with retellings based, for the most part, directly on the Roman poet's original verses, without consistent interpolation from any intermediate medieval version. The spiritual epimyths appended to the fables of this first section are rich and detailed, ranging widely among the standard works of the medieval Latin curriculum for inspiration and embellishment.

The last twenty-four fables of the vernacular Aesop are translated from a Latin commentary on the Anonymus Neveleti. Here, in contrast

---

[6] See Rüdiger Schnell, "Prosaauflösung und Geschichtsschreibung im deutschen Spät-mittelalter," in *Literatur und Laienbildung im Spätmittelalter und der frühen Neuzeit*, eds. Ludger Grenzmann and Karl Stackmann (Stuttgart: Metzler, 1984), 214–248, here 234; and Tiemann, *Fabel und Emblem*, 24–26.

[7] See Wright, "The 'Nuremberg' Aesop," 250–294, 297–299.

to the strong pedagogic emphasis evident in the Avian commentary source, the Latin commentator was satisfied with spiritual epimyths that only rarely quote other literature and are, especially in comparison to those accompanying the Avian fables, flat and perfunctory. The prose reductions of this commentary, on the other hand, were appealing and well constructed; the commentator did not scruple to abandon the verses of the Anonymus in favor of more lively and detailed retellings offered by the Romulus *recensio vetus*. Unlike the Avian commentator, this one was as much interested in the *delectatio* as in the *utilitas* of his fables, and made no special effort to import edifying material from other works.

This attitude made the Anonymus Neveleti commentary less useful to the German fabulist, and his frustration is apparent in the increasingly erratic selection of fables for translation. Where the thirty-nine German fables from Avian are translated in an order that diverges only slightly and infrequently from that maintained in most Latin manuscripts,[8] the second part of the German collection abandons the probable original arrangement of its source, presenting its final ten translations from the Anonymus Neveleti in an order unlike that in any Latin Anonymus manuscript now known.[9] This is best explained as the result of the Viennese translator's dissatisfaction with his Latin exemplar. More entertaining than edifying, the Anonymus Neveleti commentary was ultimately a source of disappointment for its translator, whose didactic sensibilities found in it too little of the "ler vnde waizzung" proclaimed as his objective.

His faltering enthusiasm notwithstanding, the Viennese translator of the Nuremberg Aesop succeeded in producing the first fable collection in German prose, unfinished though it may be. As described above, the weakening of generic constraints on the fable in the later Middle Ages created an environment in which Aesopic texts *could* be translated into prose; the precise nature of the translator's commentary sources, combined with his participation in contemporary literary movements that

---

[8] The absence in the German collection of fables corresponding to Avian's numbers 21, 39, and 40 is likely not the translator's innovation; these fables, more "novellistic" than others in the collection, are not infrequently displaced or omitted in the Latin manuscripts as well.

[9] Thus, the last ten German fables of the Nuremberg Aesop (numbers 54 to 63) correspond to fables 18, 23, 29, 20, 21, 26, 27, 22, 28, and 31 in the Latin Aesop of the Anonymus. Full concordances for the fables of the Nuremberg Aesop and its Latin sources are found in Wright, "The 'Nuremberg' Aesop," 319–320.

privileged prose over verse for edifying purposes, put him in a position uniquely apt to the realization of that potential.

The identity of the Austrian fabulist remains unknown. The implicit suggestion made some years ago by Nigel Palmer[10] of a connection between the Aesop and the prose Valerius Maximus translation of Heinrich von Mügeln remains plausible, particularly given that an obituary notice in the unique manuscript of the fable collection most likely commemorates the death of the wife of the man to whom Mügeln had dedicated his earlier work. It seems improbable, however, that the Aesop, were it the work of Heinrich von Mügeln himself, would be transmitted in only so late a copy and, in a manuscript prepared for the Viennese court circles in which that well-known poet had moved, without any mention of its author; it is noteworthy as well that the prose Aesop reveals no verbal similarities to Mügeln's strophic fables beyond those trivial echoes easily attributed to the independent use of similar Latin sources.[11]

Grubmüller's cautious identification of the Viennese translator as a member of the circle around the so-called "Nikolaus-von-Dinkelsbühl-Redaktor"[12] finds suggestive, if necessarily inconclusive, support in an entry in the fifteenth-century catalogue of the Dominican convent St. Jakob in Vienna. It is certain that at least one of the early readers of the Aesop knew that library; she or he left on the fable manuscript's flyleaf a note

> Item maister Niklas von dinkelspuchel hat ain puch gemacht dewthtsch den frawen zu sand Jacob ze wien vnd in dem puch ist das pater noster begriffen das sol gar ain ordenlich puch sein uber all dewthsche puecher dar aus wil ich schreiben es halt vil sachen von vnser frawen. dicz puch ist in der stat wien viel entten abgeschriben.[13]

---

[10] Nigel F. Palmer, "Zum Nebeneinander von Volkssprache und Latein in spätmittelalterlichen Texten," in *Literatur und Laienbildung im Spätmittelalter und in der Reformationszeit*, 579–603.

[11] See, for example, Wright, "The 'Nuremberg' Aesop," 276–277. Palmer, "Nebeneinander," in comparing the Aesop to the Valerius Maximus translation, points additionally to the use of Latin lemmata and the deictic formula "hie lert uns . . ." in both works; as the discussion in Chapter 1 above should make plain, however, those are conventions firmly established in the Latin academic tradition, and there is no reason that they could not have been imported independently into the vernacular by two different German translators.

[12] Grubmüller, *Nürnberger Prosa-Äsop*, xiv.

[13] Quoted in Wright, "The 'Nuremberg' Aesop," 32. On the Paternoster commentary

Interestingly, the catalogue of St. Jakob contains an entry for a fifteenth-century manuscript book, now lost, gathering together

> Nicolaus Dinckelpuhel super 'Pater noster'; de oracione in communi, de preceptis et caritate dei, de decem preceptis, de octo beatitudinibus, de septem donis, de septem viciis, de fraterna correccione, de oblacionibus, de penis inferni, de morte, de corpore Christi, de animalibus moralizacio eiusdem Dinkelpuhel, de quibus singulis supra. Sermones plures. Cirilli proverbia.[14]

The "moralizacio de animalibus" here attributed to the great scholar and reformer is not adduced in any of the standard registers of Dinkels-bühl's works,[15] and seems, on reflection, an odd interpolation in a

---

attributed to Nikolaus von Dinkelsbühl, see Bernd Adam, *Katechetische Vaterunserauslegungen: Texte und Untersuchungen zu deutschsprachigen Auslegungen des 14. und 15. Jahrhunderts*, Münchener Texte und Untersuchungen 55 (Munich: Artemis: 1976), 220.

[14] Theodor Gottlieb et al., eds., *Mittelalterliche Bibliothekskataloge Österreichs*, 5 vols. (Vienna: Holzhausen, 1915–1971), 1: 380; the manuscript bears the signature N 39. The fate of this manuscript is unclear, and it must for the time being be accounted lost. The typewritten catalogue of the library does not list it among the surviving codices of the Viennese Dominicans: Felix Czeike, *Verzeichnis der Handschriften des Dominikanerkonvents in Wien* (Vienna: 1952). Ulrike Bodemann's identification (*Cyrillusfabeln*, 53) of the manuscript with one now in the possession of the Schottenkloster, Vienna, does not appear to be correct, as codex 63 of that library, while it does include a copy of the "Cyrillus" fables, does not contain any of the other works listed in the fifteenth-century catalogue; compare Albert Hübl, *Catalogus codicum manu scriptorum qui in bibliotheca monasterij B. M. V. ad Scotos Vindobonae servantur* (Vienna: 1899; repr. Wiesbaden, 1970), 75–77.

The "Moralitates de naturis animalium" in Vienna, Österreichische Nationalbibliothek, cpv 1599, turn out to be a late-thirteenth-century extract, copied in the Cistercian abbey of Heiligenkreuz, from the spiritual bestiary of Heinrich von Schottenhofen, and therefore of no relevance to the question here under discussion; see Kurt Holter and Karl Oettinger, "Les principaux manuscrits à peintures de la Bibliothèque nationale de Vienne: Quatrième partie, Manuscrits allemands," *Bulletin de la Société française de Reproduction de manuscrits à peintures* 21 (1938): 57–155, here 63–64 and plate X; and Christian Hünemorder, "Des Zisterziensers Heinrich von Schüttenhofen *Moralitates de naturis animalium*. Beobachtungen zu seiner Quellenbenutzung und zur frühen Rezeptionsgeschichte von Bartholomaeus Anglicus und Thomas de Cantimpré," in *Licht der Natur: Medizin in Fachliteratur und Dichtung. Festschrift für Gundolf Keil zum 60. Geburtstag*, ed. Josef Domes, Göppinger Arbeiten zur Germanistik 585 (Göppingen: Kümerle, 1994), 195–224.

[15] Most important and most recent is Alois Madre, *Nikolaus von Dinkelsbühl*; see also the articles in the *Verfasserlexikon*, s.vv. "Nikolaus von Dinkelsbühl" and "Nikolaus-von-Dinkelsbühl-Redaktor." Neither does the manuscript or the work appear in the most authoritative studies of the medieval bestiary tradition; see, for example, Willene B. Clark and Meradith T. McMunn, "Manuscripts of Western Medieval Bestiary Versions 197–2103," in *Beasts and Birds of the Middle Ages: The Bestiary and Its Legacy* (Philadelphia: University of Pennsylvania Press, 1989); and Florence McCulloch, *Medieval Latin and French Bestiaries*, rev. ed., UNC Studies in the Romance Languages and Literatures 33 (Chapel Hill: University of North Carolina Press, 1962).

manuscript of such otherwise unrelentingly catechetic intention. It is tempting to see in the moralized zoology of this manuscript rather the work of a disciple, parading under the name of the master—and quite possibly representing a second copy of the Nuremberg Aesop.[16]

Whoever its author, the close association of the Austrian fable book with the contemporary literary production of the so-called "Vienna School" of translators is clear.[17] As I have argued elsewhere,[18] the selection of texts it includes, the dialect of its scribes, and the clues provided in the notes made by later readers all point to an origin and primary reception at the ducal court in Vienna.

The efforts of the translators of the Vienna School, beginning with the arrival in the 1380s of German-speaking professors from the University of Paris and continuing into the middle of the next century, were characterized by the attempt to reproduce in every translation not only the spirit but also the letter of its Latin original; their goal was to generate exact vernacular equivalents to Latin catechetic and devotional texts for the use of those who, semi-literate, could not gain access to the edifying content of the originals. Most of the young scholars active in this enterprise evidently found prose so overwhelmingly appropriate to their intentions that they felt no need to justify their choice, proceeding instead in many cases directly to a consideration of the particular type of prose most suitable to their ends. Only in the prologue to the German translation of William Durandus's *Rationale*, one of the earliest and most influential products of the Viennese circle, does the anonymous translator refer directly to the issue:

> Ich wil auch mein teusch nicht reimen vnde wil ez doch besliez-
> zen, so ich peste mag mit der chunste slozzen, die da haizzent
> rethorica, und daz ich bei der schrifte worten beleibe und die
> selbe mazze behalte, dï in latein geschriben ist.[19]

---

[16] The German Aesop found among the possessions of Hippolyta von Stubenberg could conceivably have been a third; she was the wife of the great-grandson of the subject of the obituary notice in the surviving manuscript described above. See Johann Loserth, "Das Archiv des Hauses Stubenberg," *Beiträge zur Erforschung Steirischer Geschichte* 37 (1914): 71–126, here 117.

[17] A convenient overview of the activities of the Viennese translators can be found in Thomas Hohmann, " 'Die recht gelerten maister': Bemerkungen zur Übersetzungsliteratur der Wiener Schule des Spätmittelalters," in *Die österreichische Literatur. Ihr Profil von den Anfängen im Mittelalter bis ins 18. Jahrhundert (1050–1750)*, eds. Herbert Zeman and Fritz Peter Knapp, 2 vols. (Graz: Akademische Druck- und Verlagsanstalt, 1986), 1: 349–365.

[18] See Wright, "The 'Nuremberg' Aesop," 7–51.

[19] G. H. Buijssen, ed., *Durandus' Rationale in mittelhochdeutscher Übersetzung*, Studia

The translator's ambition, writing a quarter of a century before the *Ac-kermann*, is to write a German

> nach der ordenunge der schrifte, dï in latein mit rechter mazze geschriben ist.

Since only the language of the Latin original can truly be commensurate with the subject matter it communicates, in the German translation, too, prose must be preferred to verse for its greater capacity to reproduce the *mazze* of the Latin prose source.

In the German *Rationale*, the need to approach as closely as possible the essential Latin text influences not only the choice of prose, but details of the syntax as well. Other Viennese works written in a Latinizing *aygen deutsch* similar to that used by the Durandus translator justify the admitted unnaturalness of their language on the grounds that only thus can the reader of the German text be assured access to the

> ganczen sin da uon ... als es latein geschriben stet.[20]

German translations, in this view, should duplicate not only the content but also the characteristic form of their Latin sources, even when that form is typified by nothing so much as obscurity:

> Auch ist ze merchen, das der tractat [that is to say, the Latin exemplar of the German text] gar pesunder vnd tewffer verstentichait ist ... vnd darümb ist die teutschz etwas seltzam vnd ist mit grossem fleiss ze merchen.[21]

This desire for a stricter approximation of the vernacular to the Latin text by mimicking the language of the original is not unique to the practitioners of the artificial, Latinizing style. The same intention is avowed by those Viennese translators who availed themselves of what has often been considered the "competing" technique of *vmbred, vber seczen,* or *gemain deutsch,* where, though fidelity to the content of the original is sought with equal eagerness, the German text largely aban-

---

Theodisca 13,6: 15/16 (Assen: 1966–1983), 15: 2 (here also the quotation immediately following).

[20] James V. MacMahon, " 'Das puech von der ordnung der fuersten': A Critical Text-Edition of the Middle High German Version of the 'De regimine principum' of Aegidius Romanus" (Ph.D. diss., University of Texas, 1967), 55.

[21] Thomas Hohmann, *Heinrichs von Langenstein 'Unterscheidung der Geister' lateinisch und deutsch: Texte und Untersuchungen zu Übersetzungsliteratur aus der Wiener Schule,* Münchener Texte und Untersuchungen 63 (Munich: Artemis, 1977), 52.

dons the syntax of its Latin source in favor of what appear to the modern reader more typical native patterns. Both styles were intentionally chosen by their adherents; the choice had to do neither with the translator's abilities nor with any prejudgment of the correctness of the one or the other style. The selection was made rather on a careful assessment of the prose style and edifying intention of the Latin original, as Ulrich von Pottenstein reveals in the preface to his monumental German catechetism:

> Nu hab ich den gemainen lauf deutscher sprach nach des lanndes gewonhait fur mich genomen, wann daz puch [that is to say, the Latin exemplar of the German work] vnd die lere die darinnen begriffen sein, schikchen sich gemainchleich. . . .[22]

Pottenstein, who in his other works is quite capable of writing an elegant, even precious *aigen deutsch*, here justifies his choice of a simpler prose style as based in the nature of his material, in precisely the same way as Heinrich von Langenstein rationalizes his use of a Latinizing technique as the only way to satisfy the demands of a subtle and challenging exemplar. The goal of translation is the same for both; but in the case of a Latin text itself homely in language and intent, German *umbred* offers the best chance to simulate the linguistic condition of the original.

Thus, the two styles of translation practiced within the Vienna School should be considered less competitors than complements, each available to every translator anxious to effect a perfect translation of Latin sources by approximating not only their content but their diction and form as well, hoping

> die *proprietas* des Lateinischen im Deutschen präzis wieder[zu]geben und dieses dadurch auf[zu]werten.[23]

In the case of the German Aesop, this mandate was made even more unbreachable by the special character of its principal Latin sources. As we have already observed in the discussion of the bilingual Munich

---

[22] Gabriele Baptist-Hlawitsch, ed., *Das katechetische Werk Ulrichs von Pottenstein*, Texte und Textgeschichte 4 (Tübingen: Niemeyer, 1980), 146.

[23] Hohmann, 'Unterscheidung', 261. Hohmann here refers only to the goals of those writing *eigen deutsch*, when in fact, the simpler style too was intended to evoke the less sophisticated Latinity of its sources.

manuscript clm 16213,[24] an Aesop seems at first an incongruous addition to a body of work so uniformly religious in content and intention as the translations of the Vienna School. Though the fable too is a didactic genre, like other moralizing texts fundamentally intended for interpretation and application, its didactic content, particularly in the Latin school traditions of Avian and the Anonymus Neveleti, is typically worldly, and its lessons all too often inconsistent with the Christian standards of virtue promulgated in the catechisms of the later Middle Ages. Charity and faith are less highly prized than success, even success attained through *calliditas* or some other species of ethical pliancy. The motivational system of the verse fable of the Middle Ages is based wholly in material profit and loss: the reader is adjured to do good not because it is right, but because it is advantageous.[25]

As we have seen in Chapter 1, the fable commentaries of the late medieval schools seized the opportunity to modify this unacceptable moral stance. Promyths were altered to exhort the reader to righteousness, changing the neutral "sic facit" to the prescriptive "non debet"; and allegorical epimyths were filled with edifying allusions and citations. The traditional school texts were thus pressed into service for much more than linguistic exercise and memory drill.

What made the commentaries so especially attractive to their Viennese translator was the inextricable connection between the supplementary religious material they offered and their own prose form. For prose was exclusively appropriate to the Latin fable commentary as to no other literary type or genre. Their purpose defined and their existence justified by their subordination to another text, the commentaries could serve their purpose of elucidation only by assuming a formal distinction from the works they accompanied. The difficulty of the verse fables lay in the rhetorical complexity of their verse form; the commentaries had therefore necessarily to be written in a Latin prose understandable to the most unsophisticated novice. To disregard in translation the fundamental formal and stylistic character of the source would have been a violation unthinkable to a translator of the Vienna School. That the essential prose form of the commentaries coincided with their moral rehabilitation of the fable made the case for its retention only the more pressing; thanks to the commentaries' close association of prose form

---

[24] See Chapter 1 above.
[25] Compare Grubmüller, *Meister Esopus*, 155.

and edifying content, it was not only possible but inevitable that both should be received intact into the vernacular.

The Viennese translator's regard for the special nature of his or her source extends to the smallest detail of the Latin commentaries' structure, a structure that is reproduced precisely in the vernacular text of the Nuremberg Aesop. Thus, each fable in the German collection has a well-marked introduction, consisting typically of a caption, a lemma, and a promyth; a narrative section, in which the plot of the fable is recited; and an allegorical epimyth, in which the story is explained or applied. As even the briefest comparison of any of the German fables with any of the Latin commentary segments discussed in Chapter 1 reveals, this formal rigor is not original or new, but is taken directly from the vernacular collection's academic sources. Where in those Latin prose texts this articulation served in the first instance practical purposes, however, these schematic elements are transformed in the German text as markers of the independence and the authority of the new work: they are not only translated, but vernacularized.

Following the familiar pattern of the Latin commentaries, each of the German fables is headed by a rubricated title; they typically name one or the other of the principal characters and then, in a dependent relative clause, introduce the remaining figures in the context of a brief but often quite informative summary of the fable's plot:

> von dem arn, der den snekken vand vnde mit im hin furt, darumb in die chra laicht.[26]

Such captions are not rare in the Latin tradition, where—as in clm 16213—they ease the reader's search for a specific text in a longer collection. In the German Aesop, however, these titles do not appear at the head of the manuscript leaf, where they should most logically be placed if they are to serve as an index; instead, they are embedded in the running text of each fable. Rather than playing a practical role in the *ordinatio* of the book, the captions in the German Aesop seem to have as their goal the establishment of a graphic and rhetorical uniformity among the fables, making of them a single collection whose integrity is assured by the formal similarities linking the individual texts.

This evident concern for similarity and unity reflects the very different status of the German Aesop from that enjoyed by its Latin coun-

---

[26] All citations to this text are to Grubmüller, *Nürnberger Prosa-Äsop*.

terparts. The prose commentary was by definition a dependent work, requiring no integrity of its own and relying for its structural and literary cohesiveness rather on its association with the verse fables it commented on. Obviously, the German Aesops' relation to the primary metric texts of Avian and the Anonymus was far more tenuous, and the vernacular work could not hope to partake of the authority of the originals to the same extent or in the same way as the Latin prose commentaries did. The Viennese translator had therefore to be solicitous of his text's unity and independence to a degree that was not necessary for the more intimately dependent Latin commentary.

In all but two of the fables of the Nuremberg Aesop, the titles are followed immediately by Latin lemmata, conspicuous for their exaggerated display script and rubricated initials and often set off from the text that follows by a fine red virgule. As expected, these Latin catchwords are taken from the incipits of the verse fables of Avian and the Anonymus Neveleti, just as in the prose commentaries that served as the exemplar of the German Aesop.

The function of these Latin insertions in the German text is less easily deduced than are their sources. In the Latin commentary tradition, such lemmata were, as we have seen, useful as guide words, their presence justified by the need to facilitate reference to another text: in many manuscripts, they assure the application of each commentary section to the correct passage in the primary text.

The Latin lemmata of the Nuremberg Aesop have been explained as meeting a similar need, possessing, besides their obvious prestige value,

> den rein praktischen Zweck, die vergleichende Lektüre von lateinischem Text und volkssprachlicher Übersetzung zu erleichtern.[27]

That German versions of Latin works did serve this function in the later Middle Ages is incontrovertibly true; there are vernacular works from the Aesop's immediate literary environment whose translators explicitly state their purely practical aim. The *De regimine principum* was translated, for example, so that the Austrian duke might read both books,

---

[27] Palmer, "Nebeneinander," 587.

latein und tewschcz, und dar aus nach syten frewd
nemen;[28]

the strictly pedagogic purpose of the Latin lemmata there is made plain
by the fact that they are themselves translated at the beginning of each
paragraph in the German rendering of the work.

The intention of the Viennese translator of the Aesop seems at first
glance similar. The prologue to the fable collection proclaims its translator's goal to be the

nucz ainualtiger layen, die dizer ler in lateinischer sprach nicht
geniezzen mochten oder dew villeicht nicht vollichleich begreif-
fen vnde versten chunden.[29]

This last clause—"or who might be unable to understand it completely"—might be read as an indication that the Aesop was intended as
a parallel text, a vernacular commentary to be read perhaps in a school,
side by side with the difficult Latin verses of Avian and the Anonymus
Neveleti. But the phrase is in fact disingenuous, its implication about the
Latin abilities of its readers a specimen of skillful flattery. The contra-
factual subjunctives "mochten" and "chunden" are part of a conditional
utterance the protasis of which is contained in the phrase "in lateinischer
sprach": the translator is musing in the abstract about what would happen
if his reader were to seek the valuable *ler* in Latin books, and not, as it
might at first appear, describing the actual use of such books.

Even if it had been the intention of the translator to provide an
easily understood gloss on the Latin texts, the lemmata would have been
of virtually no use to the project. The lemmata offer access only to the
Latin verse fables of Avian and the Anonymus, while the promised *ler*,
the unique feature of the Latin sources that prompted their selection for
translation, is to be found not in the morals of those authors, but in the
moralizations of their commentators. In effect, the lemmata in the Nuremberg Aesop refer to the wrong texts, to the untranslated fables rather
than to the translated commentaries, and can therefore play no practical
role in the realization of the translator's program.[30] They instead serve

---

[28] MacMahon, " 'Das puech von der ordnung der fuersten'," 55.

[29] Grubmüller, *Nürnberger Prosa-Äsop*, 1.

[30] That the lemmata were not meant as a reference tool is clear too from the state of
their transmission in the German text: they are completely omitted twice, and thirty of the
remaining sixty-one differ significantly from the Latin sources they claim to cite. For examples and a brief discussion, see Wright, "The 'Nuremberg' Aesop," 60–61.

a purpose less practical but no less important: they transfer some of that special authority invested in the Latin verse fable texts to their German translation.

This phenomenon can be observed in other late medieval translations as well, where the fossilized Latin lemmata function simply as markers of legitimacy; it is not necessary to understand them, or even to decipher them, for the lemmata to create their vague but significant aura of authority.[31] The translator of the German *Belial*, for example, retains his source's arcane and heavily abbreviated citations to Latin decretals even though, as he admits, they can be of no use to the reader of the vernacular text; the translator

> hat das getan, nicht darvmb das dy ainvaltigen dy maynung vnd den syn mochten dester pas versteen, nür durch das dy gelerten mochten erkennen daz er dicz püch aüs den rechtpuecheren hiet gezogen![32]

The translator goes on rather testily to suggest that those unwilling to believe him might just as well have used the Latin original in the first place.

Lemmata are similarly used in the German-language religious works associated with the same Vienna School responsible for the Aesop. Johann Bischoff, for example, a Minorite Friar writing at the end of the fourteenth century, uses Latin catchwords to introduce the biblical and patristic quotations in his German *Evangelarium*;[33] in the hands of a preacher, these citations would have been of obvious utility, but here, in a translation dedicated to the spiritual edification of a layman, they are used exclusively to invoke authority. Likewise, the Latin cross-references scattered through Nikolaus von Dinkelsbühl's German tractates were no doubt originally of real use to the scholar and his amanuenses; a mid-fifteenth-century copy, however, explains them as simple assurances of the vernacular text's orthodoxy: as the younger manuscript's anxious compiler notes, the lemmata have been preserved not for the philo-

---

[31] Compare Barbara Weinmayer, *Studien zur Gebrauchssituation früher deutscher Druckprosa*, Münchener Texte und Untersuchungen 77 (Munich: Artemis, 1982), 58.

[32] Quoted in Norbert Ott, *Rechtspraxis und Heilsgeschichte: Zu Überlieferung, Ikonographie und Gebrauchssituation des deutschen 'Belial'*, Münchener Texte und Untersuchungen 90 (Munich: Artemis, 1983), 36, n.17.

[33] See James M. Clark, "Johann Bischoff's Prologue," *English Historical Review* 47 (1932): 454–461; and Hohmann, *'Unterscheidung'*, 270–271.

logical convenience of the learned reader, but rather in order that no one doubt that the content of the vernacular works was

alles genomen aus bewärten puechern.[34]

Immediately following the lemma, the German Aesop's invocation of authority and prestige continues in the first sentence of each fable. Just as in the Latin commentaries, these introductions consist of a deictic formula,

Hie lert uns der meister ... ,

followed by a statement of the fable's moral utility; particularly in its second section, the German Aesop occasionally amplifies these pro-myths into quite lengthy, nearly homiletic excursus—again, a phenomenon observable as well in several of the Latin commentaries discussed in Chapter 1 above. The promyths conclude with a formula introducing the fable narrative itself,

und daz beweist er also,

or

und daz beweist er mit einem bispel.

In six of the German fables, the master's demonstration of wisdom is performed directly on the figures of the narrative; the fable's moral is based "an einem ritter" (no. 10) or "an einer chroten" (no. 3), in the same way as the Latin tradition lets the fabulist argue either "per fabulam" or "per cornicem."

The headmatter of the Latin commentaries—lemma, promyth, and transitional formula—plays the rhetorical role of introducing the narrative and summarizing its lesson. The first lines of each of the German fables have a similar structural significance, leading the reader gradually from the orientation provided in the lemma into the text itself. In the German Aesop, however, these elements are linguistically complex; in proceeding from lemma to promyth to text, the reader of the fable moves as well from Latin to the vernacular, a passage that each time recapitulates the act of translation responsible for the German text.

The promyths of the prose fable play a literally pivotal role in this

---

[34] Quoted in Bernhard Schnell, *Thomas Peuntners "Büchlein von der Liebhabung Gottes,"* Münchener Texte und Untersuchungen 81 (Munich: Artemis, 1984), 101.

process. They are situated in the vernacular text between the Latin lemma and the German prose retelling of the fable narrative; thus positioned, these anticipatory morals function at one and the same time as epimyths to the Latin verse fables encapsulated in the lemmata and as promyths to the vernacular retellings that follow them. Both fable versions—the Latin verse texts present as incipits, and the German prose to be read on the page—demonstrate the validity of a single, shared moral, and thus come to be seen as equivalent, with identical claims to the same stock of meaning and authority.

The stereotyped vocabulary of the German Aesop further highlights this transfer from Latin to vernacular authority. The "hie" with which the master's doctrine is introduced—adopted, of course, directly from the "hic" of the Latin commentaries—points to the original verse fable invoked by the lemma, while the concluding formula—"also," "mit einem pispel," echoing the commentaries' "per talem fabulam"—looks forward to the vernacular prose. As I have argued above, this rhetorical structure effects a displacement even in the Latin tradition between the primary verse texts and their prose annotations; in the Nuremberg Aesop, however, the introductions to the fables transfer a certain legitimacy from the antique to the modern, from verse to prose—and, most significantly, from Latin to the vernacular.

Like these formal elements, the German fables' spiritual epimyths are the immediate reflex of the translator's reliance on sources among the Latin commentaries; none of the sixty-odd allegories in the German collection is without a close parallel in one or the other of the commentary manuscripts discussed in Chapter 1. As described there, these spiritual explications served in the Latin prose tradition chiefly as a device for the demonstration of non-literal modes of interpretation; they were not meant in the first instance to communicate religious information, but rather to inspire the clever schoolboy to imitation of their form and technique. Welcome as their moral and dogmatic content must have been, it was likely only incidental to their real value as a stock of formal patterns offered for emulation.

In contrast, the translator of the Nuremberg Aesop presents the spiritual epimyths of his collection as exemplary not in form but in substance. Conspicuously and consistently introduced with the rubricated word "Gaistleich," they are a significant part of the Viennese translator's plan to provide "ler vnde waizzung," and are accordingly mentioned explicitly in the preface with which he introduces his work:

da uon ein yegleich mensch an sitten *gaistleich* vnd auch weltleich
wol mag gepezzert werden.[35]

It was the spiritual epimyths, with their biblical references and pronounced concentration on appropriate religious behavior, that attracted
the Viennese translator to his sources; their great significance to his project is apparent from his flagging enthusiasm in translating the second set
of fables, those from the Anonymus, where, as we have already seen, the
Latin commentary's explications dwindled in number and exuberance.

In the German Aesop, just as in its Latin sources, the spiritual epimyths are on occasion inconsistent with the moral sentences offered in
the fable's promyth. As the numerous examples in Chapter 1 showed,
Avian's fable of crow and pitcher, for example, functions in both the
verse fable and the promyths of the commentaries as a praise of ingenu-
ity; the point-for-point explications offered in the commentaries' epimyths, however, are as likely to take the clever bird *in malam partem*.
Precisely the same circumstance obtains in the German fable corresponding:

> Ingente. Hie beweist vns der maister, daz weizhait nüczer vnd
> löbleicher ist dann sterch, wand sich maniger offt vnd dickh mit
> weishait nert vnd sein leben frist, der sich weder mit sterch noch
> mit gut gefristen mag. Vnd daz beweist er also mit einem bispel.
> . . .[36] Gaistleich pey dem nachtraben mag man versten die haim-
> leichen, vnerbern weib, wand die selben nicht vil sterch dez leibs
> an in haben, yedoch mit irer weizhait vnd mit iren suezzen wör-
> ten vberchomen sew mangen starchen man, dez sew so gar gewal-
> tig werden, daz er in in chainen wegen wider sten mag.

The misogynous epimyth is common in the Latin commentary tradition, where it contrasts no less than here with the thoroughly positive
evaluation of the crow's behavior given in the promyth. Contradictions
of this sort were in the Latin tradition only a minor convenience, frequently reduced by the physical presence on the same manuscript folio
of both Avian's verse original and its prose derivative. For the German
translator, on the other hand, such tensions presented an eagerly seized

---

[35] Emphasis added.
[36] The prose retelling that follows has as its source one of the Avian commentaries
drawing on natural historical material; see the full text in Grubmüller, *Nürnberger Prosa-
Äsop*, 47, and the discussion in Wright, "The 'Nuremberg' Aesop," 269–275.

opportunity. The spiritual explications loosed the bond between the Latin verses and their commentaries, creating a new potential for independence in the Latin prose. The Viennese translator recognized this potential and realized it in his own work, creating a fable collection to be read and profited from without recourse to the primary Latin texts of Avian and the Anonymus Neveleti. The Latin spiritual epimyths in the commentaries were both the element that drew the vernacular fabulist to his presumed sources and the factor that rendered them susceptible to translation as a self-contained work.

Ultimately, the spiritual explications in the Nuremberg Aesop make a more ambitious claim even than that pressed in the head-matter of the individual fables. Where the progression from Latin lemma to vernacular narrative proclaims the substantial equivalence of the Latin verse fables and their remote German prose reflexes, the epimyths—conspicuously rubricated and full of religious material—invoke an authority that, because it is *gaistleich,* in fact outweighs the merely pagan legitimacy invoked by the lemmata.[37] By virtue of the superior "ler" it offers, the vernacular text participates in a new, Christianizing tradition, and asserts its own primacy over the Latin verse tradition it no longer merely comments but supplants.

Impressive as the Viennese translator's efforts are to assign new functions to the elements retained from the Latin academic tradition, the fact remains that the Nuremberg Aesop was by no measure a success. Transmitted in a single manuscript, and with no indication that it was ever intensively read by anyone before Lessing,[38] this first prose fable collection in German appears to have had no influence on the further development of the genre. As I have discussed elsewhere,[39] occasional similarities and overlaps can be observed with the texts presented in other fifteenth-century collections, but they are without exception explainable as due to a common reliance on academic Latin commentaries on Avian and the Anonymus.

The evident failure of the Nuremberg Aesop to inspire other German fabulists, and indeed even to reach readers outside the restricted circles for which it was originally composed, is due to its translator's inability to complete the process of vernacularization he had so promis-

---

[37] Recall that the German collection's preface identifies both Latin poets as "hoch haidnische maister."

[38] See Wright, "The 'Nuremberg' Aesop," 4–5, 35, 310–311.

[39] See Wright, "The 'Nuremberg' Aesop," 311–315.

ingly begun at the purely linguistic and structural level. The prose of the Nuremberg Aesop is fluent and comprehensible, among the very best specimens of *gemein deutsch* produced by the Vienna School; and, as discussed above, the translator was able to transform the programmatic retention of his Latin source's strict formal organization into a powerful assertion of the vernacular text's integrity and independence.

Effective vernacularization, however, requires a further adaptation of the translated material to the needs and interests of its intended readers. The German Aesop, however, for all its high moral intention, fails to offer meaningful instructions for the vernacular use of material that, in its original form, served specifically Latin purposes. The sources of the Nuremberg Aesop were written to help the beginning scholar overcome the initial barriers of language by substituting for the rhetorical complexity of Latin verse a more readily understandable Latin prose; at the same time, the additional material supplied by the prose commentary played a valuable exemplary role in demonstrating a variety of exegetic methods for future preachers and scholars. Both of these functions are rendered irrelevant on the translation of the prose texts into German. A vernacular text was obviously ill-suited to the teaching of Latin, and as an exposition of interpretive technique, it would have been unnecessary to those most likely to profit from it, who, themselves fully literate, would naturally have consulted Latin works for guidance.

To replace those now-lost academic functions, the translator of the Viennese Aesop claims for his work a new utility, the improvement and edification of

ein yegleich mensch an sitten gaistleich,

relying on the power of the Latin commentaries' moralized epimyths and biblical quotations to provide spiritual uplift to the readers of the German fables. Those elements, however edifying, proved an insufficient base for the reorientation of the vernacular text. Introduced into the Latin commentaries for reasons strictly pedagogic, such material remained in most cases—including the sources chosen by the translator of the Nuremberg Aesop—merely supplementary; the tendencies of the epimyths range widely from fable to fable, with no effort to subordinate them to any cohesive thematic organization. This lack of substantive coherence was easily excusable in a Latin commentary, where what mattered was less the content than the consistent form and logic of the allegories; but the absence of internal structure was fatal to a vernacular work having the stated goal of communicating religious doctrine. The

Viennese translator's faithfulness to his source prohibited the systematization of the Latin "ler," by gathering together, for example, those epimyths treating greed, or those with allegories based in New Testament history. Unable to perform the traditional functions of its Latin source and at the same time inadequate to the didactic intentions of its translator, the German Aesop was the victim of a process of vernacularization that remained only partial.

An instructive comparison is provided by the fate of a nearly contemporary product of Austrian translation, Ulrich von Pottenstein's *Cyrillus*. Composed between 1406 and 1409, Pottenstein's translation, like the Aesop, shows all the hallmarks of Vienna School prose: a primary audience firmly situated among the court nobility, a marked attention to details of style and presentation, and an explicitly stated interest in the edification, spiritual and practical, of the reader. Unlike the translator of the Nuremberg Aesop, Pottenstein's German in the *Cyrillus* is a prime example of the stiffly elegant, Latinizing language known as *eigen deutsch*; and yet his collection was exceptionally successful. It is preserved today in no fewer than nineteen fifteenth-century manuscripts, and was even the subject of an incunable edition from the press of the Augsburg printer Anton Sorg; individual texts from that printing can be traced further into the exemplum repertoire of the sixteenth century. Although both the provenance and the scribal dialect of the surviving manuscripts suggest a reception concentrated in Lower Austria, there is one copy in which Pottenstein's Austro-Bavarian text has been further translated into a Middle German dialect, providing solid evidence for the work's influence outside the city in which it was produced.

The reason for the greater success of Pottenstein's fable book seems, paradoxically, to be precisely the reason for the failure of the Nuremberg Aesop to attract a wider contemporary audience: both take the Vienna School's programmatic insistence on formal fidelity to their Latin sources to an extreme. In the case of the Aesopic collection, as we have seen, that faithfulness, the translator's adherence to a standard of accuracy requiring the virtual replication of his source, required the importation into the vernacular of formal aspects—particularly the spiritual allegories—whose primary functions had been specifically Latin; the principle of fidelity prohibited the attempt at their replacement, modification, or re-ordering so as to serve new functions more immediately apposite to the lay reader's interest in practical didactic content.

Pottenstein's German *Cyrillus* preserves the specifically Latin elements of its source with equal eagerness. Each of the German texts is headed, just as in the Latin original, with a chapter number and a brief promyth specifying its application against a given species of sin. By retaining these scholarly gestures, Pottenstein produces a German text that, but for its language, is indistinguishable on the manuscript page from its Latin counterpart.

In the case of this work, however, and in the case of those other Vienna School works whose manuscript tradition is similarly broad, the translator was fortunate or far-sighted enough to have rendered a Latin source itself composed with practical edification as its primary goal and whose original intentions thus overlapped substantially with the needs of the lay reader, requiring no further modification or expansion. The plain focus of the Latin *Cyrillus* on virtue and vice, and its clear structural organization along a scheme based on the cardinal virtues and their opposites,[40] remained relevant even after its translation into the vernacular; the gestures retained in the translated text could play a similar, and similarly important, role for the reader of the vernacular collection. The same good fortune benefited the translator of the most abundantly preserved Vienna School translation, Heinrich von Langenstein's *Erkenntnis der Sünde*, whose Latin source was likewise a compilation of materials carefully selected and sensibly arranged for the practical applicability to the life of the soul.

II

From the modern perspective, prose seems so natural a medium of narration and report that we forget at times that it even has a history. In fact, though, the completeness with which verse forms have been banished to children's books and greeting cards is both recent and hard-won; the triumph of prose, in hindsight so inevitable, is, in reality, the result of a gradual and halting process not concluded until well into the modern period.

Thus, the verse fable survived, even in Vienna, well after the first translation of an Aesopic collection in prose. Writing in part in that city nearly a half century after the composition of the Nuremberg Aesop, the professional court poet Michael Beheim included in his massive literary production a number of animal fables in strophic verse.[41]

Uniquely in the history of the German vernacular fable of the fif-

---

[40] See Elschenbroich, *Die deutsche und lateinische Fabel*, 2: 24–25.
[41] See Grubmüller, *Meister Esopus*, 426–433.

teenth century, Beheim does not limit himself to the retelling of stories from precisely identifiable sources; he instead affords himself considerable liberty in combining traditional Aesopic matter with elements and situations drawn from related genres or even newly invented.[42] It is thus not possible, as it was in the case of the Nuremberg Aesop or in the case of the earlier verse collections treated in Chapters 2 and 3, to point to specific textual echoes from the Latin prose commentaries in Beheim's German fables. Yet even here, the more general influence of that learned tradition can be discerned. Where in the Nuremberg Aesop such influence proved ultimately restrictive and was in large part responsible for the German text's failure, Beheim's reliance on patterns adopted from the commentaries had precisely the opposite effect, freeing him from the obligation to adhere strictly to the expectations of the Aesopic canon, and making of him in a new sense a vernacular fabulist.

Michael Beheim's professional activity as court poet extended from the 1440s to the 1460s, with more than half of that time spent at the ducal court in Vienna.[43] Serving as entertainer, journalist, and would-be moral conscience, Beheim had recourse in some thirty-two of his poems to fable material; in this, he continues the tradition of his *Spruchdichter* predecessors from Spervogel to Heinrich von Mügeln, who found in the Aesopic fable a ready instrument for political, religious, and aesthetic comment.[44] Beheim himself in his fables treats critically a wide variety of matters, particularly, as Grubmüller notes, the position and behavior of nobles, clerics, and poets at court.[45]

To make the application of his fables clear, Beheim uses in many of his verse epimyths the technique of allegorical equation widespread and most familiar in the Latin fable commentaries. Where in the commentaries, and in the German reflexes thus far discussed, this mode of interpretation is used chiefly to apply the fable's narrative to ethical or spiritual situations, Beheim, in keeping with his professional responsibilities, focuses rather on the political.

To all appearances, Beheim found his inspiration for such allegorical explications in the Latin tradition, and not, as one might reasonably

---

[42] Grubmüller, *Meister Esopus*, 426.

[43] Beheim's biography is sketched in Ingeborg Spriewald, *Literatur zwischen Hören und Lesen: Fallstudien zu Beheim, Folz und Sachs* (Berlin: Aufbau, 1990), 10–16.

[44] Still useful is Paul Sparmberg, "Zur Geschichte der Fabel in der mittelhochdeutschen Spruchdichtung" (Ph.D. diss., Universität Marburg, 1918).

[45] *Meister Esopus*, 426–428.

expect, the German-language Nuremberg Aesop.[46] In spite of the fact that the single known manuscript of that vernacular collection was most likely still in Vienna during Beheim's tenure at the ducal court,[47] a comparison of the poet's fables with their nearest counterparts in the Nuremberg Aesop reveals none of the close textual reminiscences so abundant in Beheim's versifications of other prose works from the Vienna School.[48] Whereas there is no evidence of any vernacular intertextuality in the strophic fables, Beheim's song number 318, "ain exempel von ainem wolff und ainem lemplein," is particularly suggestive of an affinity to the Latin commentary tradition. The strophic version of the Anonymus Neveleti's fable of wolf and lamb[49] is one of the few in which the German poet reproduces more or less closely a text from the canonical Latin collections. Beheim's version[50] follows the verses of the Anonymus quite closely, with a number of specific echoes of that Latin collection. On noticing the lamb drinking downstream, the wolf

> ... wart grimlichen taben,
> zum lemplin er da sprach:
> "Du trubest mir den bach. ...";[51]

these lines owe much to the Anonymus Neveleti's concise verses

> Hunc [namely, the lamb] timor inpugnat verba monente lupo:
> "Rupisti potumque michi riuique decorem."[52]

In several details, however, the German fable diverges from the text

---

[46] The likelihood—indeed, the near certainty—that Beheim's fables have Latin antecedents requires revision to the generally accepted notion that the sources of his *Sprüche* were exclusively German (see, for example, Spriewald, *Literatur*, 44).

[47] Compare Thomas Hohmann, "Deutsche Texte aus der 'Wiener Schule' als Quelle für Michael Beheims religiöse Gedichte," *Zeitschrift für deutsches Altertum* 107 (1978): 319–330, here 330, on Beheim's likely access to Vienna School texts at the Viennese court.

[48] For examples, see Hohmann, "Deutsche Texte," 330. All of the similarities observable between the Nuremberg Aesop and the fables of Michael Beheim can be attributed to their independent use of similar Latin sources. Compare, for example, the fox's flattery of the crow in Beheim 276 to that recounted in Nuremberg Aesop 52; the epimyth of Beheim 314 to the promyth of Nuremberg Aesop 14; the reproach of the older crab in Beheim 316 and Nuremberg Aesop 3; and Beheim's fable 320 to Nuremberg Aesop 40.

[49] Elschenbroich, " 'von unrechtem gewalte'," does not treat the version of the fable by Beheim.

[50] Hans Gille and Ingeborg Spriewald, eds., *Die Gedichte des Michel Beheim*, vol. 2, Deutsche Texte des Mittelalters 64 (Berlin: Akademie-Verlag, 1970), 637–639.

[51] Gille and Spriewald, *Gedichte*, 638, lines 13–15.

[52] Wright, *The Fables of 'Walter of England'*, 26.

provided by the Anonymus, suggesting that the vernacular poet had before him a manuscript in which the verse fables were accompanied by a prose commentary, itself based closely on the Latin verses. Where the Anonymus's lamb protests that he is not yet six months old,[53] the age of the innocent varies in the commentaries;[54] Beheim lets his lamb claim

> ". . . ich pei zwainczig jaren
> waz da noch ungeboren,
> ich pin nit aines alt!"[55]

I have encountered no identical passage in the Latin manuscripts, but this is the sort of variation one would expect from the school commentaries. Likewise, the lamb's straightforward protest,

> "daz trüb rint ab auff mich,
> nit wider auff an dich.
> waz mahtu dann gesagen?
> mir tet vil nater klagen,
> wann ich hie unden stand!"

recalls more closely passages in certain of the commentaries than the quite abstract verses of the Anonymus Neveleti themselves, in which the lamb first describes the law of gravity and then denies that the water has been sullied at all:

> ". . . vnda supremi
> Nescit iter. Nec adhuc vnda nitore caret."[56]

Many commentaries expand these verses in ways rather more similar to Beheim's text:

> "quomodo potest hoc fieri, cum non a me ad te fluat aqua sed a te ad me?"[57]

A Stuttgart manuscript adds the detail, present as well in Beheim's fable, of the wolf's slobbering into the water:

---

[53] Wright, *The Fables of 'Walter of England'*, 26.
[54] Compare Vatican, lat. ottob. cod. 2879, and Wolfenbüttel, cod. 81.16. Aug. 2o.
[55] Gille and Spriewald, *Gedichte*, 639, lines 44–46.
[56] Wright, *The Fables of 'Walter of England'*, 27.
[57] Munich, Bayerische Staatsbibliothek, clm 609, fol. 2r.

"Sed saliua tua [illegible] tu pocius poteris potum meum maculare quia de immo ab alto."[58]

Beheim gives his fable an allegorical explication:

Der wolff geleicht den hern
die mit gewalt an rechte
vil schmachait, schand und schmechte
den unschuldigen tan.
Da hor ich klagen van
auff erd so vil der armen,
daz es wol got erparmen
in seinem himel salt.[59]

Similar allegories occur in the Latin commentaries:

Per lupum intelliguntur oppressores siue calumniatores, per agnum vero innocens.[60]

Beheim's apparent close textual borrowing in this fable is exceptional; it is rather the form than the substance of any given allegorical commentary that proved productive in his composition of new fables.[61] Recognizing the flexibility and power of the "fremde glos"[62] preferred in the explications of the Latin commentaries, Beheim was inspired to work "backwards" from the desired allegorical intepretation, sketching first the political or social situation to be figured in the fable, then assigning to each actor in the real-world situation an animal role: Beheim's allegorical correspondences rely largely on patterns and motifs from the Latin tradition, and so, predictably, princes become lions, devils are made into foxes, and malicious gossips are given, if not tar, then at least feathers.[63]

Given the stereotyped nature—in both senses of the word—of the Aesopic fable, however, all of these animal fgures bring with them a burden of traditional associations, and Beheim's vernacular fables are

---

[58] Stuttgart, Württembergische Landesbibliothek, cod. HB.I.127, fol. 138v.
[59] Gille and Spriewald, *Gedichte*, 639, lines 57–64.
[60] Stuttgart, Württembergische Landesbibliothek, cod. HB XII.4o, fol. 300v.
[61] Compare Grubmüller, *Meister Esopus*, 429: "Beheims Beitrag zur geistlichen Überformung der Fabel im 15. Jahrhundert liegt in der Verbreitung dieser formalen Errungenschaft, nicht etwa in einer inhaltlich-thematischen Betonung des geistlichen Lehrbereichs."
[62] Fable 315, "Hie horent fremde glos!"
[63] Fable 276; quoted also by Grubmüller, *Meister Esopus*, 426.

eventually built upon an innovative combination of allusions and episodes from the most familiar fables associated with each of the constructed allegories' animals; the fable becomes an "Arrangement der
Details zum Zwecke ihrer Auslegbarkeit,"[64] and the story, which represents nothing more than a secondary epic elaboration of narrative
impulses already present in the allegories, is clearly subordinated, both
in order of composition and in importance, to its explication. At the
same time, however, Beheim as narrator enjoys and exploits a creative
freedom hitherto denied the vernacular fabulist, and his fables—thanks,
paradoxically, to their dependence on interpretive modes originally
Latin and academic—attain an independence unprecedented in the history of the medieval German fable.

It is not unusual that Beheim's verse fables have their most important predecessors in a Latin prose tradition. In fact, more than half of his
tremendous output of *Spruchdichtung* represents the versification, usually
with but little modification, of sources originally in German or Latin
prose.[65] In many of the *Sprüche*, particularly those based on catechetic
texts composed by members of the Vienna School, Beheim's prose
exemplar shines clearly through his verse reworking; his verse redaction,
for example, of Langenstein's *Erkenntnis* more than justifies Ingeborg
Spriewald's assessment of the work as a species of "verwandelte
Prosa,"[66] a compromise between the demand of his audience for new,
"prosaic" material and its simultaneous expectation that that material be
presented in the more traditional and more familiar form of singable
verse.[67]

Spriewald, basing her arguments on the source relationships discovered by Wachinger and Hohmann, identifies in Beheim's versifications
of prose sources the

---

[64] Grubmüller, *Meister Esopus*, 428 (without indication of what is to my mind the indispensable contribution to this freedom made by Beheim's awareness of the Latin commentary tradition).

[65] See Burghart Wachinger, "Michel Beheim: Prosabuchquelle—Liedvortrag—Buchüberlieferung," in *Poesie und Gebrauchsliteratur im deutschen Mittelalter*, ed. Volker Honemann
et al., Würzburger Colloquium 1978 (Tübingen: Niemyer, 1979), 37–75, here 67–68. Compare Spriewald, *Literatur*, 43.

[66] Spriewald, *Literatur*, 43 (and note 58). On Beheim's versification of Vienna School
prose, see Hohmann, "Deutsche Texte." As discussed above, the Nuremberg Aesop was
almost certainly not among the Viennese texts Beheim exploited; see also Wright, "The
'Nuremberg' Aesop," 313–314.

[67] See Spriewald, *Literatur*, 41, 53–55.

Versuch, *Prosa hörbar zu machen*, durch den Vortrag "singens-
weis" zum Anhören zu bringen, was nicht jeder aus dem Publi-
kum am Hof selbst lesen konnte.[68]

This hypothesis, plausible as it may be for others of Beheim's songs,
does not provide an adequate explanation for the poet's use of strophic
forms in the presentation of his fables. First, as Spriewald herself argues,[69] the Viennese court was throughout the fifteenth century an extremely literate environment, as most obviously witnessed by the production and intensive reception of Vienna School texts prepared explicitly for
the nobles in attendance there. The local preference for prose had already
extended, as we have seen, to the production of a German Aesop.

More significantly, the notion that the fable could be made more
easily "hörbar" through reworkings into strophic *Sprüche* fails to take
into account the fact that every vernacular fabulist could more easily
take advantage of the well-established alternative of the rhymed couplet,
a form with hugely successful precedent in Boner's collection and suited
at least as well as the *Spruch* to aural reception. Had effective orality
been Beheim's chief concern in the composition of his fables, he might
more likely have produced a second *Edelstein*.

A more satisfying explanation for Beheim's use of strophic verse forms
can be had by considering not the fables' reception at the Viennese
court, but rather Beheim's presentation of the texts in the manuscripts.
One notices first that the fables do not form a discrete unit within the
books transmitting them;[70] they are instead scattered, or integrated
into thematically organized song-cycles drawing on a variety of sources
and motifs. In their graphic presentation, the poems of Beheim's *Spruchdichtung* insist on their identity as a unified book; as Burghart Wachinger has observed, the gestures of performance are transformed in the
manuscripts into markers of bookish integrity, in the attempt

das Œuvre eines meisterlichen Sängers und Dichters in einer
Buchausgabe als Ganzes [zu] bewahren und dar[zu]stellen.[71]

---

[68] *Literatur*, 44 (emphasis in original); see also *Literatur*, 54: "er griff . . . auf Prosaschrift-
tum zurück, um es vortragsgerecht zu versifizieren."

[69] *Literatur*, 45–48.

[70] This is in contrast to the situation in the manuscripts of Heinrich von Mügeln's
Spruchdichtung, which effect both a formal and a thematic concentration in their grouping
of songs based in Aesopic sources. Compare Grubmüller, *Meister Esopus*, 280 ff.

[71] Wachinger, "Beheim," 48.

Even the traditional articulation of the manuscripts according to *Ton*—metric patterns permitting the association of verses to appropriate melodies—serves here to generate textual units for reading, not for singing.[72]

Beheim's composition of strophic fables can be explained quite simply as the poet's effort to maintain the uniform presentation of his life's work, fitting a variety of texts reliant on widely different sources into a single prosodic framework. In transforming the patterns of Latin prose into German verse, he likewise asserts his own identity as *meister*, highlighting the skill required to make of academic convention vernacular creativity.

---

[72] Wachinger, "Beheim," 48.

Concluding Comment

The European literature of the later Middle Ages is characterized by two developments: the growing confidence and authority of texts written in one of the national languages, and—apparently, but not in fact, paradoxically—an increasing rather than decreasing reliance in those texts on formal and rhetorical models developed for learned Latin literature. The literary enterprise of the fourteenth and fifteenth centuries became vernacular only by becoming more Latin, by adapting learned forms to a new, semi-literate readership.

The Latin models of the new vernacular, however, were written and structured with specific goals and reception situations in mind. It was the task of the translator, therefore, to remove the formal structures of the learned exemplar, to replace them, or to retain them and to assign them new functions. If translation can be understood in the first instance at a level merely lexical, this more involved process, "vernacularization," necessarily reaches into the content and ordering of the texts it confronts. This process has several steps, most of which are carried out simultaneously. To the extent that they hinder the vernacular reader's effective use of the text, the elements of its original Latin reception situation must be removed; what remains, then, must be either replaced with an entirely new framework for reception, or it must be preserved in such a way that it can play new, distinctively "vernacular" roles in the translated text.

The Aesopic fable is an ideal genre for the investigation of these phenomena. Fable collections were produced in great abundance in the late Middle Ages; on the Latin side, the texts were often bound with particular strictness to reception expectations created by the fable's use in the schools, where it was pressed into service not only for its moral utility but, equally or even more so, for its aptness to the teaching of "grammar." The linguistic sophistication of the texts of the educational enterprise, and their graphic presentation in the late-medieval school manuscripts, were both largely determined by the practical needs of the schoolmasters and their young pupils; precisely those pedagogical features, however, were most alien to the needs and expectations of a vernacular audience.

To overcome the pronounced Latinity of their schoolbook sources, the vernacular fabulists of the late Middle Ages had recourse, paradoxically, to one of the most distinctive features of late medieval hermeneutic practice, academic commentary. As I hope to have shown, the prose commentaries on the fables of Avian and the Anonymus Neveleti were in effect an intermediate literary form between the Latin and the vernacular, offering both a linguistic simplification of the difficult verse texts and, most importantly, room for intellectual maneuver in the interpretation of texts whose meaning is otherwise, per generic convention, fixed in an authoritative epimyth. The commentaries provided an opportunity to "moralize" the fable, to reconcile the fable with the Christian morality of the lay reader, to give individual texts new functions within collections.

For all its advantages, however, commentary as a genre is burdened more than most by its strict formal consistency, necessary in the Latin tradition for the orderly and systematic explication of texts otherwise excessively challenging for the youngest pupils in the cloister schools. The vernacular fabulists of the late Middle Ages dealt with that formal strictness in a variety of ways, taking advantage of it to give their collections structural integrity, exploiting it to establish their own authority as poets—and at times relying on it to their own detriment.

The foregoing investigation has sought to ask two questions: what use did the vernacular German fabulists of the fourteenth and fifteenth centuries make of academic prose sources? And how, in using those sources, did they overcome their traditional Latinity? How, in other words, does the process of vernacularization take advantage of the specifically Latin elements of its sources? On the example of five German fable collections and their late medieval reception, I have sought to show that those questions can be asked, and to some extent answered, profitably in connection with one minor genre; it seems clear already, however, that similar impulses and similar processes were at work in the broader development of vernacular literature at the close of the Middle Ages.

Translations of Medieval Texts Cited

This appendix provides translations of all texts cited in Latin or medieval languages, with the exception of lemmata and brief excerpts in my footnotes; I identify each text by page number and incipit.

Readers with highly developed aesthetic sensibilities will find the translations at times awkward; in this, however, they remain true to the Latin originals, which are themselves characterized by an inelegance that at time verges on ungrammaticality.

Introduction

ix. *Cogitanti mihi* ... I had often wondered if I could properly dedicate this work of mine to the Holy Father; and while I was worrying that it might be rejected as unworthy, there appeared to me one night in a dream the fabulist Avianus, handsome in appearance and well dressed. He began to admonish me in a kind manner and to reassure me, saying, "Why is your resolve fading with needless fear? Do as I say: for just as I offered my simple and unadorned fables to so great an emperor as Theodosius, so you too should not hesitate to offer yours, properly explicated allegorically, to Urban V, the highest spiritual leader, who is the protector of all spiritual meanings."

xv, n.19. *Secundum autem* ... According to some commentators, the efficient cause of this book was Walter, who composed this book but, contracting leprosy, did not dare to give it his own name.

Et nota ... And note that Aesop is not the name of the book's author, but some claim that Master Walther composed it; but when he had contracted leprosy, he did not want to name it with his own name lest his book be scorned by its readers.

xxi. *Illi dubiis* ... They added their interpretations to uncertain passages, poured light into the obscure verses, and added glosses everywhere; and in order to demonstrate their skill and their cleverness to their curly-haired audience, they applied their powers to the same story that they explained to the schoolboys, as if in competition with the ancient authors. And they did not hesitate to add their own fantastic creations to the works of the poets and to the authentic verses. Everyone knows that the pupils tended to mar their books with such annotations and interpretations—whether accurate or inaccurate, fitting or not as a result of laxness or ignorance.

xxiv. *Ut iuuet* ... This book intends to help and to be of use: serious images please more sweetly when mixed with wit. This garden bears fruit and flower, and both find favor: the fruit tastes good, the flower is lovely. If the fruit pleases you more than the flower, pick the fruit. If the flower pleases more than the fruit, pick the flower. If both please, pick both. In order that inactivity not dull my lazy mind, my intention is to write this book, which keeps me alert. In order that a fruitful crop grow up out of this mean field, O God, moisten these dry words with your dew. The slightness of these words bears a worthy weight, and the dry shell conceals a good kernel.

Nota per ... Note that we should understand in the "garden" this book. And in the fruit and the favor, we should understand the moral of the fable, and in the flower, we should understand the story.

Chapter 1

4. *Interdum id* ... Sometimes that which you cannot accomplish by force, you accomplish by wisdom and consideration.

7. *visum per* ... [A raven] was seen because of his thirst gathering stones into the vase of a monument, in which some rain water had collected, but which the bird could not reach; and so fearing to go down into the urn, it was seen to have pushed the water out with such a number of stones as were necessary for it to drink.

7, n.13. *Cornix sitiens* ... A thirsty crow came to a bucket and tried to tip it over. But because it stood firm, the crow could not spill it. But it gained with this strategy what it wanted: it placed pebbles into the bucket, and their number forced the water up from the bottom, and thus the crow assuaged its thirst. And so wisdom defeats strength.

8. *De cornice* ... A thirsty crow had spied a large vase, which held a little water in the bottom. It tried for a long time to spill it onto the ground, so that it might quench its great thirst with it; after its strength had failed to help, annoyed, the crow in unheard-of cleverness applied all its wits. For stones having been dropped in, the rising water provided an easy way to drink. This taught how much greater wisdom is than strength, with which the bird accomplished its task.

9. *Fabule sunt* ... Fables are to be heard, not imitated.

10. *Intentio huius* ... The intention of this author is to instruct his listeners in the morality of good things.
    Ut perlecto ... In order that when we have read this book, we are able to persist in good works.
    Contra vicium ... Moral philosophy was developed as a remedy to viciousness, and it includes in itself literature.

11. *Rustica deflentem* ... A farmwife once promised her crying child that unless he be quiet, he would be food for the ravenous wolf.
    Est ibi ... Here one tense is used for another tense.
    Pro informacione ... for the edification of pupils and children and for the convenience of their teachers, so that they might learn their text that much more easily, both to give those verse texts for Latin and to read this short book, which children can learn easily who once despised the long books, namely Aesop and Avian, on account of their long-windedness.

12. *Opus. quasi* ... In other words: wisdom of the spirit is better than strength of the body.

13. *Indignata, id* ... Frustrated, that is to say, bearing frustration because it had not been able to reach the bottom of the water.
    bene dicit ... He says correctly that the crow applied its wits.
    lapillis. id ... That is to say, onto the stones.
    Cornix est ... The crow is snow if the heart is taken away from it.

15, n.35. *Ater olor* ... A black swan, a snow-white crow, black snow, and dry water: these things are found more quickly than a chaste beauty.
    Balnea cornici ... What can baths do for a crow or a prostitute?
    Instar enim ... On the model of the crow, women first remove our eyes, then they remove our brains, to the extent that the liquid matter shows.

18. *id est* ... That is to say, tricks, fraud, or wisdom.

20. *Notandum quod* ... It is to be remembered that many say that for

"depth of water" we use the neuter *fundum*, but for "field" we use the masculine *fundus*.

21. *Grecismus. Est* ... "Dolus" is a word of two meanings, it means wisdom or trickery.

23. *Ingentem. Hic* ... Here he teaches that cleverness is better than strength; and he teaches that through a quail [!], which, when it was thirsty, found an urn half-full of water in a field, and it could not tip the urn. But using its cleverness, it filled it with stones and drew out the water. The moral is this: The wise man is better than the strong.

24. *In hoc* ... In this fable Avianus teaches that wisdom is better than strength or might.

25. *in hoc* ... In this fable we learn that there are many things which can be done more quickly by skill than by strength.

26. *hic monet* ... Here he urges us that we be more eager to acquire knowledge than power, because it is more useful.

    Hic docet ... Here the author teaches that wisdom is to be preferred to strength and urges us that we strive for all knowledge and wisdom.

    Hortatur nos ... He encourages us to seek rather wisdom than strength, because with wisdom we can sometimes accomplish what we cannot with strength, and because what we cannot manage by strength we can bring to a conclusion with wisdom.

    Vnde: Homo ... Whence the saying: A man often conquers with knowledge those things that he could not do by force. This also urges us to rely more on wisdom and cleverness than on strength.

    in hoc ... In this fable the author teaches us that we should seek wisdom, saying, "You should know that wisdom is greater than strength and more valuable, because with knowledge a man can attain what he cannot with strength." He continues saying that wisdom accomplishes the task begun by anyone. Thus Solomon in the Proverbs: "Wisdom is stronger."

28. *Ingentem sitiens* ... Here the author demonstrates that wisdom is better and greater than strength. Thus he urges us quite eagerly that we know that we should seek wisdom, which he shows by saying: A thirsty crow, flying across a field, came to a well, above which it saw a bucket hanging in which there was a little water, which it could not pour out. Then, hoping to spill the vessel onto the ground, because the crow could not tip it, it nevertheless thought up a strategy in its cleverness; and gathering pebbles it dropped them into the bucket. When they had been put in, the water rose up, and thus the crow had an easy way to drink.

30. *cum staret* ... while it was standing around in some field.
Tandem collegit ... Finally it collected little stones and put them into the ditch.
32. *Nat canis* ... A dog swims carrying a piece of meat in its mouth. The meat casts a reflection. The reflection is resolved in the water. The dog paws at the water. It desires the hope of meat more than meat itself, the image of gain more than gain. It opens its mouth, and thus both meat and hope vanish. Thus certain things should not be abandoned for uncertainties. Whoever desires what is not his, will soon be without what is.
cuius umbram ... When it saw the reflection of the meat in the water, it believed it to be larger.
33. *Quadam die* ... One day a dog, carrying meat in its mouth, was swimming across a river. Seeing the reflection and the appearance of this meat, it thought the reflection of the real meat was greater in quantity and superior in taste to the meat itself. And so desiring the reflection of the meat, it lost the meat it held in its mouth and did not gain the reflection.
34. *Cornix sitibunda* ... A very thirsty crow came to a half-full bucket, which it tried to tip over in order to extract the water that would be spilled. When that was not possible because the bucket was so stable, the crow resorted to other ideas, and when the bucket was nearly full of pebbles industriously collected according to the bird's strength, the water came up over the stones, and thus the crow relieved its thirst. The moral: It is said that skill is stronger than physical might.
35. *ut si* ... If they find water in a low place, they collect pebbles and drop them into the water until the water rises.
36. *In hoc* ... In this fable the author teaches that cleverness is more useful than might and wisdom is more useful than exertion, and he seeks to prove this with the example of a raven ...
intendit probare ... He seeks to prove this with the example of a raven which, thirsty, found a vase in the bottom of which there was a little water, which it was unable to reach. The crow had tried to spill it onto the ground so that drinking from it it might reduce its thirst. Since the vase was heavy and quite sturdy, when it could not tip it, it cast stones into the bottom so that the water, rising above the stones, gave the crow a drink.
37. *De corvis* ... It is also said of ravens that if they should find water standing in a low place, where because of the shortness of their neck

they cannot reach it at all, right away they gather stones into the water.

ita descendere ... And fearing to go down into the urn they press the water upwards with as many stones as is required for them to drink. *Ingentem cornix* ... A crow was very thirsty, and pondering this, it found a vessel in the bottom of which there was a little water, so little that the crow could not drink from it, and it did not want to enter the vessel fearing that it might be captured. Then quickly it thought up a strategy and took stones in its mouth and tossed them into the vessel such that the water steadily rose, and came up to the top of the vessel, and the crow then drank at will without any danger or dread.

37, n.86. *Animi vires* ... The strength of the soul is finer than the power of the body.

38. *Quondam fuit* ... Once there was a crow that suffered great thirst, and as it would gladly have drunk, it flew to a well and found there by the well an urn which held a little water, so little that the crow could not drink from it. And sitting above the water it strove greatly to drink the water, and tried to spill the water onto the ground in order that it might drink it and relieve its great thirst. Since it could not spill the water by force so that it could drink from it, as the crow was too weak, then, frustrated, using wisdom and cleverness, it applied all its wits and tricks. Cleverly it gathered many stones and placed them into the urn and the water in the urn rose, and thus the crow drank quite easily.

39. *Vtilitas: Sapientia* ... The moral: Wisdom is greater than strength, because many things are accomplished by skill that cannot be done by strength. Whence the verse of Cato: "We flourish by considered action ..." And thus: It is better to be a wise man than strong. And thus at times it is better to use our skill than our strength.

39, n.88. *Sic cornix* ... Thus the crow raised the water by throwing in stones.

40. *Per cornicem* ... By the crow, which provided itself with a drink, we understand those who in time of urgency look out for themselves in the same way.

In hoc ... In this fable the author shows that sometimes wisdom is better than strength of the body, and that we should act rather with cleverness than with strength. And he shows this through a crow ...

In hoc ... In this fable we are taught that there are many things that are accomplished more quickly by skill than by strength, and this is demonstrated by the fable of the crow, about which we are told in this allegory: By the crow we understand wise people. For just as the crow acts wisely, since when it could not reach the water in the bottom of the urn, it wisely made the water rise by filling the urn with stones; thus too wise men conquer and vanquish their fear and concern, just as the crow conquered its thirst, with wisdom, discernment, and patience.

41. *Licet sicud* ... Just as the crow could not spill the urn, so no student can attain any knowledge he desires; but he can acquire a certain portion of knowledge if he throws in the stone, that is to say if he applies effort and diligence.

Versus ceu ... In the same way as the author writes verses, so the crow drinks by skill.

41, n.93. *Hic ponit* ... Here the author gives this fable: Once, a very thirsty crow saw an urn in which there was water standing in a field. Again and again it tried to spill it to extinguish its thirst, but it could not get the water out of the urn by force. And so it thought up this method: it took small stones to throw into the urn, and thus the water in the bottom of the urn rose up to the mouth of the urn. When this was done, the crow quenched its thirst with the water. In this fable the author demonstrates that astuteness and cleverness or wisdom are more useful than strength. For often we gain by wisdom what we cannot acquire by strength.

42. *sic ex* ... And so from a little water, much water arises.

Allegorice per ... Allegorically by the crow we understand the sinner, who is black as a raven with sins; by the water we understand Christ or baptism; and by the stone we understand confession and good works. For when the sinner desires to cease from sin, he can come to Christ only through confession, alms, and other good works.

Allegorice per ... Allegorically the sinner, blackened by sin, is understood in the raven. Thirsty, he comes to the fountain of faith and has little moisture, that is to say wisdom, in the urn of his heart; in other words, he should rely on the son of God and take up stones, that is to say the wounds of Christ, and drop them into his heart so that the water rises, that is to say that a tear of contrition rises up, namely to Christ; and when he drinks that angelic drink, namely the tear sent forth from his heart, he shall not thirst to eternity.

42, n.95. *Si autem* ... But if we should want to extend this series, we should repeat the narrative sentence, and support it with reasons and logical confirmation.

42, n.96. *Allegoria. Per* ... Allegoria: by the thirsty crow we understand the sinner, who desires to please God with his intelligence, through confession, sincere contrition, and penance.

43. *De ghestlike* ... The allegorical sense: Whoever yearns to drink of the source of inner redemption does not find it whenever he wants, but one must make such a source flow strong by great contemplation, and very often then it arises and overflows, with which one extinguishes the thirst of the soul and is cleansed of sin.

Allegorice per ... Allegorically the heart of man, which rests in the body as if in an urn, is understood by the water in the urn. By the crow the devil is understood, who places stones, that is to say wicked thoughts, in the human heart because of his deception and wiliness, so that he might drink the water, that is to say that he might distract the human heart from good works.

44. *Utilitas quod* ... The moral is that wisdom often is worth more than great strength. Allegorically two things are understood by the crow: in its color, the devil, whom we should flee; in the action of the crow, wisdom, and that we should strive for.

Allegoria: per ... By the crow, we understand the courtesan, who though she has little strength, nevertheless has wiles with which she is always eager to deceive her lovers.

45. *Heu michi* ... Alas, how little strength a woman has, but though she is weak, she nevertheless cleverly deceives.

Sicque improba ... And so the foul bird vanquishes stronger animals; and the wicked woman defeats strong men.

46. *ieiundano, vigilando* ... by fasting, watching, and praying he lights the torch, that is to say he finds the grace of the Holy Spirit, and frees his children, that is to say his good works, from the power of the devil.

semper laudat ... he always flatters a man and inflames him with pride.

48. *Vt perimeas* ... Do not let gold persuade you to kill anyone; for your tragic lapse will take away your honor and your life.

Moraliter per ... Morally you should understand by the Jew the faithful soul that fearing the attacks of the world goes to the king, that is to say to God, asking him for an escort. God gives him the cupbearer, that is to say the body given over to pleasures, and the body kills the soul, taking from it great riches. At length, however, at the banquet, that is to say at the day of judgment, the partridges,

that is to say the sins, reproach the body, and then the king con-
demns the body to the cross, that is to say to eternal punishment.

49. *Nil fidei* ... The spirit of a woman has no fidelity. She oppresses the
living with fear and the dead with pain.

Fallere vult ... She wants to deceive today in the manner in which
she deceived yesterday. If anyone loves Thais, he should believe that
it is his belongings, and not himself, that are loved. Thais has no
love, she loves the gifts of her lover.

Moraliter per ... Morally by the young man understand any man in
his youth. By the courtesan understand youth itself, which is un-
steady and inconstant and flatters a man thus: "You are young,
enjoy your youth in pleasure and delight. There are many years left
to you to live. And so not until you have grown old will you need
to turn to the religious life."

50. *Presens appollogus* ... The present fable teaches us not to place any
trust in inconstant and unchaste women or to devote love to them.
... Every man should draw back from the love of a woman, because
the courtesan loves not him but his possessions.

Pene perit ... Both sexes nearly died of fear.

Hic docet ... Here the author teaches us not to believe the words or
the tears of women.

Moraliter per ... Morally by the woman understand the good soul;
by the man, understand good works and the chaste body, which
death, that is to say the pleasure of the world, leads into mortal sin
as if to the grave. And when death has buried him in the vanities of
this world, the soul, lingering at the grave, weeps devoutly, and at
length the guardian of the thief, that is to say the angel of every
man, hearing the weeping, joins the soul, urging it with divine inspiration to leave the dead body given over to the vanities of the world.
And if then the woman hangs the body, dead in sin, onto the gal-
lows, removing its teeth in the remorse of its conscience, then the
angel takes the soul to its heavenly home.

51. *Haec sibi* ... Let whoever would believe in feminine faithfulness consider these verses written for him, and let him take care to remember
them in his mind.

Adam Samsonem ... A woman deceived Adam, Samson, king David,
and Solomon, and captured them with her wiles. If a woman sobs
when she is not suffering, then a woman's sweet love conquers all
things.

Per rusticam ... By the woman the church is understood, and by the wolf the devil. But by the weeping child, the sinner is understood; if he does not cease from his sins, the woman, his mother, that is to say holy mother church or the confessor representing holy mother church, threatens the child that she will give him to the wolf, that is to say to the devil, if he will not cease from his sins.

52. *Allegorice per* ... Allegorically by the woman the church should be understood; by the child, the weeping sinner; by the wolf, the devil. ... Ethically, however, this author urges us not to believe the words of a woman.

Ex quo ... Thus each fable ... has a double meaning, namely the tropological, that is to say moral, and allegorical, that is to say mystical.

53. *Ex predictis* ... From these things it is plain that the literary form of the fable which the author uses throughout his work belongs to the metaphoric mode.

Si enim ... And if youth is called spring and old age winter, this is a metaphor or transsumption. If we give this the form of an analogy, saying: "As spring is to the year, so is youth to the state," it should be called a simile.

Noticia presentis ... The idea of this book is for us having read the book through to understand the truth of the fables and as a result to persist in good works and to avoid vice.

ostendere veritatem ... to show the truth ... hidden beneath the veil of the fables and to instruct the listeners in the morality of good things.

54. *Nota quod* ... Note that the author in this present book treats two things, namely pleasure and profit. The pleasure is present in the fables, in the reading of which all those who listen find pleasure. But the profit consists in the fruit of the allegories and fables, which teach good morals and instruct us in virtue.

54, n.131. *delectat, scilicet* ... This book pleases the listener in respect to the fables themselves; and it is of profit to the listener in respect to the learning of its value and the mysteries of the allegories it contains.

57. *De se* ... The foolish man, betrayed by the flurry of the tongue, is cast down by his own fault, and such a storm washes away even strong men.

Pes aquile ... The eagle's foot: The fable is that an eagle, capturing a turtle, flew high into the clouds. The turtle, however, withdrawing into its shell, could not be hurt in any way. The eagle did not know how good its prey was; a crow met up with the eagle and said: "You are carrying excellent prey, but you will not gain anything from it by strength without wisdom." The crow gave the eagle this advice: "Fly high into the sky and look below you for a rocky place and drop what you are carrying, and then, when the shell has been broken, you can eat your food." And the eagle did this. Allegory: By the turtle we understand Lucifer; by the eagle, we understand pride, by which many fall to their doom; by the crow we understand the might of God. For Lucifer in his pride wanted to ascend into the north, which was against his nature, because a creature cannot be like its creator. When the wisdom of God saw this, it cast him down into hell.

60. *Allegoria. Per* ... Allegory: By the dog the greedy man is understood; by the meat the kingdom of heaven; by the reflection the transitory goods of this world; and by the river this world or the body of a man. Beware, therefore, that we do not lose the kingdom of heaven on account of the pleasures and transitory goods of this world for which we are so eager. The kingdom of heaven is certain and eternal, and was made ready for us from the beginning of the world.

61. *Proficit exemplis* ... The lesson of a teacher is effective when properly accompanied by examples; and so let the young man rely on the knowledge of his elder.

patres spirituales ... Spiritual fathers, namely preachers, who in reproaching sinners lead them from the path of iniquity and error, teaching them by the examples of the saints, so that they, in following those examples, cease from their sins and living justly and virtuously might come to deserve eternal blessedness.

62. *ne promittamus* ... We should not claim to want to help when we mean to harm, and in general the fable teaches us that we should consider carefully whom we believe.

De mure ... On the mouse wanting to swim across the pond and the frog coming to help it: We learn that we should not plan things harmful to the well-being of others and that we should not claim to want to help when we mean to harm.

De serpente ... On the serpent living in the farmer's house, whom the farmer wounded with an ax: We learn that we should not have faith in the faithless, and that we should always be wary of those who have once attempted to harm or damage us in our possessions, our body, or our dignity.

Rustica. Fabula ... The fable is thus: A serpent was accustomed to living in the house of a farmer who fed it. But after a short while the farmer began to hate the serpent. He wounded it with an ax, and then after a short while the farmer fell into poverty. He believed the serpent was the cause of his impoverishment, and suspecting that he would be wealthy again if the serpent forgave him the sin he had committed, he pleaded with the serpent, who said to him: "I forgive you completely, but until the wound to my back is closed and healed, I am not convinced that you will keep faith completely with me. I shall return to a state of peace with you when the ax, used in perfidy, is forgotten." Now I write these verses: "Prudent reader, consider whether you are safe; consider the one wounded suspect." Allegory: You who have offended against God, if you do penance, God forgives you, but all the same your sins are always in God's sight until you do satisfaction for them. And so by the serpent we should understand the devil, by the farmer a man who, when he sins, nourishes the devil in his breast with his sins. But when he confesses, he makes an effort to expel the devil from his house, that is to say from his heart, but the devil refuses to leave until the man, having taken on true penitence, kills him as if with an ax.

63. *Allegoria: Hic* ... Understand here that faith must be kept, for we have promised to serve God faithfully in complete devotion.

65. *Cornix autem* ... But the crow was right there and buried the shell in its own stomach.

66. *Titulus huius* ... The title of this book is "Here begin the Fables of Aesop." And the fable is a plain story of brute animals adapted for the instruction of men. And the wisdom of this book has nothing to do with allegories but rather with its moral meaning. It is included in the category of moral philosophy.

Autor wlt ... The author wants the moral of every fable to be contained in the two verses placed at the very end of each fable. ... The second reason that the master puts the morals in only two verses is this: Since the fables retold here are at times quite long, if the moral were similarly extensive, it would not be willingly or easily learned. And because of its brevity and the ease of remembering the end he places his meaning in the two verses.

67. *Recte. Primus* ... Properly: The first moral. Many innocent and poor people, and at times wealthy people, are oppressed because of bad advice. The second moral: A man less experienced or unable to do something should rely on one more learned than himself.

68. *Nam miserum* ... For, he says, it is dreadful to give up what booty you have, and quite foolish to hope for the fulfillment of promises to come.

Nec est ... But it is not inconsistent with our author to say that all worldly things should be abandoned in favor of heavenly things to come, for the author's statement is understood as pertaining to worldly things and not heavenly.

Ista fabula ... This fable can be explicated allegorically such that holy mother church is understood in the woman. By the child, sinners are understood; by the wolf, the devil, for just as the wolf lives from stolen prey and is very greedy in stealing, so the devil strives to capture the souls of sinners. And so the woman, that is to say holy mother church, threatens sinners, that is to say offers them threats, that she will give them to the wolf, that is to say to the devil, if they are not quiet, that is to say if the sinners do not leave off their sinning. And when the child, that is to say the sinner, falls silent, that is to say stops sinning, then the woman disappoints the wolf, that is to say the devil, because she does not give him the sinner.

69. *insatiabilis bestia* ... An insatiable beast, the downfall of man, a lovable harm, a despicable love, the offspring of lying, the source of strife, the shackles of men, a daily offense, a burden on life's path, and the cause of everything wicked.

Avianus prohemium ... Avian does not include a prologue.

In parte ... In the prologue he does four things. First he describes his intention, the material treated in the book, describing its goal and its usefulness. Second, he provides the cause for this compilation. Third, revealing himself to be a Christian, he prays for divine assistance. Fourth, he renders his audience attentive and willing.

secundum quosdam ... According to some, the second book begins here.

70. *iste liber* ... This book is divided into as many parts as there are fables or *apologi* contained in it.

autor iste ... this author does not observe the custom of other poets, as he neither propones nor invokes, but simply narrates.

71. *huius ergo* ... You know that Aesop is our model for this material.

Esopum actor ... This author follows Aesop in this work.

Causa efficiens ... The efficient cause of this book is double, namely the "moving" cause and the "moved." The moving cause was a certain Roman emperor named Theodosius, who, seeing that Avian was skilled in the poetic art, asked him to write him some fables in which he might find distraction. The moved cause was a citizen of Rome named Avian, who on being asked by the aforementioned emperor to compose an amusing book for him, is said to have written this book of fables.

72. *Erat autem* ... This work had been written in the Greek language and was not available in translation until Tiberius, the Roman emperor, asked the poet Aesop to write some amusing fables to distract him from his outside duties.

Notandum quod ... Note that when the study of philosophy was thriving in Rome, many students, hoping to proceed to the study of the liberal arts, were frequently led astray by love for a woman. Avian means to reproach them with this fable.

73. *Tum vidit* ... When he saw in his day how many scholars and other men were puffed up in pride and seeking to go beyond their own status, which is not good, as pride is the greatest impediment to these and to other scholars; since when they desire to climb higher, it often happens that they tumble in a more serious fall; and the author explains this with a turtle ...

Ex quo ... And thus when the author in his day saw how many people reproached others, but paid no attention to their own wicked deeds, he made this statement.

Appendix

75. *Sicut ex* ... As we learn from the statement of a wise man, fables are to be heard but not imitated. They are to be heard because in them the avoidance of wickedness and the pursuit of good works or morals is demonstrated. Whence it is said: There are four impediments that impede human nature, namely ignorance, taciturnity, vice, and weakness. And against ignorance, the quadrivium or the quadrivial sciences were developed: music, arithmetic, astronomy, and geometry. Against taciturnity, the trivium or the trivial sciences were developed: grammar, logic, and rhetoric, which all concern language. Against weakness, the mechanical arts were developed: tanning, sewing, and milling. Against vice, moral philosophy was developed, which includes poetry. And so it is plain that the significance of this material is that when we have read the present book we are able to recognize the truth in the fables and with their aid persist in good works and avoid vice. The title of this text is "Here begin the

fables or *apologi* or the books of Avian." Avian was a Roman outstanding in knowledge who on the request of a certain nobleman named Theodosius put together the present material. As to the other general matters, namely the causes of the book, the same is to be said as elsewhere.

Iste liber ... This book is divided into as many parts as fables or *apologi* are contained in it. The first fable has two parts. In the first part he tells the fable, and in the second he communicates the moral of the fable; he does the same in each fable. You should know that in this first fable the author teaches us that we should not place faith in the words of women. And he demonstrates this with a certain farmwife who had a weeping son who would not stop his crying. The woman said to him, "If you do not leave off your weeping, I will give you to the wolf to devour." A wolf, standing outside in front of the door, believed the words of the woman, expecting her promise to be fulfilled. The boy, however, was tired from so much weeping and fell asleep. Then the wolf saw that he had been deceived by the woman; he went back to his woodland lair hungry. The she-wolf met him and asked why he had been away for so long and yet brought absolutely nothing with him. The wolf replied, "You should not be surprised, dear she-wolf, for the sweet words of a woman have deceived me."

From this the author teaches us that we should almost never believe the words of a woman. For "There is no head worse than the head of a serpent, and there is no deceit above the deceit of a woman." A verse: "You are foolish if you believe the words of a woman."

Allegorically by the farmwife the church is understood, and by the wolf the devil; and by the weeping boy we understand the sinner. If he will not leave off his sins, the woman, his mother, that is to say holy mother church or his confessor representing holy mother church, threatens the boy that she will give him to the wolf, that is to say to the devil, if he will not leave off his sins. But as soon as he has ceased from his wrongdoing, then he is restored to his original state of grace and is plucked from the trap of the devil, that is to say freed. Whence Ecclesiastes: "My son, be mindful of your sins and repent and you will not sin or die into eternity." It is also established by the Metrista that we should not believe women; the verse: "A woman deceived Adam, Samson, David, Lot, and Solomon; who can be safe now?"

76. *Hic autor* . . . Here the author gives another *apologus* or fable, which is as follows: When a turtle saw the beasts walking rapidly on the ground and the birds flying quickly, it was greatly saddened to be so slow by its nature even though it was the lightest among moving things. And seeing that the eagle flew higher than all other birds, the turtle promised it many things, namely precious shells and stones, if it would carry it up into the air. But when it could not fulfill its promise, the eagle let it fall down. And so the turtle, sighing as it fell through the air, died.

 With this fable the author teaches that no one should exceed the boundaries of his nature, but should rather live happily with what he has, for while he seeks the heights, he often descends to the depths. For the higher the ascent, so much worse is the fall.

 Allegorically by the turtle Lucifer, first among the angels, is designated, who was not content with his own brilliance; he desired to be like almighty God, who is figured in the eagle, and said, "I will place my throne in the north and I will be like the most High." Because of this he, with the other angels conspiring with him, fell into Hell, and thus out of the angel of light the prince of darkness was made. A verse: "Oh man, you who are proud in words and deeds, remember these words: God destroys all who are vainglorious." Also in this fable we are taught to flee the vainglory of this world, which tends to stifle the soul. If Adam, the first man, had fled vainglory, then the human race would have been firmly established. But now it has fallen because of pride, which is the root of all vices. A verse: "If wisdom, honor, or beauty is given to you, pride alone, if it is followed, will destroy all those things."

77. *In isto* . . . In this fable the author teaches us that no one should reproach another for something for which he himself could be reproached. Whence Bernard: "It must be said that he whose life is criticized will find his preaching scorned." Whence Cato: "Do not do those things yourself that you can criticize in others. It is wicked to teach others when your own fault reproaches you." And the Antigameratus: "Accuse others when you are yourself without fault." And: "Your teaching is unworthy when your own fault lingers." And it is clear in the Gospel where it is said: "Jesus did and taught."

 And the author proves this with a young crab and its mother. This young crab was reproached by its mother because it always walked backwards. It answered its mother, "O dear mother, if you would walk before me, I would walk and follow your footsteps exactly." When she was supposed to go before him, she walked backwards in just the way the young crab had been warned against.

From this fable it is clear that no one should reproach or rebuke another for any fault for which he himself should be corrected. For the one who does this, namely the one who does bad things and teaches good, is like a burning candle, which illuminates other things but consumes itself. Thus Paul: "My brothers, be doers of the word of God and not hearers." And it is said in the Gospel about such judgment of the vices of men: "He who wants to retrieve the speck from the eye of another should first cast out the beam from his own."

Allegorically by the crab the devil is understood, who made the sons of men retreat from Christian faith. But when one who is tempted by him resists, then the devil himself must move back, as it is written that he goes about "as a roaring and hungry lion, seeking someone to devour," that is to say, to lead away from Christian faith. Or differently, by the crab we understand priests and preachers on whom the law of God depends, whose life must be such that it is an example to all. And by the son of the crab we understand those subject to those prelates who foolishly do bad deeds like their superiors. To this it is said: "Let the younger ox learn to plow from the older."

78. *Hic habetur* ... Here is another fable, the sense of which is that when Boreas and Phoebus were enemies, they appeared together before a great god, namely Jove. And they agreed there that whichever of them should exert his power to the best of his ability and whichever of them should be of greater strength should rejoice in triumph over the other. When they had reached this agreement, there was a traveler walking along a road familiar to him. And Boreas and Phoebus said to each other that whichever of them could gain possession of the clothes of the traveler first must be the stronger. Then Boreas applied his great winds with a huge storm and bitter cold, with which he intended to strip the cloak from the traveler. But the traveler drew his cloak closer and closer about himself. Phoebus, soon after the storm had passed, spread his rays with warmth onto the traveler so that the traveler began to sweat from the great heat. And at length his pores opened so greatly that taking off his cloak because of the great heat and sweat, he had to sit down on the ground. And thus Phoebus gained the victory.

In this fable we are taught that we should not easily back away because of any threats from a good work we have started, but rather that we should pass right through the danger with a bold spirit and persist in our good action. Whence the Poet: "He who fears every bramble does not go to the forest." Thus a man would accomplish little if he greatly feared the words of every threat. And so in this fable it is suggested that victory often does not follow on loud words, for otherwise a brash man would be more often victorious than a restrained one. There is a double moral in this fable. The first is that no one should resist one stronger than himself lest he be put out like a light. Whence Cato: "Yield to fate, give way to the powerful one." It is no shame for the lesser to yield to the greater. The second moral is that we should vanquish our enemies rather with patience and forbearance than with threats and harshness. Accordingly, this saying: "Patience conquers wickedness." And: "Learn to endure if you wish to succeed." A verse: "No virtue is said to be so great as patience." And thus James says in his book: "God gives his grace to the humble but confounds the proud. Be subject therefore to God and resist the devil so that he will flee from you."

Allegorically or morally by Boreas we understand the foolish, by the sun however the wise. Or by Phoebus we understand almighty God, by Boreas Lucifer, who wanted to be equal to God, saying: "I will place my throne in the north and will be like the almighty." Thus there was a great battle between Boreas and Phoebus in the passion of Christ, when Christ vanquished the devil. These two likewise battled over the clothing of the traveler, that is to say over the human soul. But Phoebus, kind and gentle, using his wisdom defeated and conquered Boreas, that is to say the devil, the cruel enemy of human life.

79. *In presenti* ... In this fable or *apologus* we are taught that no man should usurp for himself any dignity that he cannot keep, which is demonstrated by a certain donkey. There was a donkey who found the skin of a lion, and said to himself: "I will put on the skin of the lion so that I seem to be a lion." When he had done this he seemed very fearsome and was an enemy of all the timid animals, bothering them every way he could. Finally a man recognized by his great long ears that he was a donkey and attacked him with blows and words, saying, "You may have deceived many by your imitation of the lion's voice, but I will always think of you as a donkey." And pulling off the lion's skin he showed that it was a donkey.

The lesson of this fable is that no one should attribute to himself any virtue or dignity that he has not earned, because if he does so, he will suffer great harm and disadvantage from it.

Allegorically by the donkey the devil is understood, who wanted to subjugate to himself the world and the people in it before the coming of Christ. When the Lord saw this, he redeemed us from the devil's control by his death. Or alternatively by the donkey is understood every wealthy and powerful man who swells up with his glory and strength and frightens other men. Then the farmer, that is to say his lord, namely the devil, tormenting him into eternity, puts on the lion's skin, that is to say that the Anti-Christ comes in a skin, that is to say under the appearance of divinity, destroying our faith, killing Christians; he does this on account of his great vainglory, for which reason vainglory must be rigorously resisted. Whence a wise man says: "God gives the humble his grace, but he resists the proud." A verse: "These words are true: God destroys every prideful man." Nothing is worse than a proud man who was once humble. A verse: "Nothing is worse than a humble man when he rises to great heights." And: "When the pitiful rise, they do not pity the pitiful." And the point of this fable is clear in these verses: "The donkey, enduring a flogging after the lion's skin was removed, reminds you not to assume undeserved praise."

80. *In presenti* ... In this fable the author means to instruct us not to boast of things we cannot accomplish. And he proves this with a frog, which climbing onto the grassy hills saw there a herd of animals, to which it said: "I am a good doctor and know how to treat the seriously ill, and I have never seen a doctor to whom I would yield in medical skill." And the animals gathered there thought that it was true. But the fox, ridiculing their naivety, said, "O, you believe the words of the frog foolishly. She is trying to deceive us with a wicked fraud. But you see that she herself is sickly pale as if she had the dropsy; such color is not suited to the healthy. If she knew how to cure the sick, she would first cure herself." And so the fox turned the animals away from such credulity.

This fable warns us that no one should attribute knowledge to himself that he does not have, and that one should not promise what one cannot bring to pass by oneself.

Allegorically by the frog we understand this world, which promises us a long and peaceful life and an opportunity to repent, in which we are often deceived. Finally we are properly ridiculed by the wise and the religious, who are compared to foxes. A verse: "The fox that showed the frog to be without medical skill teaches you that you not pretend to be an experienced teacher."

81. *In presenti* ... In this fable this author tries to instruct us not to take pride in the gifts conferred on us. For it is often doubtful and cannot easily be known namely whether they are given to us on account of our wickedness or whether they are given to us on account of our goodness. And he shows this through a fable about a dog. There was a dog that had the habit of wagging his tail at people so that quietly, without barking, it might bite them with its teeth. Seeing this, the master of this dog, or its owner, placed a bell, that is to say a small bell, on the neck of this dog, which when it moved should give a sign to people that hearing the sound of the bell they should avoid the bite of this dog. The dog, however, took great pride in the bell tied around his neck, thinking that this gift had been given because of his virtue and that it was a sign of distinction. Seeing his, an older dog approached the prideful dog and spoke to him in these words: "You really are very foolish, stupid dog, if you think and believe that these gifts, that is to say the bell, are given to you as an honor. This bell was given to you on account of your wickedness and on account of your treacherous attacks, as you used to attack people, biting them terribly."

The moral of this fable is that we should determine, when gifts or presents are given to us, whether they are given on account of our wickedness or our virtue; quite often they are not given on account of virtue, as when they are given to judges and advocates, to whom people sometimes give bribes on account of their wickedness, while they believe these bribes to have been given on account of their distinction.

Allegory: By the dog wicked and prideful men are understood; by the bell tied to the dog's neck, the power given to the wicked is understood. Just as the dog could not tell why the bell had been tied to his neck, so wicked and prideful men do not understand the privileges conferred on them by their superiors, but rather when some privileges are given to them, in their wickedness they believe that the gifts are to be attributed to the exaltedness of their honor.

82. *Hic autor* ... Here the author in this fable means to instruct us to seek those things that are proper and that cannot rightly be denied us, which we demonstrates by a camel which complained to Jove, seeing that the other animals had their defenses: lions and bears had

their claws, cattle and deer their horns and antlers; the camel, however, was deprived of all these defenses, for which reason it eagerly asked Jove to give it horns. Jupiter smiled at the camel in derision, saying, "The gifts of God are not enough for you, and so properly small ears are to be given to you in place of your long ones." And so Jupiter took away the length of its ears, saying, "Live eternally as a lesser animal, since you were not content with the gifts of fortune."

The author teaches in this fable that we should not seek anything improperly lest we suffer loss, for whoever requests something improperly does not deserve to be heard. Whence Cato: "Seek that which is proper or what seems dignified." And the mother of the sons of Zebedee because of her improper request was not heard. Or in this fable we are taught that we should be content with those advantages of the body which are given to us by nature. Or also the lesson can be had from this same fable that we should not be desirous of things that do not belong to us, but that we should rather be content with our own things, because when anyone desires to acquire things that are not his, most often he loses his own things, as we see in daily experience of thieves and robbers who want to be enriched and lose their own life for the sake of the acquisition of wealth.

Allegorically by the camel the greedy and avaricious man is understood, who often seeks and wants to have more than is proper for him. Jupiter, that is to say glorious God, who created everything out of nothing, is outraged by this improper desire and takes away from the greedy man his entire fortune, inflicting on him ill fortune or death, through which the greedy man must leave behind all the goods of the world. A verse: "The wheel of fortune is as changeable as the sphere of the moon. It waxes, it wanes, it cannot remain the same." Fortune is said to have responded to these verses in this way: "I am fortune, I am not the same fate for everyone. If I did not change, I would not be called fortune."

83. *In hoc* ... In this fable the author teaches us that no one should lightly take on a stranger as a companion, which he shows by two companions who promised each other that they would endure together anything that happened to them, both good fortune and bad. When they had agreed to this, a frightful bear came across them. When one of the companions saw the bear, he fled from the other and climbed a tree and hung onto a branch with his hands so that the bear would not see him. The other, seeing that he could not escape, fell to the ground, pretending to be dead. When the bear saw

him, it lifted him with its front paws, and when he did not move or breathe at all, the bear thought he was a rotten corpse, and leaving him behind returned to its lair. The companion who had fled came down from the tree and said to his companion, "Dear companion, tell me what secrets the bear told you when it whispered to you for so long." He replied, "The bear told me many things, but among them it urged me especially to never take on a stranger as a companion, advice I firmly intend to take."

By this fable we are taught that we should associate with those known to us rather than with strangers, because the friendship of a man known to us is proven, but that of a stranger is uncertain. Whence Cato: "Do not prefer one unknown to you over those you know. Known things are proven by judgment, unknown things by chance." And Alanus: "Often the new path, not an old one, leads the traveler astray; and so too a new friend, not an old one, leads his companion astray."

Allegorically by that companion who pretended to be dead understand our Savior, and by the companion who fled his apostles are understood, who fled from him. And by the bear the devil is understood, for just as the first traveler escaped from the bear without any injury, so Christ vanquished the devil by rising on the third day. Or differently: By the companion who climbed the tree the body is understood, because it is often eager to live in pleasure by being prideful and by receiving greater things. But the faithful soul is understood by the one who fell onto the ground, because the soul of itself always reaches for salvation, that is to say for humility, contrition, chastity and continence. Whence Saint Jerome, lecturing against the wickedness of vicious men, says, "Everyone should be wary of his neighbor and should not have faith in everyone because even a brother can cause his brother to stumble. And any friend speaks fraudulently of peace when he speaks with a friend, but secretly he sets a trap for him. And in his presence he shows himself a real friend, but in his absence he is his most bitter persecutor, for which reason the companionship of a stranger [?] is not be taken on, but rather only the companionship of those known to you." A verse: "Along the way, you will keep your old friends."

84. *Hic autor* ... Here the author teaches us in this fable that if we are laughed at by anyone, we should dispel the laughter not with anger but with a laugh. For it often happens that when someone is ridiculed, the more angry he becomes, the more the laughter increases.

He proves this in this fable. There was a bald knight who tied horsehair to his head. Once when he had done this several times it happened that he came to the tournament field with glistening weapons and steered his horse with the reins. When he was doing this with great joy, a wind, namely the north wind, rising against him blew away the hair he had fixed to his head. The people, seeing the knight with a bald head, fell into great laughter. The knight, seeing that he was ridiculed by the people, began to laugh with them, saying, "It is no wonder that the hair I fixed to my head has blown away, as my real hair has left me too." And he dispelled the laughter of the people with his own.

The moral of this fable is that we should not do anything for which we could be laughed at, and that we should not concern ourselves that artificial things do not last when even natural things cannot.

Allegorically by this knight we can understand Christ, and in the hair fixed to his head we can understand Christ's humanity, which died and slipped away, and was mocked by the Jews, saying, "He saved others, himself he cannot save." And in his resurrection he destroyed the laughter of the Jews. Or alternatively, by the crowd of those laughing, the Jews are understood, who while tearing out the beard of the knight, that is to say of Christ, ridiculed him, which he willingly accepted because all those passing on the road shook their heads as a sign of derision, but he defended himself against them with gentle words.

85. *Hic autor* ... Here the author gives another fable about two vases, and it is this: The water of a violently rushing river washed two different vases, one of bronze and the other of clay, along with it. While they were bobbing along together in the water, the clay vase avoided the bronze one, fearing that it would be harmed or broken by it. The bronze vase said to the clay pot, "Why do you avoid a friend who is eager to help you in your need?" To which the clay vase replied, "I know that the small can rely little on the great, and although you assure me with your words and promises that I will be safe, my fear cannot be put out of my mind. Whether the water pushes you toward me or me toward you, I will always be the one put in danger."

The author includes a moral for this fable, saying that the poor and the powerless should avoid the company of the powerful, for the poor cannot stand up against the powerful who wish them ill. It is said in a proverb: "The cat will find harm who plays with a dog."

Allegorically the devil is understood in the bronze pot, which is sturdy; the devil is the enemy of humankind, harsh and scheming. And in the clay pot, man is understood, who is weak and fragile; when he is lured or tempted to accompany the devil and to do his will, he should absolutely flee him and never consent to his urgings. Thus it is clear that those who are different in morals should not consort with each other. For it is said in the fourth book of the Ethics that living among good people leads to imitation in the works of virtue.

Hic autor ... Here the author gives another fable, which is this: A farmer, intending to turn his soil with the plow, found in the furrow, that is to say *eyn voer*, a great mass of purest gold. Immediately he abandoned his plow and took his oxen to a better pasture. He was very grateful and pious and began to build a temple to his field, because the field or the earth had freely given him the treasure. Fortune, however, seeing the farmer work so hard in building the temple, said, "Why do you not give these gifts to my temples? Why do you honor other gods with them? After all it was by my gift that you were made rich, and should you become poor again, then you shall pray to me with your first prayer."

The moral of this fable is that whoever has received any favor from anyone, but thanks someone else for it, sins badly, for the vice of ingratitude is a very evil and detestable sin. Whence Seneca: "He is an ingrate who ignores a favor, more of an ingrate who does not return it, and the worst ingrate of all who forgets a favor he has been granted."

Allegorically by the farmer is understood the rich man who thinks he has wealth because of his own labor and not as a gift from Fortune, that is to say from God, without whom nothing is received in this life. And if we do not give or return to him our thanks, at last he takes back from us the treasure of the everlasting kingdom because of the ingratitude we have committed.

86. *Hic autor* ... Here the author provides another fable in which he teaches that no one should harass his neighbor for no reason, lest he later be harmed by him. The author demonstrates this with a goat and a bull, saying that there was once a bull who was being chased by a large lion. This bull sought the safety of a cave in the mountains. He found a cave which a stinking, that is to say smelly, goat occupied, and, raising his head, entered into the cave. The smelly goat seeing him frightened the bull with his long beard, so that the

bull fled. The goat, after a while coming out of the cave, spoke to the bull saying, "My bravery has expelled you from my cave, and my attack has made you afraid of me." The bull replied, "O fetid and putrid goat, I would not fear your beard if not for him who follows my trail. For if he whom I truly fear were to leave me alone, then I would teach you how much greater is the strength of a bull than that of a goat."

The moral of this fable is that we should not harm those whom we can harm lest they harm us in return. Whence Cato: "Conquer with patience those whom you can overcome. Sometimes the one who could do harm can be of use."

Allegorically by the bull is understood the righteous man, and by the lion the devil, who does not cease from inflicting continual harm on man. By the goat is understood the sinner, who does not want to let the bull enter the cave when he is being pursued by the lion, because sinners always impede the good man and heap abuse on good people.

87. *Hic autor* ... Here the author in another fable teaches us that no one should praise himself, because praise of oneself is often deemed disreputable. He expresses this in this fable: Once Jupiter, wanting to know who had the most beautiful child in all the world, called together every type of bird, beast, livestock, and fish, along with humans. When they had been assembled, they came to Jove and sat together before him. The ape came and brought with it its young, asking Jove to grant it the prize on account of the beauty of its child, claiming that it was more beautiful than the other animals. When he heard this, Jupiter was moved to laughter, and growing angry, he refused to hear the petition of the ape. And when it had persisted in its pleas for a long time, not, however, making any headway with Jove, it left in great disappointment.

The moral of this story is that no one should give praise to himself because of his own opinion, because this is what the foolish do and not the wise. Likewise, we learn from this fable that no one should be swayed by pleadings or bribes, by favor or by disfavor, so as not to judge properly the truth and justice.

Allegorically by the ape we should understand the Jews and by the other animals all the other peoples. Now the synagogue says that its faith is better, which it is not; just as the ape cries to Jove, so the Jews and heretics try to destroy our Christian faith, saying that their belief is the best, although it is actually the worst.

Hic autor ... Here the author teaches that no one should be eager to fight with another in words or in deeds. Likewise he shows that no one should boast of his physical beauty. He demonstrates this with a crane and a peacock. There was a peacock, very proud of its beauty. Whenever it came among the other birds, it boasted that it was better than all the others in its beauty. The crane, hearing this, asked how this might be. The peacock replied, "The temples of the gods are adorned with my plumes, and I am the bird of lord Jove. But your feathers show that you are vile, for they have no beauty. Thus I exceed you in loveliness." The crane responded with gentle words: "Although I have plain and ugly feathers, yet I fly beyond the nearest stars, and although you have lovely plumes, yet you drag your ornate train along the ground."

The moral of this story is that the beautiful should not scorn the ugly. A verse: "Although you are beautiful, do not scorn the ugly."

Allegorically by the peacock we understand the rich and worldly people, and by its tail their worldly wealth. By the crane we understand religious men entrusted with religious duties, who scorn worldly goods. They are ridiculed by the peacocks, that is to say by the rich and worldly, because they do not have wealth. But they can respond that although they lack worldly riches, yet they fly high and always have their hearts directed towards heaven, where the riches are heavenly and everlasting. But the worldly rich remain on the ground and have their hearts oppressed by worldly wealth, so that they do not attain the heights and heavenly riches. And they are like the peacock, which has many eyes in its train but does not see anything with them.

88. *Hic autor* ... Here the author teaches us to be humble and modest and to resist with humility, which is better than annoyance and stubbornness, as he demonstrates with the oak and the reed. An oak stood on a high mountain with its branches stretched out, and it resisted every blowing wind with its strength. And while it stood there confidently, the north wind came and with its great gusts blew the oak down from the high mountain. The water took it up and floated it along a deep river; it came into the reeds and stuck there with its branches. It saw the reeds resist the winds and said, "How can you withstand the strong north wind when you are so slight in body? I have strong branches and great strength, along with strong roots, and yet I could not withstand it." Hearing this, one of the reeds said, "Do not be surprised, for though we are slight of body, when a

wind comes we yield to it. And so the wind spares us. But even though you are large, you resisted the wind and were felled, conquered by it."

The moral of this fable is that everyone should avoid pride, for according to Seneca, victory is gained more easily with humility and patience than with pride and annoyance. Thus it is said: "Learn to endure, if you wish to be victorious."

Allegorically by the oak the proud man is understood, by the reed the humble man. For the humble and lowly, in obedience to the commandments of God, bow to the blows of pride and humble themselves before their betters. But the mighty and the proud, not obedient to the commandments of God, resist those more powerful than they. In the end they are torn up and destroyed. For the Lord destroys the path of the sinner, especially of the vainglorious. Whence: "God grants his grace to the humble, but resists the proud."

89. *Hic autor* ... Here the author in another fable reproaches those who are too confident in their own strength, and believe that no one could hurt them. He demonstrates this with a hunter who took up his arms, namely arrows, and went into a very thick forest in the usual way. Seeing various animals wandering through the woods, he strung his bow and hunted them. A tiger, seeing the animals flee, soothed them, saying, "Do not be afraid, for I will provide you protection." When he had said this, the hunter took a spear and shot the tiger in the foot. The tiger wanted to flee, but the great pain took away his strength so that he could hardly breathe. A fox came up and saw that the tiger was injured and began to tease him with innocent-sounding words, saying, "O tiger, tell me who has inflicted such damage on you." The tiger replied, "When I came and wanted to defend the other animals, I was wounded with such a wound, and I don't know by whom." The fox, grinning, responded, "You know that this arrow shot at you proves that there was a man here." The hunter, standing in his hiding place, said under his breath, "This messenger will make plain who I am," and right away with an arrow pierced the insides of the animal, namely of the tiger.

The moral of this fable is that no one should risk his own life for another, lest when he has taken on that risk he become a laughingstock to the others. Whence Cato: "Be good to the good, lest harm ensue."

Allegorically by the hunter we understand the devil, who stalks us in the forest, that is to say in the pleasures of this world, and wounds us with his arrows, that is to say with his wicked urgings when we do not make an effort to draw back from those pleasures or persist in others. Whence: "Just as the forest is the home of the wild animals, so the pleasures are the home of the body."

Hic ponit ... Here the author gives another fable, which is this: Once there were four oxen bound to each other by the tie of friendship to such an extent that they had made a pact among themselves that they would bear equally whatever befell them by chance, whether good or bad. When they were going to their pasture, a hungry lion met them in the woods. When the lion saw that they were united and joined in a pact, he was afraid to attack them, as he was alone. For this reason he tried to separate them from each other by spreading discord among them with his treacherous words. The oxen, believing the lion, separated and left each other, and thus the lion attacked each of them separately and killed them. The fourth ox, seeing that his companions had been killed and that the lion was about to kill him, broke forth in these words: "Whoever wants to lead a quiet and peaceful life can learn from our deaths that he should not listen to deceptive words. According to Seneca, sweet words are mixed with poison, and so one should learn from our deaths that one should not give up an old friendship for a new one."

Whence Alanus: "Often the new path, not an old one, leads the traveler astray; and so too a new friend, not an old one, leads his companion astray." And Cato: "Do not prefer one unknown to you over those you know. Known things are proven by judgment, unknown things by chance."

Allegorically by the lion we understand the devil, and by the four oxen we can understand the four cardinal virtues. For as long as a man is bound by the four cardinal virtues to behave virtuously, and as long as he lives by them, the lion, that is to say the devil, cannot do him any harm. But after he has abandoned those virtues, right away he is subject to the devil.

90. *Hic autor* ... Here the author gives another fable, which is this: A fir tree, rooted and standing among the brambles, seeing that it rose up in height above the brambles, began to ridicule them, because it was tall and lovely and ships were built from its wood, but the bramble was plain and prickly and of no value, and because of this people did not care for the bramble, but rather despised it. Hearing this, the bramble replied, "O fir tree, though you are very tall and distinguished, nevertheless you should not assert our failings so

much while praising yourself. The time will come when the farmer will seek you out and with his ax cut you down; then you may well wish that you had had our thorns to defend yourself."

The moral of this fable is that no one should be too proud of his beauty and should not rejoice in any of his virtues, lest afterward, when he has been deprived of his distinction, he suffer. Likewise, we learn from this fable that if you are beautiful, you should not scorn the ugly, for the more beautiful the body, the more quickly its beauty fades. Beauty is a very fragile quality.

Allegorically by the fir tree the proud are understood. They tend to ridicule and to scorn the humble and rejoice so much in their vainglory that finally they are destroyed completely, while one sees the humble still standing.

91. *Hic autor* ... Here the author gives another fable which is this: A fisherman, going out to fish, pulled out a little fish on his hook. When he had removed the hook from the fish's mouth, the little fish pleaded tearfully with the fisherman that he release him, saying, "O fisherman, you will not have much profit from my tiny body, as I am young and my mother has just given birth to me and told me to swim in the water. Let me grow until I am a suitable size for eating, and then I will gladly return, fatter, to your hook." The fisherman, however, thinking it stupidity to give up something certain in return for something uncertain, did not release the fish and did not acquiesce in its pleas.

The author provides the moral that no one should give up something certain in return for something uncertain, and that no one should give up present things for those to come, even though the thing to come seem much better, for as the proverb has it, "A sparrow in the hand is worth more than an uncertain crane." And it does not contradict the author to say that we should relinquish all worldly things in return for heavenly things to come, for the statement of the author is understood of earthly and not of heavenly matters.

Allegorically by the fisherman we understand the spiritual teacher directing others, and by the little fish we understand the sinner. The sinner, corrected by his priest, although he says he intends to leave off sinning, nevertheless the good teacher, not believing the sinner's promises, urges him still to leave off his errors and his procrastination, to persist in good behavior, and to correct himself when he sins without delay, for delay is the food of the sinner. For this reason Ovid, in the *Remedia amoris*, urges us to resist evil from the start, saying: "Resist from the very beginnings, for it is too late to seek a remedy when the passage of time has strengthened evil. Hasten and do not put it off; whoever is not ready today, will be less ready tomorrow."

92. *Hic autor* ... Here another fable or *apologus* is present, which is this: There was a farmer who owned a green wheatfield in which a small bird, namely a lark, was nesting and raising its young according to the laws of nature. When the farmer saw that the grain was ripe, he asked his neighbors to help him harvest the grain. The young birds, still without feathers, that is to say featherless, heard the farmer ask for the help of his neighbors a second time. This troubled the young birds, whose mother consoled them as she had before. When the farmer noticed a third time that his neighbors were slow in helping him, he put his own hand to harvesting the grain. Seeing this, the mother of the young birds ran quickly to the nest, telling her chicks, "Run and leave your nest. It is time. The farmer has taken the sickle into his own hands."

The moral of this fable is that a man should not ask for the help of others when he is capable himself. Likewise we are taught that no one should conceal justice and the truth for the friends of another.

Allegorically by the bird we understand the devil, and by the farmer the sinner; by the grainfield we understand the hearts of men, into which the devil gives wicked thoughts and sins, even though the farmer, that is to say the devil, has been urged by others to put away the sins lurking in his heart. But this does little good if the man himself does not seek to improve himself.

Hic ponitur ... Here we have another *apologus* which is thus: Once Jupiter, wanting to understand the minds of men, sent Phoebus from heaven to investigate the spirits of men. Phoebus sought out two men, one of whom was envious, the other greedy, and said to them that they should make a request, and that whatever the one requested, the other would receive twofold. The greedy one put off his request, thinking to himself, "My companion will ask for great gifts, and I will receive twice as much." The envious one thought intently how he could change what the greedy one was hoping for into a punishment. The envious man approached and was ready to make his request. The greedy one waited eagerly to receive twice as much as the envious man requested. The envious man requested then that he be deprived of an eye so that the greedy man might lose both. And this was done. Phoebus was amazed at such great malice, namely that one had sought the torture of his own body in order that the other be punished twice as much; and he reported these events to Jove.

The moral of this fable is that we should not rejoice in the misfortune or the harm of others.

Allegorically by Jove God omnipotent is understood, who sent Phoebus, that is to say Christ, who is the true light, into this world. By the envious man the devil is understood, who seeks to be deprived of one eye, that is to say he chooses to suffer more greatly in order that he might drag the human race into perpetual suffering.

93. *In appollogo* ... In this fable it is said that a merchant exhibited in the forum a statue that he wanted to sell; the statue was beautiful and made of marble in the form of Bacchus, who was the god of wine. Two noble citizens came and wanted to buy the statue, one of them to place it at the tomb of his late father, the other to place it in a temple where people might worship it. Seeing this, the statue spoke to the merchant, saying, "While you can do me honor by selling me to the one who plans to set me in a temple so that all might worship me, you can also do me shame by selling me to the one who will place me at the tomb of his father. You should rather honor me than shame me."

By this fable we are taught that if it is in someone's power to help or to harm, he should rather help than harm. Whence Cato: "If you can, be mindful to help strangers."

Allegorically by this image worldly wealth can be understood, which is acquired so that its use can ultimately be in the service of God. Some people, though, acquire secular wealth for the sake of worldly honor or out of greed. Whereas the first circumstance is admirable, the second is despicable because we should rather work towards acquiring wealth for the glory of God omnipotent and not for the sake of worldly honor so that wealth becomes the mother of vainglory.

Hic ponitur ... Here we have another fable, which is this: A hunter and a lion were companions and friends, but as sometimes a disagreement arises between good friends, these two once argued about their nobility and their bravery. While they were arguing, that is to say in dispute, the hunter said to the lion, "Come with me and I will show you which of us is the nobler and the stronger." They went to a town where there was a picture on the wall of the tomb of some nobleman showing a man killing a lion. The hunter showed the lion the picture, saying, "Behold how much stronger the man is than the lion." The lion replied, "Who painted this picture, a man or a lion?" The hunter responded that it had been a man. The lion said, "You speak the truth. A man can paint a picture whenever he wants, but a lion cannot paint. But without a doubt, if a lion could paint as a man can, then you would see clearly the man conquered and defeated by nothing more than the roaring of the lion."

The moral of this fable is that we should not believe anyone giving testimony for himself or his friends and relatives.

Allegorically by the hunter secular men are understood who work eagerly for the goods of the world. By the lion are understood humble, devout men who do not care for worldly things. By the image secular wealth is understood, which is not a true good, but only a seeming good. The hunter, that is to say the man who acquires many goods in this world, believes that he is more worthy than the lion, that is to say than humble men without concern for the pomps of this world. And the worldly want to be revered by the humble because of their wealth, but this should not happen because the goods of this world are very inconstant, because they come and go, which is why the Psalmist says: "If riches abound, set not your heart upon them."

94. *Hic ponitur* ... Here we have another fable in which it is said that a boy sat crying beside a well and a thief approached, and asked him why he was crying. The boy, with amazing cleverness, made up a lie, and told him that the cord had broken with which he was supposed to fetch water and that his golden cup had fallen into the bottom of the well. The thief thought to increase his own wealth at the boy's expense and ascribed the boy's loss to his own good fortune. He took off his clothes and descended into the well, unaware of the deceit the boy had trickily prepared. The boy, however, took up the clothes of the thief and put them on and hid among the shadows of the thickets. The thief, when he saw that he was striving in vain, came out of the well and saw that the boy had left with his clothes, and he sat down disappointed. He bemoaned his bad fortune with these words: "Whoever would believe that a golden cup could float in liquid water should look after his clothes so as not to lose them, as I, credulous, lost mine."

The moral of this fable is that when the greedy and avaricious desire things that are not theirs, they often lose those things that are, and often the apparent innocence of some deceives the trickery of others. Thus the author says that no one should greedily desire things that belong to others, for if one did this, he might lose what he has.

Allegorically by the thief wicked and deceptive women can be understood. By the thief, the men who trust them are understood; goods and treasures are understood by the cup. For sometimes a wicked woman desires to deceive a man and utters tearful words, saying, "O dear friend, because of your love I have lost a golden cup, that is to say all my goods, my friends, and my position, which I have given up to allure you to my love." And so she tries to ensnare her lover with her tears. Whence Cato: "While a woman cries, she prepares a trap with her tears." The prudent and wise man should not entirely trust in the tears of women. And he should not enter into the well, that is to say he should not linger in misery and sin while consenting to illicit love with a woman, lest on entering that foul well of love he lose his clothing, that is to say his virtues and other goods, for lechery greatly consumes virtue and good works.

95. *Hic ponitur* ... Here we have another fable. A hungry lion saw a goat seeking food on a high mountain and said to it, "Leave the crags of the mountain, and do not seek your food at all on the rugged slopes, that is to say on the tangled sides of the mountains, but come down into the green meadows, where you will find willows and the best flowers and green grass suitable to feed you." The goat replied, "O lion, I ask you earnestly to leave me in safety, for although what you say is true, yet you conceal the greater dangers. If I should come down from the mountain, you might devour me."

The moral of this fable is that no one should readily believe the kind or flattering words of anyone else, even though sometimes those words do contain some truth. Nevertheless, one should consider the reason for which the words are spoken.

Allegorically by the lion the devil is understood, who pursues us night and day in order to drag us into his misery or torment. By the goat is understood any man who leaves off sinning and in his contrition moves on to good works and strict penitence. By the mountain we understand God almighty or the heavenly life, namely the meditative life. By the yellow flower we understand the vain pleasures of this world. The lion, that is to say the devil, advises the goat, that is to say the man who is converted to God, that he should not climb the mountain, that is to say that he should not do penance for his sins, but rather that he should come down to the green grasses, that is to say to the vain pleasures of this world and to those earthly things that are pleasing to the senses.

96. *Hec est* ... This is another fable in which it is taught that a crow was very thirsty and saw an urn standing in a field, in which there was a little water. Because the crow could not drink from it, it tried to spill the urn or to tip it onto the ground to extinguish its thirst. But being weak it could not do this. Shortly it thought up another, clever way, namely that it took up many little stones which it threw into the urn so that the water in the bottom of the urn rose up to its mouth so that the crow quenched its thirst and drank of the water of the urn.

From this fable it is clear that intelligence or cleverness is worth more than strength. Often what cannot be acquired by strength alone can be gained by wisdom or cleverness.

Allegorically by the crow we understand the devil, who constantly pursues us. By the water in the urn the heart of man is understood, which stands in the body as if in an urn. By the stones bad works and wicked thoughts are understood which the devil in his cleverness instills in the human heart so that he can drink the water, that is to say so that he can distract the heart from good thoughts and deeds. Every prudent man should beware lest the crow, that is to say the devil, in its cleverness and deceit throw stones, that is to say wicked or evil desires, into the urn, that is to say into the heart, so that it can drink the water.

Ista fabula ... This fable is about a farmer who had a young ox that was very rebellious and struck its master, namely the farmer, with its horns. The master, namely the farmer, wanted to punish the ox, and cut off its horns and yoked it to the plow, believing that he would tame it that way. But the ox shook off the chains with which it was bound and when it saw that it could do no harm with its horns, it pawed up dirt at the head of the farmer and dirtied his hair and his entire head, that is to say the hair and head of the farmer who followed the plow. The farmer, covered in dirt, said, "It is no wonder that this ox behaves in this way, for it is wicked by nature and cannot be restrained from its wickedness."

The moral of this fable is that men who are wicked by nature or accustomed to wickedness cannot easily be removed from wickedness.

Allegorically by the farmer secular judges are understood. By the rebellious ox wicked men are understood, such as thieves and robbers, who, the more they are punished, the more they are hardened in their wickedness because they are so accustomed to it that it is as if it were innate in them. For this reason habit is called "second nature."

97. *Ista fabula* ... This fable says that in winter, when a bitter cold gripped the whole earth, a traveler was walking across the middle of a field against the wind. The traveler struggled against the harshness of his path in great difficulty and the storm of the wind. When a satyr, that is to say the guardian of the forest, saw this, he admired the traveler's strength and took pity on him and asked him in to his cave to warm himself and take refreshment. The satyr had seen how the traveler, while he was on the road, had warmed his freezing fingers with the breath of his mouth and repulsed his external chill with his internal heat; the satyr was greatly amazed at this, that the traveler's natural warmth was so powerful. After they had come into the cave together and the satyr had offered the traveler his hospitality, he gave his guest delicious foods of the forest and the countryside and the rural life to eat. Finally he offered him a cup full of warm wine so that the warmth of the wine would come into the freezing limbs of the guest. The traveler, as he was going to drink, brought the hot cup to his mouth, and was startled and quickly removed it from his mouth and blowing on it with the breath from his mouth cooled the hot wine. When the satyr saw this, he was terrified of the man as if he were a monster, who before had repulsed the cold with the breath of his mouth and then with the same mouth sought to cool the intemperate heat of the wine, for which reason the satyr threw him out of his cave, saying, "We want you to leave these woods, and you will never again be welcome in our cave, for you have in your head two such different mouths."

The moral of this fable is that men who seem to have two tongues, who say good and kind things in the presence of others and bad things in their absence, should be avoided. For as Boethius says, "There is no plague more likely to do harm than a closely associated enemy."

Allegorically by the satyr every man is understood who is among the counselors of any prince and who says one thing in public and another in secret and who when he says one thing means another. This man should be expelled from the council, because he can do great harm using the secrets revealed to him there.

98. *Ista fabula* ... This fable is about a farmer who kept a field in which

much grain was growing. He found a pig in the grain and cut off one of its ears so that it would not return to his field. He caught the pig a second time in the same field and cut off its other ear. It returned a third time, and then the farmer killed the pig outright and presented it to his lord to eat. He in turn gave it to the cook and told him to dress the pig and to prepare it well. When the lord came to eat the pig, he looked for its heart and did not find it. He asked the cook sharply about it, claiming that the cook had eaten the heart of the pig or stolen it. When he heard this, the farmer said, "My lord, this pig had no heart. If it had had a heart, it would not have come back so often to the place where it had lost its ears."

The moral of this is that similarly, those who are accustomed to sinning every day can abstain from sin with difficulty. They do not care about the harm that befalls them from this.

Allegorically by the farmer every religious man is understood who punishes the sinner and urges him to leave off his sinning. By the pig every sinner is understood who, when he first runs to the field, that is to say to the delights of sin, loses an ear, that is to say he is deprived by God because of his sin, sometimes by sickness and sometimes by other various tribulations. And if he sins then a second time, he is deprived again in the same way. If he sins a third time, and our Lord sees that such correction is of no use, then at last he kills him and sends him into hellfire where there is weeping and gnashing of teeth. Whoever has fallen into sin should repent in time, making up for the sins he has committed and no longer committing them, for to sin repeatedly is to weigh down the soul the more.

Hic docetur ... Here it is taught how a little mouse with its tiny tooth wounded a great ox in the foot, and after it had bitten the ox, it ran right away back into its hole. The ox when it had been wounded grew angry and began to act menacingly, but it did not know who had wounded it. The mouse, hearing the threats of the ox, kept silent and hid in its hole until the ox had gone away. When its anger had calmed, the mouse said to the ox, "Although your parents gave you large limbs, they did not give you great effectiveness and strength in them. You should learn how much small bodies can accomplish, so that you no longer oppress them but rather faithfully fulfill whatever requests the lesser crowd makes of you."

The moral of this fable is that we should not act as the wealthy tend to, for when they cannot subject the weak and the poor to themselves they grow angry and puff up, for which reason the poor and powerless should not resist them stubbornly. For as Cato says, "Do not scorn the strength of a small body. What nature does not permit force to do, she helps good strategy to accomplish."

Allegorically by the ox the rich and powerful are understood, and by the mouse the weak and the poor. When it seems to the powerful that they are being bothered somehow by the poor, then they begin to roar and to make threats against the poor. The poor and the humble keep silent at these times until the anger of the rich and the powerful has passed and so they conceal themselves at this time. For by concealing themselves thus they injure the wealthy and the powerful more than if they spoke many words.

99. *Fabula ista* ... This fable is that a farmer was driving his cart with his oxen and drove it into a mud puddle out of which the oxen could not pull it because the cart was firmly stuck in the mud. When the farmer saw this, he fell to the ground weeping and calling on all the gods, especially on Hercules, to provide him with their help in this moment of such dire need. Hercules said to the farmer, "Get up and put your own hands to the task and whip your horses and oxen, and if you have no success, then I will help you, lazy as you are. The gods help only those who put their own hands to the task." The farmer, obeying these urgings of Hercules, stood up and put his own hands to the task and the cart came out of the mud puddle quickly.

From this fable the moral can be gathered that we should not just call on divine assistance in things we can do, but we should also apply our own efforts and labor.

Allegorically by the farmer we understand the sinner, by the puddle the human body, and by the cart stuck in it the soul in the body. The sinner who wants to be helped by God should not only call on his help, but should exert his own will by abstaining from sin, confessing his sins, and doing penance. In this way he can be helped by the grace of God.

100. *Hic docetur* ... Here it is taught about a very greedy man who had a goose that laid one golden egg every day, and it was of such a nature that it could not produce two eggs at one time. Because he was greedy, the master of this goose would gladly have been made rich all at once, and believing that the goose had several golden eggs in it, he killed it. When he had done this, he found no eggs, for which reason the goose's master, his hopes dashed, was greatly saddened.

The moral of this story is that a man should not be too greedy or too acquisitive, lest he suffer harm because of his own avarice and greed. Also, anyone wanting to accomplish any task should not set his mind to several things at once. As the poet says, "He will lose everything who has his hopes in all things."

Allegorically by the master of the goose lords or prelates are understood. By the goose their subjects are understood, by whom the prelates are fed; the prelates or lords sometimes deprive their subjects of their goods, because they must not be superior to them in wealth. *Hic autor* ... Here the author in this fable urges us to work. The fable is that an ant, providing himself with the necessities of life in the summer, stored them in his nest so that he would not die of hunger in the winter. Once when the ant had collected seeds in his nest, a grasshopper came to the ant in wintertime and asked it for help, saying that it was suffering great want in the necessities of life. The ant replied, "What did you do in the summer, when my family and I were hastening about in our great labors and gathering for our larders that from which we would live in the winter?" The grasshopper answered, "I sang then for those who were working and I received no reward from them." Then the ant said, "You would have behaved more wisely if in the summer you had looked to your future needs than now that the winter forces you to come begging at our door. If I needed anything that you could not offer me, all that would be left me would be death. And now death is all that remains for you, as your life up until now has been conducted according to your intentions and because you gave no thought to the future; I shall give you nothing."

Allegorically by the ant any wise and prudent man is understood, by the summer youth and by winter old age. By the grasshopper the foolish and perverse man is understood. Every wise man acquires in his youth those necessities that he uses in his old age. The grasshopper, that is to say the foolish man, does not take care in the time of his youth to provide himself with those things that he will need in his old age. Whence Solomon: "You sleep so much, sluggard, rise from your sleep; go to the ant, O sluggard, and learn wisdom from her who provides herself food in the summer and gathers her food in the harvest which she eats in the winter."

101. *Hic ponitur* ... Here we have another fable and it is this: There was once an ape with two children, one of whom she loved and the other of whom she hated. Once when the ape went to the forest, she was hunted by dogs, and took up both her children in a dissimilar way, for she took the beloved child into her hands and arms, and the

one she did not love on her back, so that if the dogs came, they would rather seize the unloved than the beloved child. When she had fled for a short while from the presence of the hunters, the beloved child which she held by the hands could not run. The mother, fearing the hunters, dropped the beloved child so that she might run faster. Seeing this, the unloved child clung so tightly to its mother with its arms that she could not throw it off. And when the ape had only this one child, she began to love very greatly the one whom before she had not loved.

The moral of this story is that there are many things that are at present neglected, scorned, and rejected as unworthy that later become much loved.

Allegorically the ape with two children is the sinner. The child she loves more is the world and worldly goods, which she embraces with her arms, that is to say with her affections. The child she loves less is the spirit, which she tosses onto her back as she cares little for it. When the hunter comes, that is to say death, which pursues humans, then she is forced to drop the beloved child, that is to say the world and worldly things, and the spirit, because of which she could not run, is burdened by sins and captured by the demons and led to eternal death.

Ista fabula ... This fable is that a calf was beautiful and had no work to do, leading a pampered life. It saw that the ox was plowing constantly and said to it, "Are you not ashamed at working so constantly, while I run to various pastures wherever I wish according to my own choice?" The ox was not moved to anger at these words but plowed on in the usual way until it was released from the plow. Then the ox, grazing in the grassy meadow, saw the calf being led away as a sacrifice to the gods. The ox said, "You are suffering this death on account of your luxurious habits. You would not have to die this death if you had worked as I do."

From the preceding fable the moral is derived that it is better for a man to work than that he be idle lest afterwards he die on account of that idleness. Also as the moral of this fable we have that death comes more quickly to the wealthy and the leisured than to those who lead a life of labor.

Allegorically by the ox who persevered in his work those men are understood who live in luxury but who after death are punished eternally on account of their luxury. The more intent a man was on luxury, the worse the place of torment set aside for him.

102. *Ista fabula* ... This fable consists of four parts. A very fat housedog met a gaunt lion and said to it, "Don't you see how fat I am? My neck is full and my entire body fat. I get food from the table of my master and I receive my food with an open mouth. You are very thin and wander around half starved on many forest paths wherever prey may present itself to you." The dog anticipated the objection that the lion would make to it, saying, "O lion, you might ask why I have a chain around my neck; I answer that this is so that the house of my master not be left unprotected. Although you are very thin and virtually dead, take my advice and subject your neck to a chain and so you can easily earn your food." The lion was outraged and said to the dog, "Go and have a noose around your own neck in return for your merits and let hard chains satisfy your hunger. Although I am hungry and thin, still I can run wherever I like. Do not recommend to me food for which I would have to surrender my freedom."

The moral of this fable is that no one should sell his freedom in return for luxuries. Whence Solomon in Proverbs: "Better is a morsel of bread with joy than a house full of sacrifices with strife." And "It is better to live in poverty and to have freedom than to live in luxury and to have no freedom." Whence Aesop: "Liberty should not be sold for all the gold in the world. This heavenly good exceeds the wealth of the world."

Allegorically by the lion the religious man is understood who does not care for earthly things but persists every day in worship of the divine, which is the greatest freedom. Whence Chrysostom: "No one is free of all care except for him who serves and lives for Christ. For to serve Christ is to rule." By the dog decadent men are understood who live luxuriously and would gladly attract to their company men who do penitence; every religious man should resist them.

103. *Ista fabula* ... This fable is about a fish who had grown up in fresh water but was forced by the rapid current of a flood to go into sea water where it exalted itself above all the ocean fish, claiming itself to be more noble. But a seal, that is to say a marine pig, could not bear the vanity of this foreign fish and reproached it, saying that the fish was uttering many lies. It tried to prove that the fish was uttering lies: "For if a fisherman caught both of us with his hook, then the noble and the rich people would buy me for much money. The poor people would buy you for a little money. Thus you are not more noble than I."

The moral of this fable is that a man living in a foreign land should not boast of the nobility of his family nor should he denigrate the foreigners.

Allegorically by the fish are understood men who cannot stay in one place and wander from one place to another. By the seal are understood men who are reliable and persistent in good works; they should reproach and chasten the unstable ones lest they exalt themselves excessively in their vainglory, which is the root of all vices.

Ista fabula ... This fable is about a soldier who feared that he would die in battle and promised God and all the saints that if he could be preserved from death, he would never fight again and that he would consign all his weapons to the fire. After he had returned safe to his own country, he remembered his vow and cast all his weapons into the fire. When the soldier wanted to throw his battle trumpet, that is to say his bugle, into the fire, it objected, saying that it had never inflicted any injury in battle, but that it had only inspired men to do battle. The soldier replied, "Although you were incapable and never attempted to do so, nevertheless you have sinned more than the others because you incited them to wage war with your tunes and melodies. Thus you should rightly be punished by a greater punishment."

The moral of this fable is that not only those who do wrong are to be punished, but also those who encourage others to sin. Whence Paul: "Those who do and those who consent in the doing of wrong are to be punished by the same punishment." And a verse: "If anyone has done wrong, as the apostle Paul says, whoever conspired with him is himself culpable for the deed."

Allegorically by the soldier God omnipotent is understood. By the weapons the sins of men are understood and by the trumpet their tongues. Thus God, wanting to avenge the sins of men, sends sinners to the fire of hell. But the trumpet, that is to say the tongue, would gladly excuse itself, saying, "O God, see to it that the limbs that committed the sins are punished, but I have committed no sin." God will reply, "Although you have actually committed no sin, yet by your advice and your words you have encouraged the other parts of the body to sin, for which reason you should rightly be punished with the other limbs."

104. *Ista fabula* ... This fable is that a storm, driven by the wind, flew through the fields at great speed and found a clay pot set next to a river to dry in the sun. The storm asked the name of this pot. The

pot, wanting to seem important, said, "I am called an amphora." Because the pot said this boastfully, the storm carried it into the water and completely destroyed it; it did this because the pot had boasted of its name.

The moral of this fable is that no one should assume to himself a greater or more honorable name than is owed him by right. Also we have the lesson that one should not claim to be better and of better family than he is.

Iste appollogus ... This fable is about a leopard who, because of the many spots of various colors it had on its body, despised the lion and the other animals not so distinctively marked; it said that the lion was a pitiful animal and that it was more noble than the lion. A clever fox reproached the leopard for this: "Although you are splendidly colored on the outside, inside you have no wisdom or knowledge. Wisdom of the mind is more to be valued than beauty of the body."

The moral of this fable is that we should praise and value more those who are decorated with virtues and knowledge in their minds than those who have physical beauty. Whence the poet: "Good character gives beauty, but beauty does not assure good character."

Allegorically by the leopard the proud man is understood who is wealthy in exterior goods. By the fox the man can be understood who is withdrawn from the cares of the world, who when he is scorned by the prideful can respond that exterior goods are not to be cared for but rather interior goods.

105. *Iste est* ... This is the last fable of this book; it is about a goat going to pasture. It sought the pastures close to its home and often evaded the wolf with its rapid escape. After seeking food, it went to the city with the other sheep. The wolf followed it into the center of the town and said these words to the goat: "Don't you see that your companions and the other animals are going to be killed and sacrificed to the honor of the gods, and that men will soak the earth with their blood? If you want to avoid death and to be safe, you should come with me to the field." The goat answered the wolf: "O wicked wolf, I beg of you to put away your concern and your foul mercy, for it is much better that I spill my blood for the honor of the gods than that I satisfy your hunger."

The moral of this fable is that the lesser of two evils is to be preferred, because according to Aristotle in the *Topica*, the lesser of evils when compared to the greater of evils seems to have the character of good or is placed into the category of the good.

Allegorically by the wolf the devil is understood, and by the goat seeking the fields the sinner is understood. By the blood penance is understood, and by the city the church is understood. When the devil sees the sinner hastening to church to do penance, then he tries with all his might and all his tricks to draw the sinner back so that he might not do penance for his sins; he says to him, "Come, the true penance which will be imposed on you will be very harsh, so that you will not be able to perform it. But come with me to the meadow, that is to say return to the pleasures of the world, and you will delight in the pleasures of this world." These temptations must be vigorously resisted. Nothing resists the demons so well as a devout awareness of the passion of our Lord, Jesus Christ, upon whom and upon whose mother and all the saints be blessing until the end of time. Amen.

108. *und der* ... and the one who rendered it from German into Latin should always be remembered favorably.

109. *dô Jupiter* ... When Jupiter heard the shouting, he sent a stork who should be their king. This king let none of them survive; his mouth was open, his stomach hungry, he devoured everything that he encountered.

109, n.6. *des hundes* ... The faithfulness of a dog is great. ... Its tongue can heal wounds, and his throat barks at wolves. He watches studiously and guards well. ... Teachers have the same faithfulness. The tongue of teachers is good; it heals body and soul and mind. The teacher watches for the sake of his Lord.

110. *Sepe facit* ... Sometimes fearfulness makes us fear those things that need not be feared.

In einen ... A hunter came into a forest with his dogs. The hares heard the noise.

Si vluhen ... They fled urgently: they were desperate. They thought that they would all die.

111. *wer verzwîvelt* ... Whoever despairs without good reason may well prefer death.

Quod geris ... What you are carrying in the shell is food. The shell is keeping you from that food. Break the shell and the food will fall out. To break the shell, use your brain instead of your strength. If it falls from a height, the stony earth will break it.

De se ... A foolish man, swept away by the storm of the tongue, falls of himself, and this storm can carry away strong men.

112. *diu schal* ... The shell split: the crow came up and was very pleased

with the food: it ate the snail then.

Cornix autem ... The crow was there at once and buried the food in its own stomach.

Sed quia ... But because I am not fitting to you, nor you to me, I would rather have found something less precious, namely a tiny grain that would have satisfied my hunger.

113. *alsô stât* ... Thus the desire of fools, their behavior and their longing are directed also towards the pridefulness of the world.

Per gallum ... By the chicken the foolish man is understood. By the dung this world is understood, by the jasper the heavenly kingdom or the grace of the Holy Spirit. For in the same way as the chicken did not care for the jasper, although it was worth a thousand grains of wheat, so too the foolish and the senseless man does not care for the kingdom of God.

Per gallum ... By the chicken those people are understood who, pursuing the active life, are intent on the seeds and beans of temporal wealth in the dungheap; they neglect or even scorn contemplation, that precious pearl, and the life to come, which is properly understood by the jasper.

114. *daz man* ... that one should love you, Lord.

115. *Si quis* ... If any of the birds would take it up from the earth, it would offer it shells gathered on the ruby sands.

wölt ir ... If you will teach me to fly, I would in truth give you gold and precious stones.

Indignum sibimet ... Disgusted with itself because, a lazy animal, it did nothing and got nowhere all day long.

116. *quod pocius* ... that we should conquer our foes with patience and kindness rather than with threats and harshness.

lop, daz ... Praise that comes from one's own mouth is not real praise.

117. *nemo debet* ... No one should praise himself, for praise from one's own mouth is deemed to be vile.

du solt ... You should look to the purpose of the advice and consider what could happen because of the advice.

Tamen bene ... It should be well considered to what purpose the words are said.

Montibus e ... Ripped from the highest peaks, an oak was torn from its roots, vanquished by a wild storm.

Úf einem ... On a mountain there stood an oak, which had never yielded to any wind, for it was strong, great and tall. Below the mountain there was a swamp, and through it flowed a cool stream, where one might see many reeds growing; there were flowers and grass. The oak was very well rooted: it stood without swaying. Who would have thought that if should fall down? Its strength stood in the way of that.

118. *Ein esel* ... A donkey had great labor, for which his master was very much pleased. He loaded many sacks on his back, for which reason his back often ached. I have also heard about that donkey that he had to pull and carry things: he had great labor.

119. *At mihi* ... But to me, you will always be and have always been an ass.

sîn meister ... His master suffered great distress; he thought he had lost the donkey: that was no slight source of anger to him. He looked for his donkey; he did not find it where it tended to go and look for pasture. He went out onto the heath, he looked far and wide.

Rusticus autem ... The farmer, when he had looked everywhere, happened to find his donkey by chance.

du muost ... you must be my donkey.

mea estimacione ... In my view you will always be my donkey as you were before.

120. *"Quid mirum ..."* "What surprise is it that the hair I have applied to my head has left me, when my own hair has already done the same?"

batstubenvarwe ... Cosmetic color passes away, as the natural color remains.

Ille sagax ... Wisely, because he was a source of laughter to so many thousands, he dispelled the ridicule with his cleverness.

Er dunket ... He seems to me a wise man who can dispel ridicule with laughter. That is much better than if he tried to threaten with words.

121. *hiut ist* ... Today he is poor, who once was mighty; the wheel of fortune turns unsteadily. Whoever is standing upright, if he can, he should not fall down; if he falls, he will certainly not get back up. There is no constancy in this world.

docet nos ... He teaches us that if we are ridiculed by anyone, we should not dispel the laughter with anger but with laughter ... and that we should not be eager for artificial things to last when natural things cannot last.

Notandum quod ... It is to be noted that allegorically by this knight we can understand any wise man who is constant even in adversity as to temporal things. And by the hairs fastened to his head we understand the worldly goods which arrive quickly and pass away quickly as well. ... Note that scholastically by the knight we understand the man of the church, armed with learning and virtue, and by the hairs we understand honor. So long as such a man fights to preserve justice, if he is deprived of his honor and dignity, still he will not suffer from such a loss.

122. *der hêrre* ... The lord lost the covering of his wig, that is to say the inconstancy of the world.

Allegorice per ... Allegorically by this knight we can understand Christ, by the hairs fastened on we can understand his humanity, which died and slipped away and was derided by the Jews.

123. *Diz büechlîn* ... This little book can well be called "The Gemstone."

Ein ende ... The book that is before you is now concluded.

Waz von ... If whatever is innate in a creature by nature is lost, it has been lost by consistent habit.

als hie ... As happened here in this fable.

124. *von einem* ... About a hunter and a tiger; about slander.

125. *waz diu* ... Whatever nature has provided, a man can hardly strive against that. Cuteness suits a puppy well, and a donkey should carry sacks.

die gar ... who think they are exceedingly secure; they sometimes do not survive, just as happened to the little birds, which they could easily have foreseen.

126. *wem mîn* ... Whoever does not like my stories, be it a woman, a man, young or old, that person should politely stop reading; but if he wants to continue, he should be forgiving of me, and wherever this book may have weaknesses in its content, he should disregard that.

127. *autor reprehendit* ... The author reproaches those who are so sure of their own matter and have such faith in their own defenses [?] and their own strength that they believe there to be nothing that in anger could harm them.

quamuis quedam ... Although some wild animals should be feared, yet man is more to be feared than all the animals, because when man was made and created, he was raised above all the animals because of his cleverness.

nemo periculum ... No one should put his own life at risk for the sake of another, lest when he has exposed himself to danger he become a laughingstock to the others.

Item docet ... And the author teaches too that many words are to be feared, because they leak out secretly. And they injure more than if they were said publicly because a man in this way has no way to defend himself. ... The prophet says the same thing when he says in the Psalm, "They have whetted their tongues like a sword" and so on.

128. *statim vnum* ... who turns the page right away ... as the ape does which, when it climbs up into a tree and tastes the nuts on it and finding the shell bitter, throws the shell away along with the sweet and tasty meat; if it had tasted the nutmeat, it would not throw it away but would eat it. They do likewise who, when they have seen the surface of simple and useless words scorn and undervalue the good and useful things [the words conceal].

129. *Wer die* ... Whoever wants to understand the fables should turn to their end. Their usefulness is all in the end of the fable, if anyone pays attention to it. ... The book that is written here has an end.

finem debet ... The wise reader should consider their end. For it is said in the Ethics: "Good beginnings are not praiseworthy, unless they are concluded with an appropriate end." By looking to the end, you will perceive the qualities of all things. Now we must talk about the end. The "end" is that for the purpose of which anything is. And it is twofold, namely internal and external. The internal end is that we know the things that are taught in this book and memorize their examples. The external is that once we know the things that are said here, we flee the bad and desire the good.

concludendo librum ... At the end of his book he sets the method of discovering the moral of each fable, that is how the fable should be related to its moral, that is to say applied to our life. And he intends that the moral of each fable be included in the two verses placed at the very end of each fable. The first reason why the author places the moral of each fable at the end is this: ... in the work at hand our author wants to urge us to good morals, but first he gives the narrative and then he adds the lesson. ... For all things are to be judged by their end, as Aristotle says in his book *De anima*. And the goal and intention of the author is to reproach vice and to teach good morals. ... And for the sake of brevity and the ease of memorizing he condenses the sense at the end in two verses.

131. *hic docet* ... Here the author teaches, and he demonstrates in the following fable.

132. *Bi enem* ... A stream flowed past a village; it was deep and quite

wide, and a wooden bridge spanned it, over which one used to walk. One time a dog walked over it with a piece of cheese, which he held firmly in his mouth.

Nat canis ... A dog swims, carrying a piece of meat in its mouth.

Canis per ... A dog crossed a bridge over a bright and pure stream and carried a cheese in its mouth.

133. *Des kese* ... He saw the reflection of the cheese and thought that he might find another piece of cheese on the streambed, as fine and good as this. In that hope he jumped into the water, opened his mouth greedily, and the cheese fell out onto the ground; and so by his greed he lost both the cheese and the shadow.

Cuius dum ... when he saw its reflection in the water, he thought it was a second cheese. And so throwing himself into the water in a great leap, while he wanted to grab the second one, he lost the one he was holding.

Spem carnis ... He desires the possibility of the meat more than the meat, more the sign of profit than profit. He opens his mouth, and both the meat and his hopes are lost.

134. *Do wart* ... He was sorry and said, "If I only had mine again, I would not jump down here; it was foolish of me to look [for the cheese] here, as the water is flowing here."

Aldus de ... In this way the greedy one loses what is his when he spies what is not and foolishly desires it; thereby his own property leaves him in shame and harm, just as the cheese was lost by the dog.

Sic homines ... In this way greedy men often lose the things that are theirs and cannot gain the things that are not.

Non sua ... Whoever desires what is not is, will soon lose what is.

135. *Út enem* ... A mouse, raised in a fine house, left its town and wanted to visit another town.

Mus quidam ... A certain mouse wanted to leave its town, in which it had been born and raised, to visit another town.

De andere ... The other one said, "I praise this food and this house highly; even more your spirit and your kindness are so good, that all my hunger is satisfied, for kind intentions and a generous attitude are better than all kinds of hospitality."

In mensa ... Boundless good will is enough at a slender table. A generous spirit improves coarse foods.

Ecce sere ... And late the key rattles: the door opens.

136. *Ein knape* ... A servant, while the mouse said this, put the key into the lock.

Sed modo ... But now I see your danger and the various sources of harm; you must fear men and their traps, and the ferret is your enemy; above all the treachery of the cat is to be feared, for woe is you if you fall into the hands of the cat.

De gast ... The visitor said: "I pity your young, whose life you must defend from ferrets, dogs, cats, and traps, and from all the people all the time."

138. *Út enem* ... Once a bird has escaped a snare, it will not easily be deceived afterwards.

139. *Sint heft* ... Meanwhile a man has translated into German a portion of the best fables.

140. *Wo de* ... I do not find written how they settled their business with him.

des môt ... That I can assert truthfully.

ik hân ... I have heard sometime.

Dusse mere ... This story is true and it actually happened; that was certainly long ago.

141. *Et wônde* ... There once lived a man in Judea who had a lion, huge and massive, but quite tame. The lion was more useful than the dogs, for he could protect all the livestock on the pasture and in the woods whenever he needed to.

De wart ... He quickly noticed that it was a donkey, for it was eating twigs and grass, and he saw it too by the ears.

de wulf ... The wolf bit the donkey and hacked it to pieces.

142. *Nu provet* ... Now see, dear people, what this story means.

De rike ... The rich man signifies the lords and the princes, who are experienced and have honor in their authority; but the advice and cooperation of the deputy must help the rich man if he is to set about things properly. But if that deputy, living or dead, does not remain in the employ of his master to guide his vassals, but resigns in honor, if his master then puts the lion's skin on a donkey and makes his deputy out of a peasant of the old school, who was never virtuous, wise or loyal, then he would gladly, if he could, use the donkey's braying to persecute the people and harass them and behave frightfully. If a man is faithful and experienced, he should have honor and praise from that; but if he is only wearing a skin, he will be recognized as a fool by his great foolishness, as the donkey was recognized by his ears; and so his reputation and his property will be taken from him; his behavior will be avenged in this way. Villainous deeds have that result for the wicked faithless man. I have heard sometime that one can never fully rely on a bad deputy, but that the master's estate is in honor and good reputation with a deputy who watches over his property, safeguards his land and is good for his master's honor in this way.

143. *Up enem* ... An oak tree stood on a mountain, which never yielded to the wind, for it was large and strong. Its extensive roots made it possible that it withstood many a gust, which the wind offered it often.

Haec nos ... These words remind us that we resist those greater than ourselves in vain, and that we can hardly overcome wicked threats.

144. *De êk* ... The oak tree signifies the proud man ... the reed signifies the humble.

de wisheit ...... who has wisdom and lives humbly without wealth.

Chapter 3

147. *Jm mag* ... He will have nothing of the fruit, just as they tell of the ape.

In gallo ... In the chicken you recognize the foolish man, in the jasper the precious gifts of wisdom; this fruit is of no value to the foolish man.

149. *Rumula filius* ... Rumula, the son, sends greetings to Tibernius of Athens. Aesop, a gifted Greek, was born in Phrygia and flourished there, living in honor for [illegible]. But I, Romulus, have translated this book from Greek into Latin. Its title is "Incipit Esopus, the book of fables composed by the Athenian author Aesop." Note that the final cause of poets consists in the usefulness of their language or in the delight of their material, for poets write variously. Whence Horace: "Poets seek either to delight or to profit."

151. *Vtilitas: Non* ... The moral is that it is of no use to serve or to do a favor for bad men, for [garbled] they are not mindful of favors they have received and do not remain grateful.

152. *Ossa dum* ... When a wolf was gulping down bones, one of them stuck in his throat.

Ein wolf ... A wolf was hungry for prey in the usual way. Soon he came across the prey that his heart desires. A goat chanced to come to him: voraciously he bit into it.

153. *hæt er* ... If he had not eaten the food so gluttonously, it would not have happened to him. I must say in all honesty that I wish that

every woman and every man who commit gluttony would have the same thing happen as what happened to the wolf.

155. *Cum rigido* ... While it dug with a stiff beak. This is the second introductory part of this book in which the author carries out his intention, namely discussing those things that are contained in this work; namely the delightful flower, that is to say the fables, and the very useful fruit, that is to say the allegories signified in the fables. And the book is divided into as many parts as the author gives fables and apologues. And first he presents a fable about a chicken in which he reproaches the man who scorns wisdom and philosophy. And so in this work he teaches us that we should not be foolish but intelligent, not stupid but wise. And he says in a metaphor that once a chicken seeking food in a dungheap saw a precious stone lying there which it could not use; it said to the stone, "O precious thing of great beauty, why are you lying here in this stinking place? You are of no use to me, but if someone had found you who could use you, then your shine and your splendor would be increased. But I am of no use to you and you are of no use to me, and so I would rather have found instead of you something less precious, such as a small grain of wheat with which I could fill my stomach." And then he continues: Also many stupid and ignorant men when they hear about philosophy and the moral arts and virtuous deeds, from which they gain no profit, they do not care about them but rather less valuable things, namely the pleasure of the body. And this is what is said in German as well: "A fool is like a chicken that finds a pearl in the dung. Just as the chicken does not care for the pearl, so the fool disregards whatever one teaches him." And allegorically: by the chicken the foolish man is understood, by the dungheap this world, by the jasper the heavenly kingdom or the grace of the Holy Spirit. For in the same way as the chicken did not care for the jasper, although it was worth a thousand grains of wheat, thus too the foolish and the senseless do not care for the kingdom of God. Accordingly the verse: "The foolish one does not concentrate with his mind on the kingdom of heaven." But the wise man sells all that he has and buys the kingdom and puts behind him all the human delights and concentrates on God alone, serving him in virtue. And thus he attains the kingdom of heaven and the grace of God.

157. *Eyn han* ... A chicken lived in the stinking manure and looked for food according to his skill. He found a precious jasper there, a miracle that amazed him. "O noble thing," he said, "you are lying in

filth, as I see. You bring me no profit. If someone had come to you who wanted to find you, and who would deserve to have you, he would hold you in high esteem. He would adorn you with worked gold. You would not be without delight. [corrupt] Neither am I of use to you; our value one to the other is minimal and we are not suited to each other. If there were any small insects here I would rather turn my attention to them."

158. *Den fremden* ... You, reader, should understand this new entertainment for the sake of its serious meaning: The jasper means this wise teaching, and the chicken means the uncomprehending people. Such fools consider the advice of this wisdom useless and scorn it. Similarly Solomon says: "If you do not have good listeners, rather choose silence and do not pour forth clever words."

161. *Nat canis* ... A dog swims. In this fable the author criticizes all those greedy and avaricious people who sometimes, in the hope of acquiring a small good, do not consider the great harm that can befall them. And he teaches us that when acquiring those things that are necessary we should not give up a certain thing in the pursuit of an uncertain thing, lest we lose our own things while we seek or desire to seek those things that are not ours. And to this end he presents a fable, saying that once a dog carrying meat in its mouth was swimming across a river, and when it saw the reflection of the meat in the water, it thought that the reflection of the meat was of greater quantity and better taste than its own meat. For this reason it opened its mouth and, eager to grab the reflection of the meat, lost the meat it was holding in its mouth and did not gain the reflection. And so it often happens that those who are unwilling to be content, but who strive day and night and labor to acquire riches, expose themselves and their belongings to danger. At length, when they have not acquired new goods, they also lose what they have of their own. For this reason the author reproaches them and says, "Therefore they should not" and so on, wanting us not to relinquish our property that is certain or to lose it on account of those things that are doubtful; for if anyone desires too much other people's property, it often happens to him that he loses his own. A verse: "Rightfully anyone deserves to lose his good fortune [?] if he desires things that are not his more than his own property; such people lose their belongings quickly." And it is said in German: "Certain things should not be given up in this world for appearances, for whatever man desires things that are not his is often harmed in his own prop-

erty." Allegorically by the dog understand the greedy man, by the meat the kingdom of heaven, and by the reflection the transitory goods of this world.

162. *Eyn rode* ... A dog swam across a river and took with him a piece of meat. The meat cast a reflection in the water and the dog snapped at it. He was more eager for the appearance of the food than for the meat that was his already; he preferred a sign over the real profit. His mouth gaped and his food was lost immediately, along with his ill-chosen hopes.

Nicht zolde ... We should not let go of certain things because of uncertain goods. Rightly the man loses what is his who is intent on goods that are not his.

163. *Das dy* ... Assure us properly, master Cato, that these words are correct. You say [unclear].

164. *Ein erde* ... The earth swelled to a head and lamented in pitiful screaming that it would bear a child. O how women and men were afraid that the earth would bear a monster, from which they would never be safe. The people feared dreadfully, while they would gladly have been free of fear. But the fear disappeared at the slight deed of the earth. The fear was turned into scorn; the earth, pregnant as if a woman, bore a mouse. The great fear and discomfort became a joke. The people who want to deceive me with words often end up doing small things. Very often one wants to create great fear with a little matter.

Meister Gamfred ... Master Geoffrey, give us the truth. You say, "Hurry to get ahead; death will follow your words. Whoever has much boasting in him weakens his reputation with it." And God's prophet David says likewise: "They trembled in fear when no one was doing them any harm."

164, n.47. *Terra tumet* ... The earth swells, the swelling moans and in its moaning announces that it is about to give birth. People of both sexes nearly die of fear. As much as the earth swells, it suggests that it will bear a monster. People are terrified and afraid to stand nearby. That fear gives way to laughter for the pregnant earth gives birth to a mouse. What was before fear is now laughter. Often those men who talk a lot actually do less. Often a tiny thing brings with it great fear.

167. *Proficit exemplis* ... The lesson of a teacher is effective when properly accompanied by examples; and so let the young man rely on the knowledge of his elder.

Snelle bessert ... The human mind is quickly improved where one provides a good example. The young person should be obedient to his master in matters of skill.

Aristoteles, du ... Aristotle, you master renowned in skill, long ago you said, "When we provide good examples, our students learn well. If our pupil wants to be erudite himself, he should be intent on accepting the teacher's teaching; from that, knowledge will grow [illegible] the more."

Chapter 4

173. *Item maister* ... Master Nikolaus von Dinkelsbühl has written a German book for the women of St. Jacob's in Vienna; the book treats the Lord's Prayer. That book is supposed to be a very fine book, better than all other German books; I intend to copy out of it. It has many things about the Virgin. That book has been copied in many places in the city of Vienna.

174. *Nicolaus Dinckelpuhel* ... Dinkelsbühl on the Lord's Prayer; on prayer in the community, on the commandments and the love of God, on the ten commandments, on the beatitudes, the seven gifts, the seven sins, on fraternal rebuking, on offerings, on the torments of hell, on death, on the body of Christ, and the same Dinkelsbühl's moralization on animals. Each of these is considered separately above. A number of sermons. The fables of Cyrillus.

175. *Ich wil* ... I will not rhyme my German and yet will enclose it in the chains of that art called rhetoric, in such a way that I stay close to the words of the text and maintain the same measure as in the Latin.

176. *nach der* ... according to the structure of the text, which is written in proper measure in Latin.
     ganczen sin ... the complete content of the book ... as it is written in Latin.
     Auch ist ... It is also to be noted that the Latin tract is extremely profound in its sense ... and thus the German is somewhat odd and must be considered with careful attention.

177. *Nu hab* ... Now I have adopted for my purposes the usual type of German language according to this area's custom, for this book and its teachings are appropriate to the general public.

179. *von dem* ... On the eagle that found a snail and carried it aloft, and was tricked out of it by the crow.

181. *latein und* ... in Latin and in German, and where appropriate to find pleasure in them.

nucz ainualtiger ... the profit of uneducated lay people who could not appreciate these teachings in Latin or who might not understand and comprehend them completely.

182. *hat das* ... has done this not so that the uneducated can understand the meaning and sense any better, but only so that the learned can recognize that the author has compiled this book out of the law books.

183. *alles genomen* ... compiled all from authoritative books.

Hie lert ... Here the author teaches us.

und daz ... and he demonstrates it thus; he demonstrates it with a fable.

185. *da uon* ... by which any person can be improved in morals, both spiritual and worldly.

Ingente. Hie ... Ingente. Here the author teaches us that wisdom is more useful and more praiseworthy than strength, for often many save themselves with wisdom who cannot save themselves with strength or wealth. And he demonstrates this with a fable. ... Allegorically by the raven one can understand the treacherous, faithless women, for they have little strength of body, but with their wisdom and their sweet words they can overcome many a strong man, and they gain such control over him that he can resist them in no way.

191. *wart grimlichen* ... grew furiously outraged, and he said to the lamb, "You are clouding my water."

Hunc timor ... Fear overcame the lamb while the wolf reproached it with these words: "You have disturbed my drinking and the beauty of the shore."

192. *ich pei* ... I was not yet born twenty years ago, I am not even a year old.

daz trüb ... The sullied water flows from you to me, not back to you. What are you saying? I would have more right to complain, for I am standing downstream.

vnda supremi ... The water cannot flow upstream. And anyway the water is unmuddied.

quomodo potest ... How can that be when the water flows not from me to you but from you to me?

193. *Sed saliua* ... But you can more easily sully my drinking with your slobbering since the water flows from higher to lower.

Der wolff ... The wolf is like the lord who with violence and without right subjects the innocent to much shame, slander, and harm. I hear so many poor people complain about this in the world that God in his heaven should have mercy.

Per lupum ... By the wolf oppressors and slanderers are understood, by the lamb the innocent man.

Latin Verse Fables Cited

This appendix provides the full texts of those Latin verse fables of Avian and the Anonymus Neveleti referred to but not cited in their entirety in the text (with the exception of those Avian fables referred to only in the editorial appendix that follows Chapter 1). The Avian fables are reproduced from the *editio citanda* by Guaglianone (where the "spurious" epimyths from the later manuscripts are included in square brackets); those from the Anonymus are taken from Foerster's critical edition.

Avianus

I. DE NUTRICE ET INFANTE

Rustica deflentem parvum iuraverat olim,
    Ni taceat, rabido quod foret esca lupo.
Credulus hanc vocem lupus audiit et manet ipsas
    Pervigil ante fores, irrita vota gerens.
Nam lassata puer nimiae dat membra quieti,
    Spem quoque raptori sustulit inde fames.
Hunc ubi silvarum repetentem lustra suarum
    Ieiunum coniunx sensit adesse lupa:
"Cur, inquit, nullam referens de more rapinam,
    Languida consumptis sed trahis ora genis?"
"Ne mireris, ait, deceptum fraude maligna
    Vix miserum vacua delituisse fuga.
Nam quae preda, rogas, quae spes contingere posset,
    Iurgia nutricis cum mihi verba darent?"

Haec sibi dicta putet seque hac sciat arte notari,
    Femineam quisquis credidit esse fidem.
[Adam Samsonem, regem David et Solomonem
    Femina decepit, cepit et arte sua.
Ingemiscit egens ubi non est femina, saltem
    Femineus dulcis omnia vincit amor.]

V. DE ASINO PELLE LEONIS INDUTA

[Metiri se quemque decet propriisque iuvari
    Laudibus, alterius nec bona ferre sibi,
Ne detracta gravem faciant miracula risum,
    Coeperit in solis cum remanere malis.]
Exuvias asinus Gaetuli forte leonis
    Repperit et spoliis induit ora novis,
Aptavitque suis incongrua tegmina membris,
    Et miserum tanto pressit honore caput.
Ast ubi terribilis animo circumstetit horror,
    Pigraque praesumptus venit in ossa vigor,
Mitibus ille feris communia pabula calcans,
    Turbabat pavidas per sua rura boves.
Rusticus hunc magna postquam deprendit ab aure,
    Correptum vinclis verberibusque domat.
Et simul abstracto denudans corpora tergo,
    Increpat his miserum vocibus ille pecus:
"Forsitan ignotos imitato murmure fallas,
    At mihi, qui quondam, semper asellus eris."
[Quo est ut ⟨tam⟩ penitus terrae sit homunculus expers,
    ⟨sed⟩ totam terram solus habere cupit?]

VI. DE RANA ET VULPE

Edita gurgitibus limoque immersa profundo,
    Et luteis tantum semper amica vadis,
Ad superos colles herbosaque prata recurrens
    Mulcebat miseras turgida rana feras:
Callida quod posset gravibus succurrere morbis,
    Et vitam ingenio continuare suo.
Nec se Paeonio iactat cessisse magistro,
    Quamvis perpetuos curet in orbe deos.
Tunc vulpes pecudum ridens astuta quietem,

Verborum vacuam prodidit esse fidem.
"Haec dabit aegrotis, inquit, medicamina membris,
    Pallida caeruleus cui notat ora color?"
[Ne sibimet quisquam de rebus inaniter ullis,
    Quod nequit imponat, nostra fabella monet.]

VII. DE CANE

[Haud facile est pravis innatum mentibus ut se
    Muneribus dignas suppliciove putent.]
Forte canis quondam, nullis latratibus horrens
    Nec patulis primum rictibus ora trahens,
Mollia sed pavidae submittens verbera caudae,
    Concitus audaci vulnera dente dabat.
Hunc dominus, ne quem probitas simulata lateret,
    Iusserat in rabido gutture ferre nolam.
Faucibus innexis crepitantia subligat aera,
    Quae facili motu signa cavenda darent.
Haec tamen ille sibi credebat praemia ferri,
    Et similem turbam despiciebat ovans.
Tunc insultantem senior de plebe superbum
    Aggreditur, tali singula voce monens:
"Infelix, quae tanta rapit dementia sensum,
    Munera pro meritis si cupis ista dari?
Non hoc virtutis decus ostentatur in aere,
    Nequitiae testem sed geris inde sonum."

IX. DE DUOBUS SOCIIS ET URSA

Montibus ignotis, curvisque in vallibus artum
    Cum socio quidam suscipiebat iter,
Securus, quodcumque malum fortuna tulisset,
    Robore collato posset uterque pati.
Dumque per inceptum vario sermone feruntur,
    In mediam praeceps convenit ursa viam.
Horum alter, facili comprendens robora cursu,
    In viridi trepidum fronde pependit onus.
Ille trahens nullo iacuit vestigia gressu,
    Exanimem fingens, sponte relisus humi.
Continuo praedam cupiens fera saeva cucurrit,
    Et miserum curvis unguibus ante levat.

Verum ubi concreto riguerunt membra timore
    (Nam solitus mentis liquerat ossa calor),
Tunc olidum credens, quamvis ieiuna, cadaver
    Deserit et lustris conditur ursa suis.
Sed cum securi paulatim in verba redissent,
    Liberior iusto, qui fuit ante fugax:
"Dic, sodes, quidnam trepido tibi rettulit ursa?
    Nam secreta diu multaque verba dedit."
"Magna quidem monuit, tamen haec quoque maxima iussit,
    Quae misero semper sunt facienda mihi:
"Ne facile alterius repetas consortia, dixit,
    Rursus ab insana ne capiare fera."
[Confidens homini maledicitur ore videntis,
    Indubiam cunctis non adhibeto fidem.
Fratribus in falsis exosa pericula subsunt,
    Subiectum multis lubrica, rara fides.

X. DE CALVO EQUITE

Calvus eques capiti solitus religare capillos
    Atque alias nudo vertice ferre comas,
Ad campum nitidis venit conspectus in armis
    Et facilem frenis flectere coepit equum.
Huius ab adverso Boreae spiramina praeflant
    Ridiculum populo conspiciente caput;
Nam mox deiecto nituit frons nuda galero,
    Discolor apposita quae fuit ante coma.
Ille sagax, tantis quod risus milibus esset,
    Distulit admota calliditate iocum:
"Quid mirum, referens, positos fugisse capillos,
    Quem prius aequaevae deseruere comae?"
[Ridiculus cuiquam cum sis, absolvere temet
    Apposita veri cum ratione stude.
*
Fuscata cervice stude ne prae videaris:
    Crine capillata calva secunda patent.
*
Se risu quicumque novo sciat esse retentum,
    Arte magis studeat quam prohibere minis.
*

Ferre iocos gratos calvus docet esse ligatos:
  Utile consilium risu depellere risum.]

XIII. DE TAURO ET HIRCO

Immensum taurus fugeret cum forte leonem
  Tutaque desertis quaereret antra viis,
Speluncam reperit, quam tunc hirsutus habebat
  Cinyphii ductor qui gregis esse solet.
Post ubi submissa meditantem irrumpere fronte
  Obvius obliquo terruit ore caper,
Tristis abit, longaque fugax de calle locutus
  (Nam timor expulsum iurgia ferre vetat):
"Non te demissis saetosum, putide, barbis,
  Illum, qui superest consequiturque, tremo.
Nam si discedat, nosces, stultissime, quantum
  Discrepet a tauri viribus hircus olens."
[Dum cupis illatum tibimet persolvere damnum,
  Absque tuo damno hocce caveto fore.
*

Non spernas aliquem subita de clade gementem,
  Ne quandoque minis obviet ille tuis.]

XVI. DE QUERCU ET HARUNDINE

Montibus e sumis radicitus eruta quercus
  Decidit, insani turbine victa noti.
Quam tumidis subter decurrens alveus undis
  Suscipit et fluvio praecipitante rapit.
Verum ubi diversis impellitur ardua ripis,
  In fragiles calamos grande residit onus.
Tunc sic exiguo conectens caespite ramos
  Miratur liquidis quod stet arundo vadis:
Se quoque tam vasto necdum consistere trunco,
  Ast illam tenui cortice ferre minas.
Stridula mox blando respondens canna susurro
  Seque magis tutam debilitate docet:
"Tu rabidos, inquit, ventos saevasque procellas
  Despicis, et totis viribus acta ruis.
Ast ego surgentes paulatim demoror austros,
  Et quamvis levibus provida cedo notis.

In tua praeruptus offendit robora nimbus,
    Motibus aura meis ludificata perit."
Haec nos dicta monent magnis obsistere frustra,
    Paulatimque truces exsuperare minas.
[Si fugis in bassum cupias trascendere saepe,
    Alta petunt venti tutius ima iacent.]

XVII. DE VENATORE ET TIGRIDE

Venator iaculis haud irrita vulnera torquens,
    Turbabat rapidas per sua lustra feras.
Tum pavidis audax cupiens succurrere tigris
    Verbere commotas iussit abesse minas.
Ille tamen solito contorquens tela lacerto:
    "Nunc tibi, qualis eram, nuntius iste refert."
Et simul emissum transegit vulnera ferrum,
    Perstrinxitque citos hasta cruenta pedes.
Molliter at fixum traheret cum suacia telum,
    A trepida fertur vulpe retenta diu,
Dum quisnam ille foret, qui talia vulnera ferret,
    Aut ubinam iaculum delituisset agens.
Illa gemens fractoque loqui vix murmure coepit
    (Nam solitas voces ira dolorque rapit):
"Nulla quidem medio convenit in aggere forma,
    Quaeque oculis olim sit repetenda meis;
Sed cruor et validis in nos directa lacertis
    Ostendunt aliquem tela fuisse virum."

[More volant iaculi clandestina verba nocentis,
    Nec praescire palam, laederis unde, potes.
*

Bruta licet soleant animalia cuncta timeri,
    Omnibus est illis plus metuendus homo.
*

Plus aequo pavidos confortant saepe superbi
    qui, quia confidunt viribus, hinc pereunt].

XVIII. DE QUATTUOR IUVENCIS ET LEONE

Quattor immensis quondam per prata iuvencis
    Fertur amicitiae tanta fuisse fides,

Ut simul emissos nullus divelleret error,
    Rursus et e pastu turba rediret amans.
Hos quoque collatis inter se cornibus ingens
    Dicitur in silvis pertimuisse leo,
Dum metus oblatam prohibet temptare rapinam,
    Et coniuratos horret adire boves,
Sed quamvis audax furiisque immanior esset,
    Tantorum solus viribus impar erat.
Protinus aggreditur pravis insistere verbis,
    Collisum cupiens dissociare pecus.
Sic postquam dictis animos disiunxit acerbis,
    Invasit miserum diripuitque gregem.
Tunc quidam ex illis: "Vitam servare quietam
    Qui cupiet, nostra discere morte potest.
[Neve cito admotas verbis fallacibus aures
    Impleat, aut veterem deserat ante fidem"].
[Sermones blandos blaesosque cavere memento,
    Credulitas nimia simplicitate nocet.
*
Praesens charta docet, quia lis divortiat usque:
    Foedus, amicitia, firmus amorque ligat.]

XX. DE PISCATORE ET PISCE

Piscator solitus praedam suspendere saeta,
    Exigui piscis vile trahebat onus.
Sed postquam superas captum perduxit ad auras,
    Atque avido fixum vulnus ab ore tulit:
"Parce, precor, supplex lacrimis ita dixit obortis:
    Nam quanta ex nostro corpore lucra feres?
Nunc me saxosis genitrix fecunda sub antris
    Fudit et in propriis ludere iussit aquis.
Tolle minas, tenerumque tuis sine crescere mensis:
    Haec tibi me rursum litoris ora dabit:
Protinus, immensi depastus caerula ponti,
    Pinguior ad calamum sponte recurro tuum."
Ille nefas captum referens absolvere piscem,
    Difficiles queritur casibus esse vices:
"Nam miserum est, inquit, praesentem amittere praedam,
    Stultius et rursum vota futura sequi."

[Incerta pro spe non munera certa relinque,
    Ne rursus quaeras forte nec invenias.
Unum quod tendis praepono duobus habendis,
    Plus valet "hoc tribuo" quam "tribuenda duo."
*

Quisque tenet, teneat quod cepit dextera prompta,
    Ad praesens ova sunt meliora feris.
*

Iudicio plebis non fallit "habes," sed "habebis,"
    Plus "hoc unum tribuo" quam "tribuenda duo."]

XXII. DE CUPIDO ET INVIDO

Iuppiter ambiguas hominum praediscere mentes
    Ad terras Phoebum misit ab arce poli.
Tunc duo diversis poscebant numina votis;
    Namque alter cupidus, invidus alter erat.
His sese medium Titan, scrutatus utrumque,
    Obtulit, et precibus cum peteretur, ait:
"Praestan[t] di facilis: nam quae speraverit unus,
    Protinus haec alter congeminata feret."
Sed cui longa iecur nequeat satiare cupido,
    Distulit admotas in nova damna preces;
Spem sibi confidens alieno crescere voto,
    Seque ratus solum munera ferre duo.
Ille ubi captantem socium sua praemia vidit,
    Supplicium proprii corporis optat ovans:
Nam petit exstinctus ut lumine degeret uno:
    Alter ut, hoc duplicans, vivat utroque carens.
Tum sortem sapiens humanam risit Apollo,
    Invidiaeque malum rettulit ipse Iovi;
Quae, dum proventis aliorum gaudet iniquis,
    Laetior infelix et sua damna cupit.
[Invidus ut non sis nec avarus, nostra fabella
    Casibus edocet his ne similem subeas.
*

† Omnia dat cupido, sua non petit in cupido †].

XXIII. DE VENDITORE ET MERCATORE

Venditor insignem referens de marmore Bacchum
    Expositum pretio fecerat esse deum.
Nobilis hunc quidam funesta in sede sepulcri
    Mercari cupiens compositurus erat;
Alter adoratis ut ferret numina templis,
    Redderet et sacro debita vota loco.
"Nunc, ait, ambiguum facies de mercibus omen,
    Cum spes in pretium munera dispar agit,
Et me defunctis seu malis tradere divis,
    Sive decus busti, seu velis esse deum.
Subdita namque tibi est magni reverentia fati,
    Atque eadem retines funera nostra manu."
[Convenit hoc illis quibus est permissa potestas,
    An praestare magis, seu nocuisse velint.]
[In damnum alterius spem tu tibi ponere noli,
    Fallere qui satagit, fallitur arte sua.]

XXIV. DE VENATORE ET LEONE

Certamen longa protractum lite gerebant
    Venator quondam nobilis atque leo.
Hi cum perpetuum cuperent in iurgia finem,
    Edita continuo forte sepulcra vident.
Illic docta manus flectentem colla leonem
    Fecerat in gremio procubuisse viri.
Scilicet affirmans pictura teste superbum
    Se fieri: exstinctam nam docet esse feram.
Ille, graves oculos ad inania signa retorquens,
    Infremit et rabido pectore verba dedit:
"Irrita te generis subiit fiducia vestri,
    Artificis testem si cupis esse manum.
Quod si nostra novum caperet sollertia sensum,
    Sculperet ut docili pollice saxa leo,
Tunc hominem aspiceres oppressum murmure magno,
    Conderet ut rabidis ultima fata genis."
[Ne credas aliquem, docet ista parabola forte,
    Exemplo vacuo credere velle tibi.
*
Decipiunt aures pictura oculos‹que› poesis,

Crede ‹vel› huic vel ei falleris hac vel ea.
*

Quid prodes duram ‹tibi› iacturam parituro
    Praesenti quae dat et simili modicum?
Nec pictae tabulae, nec testi credito per se,
    Nam pellectus eris, si male credideris.
*

Est homo ‹vel› simplex praecellens omnia bruta,
    Haec cum in multis sint tamen apta iocis.]

XXV. DE PUERO ET FURE

Flens puer extremam putei consedit ad undam,
    Vana supervacuis rictibus ora trahens.
Callidus hunc lacrimis postquam fur vidit obortis,
    Quaenam tristitiae sit modo causa rogat.
Ille sibi abrupti fingens discrimina funis,
    Atque auri queritur desiluisse cadum.
Nec mora, sollicitam traxit manus improba vestem,
    Exutus putei protinus ima petit.
Parvulus exiguo circumdans pallia collo,
    Sentibus immersus delituisse datur.
Sed post fallaci suscepta pericula voto
    Tristior, amissa veste, resedit humi.
Dicitur his sollers vocem rupisse querelis,
    Et gemitu summos sollicitasse deos:
"Perdita, quisquis erit, post haec bene pallia credat,
    Qui putat in liquidis quod natet urna vadis."
[Nemo nimis cupide sibi res desideret ullas,
    Ne, cum plus cupiat, perdat et id quod habet.
*

Qui videt infantem nihilominus omnia nescit,
    Quae fortuna dabit quae feret ipse puer.]

XXVI. DE LEONE ET CAPELLA

Viderat excelsa pascentem rupe capellam,
    Comminus esuriens cum leo ferret iter.
Et prior: "Heus, inquit, praeruptis ardua saxis
    Linque, nec hirsutis pascua quaere iugis;
Sed cytisi croceum per prata virentia florem

Et glaucas salices et thyma grata pete."
Illa gemens, "Desiste, precor, fallaciter, inquit,
    Securam placidis insimulare dolis.
Vera licet moneas, maiora pericula tollas,
    Tu tamen his dictis non facis esse fidem.
Nam quamvis rectis constet sententia verbis,
    Suspectam hanc rabidus consiliator habet."
[Non citius blandis cuiusquam credito verbis,
    Sed si sint fidi, prospice quid moneant.
*

Omne genus virtutum nam prudentia vincit,
    Virtutum mores regulat arte sua.]

XXVII. DE CORNICE ET URNA

Ingentem sitiens cornix aspexerat urnam,
    Quae minimam fundo continuisset aquam.
Hanc enisa diu planis effundere campis,
    Scilicet ut nimiam pelleret inde sitim,
Postquam nulla viam virtus dedit, admovet omnes
    Indignata nova calliditate dolos.
Nam brevis immersis accrescens sponte lapillis
    Potandi facilem praebuit unda viam.
Viribus haec docuit quam sit prudentia maior,
    Qua coeptum volucris explicuisset opus.

XXIX. DE VIATORE ET SATYRO

Horrida congestis cum staret bruma pruinis,
    Cunctaque durato stringeret arva gelu,
Haesit in adversa nimborum mole viator:
    Perdita nam prohibet semita ferre gradum.
Hunc nemorum custos fertur miseratus in antro
    Exceptum Satyrus continuisse suo.
Quem simul aspiciens ruris miratur alumnus,
    Vimque homini tantam protinus esse pavet.
Nam gelidos artus vitae ut revocaret in usum,
    Afflatas calido solverat ore manus.
Sed cum depulso coepisset frigore laetus
    Hospitis eximia sedulitate frui,

(Namque illi agrestem cupiens ostendere vitam,
  Silvarum referens optima quaeque dabat,
Obtulit et calido plenum cratera Lyaeo,
  Laxet ut infusus frigida membra tepor).
Ille ubi ferventem labris contingere testam
  Horruit, algenti rursus ab ore reflat.
Obstipuit duplici monstro perterritus hospes,
  Et pulsum silvis longius ire iubet:
"Nolo, ait, ut nostris unquam successerit antris
  Tam diversa duo qui simul ora ferat."
[Qui bene proloquitur coram, sed postea prave,
  Hic erit invisus bina quod ora gerat.]

XXX. DE SUE ET ILLIUS DOMINO

Vastantem segetes et pinguia culta ruentem,
  Liquerat abscisa rusticus aure suem,
Ut memor accepti referens monumenta doloris
  Ulterius teneris parceret ille satis.
Rursus in exce‹r›pti deprehensus crimine campi
  Perdidit indultae perfidus auris onus.
Nec mora, praedictae segeti caput intulit horrens,
  Poena sed indignum congeminata facit.
Tunc domini captum mensis dedit ille superbis,
  In varias epulas plurima frusta secans.
Sed cum consumpti dominus cor quaereret apri,
  Impatiens fertur quod rapuisse cocus,
Rusticus hoc iustam verbo compescuit iram,
  Affirmans stultum non habuisse suem.
"Nam cur membrorum demens in damna redisset
  Atque uno toties posset ab hoste capi?".
Haec illos descripta monent, qui saepius ausi
  Numquam peccatis abstinuere manus.

XXXI. DE MURE ET BOVE

Ingentem fertur mus quondam parvus oberrans
  Ausus ab exiguo laedere dente bovem;
Verum ubi mordaci confecit vulnera rostro,
  Tutus in amfractus conditur inde suos.
Ille licet vasta torvum cervice minetur,

Non tamen iratus quem petat esse videt.
Tunc indignantem iusto sermone fatigans,
   Distulit hostiles calliditate minas:
"Non quia magna tibi tribuerunt membra parentes,
   Viribus effectum constituere tuis."
[Disce tamen brevibus quae sit fiducia monstris
   Ut faciat quidquid parvula turba cupit].
[Cum dives persona brevem maiorve potestas
   subdere vult sibimet, si nequit, ira tumet].

XXXII. DE HOMINE ET PLAUSTRO

Haerentem luteo sub gurgite rusticus axem
   Liquerat et nexos ad iuga tarda boves,
Frustra depositis confidens numina votis
   Ferre suis rebus, cum resideret, opem.
Cui rector summis Tirynthius infit ab astris,
   (Nam vocat hunc supplex in sua vota deum):
"Perge laborantes stimulis agitare iuvencos,
   Et manibus pigras disce iuvare rotas.
Tunc quoque congressum maioraque viribus ausum
   Fas superos animis conciliare tuis.
Disce tamen pigris non flecti numina votis,
   Praesentesque adhibe, cum facis ipse, deos."

XXXIII. DE ANSERE ET SUO DOMINO

Anser erat cuidam pretioso germine feta
   Ovaque quae nidis aurea saepe daret.
Fixerat hanc volucri legem natura superbae,
   Ne liceat pariter munera ferre duo.
Sed dominus, cupidum sperans vanescere votum,
   Non tulit exosas in sua lucra moras,
Grande ratus pretium volucris de morte referre,
   Quae tam continuo munere dives erat.
Postquam nuda minax egit per viscera ferrum,
   Et vacuam solitis fetibus esse videt,
Ingemuit tantae deceptus crimine fraudis;
   Nam poenam meritis rettulit inde suis.
Sic qui cuncta deos uno male tempore poscunt,
   Iustius his etiam vota diurna negant.

[Omittit totum qui tendit ad omnia votum.
*

Cum tibi cuncta petas, aequi transcendere metas
    Desine: nulla metit qui sibi cuncta petit.
*

Vites fortunam parantem damna futura
    ‹te› docet ut caveas aurea quis det ova].

XXXXIV. DE FORMICA ET CICADA

Quisquis torpentem passus transisse iuventam
    Nec timuit vitae providus ante mala,
Confectus senio, postquam gravis affuit aetas,
    Heu frustra alterius saepe rogabit opem.
Solibus ereptos hiemi formica labores
    Distulit et brevibus condidit ante cavis.
Verum ubi candentes suscepit terra pruinas,
    Arvaque sub rigido delituere gelu,
Pigra nimis tantos non aequans corpore nimbos
    In propriis laribus umida grana legit.
Decolor hanc precibus supplex alimenta rogabat,
    Quae quondam querulo ruperat arva sono:
Se quoque, maturas cum tunderet area messes,
    Cantibus aestivos explicuisse dies.
Parvula tunc ridens sic est affata cicadam:
    (Nam vitam pariter continuare solent)
"Mi quoniam summo substantia parta labore est,
    Frigoribus mediis otia longa traho.
At tibi saltandi nunc ultima tempora restant,
    Cantibus est quoniam vita peracta prior."
[Sic, homo, grana metas ut cum tua venerit aetas,
    Ad senii metas non aliena petas.]

XXXV. DE SIMIA ET NATIS

Fama est quod geminum profundens simia partum
    Dividat in varias pignora nata vices.
Namque unum caro genetrix educit amore,
    Alterius odiis exsaturata tumet.
Coeperit ut fetam gravior terrere tumultus,
    Dissimili natos condicione rapit:

Dilectum manibus vel pectore gestat amico,
    Contemptum dorso suscipiente levat.
Sed cum lassatis nequeat consistere plantis,
    Oppositum fugiens sponte remittit onus.
Alter ab hirsuto circumdans brachia collo
    Haeret et invita cum genetrice fugit.
Mox quoque dilecti succedit in oscula fratris,
    Servatus vetulis unicus heres avis.
[Sic multos neglecta iuvant atque, ordine verso,
    Spes humiles rursus in meliora refert].
[Quod vile est carum, quod carum vile putemus,
    Sic tibi nec cupidus nec avarus eris.]

XXXVII. DE CANE ET LEONE

Pinguior exhausto canis occurrisse leoni
    Fertur et insertis verba dedisse iocis.
"Nonne vides duplici tendantur ut ilia tergo,
    Luxurietque toris nobile pectus? ait.
Proximus humanis ducor post otia mensis,
    Communem capiens largius ore cibum."
"Sed quod crassa malum circumdat guttura ferrum?"
    "Ne custodita fas sit abire domo.
At tu magna diu moribundus lustra pererras,
    Donec se silvis obvia praeda ferat.
Perge igitur nostris tua subdere colla catenis,
    Dum liceat faciles promeruisse dapes."
Protinus ille gravem gemitu collectus in iram
    Atque ferox animi nobile murmur agit.
"Vade, ait, et meritis nodum cervicibus infer,
    Compensentque tuam vincula dura famem.
At mea cum vacuis libertas redditur antris,
    Quamvis ieiunus, quae libet arva peto.
Has illis epulas potius laudare memento,
    Qui libertatem postposuere gulae."

XXXVIII. DE PISCE ET PHOCA

Dulcibus e stagnis fluvio torrente coactus
    Aequoreas praeceps piscis obibat aquas.
Illic squamigerum despectans improbus agmen

Eximium sese nobilitate refert.
Non tulit expulsum patrio sub gurgite phocis,
    Verbaque cum salibus asperiora dedit:
"Vana laboratis aufer mendacia dictis,
    Quaeque refutari te quoque teste queant.
Nam quis erit potior, populo spectante, probabo,
    Si pariter captos umida lina trahant.
Tunc me nobilior magno mercabitur emptor,
    Te simul aere brevi debile vulgus emet."
[Quisquis ab externis nuper devenerit oris,
    Non decet indigenis, ut velit, esse prior.]

Anonymus Neveleti

1. De gallo et iaspide

Dum rigido fodit ore fimum, dum queritat escam,
    Dum stupet inuenta iaspide gallus, ait:
"Res uili preciosa loco natique nitoris,
    Hac in sorde iacens nil mihi messis habes.
Si tibi nunc esset qui debuit esse repertor,
    Quem limus sepelit, uiueret arte nitor.
Nec tibi conuenio, nec tu mihi, nec tibi prosum,
    Nec mihi tu prodes, plus amo cara minus."
Tu gallo stolidum, tu iaspide pulcra sophie
    Dona notes. stolido nil sapit ista seges.

2. De lupo et agno

Est lupus, est agnus. sitit hic, sitit ille. fluentum
    Limite non uno querit uterque siti.
In summo bibit amne lupus, bibit agnus in imo.
    Hunc timor inpugnat uerba monente lupo:
Rupisti potumque michi riuoque decorem.
    Agnus utrumque negat se racione tuens:
Nec tibi nec riuo nocui. nam prona supinum
    Nescit iter nec adhuc unda nitore caret.
Sic iterum tonat ore lupus: Michi dampna minaris.
    Non minor, agnus ait. Cui lupus: Immo facis.
Fecit idem tuus ante pater sex mensibus actis.
    Cum bene patrisses, crimine patris obi.

Agnus ad hec: Tanto non uixi tempore. Predo
    Sic tonat: An loqueris, furcifer? huncque uorat.
Sic nocet innocuo nocuus, causamque nocendi
    Inuenit. Hii regnant qualibet urbe lupi.

5. De cane carnem ferente

Nat canis. ore gerit carnem, caro porrigit umbram.
    Vmbra coheret aquis. has canis urget aquas.
Spem carnis plus carne cupit, plus fenore signum
    Fenoris. os aperit, sic caro spesque perit.
Non igitur debent pro uanis certa relinqui.
    Non sua si quis auet, mox caret ipse suis.

7. De fure uxorem ducente

Femina dum nubit furi, uicinia gaudet.
    Vir bonus et prudens talia uerba mouet:
Sol pepigit sponsam. Iouis aurem terra querelis
    Perculit et causam, cur foret egra, dedit.
Sole necor solo. quid erit, si creuerit alter?
    Quid paciar? quid aget tanta caloris hyemps?
Hic prohibet sermo letum prebere fauorem,
    Qui mala fecerunt uel mala facta parant.

8. De lupo et grue

Arta lupum cruciat uia gutturis osse retento.
    Mendicat medicam multa daturus opem.
Grus promissa petit de faucibus osse reuulso.
    Cui lupus: An uiuis munere tuta meo.
Nonne tuum potui morsu precidere collum?
    Ergo tibi munus sit tua uita meum.
Nil prodest prodesse malis. mens praua malorum
    Inmemor accepti non timet esse boni.

12. De mure urbano et rustico

Rusticus urbanum mus murem suscipit ede,
    Commodat ad mensam, mensaque mente minor.
In mensa tenui satis est inmensa uoluntas.
    Nobilitat uiles frons generosa dapes.

Facto fine cibis urbanum rusticus audit.
    Vrbani socius tendit in urbis opes.
Ecce penu subeunt, inseruit amicus amico,
    Inuigilat mense, fercula mensa gerit.
Emendat conditque cibos clemencia uultus,
    Conuiuam saciat plus dape frontis honor.
Ecce sere clauis immurmurat, hostia latrant.
    Ambo timent, fugiunt ambo, nec ambo latent.
Hic latet, hic latebras cursu mendicat inepto.
    Assuitur muro reptile muris honus.
Blanda penu clauso parcit fortuna timori.
    Ille tamen febrit, teste tremore timet.
Exit qui latuit, timidum sic lenit amicum:
    Gaude, carpe cibos, hec sapit esca fauum.
Fatur qui timuit: Latet hoc in melle uenenum,
    Fellitumque metu non puto dulce bonum.
Quam timor obnubit, non est sincera uoluptas.
    Non est sollicito dulcis in ore fauus.
Rodere malo fabam, quam cura perpete rodi,
    Degenerare cibos cura diurna facit.
Hijs opibus gaude, qui gaudes turbine mentis.
    Pauperiem ditet pax opulenta michi.
Hec bona solus habe, que sunt tibi dulcia soli.
    Det precium dapibus uita quieta meis.
Finit uerba, redit. preponit tuta timendis,
    Et quia summa timet, tucius ima petit.
Pauperies si leta uenit, tutissima res est.
    Tristior inmensas pauperat usus opes.

14. De aquila et testudine

Pes aquile, predo testudinis, aera findit.
    Hanc sua conca tegit, cornua longa latent.
Hoc monitu cornix aquilam premunit ineptum:
    Fers onus. at fiat utile, crede michi.
Quod geris in conca, cibus est. tibi surripit illum
    Conca cibum. concam frange cibusque cadet.
Vt concam lanies, pro uiribus utere sensu.
    Hanc, si celsa cadat, saxea franget humus.

De se stultus homo subuersus turbine lingue
   Corruit et fortes ista procella rapit.

17. De asino et catulo et domino

Murmuris et caude studio testatus amorem
   Nunc lingua catulus, nunc pede palpat herum.
Gaudet herus comitque canem comitemque ciborum
   Efficit. alludit turba ministra cani.
Arte pari similesque cibos similemque fauorem
   Lucrari cupiens inquit asellus inhers:
Me catulo prefert uite nitor, utile tergum,
   Nec placeo fructu, sed placet ille ioco.
Ludam. lude places. sic ludit tempore uiso,
   Vt ludo placeat, ludit et instat hero.
Blandiri putat ore tonans, humerisque priorum
   Pressis mole pedum se putat esse pium.
Clamat herus. uult clamor opem. subit ordo clientum.
   Multa domat multo uerbere claua reum.
Quod natura negat, nemo feliciter audet.
   Displicet inprudens, unde placere putat.

20. De hyrundine aues monente

Vt linum pariat de lini semine semen
   Nutrit humus, sed aues tangit hyrundo metu.
Hic ager, hoc semen nobis mala uincla minatur,
   Vellite pro nostris semina sparsa malis.
Turba fugit sanos monitus uanosque timores
   Arguit. exit humo semen et herba uiret.
Rursus hyrundo monet instare pericula. rident
   Rursus aues. Hominem placat hyrundo sibi,
Cumque uiris habitans cantu blanditur amico.
   Nam preuisa minus ledere tela solent.
Iam metitur linum, iam fiunt recia, iam uir
   Fallit aues, iam se conscia culpat auis.
Vtile consilium qui spernit, inutile sumit.
   Qui nimis est tutus, recia iure subit.

21a. [Qualiter Attici elegerunt sibi regem]

Fabula nata sequi mores et pingere uitam,
    Tangit quod fugias quodue sequaris iter.
Rege carens nec regis inops, sine rege nec exlex,
    Absque iugo gessit attica terra iugum.
Libertas errore carens se sponte coegit
    Et pudor ob legem forcior ense fit.
Ne libitum faceret, regem plebs libera fecit,
    Et que non potuit pellere iussa tulit.
Rex cepit lenire truces, punire nocentes,
    Queque leuanda leuans, queque premenda premens.
Hos honerat nouitas. ciues in lege nouelli,
    Quod leuiter possent, uix potuere pati.
Vrbem triste iugum querula ceruice ferentem
    Esopus tetigit, consona uerba mouens:

21b. De ranis a Ioue querentibus regem

Cum nichil auderet ludentes ledere ranas,
    Supplicuere Ioui, ne sine rege forent.
Iupiter huic uoto risum dedit. Ausa secundas
    Rana preces subitum sensit in amne sonum.
Nam Ioue dante trabem, trabis ictu flumine moto,
    Demersit subitus guttura rauca timor.
Placito rediere metu, uidere tigillum,
    Stando procul regem pertimuere suum.
Vt nouere trabem per se non posse moueri,
    Pro duce fecerunt tercia uota Ioui.
Ira Iouem mouit, regem dedit, intulit ydrum.
    Ydrus hiante gula cepit obire lacum.
Clamitat ecce lacus: Morimur, pie Iupiter, audi,
    Jupiter, exaudi! Iupiter, affer opem!
Nos sepelit uenter, nostri sumus esca tyranni.
    Aufer cedis opus, redde quietis opes.
Ille refert: Emptum longa prece ferte magistrum.
    Vindicet eternus ocia spreta metus.
Omne boni precium nimio uilescit in usu,
    Fitque mali gustu dulcius omne bonum.
Si quis habet quod habere decet, sit letus habendo.
    Alterius non sit. qui suus esse potest.

25. De terra parturiente murem

Terra tumet. tumor ille gemit gemituque fatetur
   Partum. pene perit sexus uterque metu.
Cum tumeat tellus, monstrat se monstra daturam.
   Horrent et trepidant et prope stare cauent.
In risum timor ille redit, nam turgida murem
   Terra parit. iocus est quod timor ante fuit.
Sepe minus faciunt homines, qui magna minantur.
   Sepe gerit nimios causa pusilla metus.

26. De agno et lupo

Cum grege barbato dum ludit iunior agnus,
   Tendit in hunc menti dissona uerba lupus:
Cur olidam munda sequeris plus matre capellam?
   Lac tibi preberet dulcius ipsa parens.
Est prope, festina, matrem pete, munera matris
   Lac bibe. nam seruat ubera plena tibi.
Agnus ad hec: Pia capra michi lac dulce propinat,
   Me uice matris alit, me uice matris amat.
Non michi, sed domino prodest me uiuere. uiuo
   Vt metat in tergo uellera multa meo.
Ergo michi prestat nutriri lacte caprino,
   Quam lac matris habens mergar in ore tuo.
Omnes uincit opes securam ducere uitam.
   Pauperius nichil est, quam miser usus opum.
Nil melius sano monitu, nil peius iniquo.
   Consilium sequitur certa ruina malum.

27. De cane uetulo

Armauit natura canem pede, dente, iuuenta.
   Hinc leuis, hinc mordax, fortis et inde fuit.
Tot bona furatur senium, nam robore priuat
   Corpus, dente genas, et leuitate pedes.
Hic leporem prendit, fauces lepus exit inhermes.
   Elumbem domini uerberat ira canem.
Reddit uerba canis: Dum me pia pertulit etas,
   Nulla meum potuit fallere preda pedem.
Defendit senii culpam laus ampla iuuente.

Pro sene qui cecidit, facta priora uigent.
Nullus amor durat, nisi fructus seruet amorem.
Quilibet est tanti, munera quanta facit.
Magnus eram, dum magna dedi. nunc muscidus annis
Vileo, de ueteri mencio nulla bono.
Si laudas quod eram, quod sum culpare proteruum est.
Si iuuenem recipis, pellere turpe senem est.
Se misere seruire sciat, qui seruit iniquo.
Parcere subiectis nescit iniquus homo.

28. De leporibus et ranis

Silua sonat, fugiunt lepores, palus obuiat, herent.
Fit mora, respiciunt ante retroque, timent.
Dum librant in mente metus, se mergere pacti,
Se metui et ranas stagna subire uident.
Vnus ait: Sperare licet. non sola timoris
Turba sumus. uano rana timore latet.
Spem decet amplecti. spes est uia prima salutis.
Sepe facit metui non metuenda metus.
Corporis est leuitas et mentis inhercia nobis.
Ista fuge causam suggerit, illa fugam.
Sic metuat quicunque timet, ne mole timoris
Spe careat. grauis est spe fugiente timor.
Speret qui metuit. morituros uiuere uidi
Spe duce, uicturos spe moriente mori.

29. De lupo et edo

Capra cibum querens, edum commendat ouili,
Hunc illi solida seruat ouile sera.
Natum cauta parens monitu premunit amico,
Vt lateat, nec sit in sua dampna uagus.
Hic latet. ecce lupus mouet hostia, uoce capellam
Exprimit, ut pateant hostia clausa petit.
Sta procul, edus ait, caprizas gutture falso.
Cum bene caprizes, te procul esse uolo.
Quod mea sis mater, mentitur ymago loquendi.
Rimula, qua uideo, te docet esse lupum.
Insita natorum cordi doctrina parentum
Cum pariat fructum, spreta nocere solet.

34. De lupo et capite

Dum legit arua lupus, reperit caput arte superbum.
　　Hoc beat humanis ars preciosa genis.
Hoc lupus alterno uoluit pede, uerba resoluit:
　　O sine uoce genas, o sine mente caput!
Fuscat et extinguit cordis caligo nitorem
　　Corporis, est animi solus in orbe nitor.

48. De uiro et uxore

Dum uir et uxor amant, uxorem priuat amato
　　Parca uiro, nec eam priuat amore uiri.
Coniugis amplectens tumulum pro coniuge uexat
　　Vngue genas, oculos fletibus, ora sono.
Hanc iuuat ipse dolor, nequit hac de sede reuelli
　　Grandine seu tenebris seu prece siue minis.
Ecce reum dampnat iudex, crux horrida punit.
　　In cruce custodit tempore noctis eques.
Hic sitit, ad tumulum uocat hunc et clamor et ignis,
　　Orat aque munus. hec dat et ille bibit.
Egrum nectareis audet cor inungere uerbis,
　　Hunc uocat ad primum cura timoris opus.
Sed redit et dulces monitus intexat amaro
　　Cordi. uicta subit castra doloris amor.
Vir metuens furi furem, suspendia furis
　　Visit, sed uiduam tactus amore petit.
Hanc ligat amplexu fructumque ligurit amoris.
　　Hinc redit ad furem, sed loca fure carent.
Hic dolet, hoc questu dolor hic instigat amicam:
　　Non bene seruato fure, timore premor.
Rex michi seruandum dederat, me regius ensis
　　Terret, et extorrem me iubet esse timor.
Hec ait: Inueni, que spem tibi suscitet, artem.
　　Vir meus inplebit in cruce furis honus.
Ipsa uiri bustum reserat, pro fure cathenat
　　Ipsa uirum, restem subligat ipsa uiro.
Huic merito succumbit eques. succumbit amori
　　Illa nouo, ligat hos firmus amore thorus.
Sola premit uiuosque metu penaque sepultos
　　Femina. femineum nil bene finit opus.

49. De iuuene et Thayde

Arte sua Thays iuuenes irretit, amorem
  Fingit, et ex ficto fructus amore uenit.
A multis fert multa procis, ex omnibus unum
  Eligit, huic ueri spondet amoris opes.
Sum tua, sisque meus, cupio. plus omnibus unum
  Te uolo, sed nolo munus habere tuum.
Percipit ille dolos et reddit qualia sumpsit:
  Sis mea, simque tuus. nos decet equs amor.
Viuere non uellem, nisi mecum uiuere uelles.
  Tu michi sola salus, tu michi sola quies.
Sed falli timeo, quia me tua lingua fefellit,
  Preteriti racio scire futura facit.
Vitat auis taxum, quam gustu teste probauit.
  Fallere uult hodie, si qua fefellit heri.
Thayda si quis amat, sua, non se, credat amari.
  Thays amore caret, munus amantis amat.

50. De patre et filio

Est pater, huic natus. hic patri cedere nescit,
  Nam fugienda facit et facienda fugit.
Mens uaga discurrit et menti consonat etas:
  Mentis et etatis turbine frena fugit.
Ira senis punit pro nati crimine seruos,
  Instruit ista senem fabula nota seni.
Cauta bouem uitulumque manus supponit aratro.
  Hic subit, ille iugum pellit. arator ait:
Gaude, letus ara, tu quem domat usus arandi.
  A boue maiore discat arare minor.
Non placet, ut sudes, sed des exempla minori,
  Qui pede, qui cornu pugnat abire iugo.
Sic domat indomitum domitoque boue cautus arator,
  Sic ueterem sequitur iunior ille bouem.
Proficit exempli merito cautela docendi,
  Maiorique sua credat in arte minor.

54. De cane et lupo

Cum cane silua lupum sociat. Lupus inquit: Amena
    Pelle nites, in te copia sancta patet.
Pro uerbis dat uerba canis: Me ditat herilis
    Gracia, cum domino me cibat ipsa domus.
Nocte uigil fures latratu nuncio, tutam
    Seruo domum. michi dat culmus in edo thorum.
Hec mouet ore lupus: Cupio me uiuere tecum,
    Communem capiant ocia nostra cibum.
Reddit uerba canis: Cupio te uiuere mecum.
    Vna dabit nobis mensa manusque cibum.
Ille fauet sequiturque canem, gutturque caninum
    Respicit et querit: Cur cecidere pili?
Inquit: Ne ualeam morsu peccare diurno,
    Vincla diurna fero, nocte iubente uagor.
Reddet uerba lupus: Non est michi copia tanti,
    Vt fieri seruus uentris amore uelim.
Dicior est liber mendicus diuite seruo.
    Servuus habet nec se nec sua, liber habet.
Libertas, predulce bonum, bona cetera condit.
    Qua nisi conditur, nil sapit esca michi.
Libertas animi cibus est et uera uoluptas.
    Qua qui diues erit, dicior esse nequit.
Nolo uelle meum pro turpi uendere lucro.
    Has qui uendit opes, hic agit ut sit inops.
Non bene pro toto libertas uenditur auro,
    Hoc celeste bonum preterit orbis opes.

59. De iudeo et pincerna

Fert iudeus opes, sed honus fert pectore maius.
    Intus adurit eum cura, laborque foris.
Ergo metu dampni sibi munere regis amorem
    Firmat, ut accepto preduce tutus eat.
Regius hunc pincerna regit, cor cuius adurit
    Auri dira sitis, qui parat ense nefas.
Silua patet, subeunt. Iudeus in ore sequentis
    Cor notat: Ipse sequar, inquit. at ille negat
Et gladium nudans: Nemo sciet, inquit, obito.
    Ille refert: Scelus hoc ista loquetur auis.

Prosilit a dumo perdix. hanc indice signat.
    Alter ait: Scelus hoc ista loquetur auis?
Et rapit ense caput et opes petit et scrobe funus
    Celat. agit celeres annus in orbe rotas.
Perdices domini cene pincerna ministrat,
    Ridet et a risu uix uacat ille suo.
Rex audire sitit. hic differt dicere causam.
    Fit locus, ambo sedent. hic petit, ille refert.
Rex dolet et leto mentitur gaudia uultu.
    Regis consilium consiliumque sedet.
Pincernam crucis esse reum sentencia prodit,
    Crux punit meritum iure fauente cruci.
Vt perimas quenquam, nullum tibi swadeat aurum.
    Nam decus et uitam mesta ruina rapit.

Bibliography

Texts

["Aesop"] Léopold Hervieux. *Les fabulistes latins depuis le siècle d'Auguste jusqu'à la fin du moyen âge.* 2d ed. 5 vols. Paris: Firmin-Didot, 1893–1899.

[Alanus] Alanus ab Insulis. *Doctrinale altum sive liber parabolarum metrice descriptus cum expositionibus.* In *Patrologia latina* 210: 579–592.

[Anonymus Neveleti] Wendelin Foerster, ed. *Lyoner Yzopet: Altfranzösische Übersetzung des XIII. Jahrhunderts in der Mundart der Franche-Comté mit dem kritischen Text des lateinischen Originals (sog. Anonymus Neveleti).* Altfranzösische Textbibliothek, 5. Heilbronn: Henninger, 1882.

[Anonymus Neveleti] A. E. Wright, ed. *The Fables of 'Walter of England.'* Toronto Medieval Latin Texts, 25. Toronto: Pontifical Institute of Mediaeval Studies, 1997.

[Avianus] Antonius Guaglianone, ed. *Aviani Fabulae.* Turin: Paravia, 1958.

[Avianus] *Apologus Aviani.* Cologne: Quentell, 1494.

[Avianus] Robert Gregory Risse, Jr. "An Edition of the Commentary on the Fables of Avianus in Erfurt Ms. Amplon. Q.21.: The Text and Its Place in Medieval Literary Culture." Ph.D. Diss., Washington University, 1964.

[Babrius] Léon Herrmann. *Babrius et ses poèmes.* Collection Latomus, 135. Brussels: Latomus, 1973.

[Babrius] M. J. Luzzata and A. LaPenna. *Babrius: Mythiamboi Aesopei.* Leipzig: Teubner, 1986.

[Michel Beheim] Ed. Hans Gille and Ingeborg Spriewald. *Die Gedichte des Michel Beheim.* Vol. 2. Deutsche Texte des Mittelalters, 64. Berlin: Akademie-Verlag, 1970.

[Boethius] Boethius. *Anicii Manlii Severini Boethii philosophiae consolatio.* Ed. L. Bieler. Turnhout: Brepols, 1957.

[Ulrich Boner] Franz Pfeiffer, ed. *Ulrich Boner: Der Edelstein.* Leipzig: Göschen, 1844.

[Bono Stoppani] Ambrogio Oldrini. "L'ultimo favolista medievale: Frate Bono Stoppani da Como e le sue *Fabulæ mistice declaratæ.*" *Studi medievali* 2 (1906/1907): 155–218.

[Pseudo-Cato] Marcus Boas, ed. *Disticha Catonis.* Amsterdam: North-Holland Publishing, 1952.

[Conrad of Hirschau] R. B. C. Huygens, ed. *Dialogus super Auctores.* Collection Latomus, 17. Brussels: Latomus, 1955.

[Aesopus Dorpii] Martin Dorp, ed. *Aesopi Phrygis et vita ex Maximo Planude desumpta, et fabellae iucundissimae.* ... Strasbourg: Schurer, 1544.

[Pseudo-Dositheus] G. Goetze, ed. *Hermeneumata Pseudodositheana.* Corpus Glossariorum Latinorum 3. Leipzig: Teubner, 1892.

[Eberhard] Johann Wrobel, ed. *Grecismus.* Corpus grammaticorum medii aevi, 1. Wrocław: Koebner, 1887; repr. Hildesheim: Olms, 1987.

[Frowin of Cracow] Edwin Habel, ed. "Der Antigameratus des Frowinus von Krakau." In *Studien zur lateinischen Dichtung des Mittelalters: Ehrengabe für Karl Strecker,* 60–77. Dresden: Baensch, 1931.

[Geoffrey of Vinsauf] Edmond Faral. *Les arts poétiques du xiie et xiiie siècle.* Bibliothèque de l'école des hautes études, 238. Paris: Champion, 1924; repr. Geneva: Slatkine, 1982.

[Gregory the Great] Marcus Adriaen, ed. *S. Gregorii Magni Moralia in Job.* Corpus Christianorum Series Latin, 143. 3 vols. Turnhout: Brepols, 1979.

[Robert Henryson] H. Harvey Wood, ed. *The Poems and Fables of Robert Henryson.* Edinburgh: Thin, 1978.

[Hildegard of Bingen] *Physica. Patrologia latina* 197: 1117–1352.

[Hugh of St. Victor] "De fructibus carnis et spiritus." *Patrologia latina* 176: 997–1010.

["Iocalis"] Paul Lehmann, ed. "Der *Liber Iocalis.*" *Sitzungsberichte der Philosophisch-historischen Abteilung der Bayerischen Akademie der Wissenschaften zu München* (1938): 55–93.

[Isidor] *Isidori Hispalensis Episcopi Etymologiarum sive Originum Libri xx.* Ed. J. W. M. Lindsay. 2 vols. Oxford: Oxford University Press, 1911.

[Magdeburg Aesop] W. Seelmann, ed. *Gerhard von Minden*. Niederdeutsche Denkmäler, 2. Bremen: Kühtmann, 1878.

[Alexander Neckam] Thomas Wright, ed. *Alexandri Neckam De naturis rerum libri duo, With the Poem of the Same Author, De laudibus divinæ sapientiæ*. Rolls Series, 34. London: 1863; repr. Nendeln: Kraus, 1967.

[Nuremberg Aesop] Klaus Grubmüller, ed. *Nürnberger Prosa-Äsop*. Altdeutsche Textbibliothek, 105. Tübingen: Niemeyer, 1996.

[Ovid] E. J. Kenney, ed. *Amores; Medicamina faciei femineae; Ars amatoria; Remedia amoris P. Ovidi Nasonis*. Oxford: Clarendon Press, 1994.

[Romulus] Georg Thiele. *Der lateinische Äsop des Romulus*. Heidelberg: Winter, 1910.

[Seneca] L. D. Reynolds, ed. *Ad Lucilium epistolae morales*. Oxford: Clarendon Press, 1965.

[Thomas of Cantimpré] Helmut Boese, ed. *Thomas Cantimpratensis: Liber de natura rerum*. Text (all published). Berlin: De Gruyter, 1973.

[Vincent of Beauvais] *Speculum naturale*. Douay: Beller, 1624; repr. Graz: Akademische Druck- und Verlagsanstalt, 1964.

[Ysopet-Avionnet] Kenneth McKenzie and William A. Oldfather. *Ysopet–Avionnet: The Latin and French Texts*. Urbana: University of Illinois Pres, 1919.

Secondary Literature

Adam, Bernd. *Katechetische Vaterunserauslegungen: Texte und Untersuchungen zu deutschsprachigen Auslegungen des 14. und 15. Jahrhunderts*. Münchener Texte und Untersuchungen, 55. Munich: Artemis, 1976.

Allen, J. B. *The Ethical Poetic of the Later Middle Ages: A Decorum of Convenient Distinctions*. Toronto: University of Toronto Press, 1982.

Baptist-Hlawitsch, Gabriele, ed. *Das katechetische Werk Ulrichs von Pottenstein*. Texte und Textgeschichte, 4. Tübingen: Niemeyer, 1980.

Baswell, Christopher. *Virgil in Medieval England: Figuring the Aeneid from the twelfth century to Chaucer*. Cambridge Studies in Medieval Literature, 24. Cambridge: Cambridge University Press, 1995.

Bedrick, Theodore. "The Prose Adaptations of Avianus." Ph.D. Diss., University of Illinois, 1944.

Beringer, Alison L. P. "Comments on Commentaries on Avian 25." Unpublished paper, University of Illinois, 1998.

Binkley, Peter. "Thirteenth Century Latin Poetry Contests Associated with Henry of Avranches: With an Appendix of Newly Edited Texts." Ph.D. Diss., University of Toronto, 1990.

Bisanti, Armando. "L'*ornatus* in funzione didascalica nel prologo di Gualterio Anglico." *Sandalion* 12/13 (1989/90): 139–163.

Blaser, Robert-Henri. *Ulrich Boner: Un Fabuliste suisse du xiv*ᵉ *siècle*. Mulhouse: Baly, 1949.

Bodemann, Ulrike. *Die Cyrillusfabeln und ihre deutsche Übersetzung durch Ulrich von Pottenstein: Untersuchungen und Editionsprobe.* Münchener Texte und Untersuchungen, 93. Munich: Artemis, 1988.

––––– and Gerd Dicke. "Grundzüge einer Überlieferungs- und Textgeschichte von Boners 'Edelstein'." In *Deutsche Handschriften 1100–1400: Oxforder Kolloquium 1985*, ed. Volker Honemann and Nigel F. Palmer, 424–468. Tübingen: Niemeyer, 1988.

Boldrini, Sandro. "Una testimonianza delle 'favole nuove' di Fedro prima di Perotti: Gualterio Anglico XLVIII." *Res publica litterarum* 13 (1990): 19–26.

Borst, Arno. *Das Buch der Naturgeschichte*. Heidelberg: Carl Winter, 1994.

Buijssen, G. H., ed. *Durandus' Rationale in mittelhochdeutscher Übersetzung*. 4 vols. Studia Theodisca, 6, 13, 15, 16. Assen: Van Gorcum, 1966–1983.

Cameron, Alan. "The Date and Identity of Macrobius." *Journal of Roman Studies* 56 (1966): 25–38.

–––––. "Macrobius, Avienus, and Avianus." *Classical Quarterly* 17 (1967): 385–399.

Cannegieter, Henricus. *Flavii Aviani Fabulae: cum commentariis selectis Albini scholiastae veteris, notisque integris Isaaci Nicolai Neveleti et Casparis Barthii: quibus animadversiones suas adjecit Henricus Cannegieter: accedit ejusdem dissertatio de aetate et stilo Flavii Aviani*. Amsterdam: Martin Schagen, 1731.

Clark, James M. "Johann Bischoff's Prologue." *English Historical Review* 47 (1932): 454–461.

Clark, Willene B. and Meradith T. McMunn. "Manuscripts of Western Medieval Bestiary Versions." In *Beasts and Birds of the Middle Ages: The Bestiary and Its Legacy*, 197–203. Philadelphia: University of Pennsylvania Press, 1989.

Cramer, Thomas. "AEsopi wolff." In *Festschrift Walter Haug und Burghart Wachinger*, eds. Johannes Janota et al., 955–966. Tübingen: Niemeyer, 1995.

Curschmann, Michael. "Marcolfus deutsch." In *Kleinere Erzählformen des 15. und 16. Jahrhunderts*, eds. Walter Haug and Burghart Wachinger, 151–256. Fortuna vitrea, 8. Tübingen: Niemeyer, 1993.

Czeike, Felix. *Verzeichnis der Handschriften des Dominikanerkonvents in Wien bis zum Ende des 16. Jahrhunderts.* Vienna: n.p., 1952.

Dicke, Gerd. *Heinrich Steinhöwels «Esopus» und seine Fortsetzer: Untersuchungen zu einem Bucherfolg der Frühdruckzeit.* Münchener Texte und Untersuchungen, 103. Tübingen: Niemeyer, 1994.

—— and Klaus Grubmüller. *Die Fabeln des Mittelalters und der frühen Neuzeit: Ein Katalog der deutschen Versionen und ihrer lateinischen Entsprechungen.* Münstersche Mittelalter-Schriften, 60. Munich: Fink, 1987.

Elschenbroich, Adalbert. *Die deutsche und lateinische Fabel in der Frühen Neuzeit: Grundzüge einer Geschichte der Fabel in der Frühen Neuzeit.* 2 vols. Tübingen: Niemeyer, 1990.

——. *"Von unrechtem gewalte.* Weltlicher und geistlicher Sinn der Fabel vom 'Wolf und Lamm' von der Spätantike bis zum Beginn der Neuzeit." In *Sub tua platano: Festgabe für Alexander Beinlich*, 420–451. Emsdetten: Lechte, 1981.

Fouquet, Doris. *Ulrich Boner: Der Edelstein. Faksimile der ersten Druckausgabe Bamberg 1461, 16.1 Eth. 2o der Herzog August Bibliothek Wolfenbüttel.* Stuttgart: Metzler, 1972.

Franz, Adolph. *Die Messe im deutschen Mittelalter.* Freiburg: 1902; reprint Damrstadt: Wissenschaftliche Buchgesellschaft, 1963.

Goldschmidt, Adolph. *An Early Manuscript of the Aesop Fables of Avianus and Related Manuscripts.* Studies in Manuscript Illumination, 1. Princeton: Princeton University Press, 1947.

Gottlieb, Theodor. *Mittelalterliche Bibliothekskataloge Österreichs.* 5 vols. Vienna: Holzhausen, 1915–1971.

Gottschick, R. "Ueber die Quellen zu Boners Edelstein." *Königliches Gymnasium zu Charlottenburg Jahresbericht* 6 (Berlin, 1875): 1–13.

——. "Über die Benutzung Avians durch Boner." *Zeitschrift für deutsche Philologie* 7 (1876): 237–243.

Grubmüller, Klaus. "Elemente einer literarischen Gebrauchssituation: Zur Rezeption der aesopischen Fabel im 15. Jahrhundert." In *Würzburger Prosastudien* II, ed. Peter Kestig, 139–159. Medium Aevum, 31. Munich: Fink, 1975.

——. *Meister Esopus: Untersuchungen zu Geschichte und Funktion der Fabel im Mittelalter.* Münchener Texte und Untersuchungen, 56. Munich: Artemis, 1977.

——. "Fabel, Exempel, Allegorese: Über Sinnbildungsverfahren und

Verwendungszusammenhänge." In *Exempel und Exempelsammlungen*, eds. Walter Haug and Burghart Wachinger, 58–76. Fortuna vitrea, 2. Tübingen: Niemeyer, 1991.

Henkel, Nikolaus. *Deutsche Übersetzungen lateinischer Schultexte.* Münchener Texte und Untersuchungen, 90. Munich: Artemis, 1988.

Herlet, Bruno. *Studien über die sog. Yzopets (Lyoner Yzopet, Yzopet I und Yzopet II).* Leipzig: Fock, 1889.

Hilka, Alfons. "Beiträge zur mittelalterlichen Fabelliteratur." *Jahresberichte der Schlesischen Gesellschaft für vaterländische Cultur* 91, Abt. IV, Sect. C (1913): 1–21.

Hohmann, Thomas. *Heinrichs von Langenstein 'Unterscheidung der Geister' lateinisch und deutsch: Texte und Untersuchungen zu Übersetzungsliteratur aus der Wiener Schule.* Münchener Texte und Untersuchungen, 63. Munich: Artemis, 1977.

——. "Deutsche Texte aus der 'Wiener Schule' als Quelle für Michel Beheims religiöse Gedichte." *Zeitschrift für deutsches Altertum* 107 (1978): 319–330.

——. " 'Die recht gelerten maister.' Bemerkungen zur Übersetzungsliteratur der Wiener Schule des Spätmittelalters." In *Die österreichische Literatur. Ihr Profil von den Anfängen bis ins 18. Jahrhundert (1050–1750)*, ed. Herbert Zeman and Fritz Peter Knapp, Teil I: Mittelalter, 349–365. Graz: Akademische Druck- und Verlagsanstalt, 1986.

Holzberg, Niklas. *Die antike Fabel: Eine Einführung.* Darmstadt: Wissenschaftliche Buchgesellschaft, 1993.

Hübl, Albert. *Catalogus codicum manu scriptorum qui in bibliotheca monasterij B. M. V. ad Scotos Vindobonae servantur.* Vienna: 1899.

Hünemorder, Christian. "Des Zisterziensers Heinrich von Schüttenhofen *Moralitates de naturis animalium.* Beobachtungen zu seiner Quellenbenutzung und zur frühen Rezeptionsgeschichte von Bartholomaeus Anglicus und Thomas de Cantimpré." In *Licht der Natur: Medizing in Fachliteratur und Dichtung. Festschrift für Gundolf Keil zum 60. Geburtstag*, ed. Josef Domes, 915–224. Göppinger Arbeiten zur Germanistik, 585. Göppingen: Kümmerle, 1994.

Hunt, Tony. *Teaching and Learning Latin in Thirteenth-Century England.* 3 vols. Cambridge: Brewer, 1991.

Huber, Gerlinde. *Das Motiv der 'Witwe von Ephesus' in lateinischen Texten der Antike und des Mittelalters.* Tübingen: Narr, 1990.

Hunger, H. *Die hochsprachliche profane Literatur der Byzantiner.* 2 vols. Munich: Beck, 1978.

Janson, H. W. *Apes and Ape Lore in the Middle Ages and the Renaissance.*

Studies of the Warburg Institute, 20. London: Warburg Institute, 1952.

Jones, Edith Carrington. "Avianus in the Middle Ages: Manuscripts and Other Evidence of Nachleben." Ph.D. Diss., University of Illinois, 1944.

Jones, W. Robert. "Avianus, Flavianus, Theodosius, and Macrobius." In *Classical Studies Presented to Ben Edwin Perry*, 203–209. Urbana, Ill.: University of Illinois Press, 1969.

Kaster, Robert A. *Guardians of Language: The Grammarian and Society in Late Antiquity.* Berkeley: University of California Press, 1988.

Klein, Dorothea. "*Ad memoriam firmiorem*: Merkverse in lateinisch-deutscher Lexikographie des späteren Mittelalters." In *Überlieferungsgeschichtliche Editionen und Studien zur deutschen Literatur des Mittelalters: Kurt Ruh zum 75. Geburtstag*, ed. Konrad Kunze et al., 131–135. Texte und Textgeschichte, 31. Tubingen: Niemeyer, 1989.

Knapp, Fritz Peter. "Von der antiken Fabel zum lateinischen Tierepos des Mittelalters." In *La fable*, 253–306. Entretiens sur l'antiquité classique, 30. Geneva: Fondation Hardt, 1984.

Kraume, Herbert. *Die Gerson-Übersetzungen Geilers von Kaysersberg.* Münchener Texte und Untersuchungen, 71. Munich: Artemis, 1980.

Kuhn, Hugo. "Versuch über das 15. Jahrhundert." In *Entwürfe zu einer Literatursystematik des Spätmittelalters*, 77–101. Tübingen: Niemeyer, 1980.

Küppers, Jochen. *Die Fabeln Avians: Studien zu Darstellung und Erzählweise spätantiker Fabeldichtung.* Bonn: Habelt, 1977.

Loserth, Johann. "Das Archiv des Hauses Stubenberg." *Beiträge zur Erforschung Steirischer Geschichte* 37 (1914): 71–126.

Madre, Alois. *Nikolaus von Dinkelsbühl: Leben und Schriften.* Beiträge zur Geschichte und Theologie des Mittelalters, 40. Münster: Aschendorff, 1965.

McCulloch, Florence. *Medieval Latin and French Bestiaries.* Rev. ed. University of North Carolina Studies in the Romance Languages and Literatures, 33. Chapel Hill: University of North Carolina Press, 1962.

McKenzie, Kenneth. "Note sulle antiche favole italiane." In *Miscellanea di studi critici in onore di V. Crescini*, 59–72. Rome: Stagni, 1910.

MacMahon, James V., ed. " 'Das puech von der ordnung der fuersten': A Critical Text-Edition of the Middle High German Version of the 'De regimine principum' of Aegidius Romanus." Ph.D. Diss., University of Texas, 1967.

Nichols, Stephen G. and Siegfried Wenzel, eds. *The Whole Book: Cul-*

tural Perspectives on the Medieval Miscellany. Ann Arbor: University of Michigan Press, 1996.

Oldfather, William A. "New Manuscript Material for the Study of Avianus." *Transactions of the American Philological Association* 42 (1911): 105–129.

Ott, Norbert. *Rechtspraxis und Heilsgeschichte: Zu Überlieferung, Ikonographie und Gebrauchssituation des deutschen 'Belial'*. Münchener Texte und Untersuchungen, 90. Munich: Artemis, 1983.

Palmer, Nigel F. "Zum Nebeneinander von Volkssprache und Latein in spätmittelalterlichen Texten." In *Literatur und Laienbildung im Spätmittelalter und in der Reformationszeit*, eds. Ludger Grenzmann and Karl Stackmann, 579–603. Stuttgart: Metzler, 1984.

Peet, Celena. *"De leone et mure*: Rhetorical Devices in Aesop's 'The Lion and the Mouse'." Unpublished paper, Carleton College, 1996.

Peil, Dietmar. *Der Streit der Glieder mit dem Magen*. Mikrokosmos, 16. Frankfurt: Peter Lang, 1985.

Perry, B. E. "Fable." *Studium generale* 12 (1959): 17–37.

Pintus, Giovanna Maria. "Il Bestiario del diavolo: l'Esegesi biblica nelle 'Formulae spiritalis intelligentiae' di Eucherio de Lione." *Sandalion* 12–13 (1989–90): 99–114.

Proctor, Robert George Collier. "The Accipies Woodcut." In *Bibliographical Essays*, ed. A. W. Pollard, 1–12. London: Chiswick Press, 1905.

Provenzo, Eugene F. "Education and the Aesopic Tradition." Ph.D. Diss., Harvard University, 1976.

Risse, Robert G. "The Augustinian Paraphrase of Isaiah 14.13–14 in *Piers Plowman* and the Commentary on the *Fables* of Avianus." *Philological Quarterly* 45.4 (1966): 712–717.

Rudolf, Rainer. "Der Verfasser des *Speculum artis bene moriendi*." *Anzeiger der Österreichischen Akademie der Wissenschaften, phil.-hist. Klasse* 88 (1951): 387–98.

Ruf, Paul, et al., eds. *Mittelalterliche Bibliothekskataloge Deutschlands und der Schweiz*. 4 vols. Munich: Beck, 1918–1977.

Ruh, Kurt. "Heinrich Wittenwilers 'Ring.' " In *Festschrift Herbert Siebenhüner*, ed. Erich Hubala, 59–70. Würzburg: Schöningh, 1978.

Schmidtke, Dietrich. "Geistliche Tierinterpretation in der deutschsprachigen Literatur des Mittelalters (1100–1500)." 2 vols. Ph.D. Dissertation, Freie Universität Berlin, 1968.

Schnell, Bernhard. *Thomas Peuntners "Büchlein von der Liebhabung Gottes."* Münchener Texte und Untersuchungen, 81. Munich: Artemis, 1984.

Schnell, Rüdiger. "Prosaauflösung und Geschichtsschreibung im deutschen Spätmittelalter." In *Literatur und Laienbildung im Spätmittelalter und der frühen Neuzeit*, eds. Ludger Grenzmann and Karl Stackmann, 214–248. Stuttgart: Metzler, 1984.

Schnyder, Mireille. " 'sunder ich pin ein armer rab': Zu einer autobiographischen Anekdote in Konrads von Megenberg 'Buch der Natur'." *Wirkendes Wort* 1 (1994): 1–6.

Schönbach, A. E. "Zur Kritik Boners." *Zeitschrift für deutsche Philologie* 6 (1875): 251–290.

Schönbach, Anton. *Über Hartmann von Aue: Drei Bücher Untersuchungen*. Graz: 1894.

Seemann, Erich. *Hugo von Trimberg und die Fabeln seines Renners*. Munich: Kastner und Callwey, 1921.

Sparmberg, Paul. "Zur Geschichte der Fabel in der mittelhochdeutschen Spruchdichtung." Ph.D. Diss., Universität Marburg, 1918.

Speckenbach, Klaus. "Die Fabel von der Fabel: Zur Überlieferungsgeschichte der Fabel von Hahn und Perle." *Frühmittelalterliche Studien* 12 (1978): 178–229.

Spriewald, Ingeborg. *Literatur zwischen Hören und Lesen: Fallstudien zu Beheim, Folz und Sachs*. Berlin: Aufbau, 1990.

Thite, G. U. "Indian Fable." In *La fable*, 33–60. Entretiens sur l'antiquité classique, 30. Geneva: Fondation Hardt, 1984.

Thoen, Paul. "*Aesopus Dorpii*: Essai sur l'Esope latin des temps modernes." *Humanistica Lovaniensia* 19 (1970): 241–316.

——. "Les grands recueils ésopiques latins des XVe et XVIe siècles et leur importance pour les littératures des temps modernes." In *Acta Conventus Neo-Latini Lovaniensis; Proceedings of the First International Congress of Neo-Latin Studies, Louvain, 23–28 August 1971*, ed. J. Ijsewijn and E. Keßler, 659–679. Humanistische Bibliothek, I.20. Munich: Fink, 1973.

Tiemann, Barbara. *Fabel und Emblem: Gilles Corrozet und die französische Renaissance-Fabel*. Humanistische Bibliothek, 18. Munich: Fink, 1974.

Vaio, John. "Babrius and the Byzantine Fable." In *La fable*, 197–224. Entretiens sur l'antiquité classique, 30. Geneva: Fondation Hardt, 1984.

Wachinger, Burghart. "Michel Beheim: Prosabuchquelle — Liedvortrag — Buchüberlieferung." In *Poesie und Gebrauchsliteratur im deutschen Mittelalter: Würzburger Colloquium 1978*, eds. Volker Honemann et al., 37–75. Tübingen: Niemyer, 1979.

Walther, Hans. *Proverbia sententiaeque Latinitatis Medii ac Recentioris Aevi*. 6 vols. Carmina Medii Aevi Posterioris Latina, 2. Göttingen: Vandenhoeck und Ruprecht, 1963–69.

Weinmayer, Barbara. *Studien zur Gebrauchssituation früher deutscher Druckprosa*. Münchener Texte und Untersuchungen, 77. Munich: Artemis, 1982.

Weitemeier, Bernd. "Latin Adaptation and German Translation: The Late Medieval German D-Translation of the *Visiones Georgii* and Its Source Text." In *The Medieval Translator. Traduire au Moyen Age. Proceedings of the International Conference of Conques (26–29 July 1993). Actes du Colloque international de Conques (26–29 juillet 1993)*, eds. Roger Ellis and René Tixier, vol. 5: 99–119. Turnhout: Brepols, 1996.

Westphal, Sarah. *Textual Poetics of German Manuscripts, 1300–1500*. Studies in German Literature, Linguistics, and Culture. Columbia, S.C.: Camden House, 1993.

Wheatley, Edward. "The 'Fabulae' of Walter of England, the Medieval Scholastic Tradition, and the British Vernacular Fable." Ph.D. Diss., University of Virginia, 1991.

———. "Scholastic Commentary and Robert Henryson's *Morall Fabillis*." *Studies in Philology* 91 (1994): 70–99.

Wieland, Gernot Rudolf. *The Latin Glosses on Arator and Prudentius in Cambridge University Library, Ms. GG 5.35*. Studies and Texts, 61. Toronto: Pontifical Institute of Medieval Studies, 1983.

Wright, Aaron E. "The 'Nuremberg' Aesop and Its Sources." Ph.D. Diss., Princeton University, 1991.

———. "Hartmann and the Fable: On *Erec* 9049 ff." *Beiträge zur Geschichte der deutschen Sprache und Literatur* 116 (1994): 27–36.

———. " 'Le voir ne l'en osa dire': An Aesopic Reminiscence in Chrétien de Troyes." *Romance Notes* 36 (1996): 125–131.

———. "*Fabule vtilitatem in se continentes*: Der kommentierte Äsop der Handschrift St. God. 27." In *Bücherschicksale*, Jochen Bepler et al., eds., 255–270. Hildesheim: Dombibliothek, 1997.

———. "*Iste auctor ab aliis differt*: Avianus and His Medieval Readers." In *Fremdes wahrnehmen — fremdes Wahrnehmen*, eds. W. Harms and C. S. Jaeger, 9–19. Stuttgart: Hirzel, 1997.

———. "A Cistercian Figure Initial in Vienna." *Wolfenbütteler Beiträge* 11 (1997): 1–7.

———. "Kommentar und Übersetzung: Zur Entlatinisierung der Fabel im ausgehenden Mittelalter." *Wolfenbütteler Beiträge* 11 (1997): 21–31.

——. "Readers and Wolves: Late-Medieval Commentaries on 'De lupo et capite'." *Journal of Medieval Latin* 8 (1998): 72–79.

——. "Aesop, Hyssop, and Brass: Two Late-Medieval Latin *Merkverse*." *Fifteenth Century Studies* 30 (1999): forthcoming.

Zurli, Loriano. "L'"Avianus Astensis' e l'"Avianus Vindobonensis': Considerazioni sulla nazionalità dell' "Astensis' e sulla cronologia relativa." In *La favolistica latina in distici elegiaci: Atti de Convegno Internazionale Assisi, 26–28 ottober 1990*, eds. Giuseppe Catanzaro and Francesco Santucci, 63–78. Assisi: Accademia Properziana, 1991.

Manuscripts and Incunables

Augsburg, Universitätsbibliothek
Cod. II.1.4o.27
Berlin, Staatsbibliothek Preußischer Kulturbesitz
Ms. Diez B Sant. 4
Ms. Hamilton 6
Ms. lat. qu. 177
Ms. lat. qu. 536
Budapest, National Széchényi Library
Cod. Nem. Muz. 123
Cambridge, Peterhouse
Cod. 2.1.0
Colmar, Bibliothèque de la Ville
Ms. 78
Copenhagen, Kongelige Bibl.
GKS 1905, 4o
NKS 213 b, 4o
Cracow, Bibliotheca Jagiellonica
Cod. 1891
Cod. 2195
Darmstadt, Hessische Landesbibliothek
Ms. 23
Ms. 2780
Dijon, Bibliothèque communale
Ms. 497
Donaueschingen, Fürstlich Fürstenbergische Hofbibliothek
Cod. 27
Erfurt, Stadtbücherei
Cod. Amplon.Q.21

Freiburg, Universitätsbibliothek
    Cod. 21
Hannover, Stadtbibliothek
    Ms. Mag. 15
Hildesheim, Dombibliothek
    Hs. St. God. 27
Kampen, Archief der Gemeente
    no signature
Leipzig, Universitätsbibliothek
    Ms. Haenel 3475
Lincoln, Cathedral Library
    Ms. C.5.8.
London, British Library
    Additional 10090
    Additional 11897
    Additional 33781
    Harley 4967
Mainz, Stadtbibliothek
    Cod. I.540
Munich, Bayerische Staatsbibliothek
    cgm 3974
    clm 237
    clm 391
    clm 609
    clm 631
    clm 4409
    clm 7680
    clm 14703
    clm 16213
    clm 19667
    clm 19826
    clm 22404
Ottobeuren, Stiftsbibliothek
    Ms. 0.82
Paris, Bibliothèque nationale
    Ms. Fr. 1594
St. Petersburg, Publichnaia biblioteka im. M.E. Saltykova-Shchedrina
    QvCl.Lat.N.6
Prague, National Library
    Ms. XI.C.4

Prague, Universitní Knihovna
  Ms. 546
Rome, Biblioteca Apostolica Vaticana
  Ottobon. lat. 1297
  Ottobon. lat. 2879
  Pal. lat. 1573
  Reg. lat. 1424
  Reg. lat. 1556
  Reg. lat. 2080
Salzburg, Stiftsbibliothek St. Peter
  Ms. b.ix.1
Stuttgart, Württembergische Landesbibliothek
  Ms. 34
  HB i. 127
  HB vi. 128
  HB xii. 40
Trier, Stadtbibliothek
  Cod. 1106/15
  Cod. 1109/31 8°
Urbana, University of Illinois Library
  x871A8.1400
Vienna, Österreichische Nationalbibliothek
  cpv 303
  cpv 15071
Winchester, Cathedral Library
  Ms. III,A
Wolfenbüttel, Herzog August Bibliothek
  288 Gud. lat.
  81.16. Aug. fol.
  185 Helmst.
  13.10.Aug.4o
  Alleg. 17524
  Aug. 4o 34
Wrocław, Biblioteka Uniwersytecka
  Ms. cod. IV.Q.81
  Ms. cod. IV.Q.126
Würzburg, Bibliothek der Franziskaner-Minoriten
  Cod. I.42